ISAAC LA PEYRÈRE
(1596-1676)

BRILL'S STUDIES
IN
INTELLECTUAL HISTORY

To help bring this about, La Peyrère said in *Du Rappel des Juifs*, certain steps can be taken by Christians. The recall of the Jews involves their uniting with the Christians. To accomplish this, first Jews have to be treated well. Anti-Jewish activity must be halted. The Jews must be recognized as benefactors. To persecute them is to persecute the sons of God. And that is almost as bad as persecuting the Son of God. Were hatred of the Jews to be eliminated, Jews should be ready to convert to Christianity, if they were made to see that Christianity is practically the same as Judaism. To help them to this view, La Peyrère proposed the creation of a Jewish Christian Church which would have no doctrines or dogmas offensive to Jews.[22] He claimed that Jewish Messianism and Christian Messianism were two distinct views, which described two different roles of Jesus, as Christian Messiah in the first century, and as Jewish political Messiah in the seventeenth century. If this were accepted, Jewish converts would find no trouble in joining his church for it would have no rational theology, and only a minimum of ceremony. La Peyrère's philosemitism is significantly different from that of the views usually offered at the time. Although his aim is similar to that of John Dury, Peter Serrarius, and a host of others, who wanted to bring about the conversion of the Jews, La Peyrère put practically none of the onus on the Jews. It is the Christians who are responsible for the failure of the Jews to convert because they fail to see the merits of the Jews, and they engage in anti-semitic practices. Other philosemites saw part of the problem as Jewish stubbornness and blindness, and part the corruption of Christianity. They claimed that the purification of Christianity taking place in England during the Puritan Revolution would make the Jews see the light. In La Peyrère's view, most of Christian theory and practice was to be dropped so Jews would not object to it. Then once the Jews joined the Christians, the Gentiles would also become Christians. The whole human race would be joined together. Jesus would return, and He and the King of France and the Jewish Christians in Palestine would rule the world in the wonderful Messianic Age.[23]

Due to the scarcity of information we have about La Peyrère's early years, it is hard to tell when he developed his vision of the Judeo-Christian Messianic Age. It is a view that flies in the face of most Christian Millenarian theories, in minimizing the Christian role and maximizing the Jewish one. It has no Anti-Christ in its scenario, as King of the Jews or ruler of Rome or Babylon, who has to be overcome. It also conflicts with Jewish Messianic views in giving Jesus the key role in the future of Jewish redemption, and in requiring the Jews to become minimal Christians (as the Marranos, the Jewish converts to Christianity, of Spain and Portugal were accused of being). Even though some of

Spon, André Rivet and Christian Du Puy all thought the book was pretty awful, but seem only to have grumbled their misgivings to each other. Cardinal Barberini was apparently shown a copy by Bourdelot. There is no evidence that he complained or tried to have the work suppressed.[13]

Du Rappel des Juifs presents a radical program for Christians to accept and act upon in preparing for the Messianic Age. Other works, like Sir Henry Finch's *The World's Great Restauration, or the Calling of the Jewes and with them of all the Nations and Kingdomes of the Earth, to the Faith of Christ* (London, 1621), indicate the rising interest in such eschatological themes.[14] Throughout the sixteenth and the early part of the seventeenth century many theological authors saw signs of the imminent fulfillment of the prophecies in the books of Daniel and Revelation, especially concerning the recall (and conversion) of the Jews and the arrival of the Millenarian state and the Messianic Age.[15] What had been taken by English Protestants as the most important text on how to decipher the prophecies in Scripture, and how to predict when the end will come, was the much republished work of Joseph Mede, *Clavis Apocalyptica* (London, 1627).[16] A somewhat similar literature was being developed by the Jewish Kabbalistic writers, especially Isaac Luria and his disciples.[17] Their work was used by Christian Kabbalists to dig deeper for reasons for their interpretations.[18] Of the works about the impending culmination of the world, La Peyrère's was definitely one of the more favorable to the Jews. He offered little argument and source material to justify his amazing proposals, though some may come from the unusual theological writings of Guillaume Postel (who, however, is never directly cited), or possibly from some of the medieval Joachimite sources (also never directly cited).[19]

Du Rappel des Juifs was probably the third part of La Peyrère's theological project. At times he indicated that his overall thesis was to be presented in three sections, (1) the election of the Jews, (2) the rejection of the Jews, and (3) the recall of the Jews. The first section appears in his later published work on the pre-Adamites. The second exists in an unpublished manuscript, and the third in his first published book.[20] The latter is completely silent about La Peyrère's radical views on biblical criticism and the existence of pre-Adamites.

The book deals with the way in which the Jews are to be recalled. For many, mainly Kabbalistic reasons, similar to those offered by Postel a couple of generations earlier, the recall is to take place in France, which has been chosen as the special territory for this crucial event in Providential History. After the recall of the Jews, they will be led back to Palestine by the King of France. Palestine will be rebuilt, and Jerusalem will be the center of the universe, from which the world will be governed by the recalled Jews and 'le roi universal,' the King of France.[21]

did for the Prince as his secretary, we are told that he often discussed metaphysics and theology with him.[7] In his spare time he was also writing his major work. Gabriel Naudé informed Cardinal Barberini in the Vatican in 1641 that La Peyrère's opus had already been completed, and that because Cardinal Richelieu (to whom the work was dedicated) had carefully banned it, many people were trying to obtain copies of it in manuscript form.[8] This original formulation of his message apparently included both his pre-Adamite theory and his Messianic view. Then it seems that La Peyrère subsequently showed the banned manuscript to the very pious Father Mersenne, who showed it to various members of their circle, including Hugo Grotius.[9] The latter published the first refutation of La Peyrère's views in his *Dissertatio altera de origine Gentium Americanarum adversus obtrectatorem* of 1643, because he thought that the pre-Adamite theory was a grave threat to religion. Grotius's own explanation of the origins of the inhabitants of America was that they were Norwegians or Germans whose ancestry went back to the Viking expeditions of Eric the Red and Leif Erikson. If this were not the case, Grotius declared, then either the Americans would not be the offspring of any nation, or they existed from eternity, or were born of the earth or the ocean, 'or that there were some men before Adam, as one in France lateley dream'd. If such things be believed, I see a great danger imminent to religion.'[10] (We will consider La Peyrère's answer to Grotius later on, when we examine the former's justification of his theory as an explanation of the existence of the people in the New World.) La Peyrère felt Grotius was presuming on their friendship by taking an undigested, unrevised manuscript that had been lent to him at Mersenne's request, and then sharply attacking the unfinished work in print.[11]

At any rate, in the period between 1641-1643, La Peyrère did revise his manuscript drastically. He removed all the material about the pre-Adamites, all the material about the history of the Jews, and left only the Messianic part about the role the Jews were to play in the immediate future with the coming of the Jewish Messiah. This part was published anonymously in 1643, in the year after Richelieu's death, without the name of the publisher, the place of publication, or the permission to publish it, under the title, *Du Rappel des Juifs*. Friends such as Guy Patin knew who the author and the printer were. Mersenne, Patin, Bourdelot (the Prince of Condé's doctor), La Peyrère himself and others distributed both his printed work and the manuscript of the rest of his theory.[12]

Although *Du Rappel des Juifs* contains many bizarre and heretical interpretations of the Jewish and Christian roles in the events leading to the end of time, the work did not seem to cause much excitement. Mersenne, Patin and a few others found interesting things in it. Charles

THE LIFE OF ISAAC LA PEYRÈRE

Isaac La Peyrère was probably born in 1596 in Bordeaux, the first child of a well-to-do family. Many catalogues, encyclopedias, and other reference works record him as having been born in 1594.[1] The notorial records, however, list his parents, Bernard de La Peyrère and Marthe Malet, as having been married on January 15, 1595. The mother was the daughter of the General Treasurer of the House of Navarre and the father was the private secretary of the Maréchal de Matignon, Lieutenant General of Guyenne. Both sides of the family were prosperous Calvinists. La Peyrère's father was a fairly influential Protestant in the Bordeaux milieu[2] where many of the Protestants were suspected of being secret Jews, or Marranos of Portugese origin.

Bernard de La Peyrère and his wife had nine children. The best known one after Isaac was his brother Abraham who became an important jurist, and published a work on royal decisions that was reissued up to 1808 (when presumably the Code Napoléon made it obsolete).[3]

We know practically nothing about Isaac's upbringing and education. On November 10, 1624, when he was twenty-eight, he married Suzanne Petit. By then he was a qualified lawyer.[4] A couple of years later, he was apparently starting to show heretical tendencies.

In 1626 he was accused by an unknown party of atheism and impiety before a provincial synod of the French Reformed Church. Unfortunately, not enough detail has survived to enable us to hazard a guess as to what La Peyrère's outlook was at this time. However, and this may indicate how powerful the La Peyrère family was, sixty pastors supported Isaac, and the charges were dropped. One pastor, M. Jean Alba, whose views we have, wrote a letter supporting La Peyrère in which he said Isaac was a 'homme duquel le merite et la pieté, receus comme par heritage de la maison d'où il sort, ont acquis mon affection toute entiere.'[5]

The La Peyrère family had had some business dealings with the Prince of Condé. In 1640 Isaac went from the provinces to Paris to become a secretary to this very important nobleman. He now found himself in the circle of philosophers, scientists, and writers who were being sponsored by Condé, including Father Marin Mersenne, Father Pierre Gassendi, François La Mothe le Vayer, Gabriel Naudé, Guy Patin, Blaise Pascal, Hugo Grotius and probably Thomas Hobbes.[6] Whatever else La Peyrère

Isaac La Peyrère and his influence definitely deserve a full length study. He was a man who had shocked his age; he was an associate of many of the leading figures of the time and his ideas have had great influence in shaping basic aspects of our intellectual world. In spite of all this, he is very little known at present. There has been only one thesis (that of Jean Oddos) and one long monograph (that of Dino Pastine) on La Peyrère's life and works. While there have been a reasonable number of recent articles and chapters of books dealing with one facet or another of La Peyrère's career, his doctrines, or his influence, there has not been up to now an attempt to examine all of these sides in a book length volume, or an attempt to offer an overall interpretation of what he was trying to accomplish in his central theory and its later development. (There are three as yet unpublished works of La Peyrère, one containing the only known answer he wrote to one of his critics, the other two, late revisions near the end of his life of his theory of Jewish history.) Little attempt has been made to examine the antecedents of La Peyrère's theory in Jewish and Christian theology, or in the writings from 1492 onward about the American Indians. The subsequent uses to which portions of his theory were put in re-evaluating the Judeo-Christian world view have also not been fully examined. His theory was used to justify slavery and the subjection of Africans and American Indians, and it was also widely used as a major theory about the origins of the human race.

In examining La Peyrère's views and their influence on theology, we will start with his biography, as far as it is presently known. Unfortunately we lack some of the crucial data which might make it possible to give a definite account of his personal background and his intentions in launching his theory. After presenting the biographical details, we shall examine the three main aspects of his view, the pre-Adamite theory, his biblical criticism, and his French-oriented Messianism in light of their antecedents in order to demonstrate the extent of La Peyrère's original contribution. The influence of each of these main features of his view will be examined, on his contemporaries like Spinoza and Richard Simon, on leading Messianists and Millenarians like Menasseh ben Israel, Antonio de Vieira, and Pierre Jurieu. His influence on later thinkers in advancing a basic anthropological view that was to be taken as a formulation for modern racism will be examined as well as a nationalist view of his that was to be revived by the French Revolution leader, the abbé Henri Grégoire, and by Napoleon Bonaparte. Finally we shall see what remaining legacy there is of La Peyrère's views in the present day.

The overall point in La Peyrère's great array of heretical theses was to establish what the author regarded as his most important message for mankind, namely that the long awaited arrival of the Messiah of the Jews was about to occur. This would bring about the Messianic Age, in which the Jewish Messiah would rule the world (along with the King of France) from the rebuilt capital of the Jews in Jerusalem. And in this wonderful transformation, everyone, Jew, Christian, pre-Adamite, post-Adamite, would be saved. La Peyrère's friend, Father Richard Simon, told him that his theory that there would be two Messiahs, one for the Jews and one for the Christians, would totally destroy Christianity. But long before that point, La Peyrère's antecedent claims about the authorship, authenticity, accuracy, and purview of the Bible, would have taken their toll. In order for the author to justify his Messianic-Millenarian prediction of the imminent transformation of the world, he first had to make it necessary to reconstruct the 'actual' text of the Bible, and to reinterpret what it was actually about (namely Jewish history from its beginnings to its projected end.) Added to this was his unCalvinist view, that in the world to come, everyone, yes, everyone, would be saved. The damned and elect classification of the church he belonged to when he published his doctrines is completely missing in his overall conception. Also missing is any mention of an Anti-Christ to be overcome before the Messianic Age, a critical feature of all other Millenarian theories of the time.

The effect of the appearance of such a set of heresies challenging basic tenets of Judaism and Christianity was to produce counterattacks of two kinds, one a stream of refutations starting even before his book was published, and continuing roughly down to the end of the eighteenth century; the other, a personal challenge to the unhappy author by the Catholic authorities in Belgium who placed him in jail until he recanted. La Peyrère was certainly one of the most frequently refuted authors in the period 1655-1800.

Although the author may have been forced, or led to recant, and was then unable to publish answers to his critics, or offer further arguments and evidence in favor of his theories, it is interesting that no significant intellectual figure (prior to Voltaire) was willing to state publicly that he or she believed the pre-Adamite theory. Nonetheless various, central heretical ideas of La Peyrère's were constantly being reassessed and revived by leading liberal theologians and early anthropologists. These seminal, heretical ideas of La Peyrère influenced biblical criticism, the historical social sciences, anthropology, racial theories, and later religious and secular Messianic theories in France. There is even, as we shall see, some evidence that La Peyrère's French nationalist Messianism played some, not yet clearly understood, role in Napoleon's imperial projects.

Moses could not have been the author of all of the Pentateuch (since part of it describes what happened after the death of Moses). La Peyrère's friend and contemporary, Thomas Hobbes, asserted that Moses wrote only those portions of the text directly attributed to him. La Peyrère went much further both in denying that Moses was the author of the work, or (and this may have been more seditious) that the scriptural text we now possess is completely accurate. La Peyrère pressed the data about inconsistencies and variants among the multitude of biblical manuscripts in order to question whether there was then any copy of the book which we could really rely on for the exact statement of the Divine Message. This questioning of the authorship and the accuracy of the biblical texts subsequently opened the door to the development of modern biblical criticism. La Peyrère's friend and younger contemporary, Richard Simon, carried out a systematic examination of the Bible. Shortly after La Peyrère died, Simon published his results which have since served as the basis for the so-called 'Higher Criticism' of Scripture.

What was considered La Peyrère's greatest heresy in his day, and throughout the next two centuries, was the startling thesis that there were men (and women) before Adam. La Peyrère offered internal evidence from the Bible, evidence from classical antiquity, and, more important for his time, from the Voyages of Discovery. Out of these three types of data, La Peyrère presented what he thought was a compelling case for a polygenetic account of human origins and development. Such data also pointed to an indefinite or infinite duration of the world. It also suggested that there were multiple sources of human beings and that many of these peoples had commenced their existence prior to the arrival of Adam. If that were the case, then the account of human history given in Genesis could only be a partial one. It does not tell us about the pre-Adamites, the people before Adam, but only about that part of mankind that descended from Adam and Eve and from the survivors of Noah's Flood. Noah's Flood, La Peyrère claimed, was only a local event in Palestine, and did not affect people in the rest of the world. The group which was inundated was the Jews. Hence, biblical history is not world history, but Jewish history. This idea plus the pre-Adamite theory seemed to La Peyrère's contemporaries to be the heretical core of his main book, arousing the most immediate criticism. And, in spite of the fact that pre-Adamism was to be attacked for a long time thereafter, La Peyrère's version soon began to have some major consequences in the budding field of anthropology. It was quickly to be transformed into a justification for the racist exploitation of Africans and American Indians, among others. (There seems, unfortunately, to be a lingering trace of this element in some current racist theories.)

CHAPTER ONE

INTRODUCTION

Some of the most revolutionary ideas in biblical criticism and in Judeo-Christian theology were advanced by the French Millenarian, Isaac La Peyrère, in the middle of the seventeenth century. His questioning of the Mosaic authorship of the Pentateuch, of the authenticity of the present text of Scripture, and of the accuracy of Scripture with regard to its account of the history of mankind had tremendous effects on his contemporaries as well as thinkers of later times. He was regarded as perhaps the greatest heretic of the age, even worse than Spinoza, who took over some of his most challenging ideas. He was refuted over and over again by leading Jewish, Catholic, and Protestant theologians. Nonetheless some of his ideas gradually became a basic part of biblical scholarship, greatly influenced the development of anthropology, and affected Millenarian political history.

However, the man who could contend that the Bible was not accurate, that there were men before Adam, and that the Bible was only the account of Jewish history; who could shock the philosophical-theological world of his time, is hardly known today. He is remembered, if at all, as a footnote to the biblical criticism of Spinoza, Richard Simon and Jean Astruc, and as a footnote in the history of anthropology. He has been reduced to a small paragraph in encyclopedias which present him as the formulator of the pre-Adamite theory. Only in the last few years has there been a revival of interest in La Peyrère and his revolutionary ideas.

In the present volume I shall present an intellectual biography of the man, and place him in the history of the religious ideas of his predecessors, and trace his influence from the mid seventeenth century onward. In so doing I hope it will become clearer how certain aspects of the secular world view emerged from various Renaissance and Reformation speculations. Some of the challenges to the biblical world view offered by La Peyrère, whether so intended or not, set the stage for understanding the world without reference to the supernatural.

When La Peyrère expounded his views on the Bible and its real message, he based his interpretation on a series of radical challenges to the religious traditions of both Judaism and Christianity. First, La Peyrère denied that Moses was the author of the Pentateuch. Others, such as Rabbi Ibn Ezra in the Middle Ages, had raised the point that

British Library, the Mocatta Library of the University of London, the library of the Warburg Institute of the University of London, Dr. Williams Library, the Royal Library, Brussels, the Royal Library, Copenhagen, and the National Library, Israel.

And, I should like to thank the following people for their aid and comfort in discussing aspects of the topic with me: Joseph Agassi, Susanna Akerman, Sir Isaiah Berlin, Harry Bracken, Norman Cohn, Paul Dibon, Shmuel Ettinger, James Force, Amos Funkenstein, Patrick Gerard, Judah Goldin, James Groves, Moshe Idel, Yosef Kaplan, Karl Kottman, Paul O. Kristeller, Marion Kuntz, Elisabeth Labrousse, Imre Lakatos, Arnoldo Momigliano, Ruth Necheles, David F. Norton, Shlomo Pines, Leon Poliakov, Leonora C. Rosenfield, H. P. Salomon, Charles Schmitt, Gerschom Scholem, Steven S. Schwarzschild, Giorgio Tonelli, Mayir Vereté, John N. Watkins and Richard A. Watson.

My colleague, Seymour Pollack, has been of great assistance in the technical preparation of the text.

And, Mary L. D. Scott, Melanie Miller, Dorothy Fleck, Shaaron Benjamin and Melissa Hall have kindly labored to type and word-process the manuscript.

ACKNOWLEDGMENTS

I first became seriously interested in Isaac La Peyrère in 1960, when I read his *Men Before Adam* at the William Andrews Clark Library of UCLA. I had heard of him earlier, when working on my *History of Scepticism*, but did not see at the time that he played any special role. From 1960 onward I have been exploring La Peyrère's theory, his influence on scepticism about the Bible, racism, Jewish-Christian Messianic and Millenarian developments, French nationalism, etc. Each time I thought I was done, either someone brought new material or perspectives to me, or I stumbled on to something I had not seen before. I have just added four new items to the text, before sending the manuscript off to the publisher.

I should now like to thank the many foundations, institutions, libraries and persons who have helped me in this work. Of course some of those acknowledged do not agree with some of my conclusions, but their aid was of great importance. I have also acknowledged some people's specific help in some of the footnotes.

I am grateful too for fellowships given me by the Alexander Kohut Foundation, the American Council of Learned Societies, the John Simon Guggenheim Foundation, the American Philosophical Society, the Memorial Foundation for Jewish Culture, The National Endowment for the Humanities, as well as for research grants from Harvey Mudd College, The University of California San Diego and Washington University, St. Louis, to work on this project.

The following libraries have been most helpful and generous in letting me use their materials: In the United States: The Boston Public Library, the William Andrews Clark Library and the Research Library of the University of California Los Angeles, the libraries of the University of California Berkeley and the University of California San Diego; the Folger Shakespeare Library, Harvard University Library, the Hoose Library of the University of Southern California, the Huntington Library, the Newberry Library, the New York Public Library. Abroad: The Bibliothèque de Chantilly, Bibliothèque Mazarin, Bibliothèque Nationale of Paris, Bibliothèque de Port Royal, Bibliothèque Ste. Genevieve, Bibliothèque Municipale of Sémur, Bibliothèque Municipale of Toulouse, the library of the University of Toulouse, the library of the University of Amsterdam, the library of the University of Leiden, the Rosenthaliana Library of Amsterdam, the library of Ets Haim, Amsterdam, the Royal Library of the Hague, the Bodleian Library, Oxford, the

CONTENTS

To my beloved wife Juliet who has patiently encouraged me and assisted me in this research over twenty-five years. And in memory of my good friend, Charles B. Schmitt, whose interest and concern about the subject were of the greatest help.

Library of Congress Cataloging-in-Publication Data

Popkin, Richard Henry, 1923-
  Isaac La Peyrère (1596-1676).

  (Brill's studies in intellectual history, ISSN 0920-8607; v. 1)
  Bibliography: p.
  Includes index.
  1. La Peyrère, Isaac de, 1594-1676. I. Title.
II. Series.
BR1725.L2P67   1987   230   87-14599
ISBN 90-04-08157-7

ISSN 0920-8607
ISBN 90 04 08157 7

PRINTED IN THE NETHERLANDS BY E. J. BRILL

ISAAC LA PEYRÈRE
(1596-1676)

HIS LIFE, WORK AND INFLUENCE

BY

RICHARD H. POPKIN

E.J. BRILL
LEIDEN · NEW YORK · KØBENHAVN · KÖLN
1987

La Peyrère's friends such as Father Mersenne thought it an interesting work, it nonetheless reeked of heresy, from Jewish, Catholic, and Protestant points of view. He made no serious effort to argue the case, simply offering personal and Kabbalistic biblical interpretations, biblical quotations, and unsupported exposition.[24] Oddos suggests that La Peyrère got some, if not all of this, from Tommaso Campanella.[25] They may both have had a common source.

No matter what the source of his view, the book was largely ignored, though a few Christian and Jewish thinkers did take it seriously.[26] It does not read like the many tracts of the time reporting the imminent end of the world. It offered no tremendous impending events—natural disasters, wars, destruction of Satan, and so forth, to precede the Millenium. And La Peyrère, unlike many Christian Millenarians and Jewish Messianists denied that one could offer a precise date for the advent of the Messianic Age. He also made no effort that we know of to connect his vision with the current events on earth, unlike Messianic and Millenarian theorists such as Joseph Mede, Menasseh ben Israel, John Dury, Abraham von Frankenburg, and Antonio de Vieira.[27] No interpretations of the Thirty Years War, the Puritan Revolution, or developments in France, are offered as signs of the beginning of the fulfillment of the prophecies in Scripture. The struggle of the French Protestants to survive is not mentioned as related to the Millennial events to come. Later on when Richard Simon suggested that La Peyrère could apply his theory to the Jewish Messianic movement of Sabbatai Zevi, he showed no interest at all.[28]

The only fact I have come across that may explain why the secretary of the Prince of Condé published such a remarkably philosemitic theory, is that it had been reported in France that a rabbi in Constantinople had said that a future king of France had been born in 1588. No member of the royal house of France who subsequently became king was born in that year. However, perhaps significantly, Condé, the father of *le grand* Condé, was born in 1588.[29]

From what we presently know of La Peyrère's activities at the time of the publication of *Du Rappel des Juifs*, and thereafter, there is no evidence that the author took any practical steps to bring about the pre-conditions of the Messianic Age. However, a scholar of French Protestant literature of the time, tells me that he has run across indications that La Peyrère attended regular 'secret' Millenarian gatherings in Paris, and was accompanied by an unnamed Jewish friend.[30] This would be the only indication that he himself did befriend any Jew. He did not try to establish his envisaged Jewish Christian Church, nor did he start a campaign to end persecution of Jews. Instead, as we will now see, he apparently lived comfortably most of the time in European high society, and among the most learned scholars. A Jew he may have met was Rabbi Menasseh ben Israel, who we know was impressed by La Peyrère's Messianic theory, but not by his pre-Adamite views.[31]

Political conditions after Richelieu's regime led to a decline in the fortunes of the Prince of Condé and his circle. Possibly in order to find a way of publishing the pre-Adamite theory, and possibly because there were some indications the Vatican might attack him and cause him trouble, La Peyrère accepted a proposal from Doctor Bourdelot that they both join the French ambassador in Holland who was going on a diplomatic mission to Scandinavia. This would give him the opportunity to meet many of the Dutch scholars and to see if they thought better of his efforts than did Hugo Grotius. La Peyrère was so annoyed by Grotius at this point that he was going to entitle his suppressed work 'The dream of a gentleman from Gascony concerning the pre-Adamites.'[32]

By April 1644, La Peyrère had arrived in Holland where he met André Rivet and Claude Sarrau, both of whom commented at the time that they found him 'un bel et agreable esprit,' while they found his ideas very paradoxical. Rivet commented that he found *Du Rappel des Juifs* 'bien extravagant' and that it 'tire l'escriture par les cheveux.' La Peyrère offered to show him his work on the pre-Adamites, which Rivet said 'me semble aussi un grand Paradoxe.'[33]

Next, our author travelled with the diplomatic mission, in which he does not seem to have had any actual function, into Germany, and then to Denmark. Denmark had been invaded by France's ally, Sweden, so the Danes were not particularly happy to greet a French diplomatic mission. Then the diplomats went to Stockholm, after which they settled down for the winter in Copenhagen. It was here that La Peyrère met the Danish scholar and scientist, Ole Worm, who was to become one of his best friends. Worm was extremely helpful to La Peyrère, lending him books and documents.[34] Using these, La Peyrère completed his *Relation de l'Islande* in 1644, which was written as a letter to La Mothe le Vayer. It was not published until 1663. The published copy is dedicated to the Prince of Condé. In the dedication, which is undated, a text from Isaiah 55 is cited to the effect that there will be a universal king who will spread God's message. Next it is said that this King is Louis XIV, who with the help of the Prince of Condé, will commence the conquest of the world. And finally La Peyrère suggested that perhaps his successor would finish the task.[35] Clearly La Peyrère brought up his Messianic scenario wherever he could.

Also at this time La Peyrère met the young Queen Christina of Sweden. She was then just nineteen. A decade later she was to play a decisive role in La Peyrère's life.[36]

One of the most important sources for understanding La Peyrère's thought comes from this Scandinavian period. There is a lengthy correspondence with Worm, covering the period 1645-1649.[37] A lot of it concerns current events, but some of it deals with La Peyrère's researches. In a letter of April 17, 1645, he described the reaction of his Parisian friends to his writing on Iceland, and asked Worm if there were any experts on Icelandic conditions in Copenhagen who could confirm or deny certain details. Worm supplied him with the data he needed (which incidentally made La Peyrère the leading authority on Iceland and Greenland well into the nineteenth century).[38] In a very important letter to La Peyrère of June 12, 1646, Worm asked if he had given his dissertation on the pre-Adamites to a publisher 'as was your intention.' Worm also wanted a copy of Du Rappel des Juifs and asked the author for one.[39] His attitude toward La Peyrère's heretical views seems to have been very positive, unlike some of the Danish theologians, such as Thomas Bangius (who later wrote a refutation of La Peyrère's theory about the pre-Adamites).[40] In a letter of March 5, 1647, Worm told La Peyrère that he, Worm, had explained the pre-Adamite theory to the Prince of Denmark, and presented the evidence for the theory. According to Worm, the Prince was pleased to learn of such a novel view.[41] The correspondence shows that a major concern of La Peyrère's was how to account for the origins of the American Indians. From his researches in Scandinavia, and his discussions with Worm, La Peyrère came to see that there was a similar problem in accounting for the Eskimos. Hence, the question of whether the Bible is adequate as an account of how the world developed was challenged both geographically and anthropologically by what was then known about the Americas and about the far north. La Peyrère developed his Eskimo material into an answer to Grotius. If Eskimos were found in Greenland by the Viking explorers, where did they come from? Grotius may have thought he had solved one problem, that of the origin of the Indians, but he had acquired a second one concerning the origins of the Eskimos.[42]

The French mission to which La Peyrère belonged left Scandinavia in the spring of 1646, stopping in Holland again for a few months. While there, La Peyrère finished his Relation du Groenland which was published upon his return to France.[43] He also seems to have gotten to know Samuel Sorbière, Gassendi's chief disciple and the translator of Hobbes' De Cive; and to have renewed his acquaintance with the very learned Claude Saumaise, the leading opponent of John Milton, who supplied him with some additional data for the pre-Adamite theory. Apparently due to the discussions with Saumaise, La Peyrère felt that he had to redo his great work on the pre-Adamites, since Saumaise, in his work on the history of astrology, had found much material about ancient chronologies far older than the biblical one. La Peyrère, in fact, used so much material from Saumaise that he later said Saumaise was the mid-wife of his pre-Adamites, and that they owed their life to him.[44]

La Peyrère returned to Paris in the fall of 1646,[45] taking his place again among the avant-garde intellectuals. When the Prince of Condé died at the end of the year, La Peyrère was appointed to the retinue of his successor a year later. Early in 1648, he received a copy of Saumaise's new work, *De annis climacteris*, in which his friend announced that if we believe the Chaldeans and the Egyptians, creation had to have been more than thirty thousand years earlier, a view which was more ammunition for the pre-Adamite theory! The rest of the year La Peyrère worked feverishly on his manuscript.[46] He wrote a brief piece, *Bataille de Lents*, to describe the courage of his employer, the Prince of Condé, and the noble character of the Prince's friend, Queen Christina.[47] La Peyrère's fortunes fluctuated as Condé's did, so that when Condé was in jail, La Peyrère seems to have languished. Finally he moved to Belgium with Condé in the early 1650s after the Fronde. From there, he went on a delicate mission for the Count to Spain in 1653, dangerous because neither Protestants nor Jews were tolerated in Inquisitorial Spain. In Spain, La Peyrère reported he was regarded as some truly strange type of being, a Protestant and a pre-Adamite. But when Spaniards saw that he was as reasonable as other men and a learned man, he gained some respect.[48]

At the end of 1653, La Peyrère left Spain and went with Condé's emissaries to England. All that we know as yet about his stay in London is that he became very ill there and almost died.[49] We do not know if he met any English intellectuals, nor if he made any of the contacts that were responsible for the publication in 1656 of a translation of the work on the pre-Adamites. His trip to England was his last diplomatic mission.

The decisive period for this peripatetic intellectual was 1654-1655. He had returned to Belgium where Queen Christina who had just abdicated her throne was residing in Antwerp. The Prince of Condé, who sought an alliance, perhaps marital, with her, got into a comedy of etiquette as to whether she should come to him, or he to her. Unable to resolve this, he placed La Peyrère as an intermediary, living next door to her. During this period Christina seems to have had a good deal of intellectual contact with La Peyrère. Despite her preparations for her official conversion to Catholicism (which occurred on Christmas eve, 1654) she was extremely interested in La Peyrère's ideas as well as in her search for irreligious literature, especially the notorious *De Tribus Impostoribus* or *Les Trois Imposteurs*, both of which supposedly exposed Moses, Jesus and Mohammed as the impostors. It is not clear whether either of these works, in the form in which they were published in the eighteenth century, then existed. Christina indicated to La Peyrère that she was willing to pay a fortune for a copy. This may account for indications that part of *Les Trois Imposteurs* existed by 1656. Her search may have inspired someone to start writing the work.

Shortly before her official conversion, Christina was visited by the famous Amsterdam rabbi, Menassah ben Israel, who apparently first read or learned about La Peyrère's views about the recall of the Jews at this point. Whether he met La Peyrère in Brussels is uncertain. He was overwhelmed by La Peyrère's picture of what was about to happen, and rushed back to Amsterdam to tell the Millenarians there that the coming of the Messiah was imminent.[49a]

Soon after her conversion, Christina is reported to have been listening to the charming courtier, Isaac La Peyrère, reading to her his still unpublished manuscript about the pre-Adamites. In spite of her new found religion, she urged him to go to Holland to publish it, and she probably financed the publication.[50] In a later account of why the work was finally printed, La Peyrère said he had completed the manuscript when he was in Paris, and left it with a friend who sent it to him in Brussels. When La Peyrère had to go to Amsterdam on Condé's business, he carried the manuscript with him. There he fell into a crowd of publishers who wanted to publish the work he was carrying. Since he could not take the bulky manuscript with him everywhere and he was very much afraid of losing it, he said he felt obliged to take advantage of the convenience of the Dutch printers, and also, almost as an afterthought, of the freedom that he had in Amsterdam to publish his book.[51]

La Peyrère did not stay in Holland until the book appeared. We know that he stayed at the Montagne d'Argent in Amsterdam, that he met the secretary of the Queen of Poland there,[52] and that he refused to get into a public debate over the pre-Adamite theory with the Millenarian Paul Felgenhauer who was a good friend of Menasseh ben Israel.[53] Menasseh had a copy of La Peyrère's work before its publication, and was working on a refutation of it. Considering that La Peyrère knew several Dutch scholars (Saumaise was dead), one would expect him to have contacted them. But there is no evidence that this was the case. A Millenarian work by Felgenhauer, published early in 1655, with the lively title, *Good News for the Jews*, contains a letter of Menasseh ben Israel in which he mentions the few people he knows of who are aware that the coming of the Messiah is imminent. One is the anonymous French author of *Du Rappel des Juifs* (who is not named or connected with the forthcoming work on the pre-Adamites). With such a testimonial, La Peyrère would certainly have been most welcome among the many Millenarian and Messianic circles in Amsterdam.[54]

In any case, La Peyrère's most notorious literary effort was published in five editions in 1655. Three of these were done by the Dutch publisher, Elzevier, one by a printer in Basel, and the last has not been identified. The following year an English translation appeared, and in 1661 a Dutch one came out. While the intellectual world was being shaken by his views, the author was actually spending six peaceful months in Namur in Belgium.[55] Although the work was published anonymously, enough people knew La Peyrère's ideas, so that his authorship was easily recognized. Condemnations and refutations began to appear. What seems to be the first one is that of the President and Council of Holland and Zeeland, The Hague, November 26, 1655.[56] La Peyrère's book was condemned among other things for being false, shameful, against the teaching of God's word, as well as being scandalous, godless, and against the interests of the state. On Christmas Day a month later, the Bishop of Namur published a condemnation of the *Prae-Adamitae* in all of the churches in the city (where La Peyrère was then living). As the author said, 'I was censored as a Calvinist and as Jew.'[57]

As more and more condemnations and refutations appeared, La Peyrère went to Brussels to try to get Condé to protect him. However, one day in February 1656, thirty armed men entered his room and carried him off to jail.[58] There, as he was interrogated over and over again, he felt that he had been abandoned by the Protestants (who had been quick to denounce him), and even by his Prince.[59] For a while he rebutted his accusers and refused to retract his views. Finally, it was gently suggested to him that if he repented, apologized to the Pope and became a Catholic, he would be forgiven. By June 1656, a worn out La Peyrère accepted this solution. He arrived in Rome on January 17, 1657.[60] We are told that when he got to the Vatican and met the Pope, Alexander VII smiled at him and said '...let us embrace this man who is before Adam.'[61] Later on La Peyrère described his audience with the Pope to Christian Huygens. At the audience the General of the Jesuit order told La Peyrère that both the General and the Pope had laughed delightedly when they read *Prae-Adamitae*.[62]

In Rome, it seemed prudent to La Peyrère to begin work on his apology, abjuration or recantation, which went through a few versions before it became acceptable. With his usual finesse, La Peyrère tried to formulate his recantation in such a way that neither the pre-Adamite theory, nor the theory of the role of the Jews in Divine History, had to be declared contrary to reason and evidence. And, wisely, to make the recantation more acceptable to the authorities, La Peyrère found a major place for his new master, the Pope, in the Messianic scenario.[63]

Basically La Peyrère contended that he had been led astray by his Calvinist upbringing. As a Calvinist he had to interpret Scripture according to reason and according to his individual conscience. Hence, he had to believe in the pre-Adamite theory. When his book came out, his adversaries maintained that his interpretations of Scripture were contrary to those of all the rabbis, all the Church Fathers and all the Doctors of Theology. However, La Peyrère pointed out, his opponents did not offer any evidence against the theory. They produced neither arguments nor scriptural texts to show it was false. Finally to determine who was right, La Peyrère or his opponents, one had to appeal to some authority. Who could this authority be? The Pope, of course. Now, when the Pope said his theory was false, then La Peyrère had no choice but to abjure it.

In setting up the recantation in this manner, La Peyrère never had to say that he believed his own theory was false or that there was evidence against it. He had only to say that he accepted what the Pope told him on this subject. With the assistance of Cardinals Albizi and Barberini, La Peyrère made his apology to the Pope.[64] From its initial claim that it was Calvinism that led him astray, to his contention that as far as La Peyrère was now concerned, the Pope's will shall be La Peyrère's reason and law, to his conclusion that Pope Alexander VII would accomplish what Alexander the Great started, namely uniting all mankind, the apology reeks with hypocrisy. Pope Alexander, according to La Peyrère's finale, was going to play the role previously given to the King of France. He would reunite all of the schismatics and bring about the conversion of the Jews.[65]

Besides these pious pronouncements, La Peyrère attempted to steer a careful course that would allow some acceptable sense in which the pre-Adamite theory was not condemned, and some meaningful way in which his Messianism could be squared with the Church's view. To accomplish these difficult tasks, La Peyrère began by saying that as a Calvinist he had to accept the pre-Adamite theory, for it accorded better with right reason and the natural sense of Scripture. He thought that the Christian faith could be more solidly, more easily and more clearly demonstrated on the basis of this hypothesis.[66] (And in *Prae-Adamitae* it is called an hypothesis.[67]) It also fitted better with what was known of the histories of pagan nations, with the information about the recently discovered peoples around the world, and with the theory that the world is eternal.[68] La Peyrère pointed out in his apology that he set forth his view tentatively. In the book, he asked people to tell him if anything he said was contrary to Scripture, or to any article of the Christian faith. Once all the controversy about his views took place, La Peyrère realized he had to find a judge of the matter. The Pope was such a judge. A papal letter, issued while La Peyrère was in prison, accused him of being 'un heriti-que détestable.' He felt, when he learned of this, that he should go to Rome and submit himself and his book to the Pope's judgment. There-fore he abjured all those claims in his two books that the Pope had said were wrong. Nevertheless, to the end of his life, La Peyrère contended that no one had shown him any evidence, natural or scriptural, that op-posed his theory, or any arguments that disproved it. So the pre-Adamite theory was wrong just because the Pope said it was wrong.[69] As a last word on the subject, La Peyrère said the theory was like the Copernican hypothesis. It did not change anything in the world. It only changed how one looked at things in the world.[70]

In the rest of the apology, La Peyrère tried to make his Messianic theories compatible with Christian teachings. The recognition of the crucial role of the Jews in Divine History, and the conversion of the Jews would bring about rewards for everybody. It would also lead to the resur-rection of the world. La Peyrère insisted that he still thought that conver-sion was possible, in spite of Jewish obstancy. His programme of kindness, suppression of anti-Jewish activities, and construction of a Judaized Church should work.[71] However, a conversion policy based on the pre-Adamite theory should be given up. Not only had the church con-demned the theory, but he had also learned that the Synagogue had re-jected it.[72] Therefore, the programme to unite Jews and Christians has to go on without the theory. Since, as La Peyrère was convinced, the time was not far off when an accord between Jews and Christians would take place, it would be the Pope who played a central role in bringing this about.

La Peyrère ended with a glorious mystical picture of the world to come, plus the announcement that he was now ready to abjure the pre-Adamite hypothesis. He was simply waiting to learn what were the terms of the abjuration.[73] When he was given them, with the help of the two Cardinals Albizi and Barberini, a lengthy list was prepared of his biblical interpretations, his claims about creation, his denial of the Mosaic authorship, his view that the Flood was not universal, his claim that the world was eternal, he abjured anything in his book that was contrary to the articles of the Christian faith and the Church Councils, and conclud-ed, 'j'abjure et detéste toute autre hérésie contraire à la Sainte Eglise Apostolique Romaine, captivant comme cy-dessus mon entendement, renonçant à ma raison, et renonçant à moi-même, pour me ranger sous l'obeissance de l'Eglise Catholique'[74] The abjuration was accepted on March 11, 1657. There are indications that the church expected La Peyrère's conversion to be followed by that of many more people; in fact, there is only one case that we know of where La Peyrère tried to influence anyone to become a Catholic, namely le Comte de la Suze.[75]

For a time La Peyrère settled down in Rome. During this period he apparently discussed mathematics with the English Catholic philosopher, Thomas White (Albius).[76] But there is no data that indicates La Peyrère was in contact with his friend, Queen Christina, who had also turned Catholic and settled down in Rome. She was in France much of the time that he was in Italy.[77]

In spite of, or perhaps because of his ideas, the Pope was apparently more than pleased with La Peyrère, and urged him to stay in Rome and accept a benefice.[78] Possibly out of prudence, La Peyrère decided to decline, returning to Paris instead. Guy Patin wrote to Charles Spon on April 9, 1658 that 'L'auteur du livre des Préadamites est ici de retour de Rome.'[79] He rejoined his patron, the Prince of Condé, who was still in exile. Finally at the end of 1659, Condé and his entourage were able to return to Paris. La Peyrère was made Condé's librarian. His correspondence at this time with Philibert de la Mare clearly indicates that he had not really changed his opinions about the pre-Adamite theory.[80] Nonetheless, in 1660 he published his *Lettre à Mr. le Comte de la Suze pour l'obliger par la raison à se faire catholique* in which he again went over his official explanation of how he was led astray by Calvinism, and why he had abjured his former theories. The book and some supplements to it contain a great deal of La Peyrère's theory from *Du Rappel des Juifs*. In fact, La Peyrère waxed eloquent about his desire to be Jewish. When some unknown opponent whose views are included in the book accused La Peyrère of, in fact, being Jewish, he replied that he was not Jewish in the sense intended by his challengers, 'mais je me fais gloire de l'estre comme saint Paul l'a entendu et l'a escrit.'[81] Since Saint Paul was a *Jewish* Christian who claimed he kept all the Jewish laws, perhaps La Peyrère was telling the world that he, too, was a Jewish Christian, a Marrano in the full sense of the term, both Jewish and Christian.

In the next few years La Peyrère published a continuation of his letters to le Comte de la Suze, who did not actually become a Catholic.[82] He also finally published his study on Iceland in 1663. In the prefaces to these works he outlined a phonetic system of orthography for the French language. He began using it in the continuation of the controversies about his letters to le Comte de la Suze. His unpublished work, *Des Iuifs, Elus, Reietés et Rapelés*, finished in 1673, is written in this orthographic system. In the preface La Peyrère explained and justified his new spelling. He also said that his views on this matter had been adopted by 'un Filosofe d'importance.' This individual was not identified by La Peyrère, nor has he been, as far as I know, by any present day scholars.[83]

Also in 1663, La Peyrère wrote his explanation for the Prince of Condé of his conversion and abjuration. Again, the same basic explanation is offered about how Calvinism led him astray. But this time La Peyrère also stressed the great explanatory power of his pre-Adamite hypothesis, and the role the theory should play in reconciling the Jews and the Christians. And what could be better than explaining and reconciling biblical history, pagan history and modern discoveries under one hypothesis, without destroying any article of faith, and without altering anything in Scripture. Whether the hypothesis was true or false, it seemed to explain more things in a reasonable manner. La Peyrère reiterated that his hypothesis was like that of Copernicus. It changed nothing, but made matters clearer than the Ptolemaic theory. Besides, all of science and mathematics were built on the use of imaginary hypotheses, which lead to thousands of real truths.[84]

Having made allowances for his theory, La Peyrère then insisted once more that there was no evidence or argument against it. But since the theory was opposed by all Christians and Jews, La Peyrère had to find a judge. The Pope was such a judge, and this accounts for La Peyrère's abjuration and conversion. This time a little more room was left for considering the pre-Adamite theory as an imaginary hypothesis, even if it had been abjured as a true hypothesis.[85] The *Apologie* received an approbation from two Doctors of the Sorbonne, stating that this is an 'ouvrage dans lequel la raison éclaire la Foy et la Foy donne du mérite à la raison!'[86]

In 1665, La Peyrère decided to retire. He was already 69 years old, had little money, and did not receive great wages as a librarian. There is no evidence of the continued existence of his wife or of any children. He joined the Seminary of the Oratorians, Notre Dame des Vertus, at Aubervilliers outside Paris, as a lay member.[87] There, we are told, he continued looking for more evidence for the pre-Adamite theory. He discovered that Maimonides had described a group, the Sabeans, who were supposed to have held that Adam had parents and had come from India. He heard that it was claimed that Adam died of gout. Since gout is a hereditary disease, Adam must have inherited it from his parents. La Peyrère also found out about a Kabbalistic claim that Adam had had a teacher, and a Moslem assertion that there were two or three men before Adam.[88] His friends recognized that he was 'fort enteté de son idée des Pre-Adamites.'[89] The great biblical scholar, Father Richard Simon, who was an Oratorian, tried to explain the evidentiary merits of these points that La Peyrère kept bringing up. Simon wrote a brief biography of La Peyrère after he died. In it he asserted that all that La Peyrère did in his religious retreat was to read the text of the Bible in order to fortify certain visions he had about the coming of a new Messiah who would soon reestablish the Jewish nation in Jerusalem. Simon added that La Peyrère was not much of a scholar, since he knew neither Hebrew nor Greek.[90]

During his retirement, La Peyrère tried in different ways to propagate his views. He wrote the only actual answer to a critic, Samuel Desmarets of Groningen, who had severely attacked his ideas. The answer was not published, probably because La Peyrère was honoring his commitment to the Pope that he would not publish any advocacy of the pre-Adamite theory.[91] A more subtle approach appeared in his notes to Michel de Marolles's French translation of the Bible. This work was being printed in 1671. The publication was suppressed by the Archbishop of Paris when it got as far as the 23rd chapter of Leviticus. In the notes, beginning with Genesis 1:27, when men appear on the scene, La Peyrère began by discussing a theory, which he said the Church had condemned as false, that there were men before Adam. He then presented evidence for the theory, and ended accepting the Church's decision. 'Mais l'Eglise en ayant autrement jugé, on s'est soûmis à ses Decrets, & aux sentimens de tous les Saints Peres.' Using this formulation he got in his points about the flood being a local event in Palestine, and about the problem of accounting for human dispersion as well as other matters.[92]

With the biblical commentary venture halted, La Peyrère turned to writing a new version of his *Recall of the Jews* .In May of 1670, he sent the manuscript to Richard Simon, who told him right away that the work could not possibly be published. Simon said the censors would turn it down because of its presentation of the pre-Adamite theory and because of its claim that there are two Messiahs. Both Jews and Christians would be displeased.[93] On the basis of this critique, La Peyrère changed the manuscript and submitted it to the censor, who refused to give permission for the publication of the work. Then he rewrote the manuscript once more, but still could not obtain the needed permission. The text that remains is apparently from 1673.[94] It was preserved because it was deposited in the Prince of Condé's archives.[95]

This last work, *Des Iuifs, Elus, Reietés, et Rapelés* is La Peyrère's testament. First of all, it is written in his phonetic French. Second, and of much more significance, the author had finally abandoned his pre-Adamite hypothesis in order to defend his Messianism. He insisted that he had only developed the pre-Adamite theory in order to buttress his vision of recalling the Jews. Originally La Peyrère expected that both Jews and Christians would happily accept his pre-Adamite theory, and then would accept their roles in the Messianic dramas. But just the opposite occurred. Christians of all sects attacked him. The Jews disavowed him. As we know he gave up the hypothesis because the Pope told him to. He also now asserted, sadly we may suppose, that the theory had been counter-productive to the plan of bringing the Jews and the Christians together. So, in order to regain contact with both groups, La Peyrère said he would adopt the Adamic hypothesis, that Adam was the first man, and that all people are descendants of Adam.[96] The rest of the manuscript is the final presentation of La Peyrère's picture of Jewish history, and shows how the central event, the coming of the Jewish Messiah is going to transform the world.

It is curious that La Peyrère, filled with a Messianic, Zionistic vision, never seems to have tried to place his idea in the current series of events. For he seems to have had no contact with the leading Millenarians in Europe, not to have read their literature, nor was he the least interested in dating when all the great events would occur. He never described any of the great political events that occurred in his lifetime as having significance for the world to come. And as mentioned before, he also completely omitted the Anti-Christ from his theory, so he could not make it as topical as many sixteenth and seventeenth century Protestant writers did.[97] He was apparently completely uninterested when Richard Simon told him about the alleged Jewish Messiah, Sabbatai Zevi, who was alive at the time.[98]

Even though La Peyrère's testament shows that he still entertained many heretical views, his behavior in the Seminary was such that 'il n'a rien fait paroître dans le Seminaire des Vertus, qui pût donner le moindre atteinte à la pureté de sa Religion.'[99] Another friend told Pierre Bayle that La Peyrère was 'très-peu Papiste, mais fort entêté de son idée des Preadamites' which he secretly discussed with his friends up to his death. The head of the religious order said that La Peyrère was constantly writing books that would be burned just as soon as he died. Bayle's informant told him that 'La Peirere etoit le meilleur homme du monde, le plus doux, & qui tranquillement croyoit fort peu des choses.'[100]

La Peyrère died a pauper with many debts on January 30, 1676.[101] Father Simon said that he heard that even on his death bed when he was asked to deny his pre-Adamite theory, and to retract all of his errors, La Peyrère refused. Instead he quoted the words of St. Jude, 'Hi quaecumque ignorant blasphemant.'[102] His epitaph, attributed to La Monnoye, stated,

> Here lies La Peyrère, that good Israelite
> Hugenot, Catholic, finally Preadamite
> Four religions pleased him at the same time
> And his indifference was so uncommon
> That after eighty years when he had to make a choice
> That good man left and did not choose any of them.[103]

During La Peyrère's long life, with its dramatic episodes, he introduced some revolutionary ideas concerning the Bible, the history and development of mankind, and of the future world. Rejected by almost

everyone, his ideas nonetheless were yet to have a great effect on the intellectual world. The rest of this volume will be devoted to examining this
influence.

One of the basic problems in evaluating La Peyrère's thought arises
from trying to ascertain what the 'real' purpose of his theology was.
Scholars such as René Pintard, Don Cameron Allen, and David McKee
have interpreted him as a *libertin* or a premature Deist deliberately attacking Judaism and Christianity because he did not believe in either of
them.[104] This type of reading of La Peyrère does not account for his other
writings besides *Prae-Adamitae*, especially his *Du Rappel des Juifs* and the
unpublished manuscript with the same title. It also does not account for
the fact that after La Peyrère became notorious, he chose to live in a very
pious monastery. It also fails to account for the Pope's attitude towards
him.

Some scholars who have studied more of La Peyrère's writings have
offered the interpretation that he was really Jewish, though living as a
Christian; that is, that he was a Marrano. This view has been presented
by Cecil Roth, Leo Strauss, Hans Joachim Schoeps, and Léon
Poliakov.[105] They have appealed not only to the philosemitism in La
Peyrère's works, but also to the fact that such friends as Guy Patin and
Richard Simon, and those in the circle of Condé who knew him well,
thought he was a Marrano.[106] Pierre Jurieu just stated bluntly that he
was a Jew.[107] In addition, La Peyrère came from Bordeaux, a center of
Marranism, and his name looked like a French version of 'Pereira.'
These scholars did not, however, press the Marrano aspect as a way of
making sense of the broad spectrum of La Peyrère's opinions.

More recently, four studies on La Peyrère have either held a noncom-
mittal view about his possible Jewish origins or have denied this entirely.
Articles by Myriam Yardeni and Ira Robinson try to interpret La
Peyrère in terms of the widespread views of the time which may best be
described as philosemitic and French nationalist. Yardeni suggests that
La Peyrère's theories might have some relation to Marrano or Jewish
views current in the Bordeaux milieu in which he grew up, if in fact he
belonged to this milieu. She interprets La Peyrère's theory as a political
doctrine intended to show the importance of France in the Messianic
Age. This doctrine was addressed to two audiences, the French nationalists and the Jews.[108]

Another recent interpretation, that of Ira Robinson, seeks to place La
Peyrère's efforts in the ranks of philosemitic Millenarian literature of the
time, especially that which also contends that France is to have a special
role in these religious developments. He even declares that, 'La Peyrère
thus, far from being out of step with his time and locale, emerges out of

traditions which were widespread among apocalyptic circles both in his
vision of the recall of the Jews and in his conception of the role France
and the Pope were to play in that recall.' Robinson points out that the
evidence offered by those of us who believe La Peyrère was a Marrano
is only circumstantial, therefore not conclusive. The most he is willing
to say is that La Peyrère's Jewish origins cannot be categorically denied,
but they also cannot be affirmed given the present state of our
evidence.[109]

A quite different view is presented in the thesis of Jean-Paul Oddos
and the monograph of Dino Pastine. They directly challenge the Jewish
origin theory, first by showing that there were old Christian families in
the Bordeaux area with the names 'La Peyrèrea' and 'Lapeyrere,' and
that these families could be traced back to the Middle Ages.[110] Then, if
the family of Isaac La Peyrère were a continuation of either of these old
French families, they were genuine Christians who had become
Calvinists during the Reformation. Oddos attributed La Peyrère's
outlook first to his Calvinism and second to the philosemitism of the time
that was so widespread in England and Holland. Philosemitic views
could easily have travelled from those lands to Bordeaux. And young La
Peyrère could well have come into contact with them. He also could have
known Marranos in Bordeaux. Oddos saw La Peyrère constructing a sort
of combination of Judaism and Christianity built around both Jewish
Messianic currents and Christian Millenarianism, but still Christian.[111]
Pastine just attributes La Peyrère's views to the admiration of various
French Calvinist leaders, like Plessis du Mornay and Du Moulin, for the
ancient Jewish tradition and the Old Testament.[112] Pastine ignores, however, how strongly Plessis du Mornay criticized and castigated contemporary Jews.[113] Both Oddos and Pastine seem to be oblivious to the case
of Nicholas Antoine, a French Protestant who became a Jew, and who
was burned to death in 1632 in Geneva when he refused to deny that
Judaism is the true religion.[114] Both Oddos and Pastine leave out the
hostility that still existed between Protestants and Jews, except among
the most radical Millenarians, whose philosemitism flourished after the
Puritan victory in England, and especially in the decade after La
Peyrère's work appeared.[115]

My own view is that the most likely explanation of La Peyrère's
outlook was that he was of Jewish origins. The evidence, as we have seen,
is not overwhelming. Some of his friends who knew him well, called him
either a Jew or a Marrano. He said at one point he was a Jew, but a Jew
like St. Paul. One obvious interpretation of that remark is that he was
a convert. There were Marrano families with names like La Peyrère, and
there were many Marranos who were Calvinists at the time. The epitaph

written for him calls him 'that good Israelite.' This, I admit, is not decisive. One would like either some archival evidence that traced his ancestors back to Spain or Portugal, or some document by La Peyrère or a close friend describing the family background. Since we have neither, we can only see what interpretation seems most probable. And it seems to me that the one that says he was a Marrano best fits the data.

Whether he was or was not a Marrano, his theory, I believe, is best explained as a vision of the world for the Marranos. It was said in Spain that the Marranos were like Mohammed's horse, who was neither horse, nor bird, nor any other kind of animal. The Marranos were neither Jewish nor Christian. Neither the unconverted Jews nor the old Christians liked the Marranos, nor did they trust them or accept them. Nonetheless, in La Peyrère's vision, the Marranos (that is, Jews converted to Christianity while remaining Jews) are and will be the most important people in the world when the Messiah comes. According to La Peyrère's theory everyone's fate will depend upon the actions of the Marranos in the world to come. Salvation will result from the activities of the Marranos in transforming the world, and from the providential events that will bring about its end.

La Peyrère presented a three point program that human beings could carry out at the time in order to prepare for the Messianic Age. First of all, Christians could cease their social and political mistreatment of Jews. In this way life would become more pleasant for the Jews. Perhaps, in this improved state of affairs, they would be encouraged to become Jewish Christians, or maybe Christian Jews.

The second step to be taken would be for Christians to reduce Christianity to a religion whose creeds and practices made it acceptable to Jews. In such a religion Jews could retain their own Messianic expectations and hopes without becoming involved in religious activities they abhorred and without accepting any dogmas that they might find offensive. For one hundred and fifty years before La Peyrère wrote, Spanish and Portugese Marranos had sought ways of interpreting Christianity so that doctrines like that of the Trinity did not have to be accepted literally, and so that various Jewish practices, such as fasting on Yom Kippur, did not have to be abandoned. The Marranos in Spain and Portugal gravitated towards Erasmian anti-Trinitarian views until they were condemned. Next they turned towards mysticism and towards some of the Protestant views and practices. Many would have been delighted with La Peyrère's description of a form of Christianity which was not offensive to them.

The first two points state actions that Christians can take before the beginning of the Messianic age. The third, and most crucial one, is that

Jews can become Jewish Christians. In so doing they would be in the
same situation as the Marranos in that they would be Jewish converts to
Christianity who still retained some essential Jewish beliefs. Of course,
unlike the Marranos, these Jewish Christians would not be forced converts. Instead, presumably, they would have converted because they
wanted to, and because they understood their role in world history.

La Peyrère's program differs significantly from that of the Dutch and
English Millenarians of the time. They would agree with the last point—
that the Jews should willingly convert to Christianity. On the other hand,
the Millenarians did not want to strip Christianity of some of its claims.
Many Dutch and English Millenarians wanted to convert the Jews to
genuine and complete Christianity, and not to a view that contained
some inoffensive Christian elements. La Peyrère, advocating his two
Messiah theory, obviously was not in harmony with these Millenarians.
Some, however, sought for some kind of Judeo-Christian formulation in
which what happened in the past could be stated acceptably to both Jews
and Christians, and that what is expected to happen in the future is the
same for both groups. Menasseh ben Israel had explained to various
Millenarians a Jewish doctrine that there would be two Messiahs, a
Messiah from the family of Joseph and one from the family of David.
This view was taken up by some of the Dutch and English Millenarians
(and led some to accept Sabbatai Zevi as the second appearance of the
Messiah.) La Peyrère's formulation was considered completely destruc-
tive to Christianity by Father Richard Simon. Nonetheless we shall see
that Rabbi Menasseh ben Israel, and Father Antonio de Vieira adopted
it, and tried to convince other Millenarians and Messianists of this.[116]
Also John Dury and Samuel Hartlib shared La Peyrère's desire to make
Christianity less offensive to the Jews, but they were not going to do this
by gutting Christianity of any essential doctrines.

The human activities leading up to the climax of history in La
Peyrère's theory would be followed in God's good time by the events that
lead to the Messianic Age. At that time, the Marranos, the elect, and the
King of France would play the central human roles. From La Peyrère's
perspective in the mid-seventeenth century it would be better to be a
Marrano in the Messianic Age than to be either a Jew or an old Christian. Being a Jew was better than being an old Christian, because a Jew
could always become a Marrano whereas an old Christian could not,
since he or she could not suddenly become a Christian all over again.
Similarly a Marrano, since he or she was of Jewish origins, could possibly
be one of the elect, whereas an old Christian with no Jewish roots could
not. Hence, if the Marranos were portrayed as having very privileged
positions in the world to come, then the pains, torments and social dif-

ficulties that they were suffering might be excused or justified. In fact, if this is a proper reading of La Peyrère's message, then the contemporary Marrano would have no reason to give up his or her present status in order to become either a Jew or an ordinary Christian. Only by preserving his or her present status could the Marrano play a central role in the Divine Drama. Thus the Marrano should want to be authentically what he or she is, namely a Jewish Christian.

Looking at the matter in this way, La Peyrère can be interpreted as a theologian who was explaining to the world why the forthcoming transformation would make it the case that the present victims, the Marranos, would become the victors. The author did not say this, but it seems a reasonable implication from what he was asserting. He did use one of the then current terms for Marrano, namely 'Christianos nuevos,' in describing God's recall of the converted Jews.[117] The Divine Plan that La Peyrère described was one in which being a Jewish convert to Christianity was the best thing that could happen to a human being in view of the imminence of the epoch of the Recall of the Jews. Only such a convert or a member of the elect would play a vital role at that time. The Jews might view the conversion of some of their brothers and sisters as catastrophic. The Spanish Inquisition might see the new converts as a potential fifth column, since they might not really believe in Christianity. However, from the perspective of the Marranos, if they looked at the world as La Peyrère described it, the conversion of the Jews would represent the next stage in the march towards the Messianic Age.

Thus the program of human action set forth in *Du Rappel des Juifs* can, I believe, be characterized as a Marrano theology. It appealed to Jews to become Marranos and to join the legion of converts who would play a central role in the Messianic culmination of human history. It provided a prospective monumental reward for the Marranos to make up for their present sufferings. They were to be the main agents of God in the Messianic Age. La Peyrère appears to have inflated the role of the converts beyond the usual picture given in the Millenial theories of the time in which the conversion of the Jews was seen as a precondition of the Christian Millenium. Even those theories that foresaw a Jewish reign during the Millenium, still saw a major or vital role for the true Christians. Some Calvinists designated this group as the elect, while La Peyrère saw the elect as just 'seven thousand' hidden Jews. Hence, the emphasis in *Du Rappel des Juifs* seems much more in favor of Jews, and converted Jews, than was typical around the mid-seventeenth century. Yet it is an emphasis that would be rejected equally by most Jewish and most Christian theologians. Thus, perhaps only Marranos would really be happy with this picture of the world to come.[118]

CHAPTER THREE

THE HISTORY OF THE PRE-ADAMITE THEORY
FROM ANCIENT TIMES TO LA PEYRÈRE

Like all interesting theories, the pre-Adamite hypothesis was not really original with La Peyrère who made it famous. It has a very long history, in which it played a variety of roles. We shall first consider the development of the theory among ancient and medieval thinkers.

We will probably never know exactly when the theory was first stated. It most likely arose as a pagan answer to the Jewish and Christian claims about the origin of the human race. Pagans, when confronted with what Jews and Christians asserted about history, must have realized that their own accounts of the origins of mankind long pre-dated the scriptural one. Probably when the first Greek to meet a Jew heard what the Bible said about human origins, he retorted with a version of the pre-Adamite theory. Be this as it may, the first case that we know of is that of a Christian, Theophilus of Antioch, who around A.D. 170 was debating the contention of the pagan, Apollonius, the Egyptian, that the world was 153,075 years old.[1] Since there are some figures of this kind in Greek and Roman literature, conflicts over chronology must have come up often. There were also various claims that mankind had no actual beginning, but has existed eternally as the world has.[2]

A serious challenge to biblical Adamism came from the last opponent of Christianity among the Roman Emperors, Julian the Apostate. Julian had been a Christian, presumably accepting the standard picture of the biblical world. After his return to paganism, he tried to defend his picture of the world against the Christian one maintaining that it was just as easy for the gods to have created a single original pair of people, as to have created many pairs.[3] 'Therefore,... we are all kinsmen, whether many men and women as we are, we come from two human beings, we all spring from one male and one female..., or whether there were many.' The second possibility, Julian contended, fits more with the variety of customs and laws among people, and with pagan tradition.[4] Unfortunately for the history of pre-Adamism, Julian died quite young, before he had a chance to challenge strongly the Christian leaders of the time. Julian seems to have worked out his case only as far as presenting some kind of co-Adamism, or multiple-Adamism as a plausible alternative to the Christian view. There is no indication that his defense of paganism had any lasting effect, or that it was taken up by others. Julian was pro-

Jewish, while strongly opposing Christianity. He hoped to join together Judaism and paganism. In fact, we are told that he actually tried to rebuild the temple in Jerusalem, and intended to worship there with the Jews. He, therefore, did not rule out Jewish claims, such as a Mosaic account of creation, but rather sought to show that these claims were similar to pagan ones such as Plato's creation story in the *Timaeus*, and that the pagan versions were more believable. Hence, co-Adamism or multi-Adamism could encompass both the Jewish and pagan traditions.[5]

Two chapters in St. Augustine's *City of God* indicate that there had been an ongoing argument over chronology between the pagans and those who accepted the Bible. Book XII, chap. 10 of St. Augustine's work is entitled 'Of the falsenesse of the History that the world hath continued many thousand yeares.'[6] The title of Book XVIII, chap. 40 is even stronger; 'The Aegyptians abbominable lyings, to claime their wisdom the age of 100,000 yeares.'[7] The titles alone show St. Augustine's attitude, namely that the pagan chronological accounts are false, and that those who promulgate them are lying. In these chapters St. Augustine went further to explain why the pagans stated false information. The pagans are ridiculous to begin with since the world is not yet six thousand years old. The reason they are ridiculous is that they are faced with a wide range of conflicting accounts of the history of the world and of mankind. The pagans do not know what to believe when presented with these differing relations. We, on the other hand, are not in such a situation, 'we have a divine historie to undershore us, and we know that what so ever secular author he bee, famous or obscure, if hee conradict that, hee goeth farre astray from truth. But bee his words true or false, they are of no valew to the attainment of true felicitie'.[8]

St. Augustine's explanation is the position that was adhered to by most of the rabbis and church fathers. They contended that the pagan claims about history and chronology were fables and myths. On the other hand, the Jewish and Christian claims were based on revealed truth. One could cite many, many forms of the response to paganism. An interesting one that may have influenced La Peyrère appears in the writing of the Jewish poet, Judah Halevi. In his work, *The Kuzari*, written in Spain between 1130 and 1140, the author presents a discussion between the King of the Khazars and a Jew, a Christian, and a Moslem theologian. The King is seeking to find out which is the true religion. Early in the work, the King asks the rabbi, 'Does it not weaken thy belief if thou are told that the Indians have antiquities and buildings which they consider to be millions of years old?' The rabbi, instead of being worried by this challenge, simply responded, 'It would, indeed, weaken my belief had they a fixed form of religion, or a book concerning which a multitude of people held the same opinion, and in which no historical discrepancy could be found. Such a book, however, does not exist. Apart from this, they are a dissolute, unreliable people, and arouse the indignation of the followers of religions through their talk, whilst they anger them with their idols, talismans, and witchcraft.'[9] In essence, Judah Halevi's rabbi simply pointed to the kind of evidence the Indians do (or do not have), and to the kind of people they are. In view of this their pre-Adamite claims could be ignored.

Later on in his book, Judah Halevi attacked a specific pre-Adamite claim that had appeared in a work called *Nabatean Agriculture*, which was written or translated by Ibn Wahshiyya in 904.[10] The view was attributed to the Sabeans that there were people before Adam, that Adam had parents and that he came from India. All of this was known to La Peyrère through Maimonides' famous discussion of the matter.[11] Judah Halevi brushed all of this aside on the grounds that these people did not know the Revelation contained in Scripture. Similarly, Halevi rejected Greek theories that the world is eternal. He also rejected the pagan views of the Chaldeans.[12] However, at the end of his rejection of these pre-Adamite possibilities, Judah Halevi gave his final opinion, which indicated he really did take seriously some pre-Adamite possibilities, and that he really only wanted to defend the idea that Adam was the first man in this world. 'If, after all, a believer in the Law finds himself compelled to admit an eternal matter and the existence of many worlds prior to this one, this would not impair his belief that this world was created at a certain epoch, and that Adam and Noah were the first human beings.'[13].

Both Augustine and Halevi were important in showing the perplexed how to deal with the evidences of a much older world different from that described in the book of Genesis. Halevi opened the door a crack to accepting the possibility of worlds before this world, while insisting the origins of *this* world are what are described in Genesis. A possible reason for this concession on Halevi's part may have been the growing use of pre-Adamite themes to embellish the stories in the Bible. These embellishments were presumably to make the stories sound better, sometimes by amalgamating them with other non-biblical traditional materials. So, for example, stories arose that Adam had a teacher. La Peyrère was very excited when he heard about this, until Richard Simon told him that in the story the teacher was an angel.[14]

A stronger embellishment that may be related to Halevi's position appears in some of the medieval Jewish Midrashim and in some of the Kabbalistic writings. These writers were trying to understand why God created *this* world. They assumed that God had previously created other worlds. The writers went further in saying that these other worlds contained human beings. But then they claimed those previous worlds were destroyed by God because the people in them had not been sufficiently virtuous. And then, according to this interpretation, God finally created our world. The Midrash Rabba says, in discussing the creation story in Genesis, 'The Holy One Blessed be He, created many worlds, and destroyed them one after another until He consulted the Torah, and created this that endured.' And another Jewish pre-Adamite view appears in the explanation of why the Bible begins with the Hebrew letter Beth, instead of with the first letter of the Hebrew alphabet, Aleph. A reason given is that there must have been a previous Bible, beginning with an Aleph describing a previous world that has now disappeared. This theory also includes the claim that there will be worlds after ours, the next one will be described in a Bible beginning with the third letter of the Hebrew alphabet, Gimel.[15]

Another view that might be considered as a kind of embellishment is one that is explicit or implicit in various neo-Platonic theories about the metaphysical (not historical) origin of man. Starting with Philo Judaeus, the metaphysical creation of the Idea of Man is a precondition for the actual creation of a person. The former is spirit, the latter a combination of spirit and body. The first is a divine creation, the second the result of the actions of the Logos. The spiritual man would precede the actual man, Adam, in the chain of being. The church father, Origen, has been interpreted as holding that man as spiritual being was made in the image of God, and man as human being was made from the slime of the earth. In both of these views the closeness of the human spirit to Divinity is being emphasized at the expense of adding a separate, and maybe later creation of the actual historical first man, Adam.[16]

Of all these views mentioned above, none poses the possibility that there have been any human beings in *this* world who existed prior to Adam. One finds an important statement of just such a possibility in the well known chap. 29, Book III of the *Guide for the Perplexed*. When Maimonides discussed the same Sabeans that Judah Halevi had dealt with, he reported that 'They deem *Adam* to have been an individual born of male and female like any other human individuals, but they glorify him and say that he was a prophet, the envoy of the moon.'[17] Maimonides' source is the same as Halevi's, namely Ibn Wahshiyya's *Nabatean Agriculture*. Some present day interpreters think this work was supposed to be a critique of Mohammedanism, and a glorification of the Nabateans over the Arabs.[18] Maimonides treats the Sabean views fairly neutrally. He listed their further claims, that Adam came from India, and that he went on to Babylon. The Sabean view as stated by Maimonides involved only a minimal pre-Adamite theory, namely that there were at least two people before Adam—his parents. Actually the pre-Adamism in *Nabatean Agriculture* goes far beyond this. However, why stop at two? The interest in this chapter of Maimonides from the time he wrote it until today suggests that it may have been a source for speculations about pre-Adamism. This chapter was pointed out to La Peyrère, so many scholars must have noticed it.[19] And they may have pondered if there were parents of Adam's parents, or something of this kind.

Dr. Moshe Idel of the Hebrew University, Jerusalem, has pointed out to me that there were other Islamic and perhaps Indian theories that contained forms of pre-Adamism. One of them, of the Ihwan Al-Safa, speaks of djinns who are on the one hand angels, and on the other hand, men before Adam. A whole history of what happened before Adam was presented, a history of the world before the present cycle in which Adam was made calif of the earth.[19a] Dr. Idel tells me that there are other such theories in Middle Eastern and Eastern literature of the Middle Ages. It is as yet hard to tell if they affected Jewish and Christian thought.

The nineteenth century German scholar, Otto Zöckler, who investigated the intellectual antecedents of La Peyrère, found that a form of pre-Adamism developed out of the discussions about what was or could be going on in the Antipodes. Could pre-Adamite people be living there? Or, to move a step further, could there have been two Adams who were created by God, one who was the father of all of the people living on this side of the world, and the other who was the father of all those in the Antipodes?[20]

In the fifteenth century a canon, Zaninus de Solcia, appears to have gone too far in these kinds of speculations. He was condemned in 1459 for holding that Adam was not the first man. The condemnation indicates that he held the view that God had created other worlds and that in these worlds there were other men and women who had existed prior to Adam. He was not, however, holding that there were people before Adam in our world. Zaninus de Solcia's heresy revolved around the role of Jesus in such a situation. Was Jesus the savior of all mankind, or just that portion of mankind that is in our world? Zaninus de Solcia's multi-world theory came, according to his condemnation, from his accepting Epicurus's cosmology.[21]

There seems to have been a more heretical case in the fourteenth century concerning a Father Tomas Scoto. Unfortunately, as in the above one, all that we possess are the accusations of heresy made against these men. We do not have any statement of their views by themselves. Father Scoto was accused of holding a series of propositions that amount to a pretty thorough denial of Judaism and Christianity. One of his heretical propositions, we are told, asserted that there were men before Adam, and that Adam was the descendant of these men. Also he is supposed to have held that the world is eternal, and that it was always populated. Unfortunately, one cannot tell from the propositions what evidence might have led Scoto to these conclusions. We also cannot ascertain what philosophical basis he may have had for his theories.[22] Pastine examined the documents very carefully and suggested that Scoto may have gotten some of his theory from the original *Three Impostors* that supposedly came from the court of Frederick II. (The seventeenth and eighteenth century versions do not deal with pre-Adamism.) The full text indicates that Scoto held there were always people in the world, and that Adam was therefore the natural descendant of pre-Adamites. The eternal world theory may be based on Aristotelian and/or Averroist sources.[23]

Another equally mysterious case is that of a Jew named Samuel Sarsa. He is reported to have been killed by being burned at the stake in 1463 in Persia because he told a rabbi that the world was of great antiquity. Again we do not know his theory or the evidence for it. Thus, we cannot really tell if this is a case of incipient pre-Adamism.[24]

The considerations of the pre-Adamite theory in antiquity and in the Middle Ages do not seem to have created much controversy. They do not appear to have raised basic challenges to the biblical picture of the world. And, as St. Augustine and Judah Halevi pointed out, if one accepts the biblical Revelation then all the evidence that suggests a pre-Adamite solution is to be set aside as mythical, false, and even as deliberate lies. The brief mention above of a few cases indicates that there may have been a very limited number of individuals who had irreligious or bizarre views that led them to pre-Adamism. But these few people do not seem to have made any serious dent in the official biblical picture of the world, accepted both by Jews and Christians.

However, by the sixteenth century, certain new information about the world had come to light, and this new information made the pre-Adamite theory an important hypothesis that might explain what was really going on. The earlier pre-Adamite speculations and legends were now in fact transformed into a very serious alternative theory to that presented in the Bible. What led to this change were two developments during the Renaissance. The first was the humanistic rediscovery of the pagan past of 'antiquity.' The second was the discovery of other peoples and other cultures as the result of the expansion of Europe through the voyages of discovery. Those who studied the ancient pagan historians found that there was a great deal of data in those writers that conflicted with the scriptural picture of the origins of the human race. In fact, the great

Spanish humanist, Juan Luis Vives, when he put together his edition of St. Augustine's *The City of God*, included a long note listing all of the people he knew about in ancient literature who were said to have lived long before Adam and Eve.[25] As mentioned earlier, St. Augustine had said that when he wrote the book, the world was not yet six thousand years old. Nonetheless Vives mentioned Chaldean figures that went back four hundred seventy thousand, and Egyptian ones over fifty thousand years. Vives did not draw any unusual conclusion from this data, nor did he ask any touchy questions about it . Vives's actual religious views have been debated. He has been seen by some as a religious sceptic and a philosophical naturalist.[26] Nonetheless when he compiled this data that pointed to a pre-Adamite conclusion, Vives, like other Renaissance humanists, offered the usual explanation of these facts, namely that the ancient pagans invented these chronological claims so that they could make themselves appear as the creators of everything in the human world. The historically minded humanists who carefully gathered the data about antiquity that were apparently incompatible with official religious views, were not prepared to challenge the biblical world view in print or in theory. However, by gathering together such a mass of data, and by publishing it so that other scholars could learn of it, these humanists made European intellectuals aware of a looming crisis, that of reconciling the pagan data with Judaism and Christianity, or else finding some way of accounting for it. Not only were the claims of European and Near Eastern writers of antiquity revived and studied, but also new data such as the Aztec Calendar Stone were found and interpreted which definitely seemed to point to ages long before the biblical creation.[27] The data compiled by these humanists provided some of the chief information that La Peyrère and Saumaise used in questioning the biblical chronology.

As difficult to assimilate as all of this data may have been, still more disturbing to European intellectuals was information resulting from the discovery of America. From the times of Columbus's and Vespucci's voyages, questions must have come to mind concerning who these inhabitants of the New World were, where they came from, and where they fit in our world. Although it does not seem that either Columbus or Vespucci was worried about these matters, it appears that various thinkers in the Spanish and Portuguese world began examining them. This took place not just out of idle curiosity, but because after the first settlements in America, it became necessary to determine the status of the Indians in the human world in order to see if they had any human rights. The early historian of anthropology, Thomas Bendysche, claimed that by 1512 a declaration had been made that the Indians were descended from Adam and Eve.[28] Bartholemé de las Casas, the protector of the Indians, in his long polemic with Sepulveda, finally got Pope Paul III to declare in 1537 that 'We…consider however, that the Indians are truly men.'[29] But then what kind of men, and where did they come from?

Lee Eldridge Huddleston, who wrote *Origins of the American Indians, European Concepts, 1492-1729*, pointed out that Columbus had no Indian origin problem. The Admiral thought that the land and the people he discovered were located right off the coast of Cathay. If so, there was no great mystery about where they came from. A bit later, Pedro Martin de Angleria, and perhaps Columbus too, claimed Hispaniola was actually Solomon's Ophir. If so, then the land and its inhabitants would fit neatly into the geography described in the Bible. Other theories were offered which assumed that the inhabitants of the New World came from some place in the Old World. Still others were offered claiming that the Indians came from Phoenicia, from China, from Arab lands, and, as we have seen, from Norway as Hugo Grotius contended. The most alluring and significant possibility, in terms of European theology, was that the Indians were the Lost Tribes of Israel, and hence, that the Indians were those Jews who were to be discovered just before the commencement of the Messianic Age. Debates raged over different possibilities. All of those listed above would make the Indians part of the same human group as the Europeans, Near Easterners and Asiatics. Any differences between the Indians and the rest of mankind would have to be accounted for by the long isolation of the Indians from everybody else.[30]

The first theory that posed a separate origin for the American Indians was offered by Paracelsus in 1520. In that same year the poet-dramatist, John Rastell, had written: 'But howe the people furst began, In that countrey or whens they cam, For clerkes it is a quesyon.'[31] Paracelsus tried to construct an answer that was both in keeping with his version of Christian theology, and yet admitted that the Indians and the rest of mankind had separate origins. In his work, the *Astronomia magna*, he wrote,

> We are all descended from Adam. And I cannot refrain from making a brief mention of those who have been found in hidden Islands and are still little known. To believe they have descended from Adam is difficult to conceive—that Adam's children have gone to the hidden islands. But one should well consider, that these people are from a different Adam. It will be difficult to maintain, that they are related on the basis of flesh and blood.'[32]

This much of Paracelsus's view would make it look as if he thought there were two co-equal Adams with co-equal descendants. Such a theory would seem to be heretical, similar to one of those condemned in the

Middle Ages. To clarify his position he said, 'It is credible that they (the Indians) were born there after the Deluge,' and also that 'perhaps they have no souls.'[33] If the first of these were to be the case, then it would not be necessary that the theory of two Adams conflict with Scripture. The scriptural account could be accepted as accurate. The second Adam theory would just be an addition to the history presented in Genesis. Paracelsus's second point should eliminate any lingering hint of theological difficulty. If the Indians have no souls they are not involved in the Divine drama that gave rise to the human Adam and all of his descendants. The Indians would simply not be participants in Providential history. To make the separation of the Indians from mankind more complete, Paracelsus suggested that the Indians were created after the Flood. This would eliminate the question of how they survived the Deluge, and would also eliminate the need to explain how the Indians had migrated from the Middle East to America. Theories like this were held up to the eighteenth century, I suppose, because they allowed the holder to assert simultaneously that the Indians had a separate creation, and that the biblical picture of the Adamic creation is true. One of the last to offer this theory was Henry Home, Lord Kames, in his *Sketches of the History of Man*.[34]

Paracelsus is often given credit for being the first modern thinker to offer a polygenetic theory of human origins. I think this is going a bit too far. After Paracelsus made his claim that it is possible that Indians do not have souls, he linked this with consideration of the cases of nymphs, sirens, sylphs, salamanders, and so on. Walter Pagel, whose studies on Paracelsus are of the highest importance in understanding him, has told me that all of the entities listed above that are compared with Indians are categorized as wild spirits in Paracelsus's theory. These wild spirits pervade the world. However, one has to take note, that these wild spirits are not other kinds of human beings. Instead they are sub-human beings. Thus, their separate creation from that of human beings does not involve a polygenetic theory.[35]

Even if Paracelsus did not actually advance a polygenetic point of view, he did set the stage for the emergence of such a daring theory. Once he had proposed considering a separate origin thesis to account for the American Indians, then other hardy thinkers could develop explanations that challenged biblical history. The full pre-Adamite theory of La Peyrère is the consequence of a century of analysis of explorer data. (La Peyrère's strongest opponent, Samuel Desmarets, said that Paracelsus and Maimonides were among the main sources for La Peyrère's theory.)[36]

Another important Renaissance thinker who speculated on possible origins of the Indians, and also by then, the Africans, was Giordano Bruno. In considering the differences between the Ethiopians (Africans), the American Indians, and various special or mythical beings such as those in the caves of Neptune, the Pygmies, the Giants, and so forth, Bruno felt that all of those beings 'cannot be traced to the same descent, nor are they sprung from the generative force of a single progenitor.'[37] Bruno had read a theory in the Kabbalistic literature to the effect that mankind had come from three protoplasts. The first gave rise to the Jews. Then the other two which were created two days earlier (and hence pre-Adamic) gave rise to the rest of mankind. Bruno had learned from another source that there was a Chinese theory that also claimed that mankind arose from three differently named protoplasts some twenty thousand years ago.[38]

Besides putting this in terms of Renaissance speculations, Bruno was concerned with the problem of the actual evidence coming to light in his time, and whether it could fit into a consistent (and preferably orthodox) cosmology. The evidence of the explorer literature, of the physical artifacts like the Aztec Calendar Stone (which, hidden after the Conquest of Mexico, was rediscovered in 1551, buried again by Spanish Church authorities in 1558, and not rediscovered again until 1790),[39] seems to have led Bruno to discuss, in his *Spaccio della Bestia trionfante* (1584), how the gods could deceive men about the true chronology of the world. Bruno posed the problem of how men could be made to believe counter to the evidence. The evidence includes pagan records that the world is over twenty thousand years old. It also includes discoveries about 'a new part of the world, where are found memorials of ten thousand years and more.'[40] If people are to be made to believe the biblical cosmology in spite of the evidence, then Bruno suggested it had better be asserted that the American Indians are not men, even though they resemble them in several respects, including intelligence. Besides seeing what the real conflict between the new data and the Bible was, and what one would have to do to save the biblical view (which, on the other hand, there is no evidence Bruno wanted to), Bruno was developing a naturalistic cosmology. In this theory everything is created out of Nature, including plants, animals and people. If this were so, no theory would be needed about the special creation of the human race.[41]

Bruno went to England in 1583-1585. It was there that he wrote the *Spaccio* where he discussed matters bordering on a pre-Adamite theory. He may have met or influenced some English thinkers who were accused of holding to the pre-Adamite theory, and of believing in a naturalistic or atheistical picture of the world. The chief of those so accused was Sir

Walter Ralegh. One of the accusations leveled against him was that he ran a school for atheists from 1592 onward.[42] Some of what was going on, according to the accusers, was described by the poet, Thomas Nashe. 'I heare say there be mathematicians abroad that will proove men before Adam.' Also, Nashe said, 'Impudently they persist in it, that the late discovered Indians are able to shew antiquities thousands before Adam.'[43] The targets of these charges were presumably Ralegh's friends, the mathematician, Thomas Harriot, and the playwright, Christopher Marlowe. After Marlowe was killed, a government agent who had been spying on him reported that Marlowe had read an atheist lecture to Sir Walter Ralegh and his guests.[44] Another agent, whose report was sent to Queen Elizabeth, gave some details about the alleged lecture of Marlowe. We are told that he stressed that there was a conflict between the biblical account of the world, which makes it to be about six thousand years old, and the American Indian and pagan accounts which make the world out to about sixteen thousand years old.[45] After Marlowe's death, Ralegh was accused over and over again of being irreligious, of having friends who were irreligious, and of encouraging disbelief in Christianity. Finally he was imprisoned in 1603.

A great deal of scholarly research has been carried on about the question of whether or not Harriot, Marlowe, or Ralegh really believed in the pre-Adamite theory, or whether they were actually atheists. Nothing that appears in the published writings of these three men states such views. The examination of the unpublished papers also provides no indications of pre-Adamism or atheism. Both Ralegh and Harriot had been in America, and had first hand knowledge of the Indians. In 1588 Harriot published *A Briefe and True Report of the New Found Land of Virginia*. In this work he described his discussion with the Indians about their views concerning the creation of the human race. Later on Harriot worked on biblical chronology, and is believed to have worked out the dating system, starting with the Creation, that was used in Ralegh's *Historie of the World*.[46]

So, on the one hand, no printed or manuscript document by Harriot, Marlowe, or Ralegh indicates that they held daring, irreligious views like the pre-Adamite theory. They did, however, have access to the raw material for forming the theory, namely the Indian creation views versus the Bible. There is evidence they all knew about some of Bruno's ideas. None of this shows they used the materials they were aware of to set forth a form of atheism. In fact, when Ralegh wrote his most extended picture of what he thought the world was like, the *Historie of the World*, it is put entirely into a biblical framework. On the other hand, however, there are the continuous statements of charges. Were they just a way of blackening the characters of the people involved, or did they reflect what was really going on? I think that when one examines the quantity and the quality of the attacks, it seems reasonable to suppose there was some radical thinking in the circle around Ralegh. The reports indicate a much more specific pre-Adamite theory than any that had been proposed up to then. Could the spies have invented the specific Indian claims that conflicted with the Bible? Obviously, Harriot and Ralegh could have heard the claims when they were in Virginia, and could have reported them to Marlowe. Thus, it seems plausible that the Ralegh group, in the 1590s, in some way raised the possibility of the pre-Adamite theory, especially with reference to the explorer data, probably based on the direct information that they had. However the Ralegh circle seems to have been either too fearful or too tentative to have been willing to write down even the most tenuous form of the pre-Adamite theory. Because of this, the Ralegh circle does not seem to have had any influence in the development of pre-Adamite or polygenetic theory.

Elizabethan pre-Adamism, whether an actual theory, or an accusation, was by far the most advanced form of the view to be presented during the Renaissance. It set forth the conflict between the biblical view, and that of the other chronologies, pagan or Indian. It did not, from what we are told, set forth a non-biblical picture of the world. And, unfortunately, we have no statement from either Harriot or Marlowe or Ralegh dealing with the nature of their pre-Adamic views, and how they would explain the world accordingly. There is no evidence at all that any rumors, discussions, hints about the pre-Adamism of the Ralegh group played any role whatsoever in the future development of the theory. It is striking that in the mid-seventeenth century, when La Peyrère's pre-Adamism was being hotly discussed everywhere, including England, nobody made any reference to an earlier English version of the theory.

So, as we have seen, during the sixteenth century, the study of pagan historical accounts, and the perplexing explorer data, led some bold thinkers to raise radical versions of the pre-Adamite theory. This was seen as a danger to the Christian world view, at least in England. Theoreticians such as Paracelsus and Bruno apparently had cosmologies too bizarre to be employed as adequate explanations of the new data. The English pre-Adamite theorists, if there actually were any, offered no theory. They are accused only of presenting the conflict between biblical chronology and other data. Were it not for the fact that the pre-Adamite theory was accepted by many anthropologists in the nineteenth century, the few versions of the theory that were presented in the Renaissance would probably be considered as the isolated reflection of some of the strange thinkers of the time. But, in view of what was to happen, the

Renaissance turned out to be a period in which there was a transformation from odd speculations that were intended mainly to embellish and reinforce the biblical picture of the world, to theorizing that presented a jarring confrontation of the then accepted world view concerning the nature and destiny of man with the ancient and modern facts that simply did not fit it. The polygenetic theory was to offer a most basic challenge to Judaism and Christianity.[47]

Huddleston, who has examined a wide range of the writings on the origins of the American Indians during the sixteenth century, found that they all held that the Indians were part of the Adamic world. The Church held that the Indians were truly men. What was debated among the experts was whether the Indians got to America from an ancestral home in Carthage, or Atlantis, or China, or Palestine, or some place else. Classical as well as Jewish and Christian literature were scrutinized for clues to the possible origins of the Indians.[48] The guiding principle of this research was stated late in the century by the important Spanish historian, Joseph de Acosta. He said, 'The reason which forces me to say that the first men of these Indies came from Europe or Asia is so as not to contradict the Holy Scripture which clearly teaches that all men descended from Adam, and thus we can give no other origin to man in the Indies.'[49] In this light, the best theory that Acosta could work out was that there must have been a land bridge in the past. Another important writer, Gregorio Garcia, wrote, in 1607, in his *Origen de los indios*, that the basic premise in considering where the Indians have come from is that all 'men and women had, and have, since the beginning of the World, proceeded, and taken their beginning and origin from our first parents Adam and Eve; and subsequently from Noah and his sons, who were all who remained alive after the General Deluge.'[50] The writers on the Indian question clung to a biblical monogenetic explanation, trying to find ways within it to account for the migrations of the Indians. While they were doing this, another development was also occurring. Some radical speculative thinkers of the Renaissance had already set the stage for a revolutionary reconsideration first of the question of the origins of the American Indians, and second, and more fundamental, of the question of the authenticity of the biblical account itself.

In the fifty or sixty years between the speculations of Giordano Bruno and the possible heresies of Harriot, Marlowe, and Ralegh, and the appearance of Isaac La Peyrère's theory, there is very little in the intellectual world that could have contributed to the development of his hypothesis. Among the few items are some comments by Lucilio Vanini, Francis Bacon, and Tommaso Campanella. In Vanini's *De admirandis naturae reginae deaeque mortalium arcanis*, he offered the view that some 'have dreamed' that the first man originated from mud, putrified by monkeys, swine and frogs. Further, Vanini reported, there have been other atheists who have maintained that only the Ethiopians came from monkeys.[51]

Francis Bacon, in his essay, 'Of vicissitude of things,' calmly commented that 'if you consider well, of the people of the *West Indies*, it is very probable that they are a Newer, or a Younger People, than the People of the Old World.'[52] Bacon dropped the subject, and offered no explanation about how he was going to square this with the account of man's origins in the Bible.

Tommaso Campanella, in his *Apologia pro Galileo* had offered his theory of the plurality of worlds. Other men may inhabit other stars. If they do, then these inhabitants 'did not originate from Adam and are not infected by his sin.' So, according to Campanella's pre-Adamism, only human beings from other planets could be pre-Adamites.[53] La Peyrère knew about Campanella and his views through Mersenne and Bourdelot. There is even some indication that La Peyrère met Campanella and discussed the pomp of the Papacy with him.[54] However, as far as we know, La Peyrère only settled in Paris in 1640, a year after the death of Campanella. Of course, it is always possible that he made earlier visits before becoming Condé's secretary. However, whether he actually met and conversed with Campanella or not, he most probably would have been introduced to his ideas by Campanella's admirers, Boudelot and Mersenne, who became close friends of La Peyrère in the early 1640s.

Apparently coincidentally a less learned but forceful expression of pre-Adamism appeared in some of the extreme radicals in the Puritan Revolution. The Levellers, Ranters and the Diggers questioned not only the authority of the Church, but also of Scripture. The great Leveller leader of the Puritan Revolution, Gerard Winstanley, saw that the Bible suggested there were men before Adam. To him this did not show the Bible was inaccurate, but that it should be interpreted metaphorically, not literally. This allowed him to justify his egalitarian version in terms of using Scripture as allegory, not historical fact.[55]

Some radicals went even further. William Walwyn is supposed to have questioned whether the Bible was the word of God. The Ranter, Laurence Clarkson, contended God was in all living things and in all matter. 'I really believed no Moses, Prophets, Christ or Apostles.'[56] He found 'so much contradiction' in the Bible and saw it as only a history. There were men before Adam and the world will go on eternally.[57]

The radical English attack on the Bible, and its inclusion of claims of the existence of men before Adam, seems to grow out of concerns to justify the egalitarian political views of the left wing of the Puritan Revolution. It was not based on classical evidence, theology, or reconciling the explorer data, and seems to have had little intellectual structure except the need to brush aside accepted authority in order to allow for the personal message of God to men to construct an earthly Utopia. Jacob Boehme's personal mysticism seems to have influenced those questioning or allegorizing the Bible.

There is an intriguing fragment in the British Library that may belong to this radical English discussion. It is entitled 'Whey^{re} there were any men before Adam? Answ^{re}.' The item is three pages long, and is anonymous. It is bound with material from 1667, but is in a different hand. The answer offered is that 'The Great God' from eternity was communicating His Goodness. To do this there must be rational creatures to receive those communications. 'hence it is y^t men were from everlasting.' The rationale for this seems to come from a Neo-Platonic view of God's overflowing nature. The anonymous author considers the apparent contradiction between the eternal existence of men, and the Biblical view that the creation occurred about 6,000 years ago. This difficulty is overcome by claiming this must be a new creation to replace the earlier creation of corrupt, abominably wicked people. The only point raised that also appears in La Peyrère's view is that the Biblical story about Cain is evidence that there were people other than those who descend from the Adamic creation.[58]

In spite of the fact that this radical political biblical criticism with an avowal of pre-Adamism appeared in the same period as La Peyrère's work, there seems to be no connection whatsoever. I say 'seems,' (a) since it is possible that La Peyrère's theory became known in the 1640s in some form in England, from people who had encountered it either in France or Holland, and (b) since some one, not yet known, thought it appropriate to translate and publish La Peyrère's *Prae-Adamitae* as *Men Before Adam* in 1656, at the height of the Puritan Revolution. However I have not any seen Leveller, Digger or Ranter text taken from La Peyrère's material, nor any reference in La Peyrère to what was going on in England which he might have heard about from Hobbes or other English refugees. La Peyrère, as mentioned earlier, was in England in 1654 on Condé's business, but so far we know nothing of whom he saw or what he learned there.

A radical English theologian, who may have interrelated with La Peyrère either in person or through some kind of intellectual exchange, was Samuel Fisher, an Oxford trained Baptist, who became a Quaker, and developed a most forceful attack on the accuracy of existing scriptural texts as The Word of God. We will discuss his views in relation to those of La Peyrère and Spinoza (whom Fisher probably knew personally) in the next chapter.

As these various thinkers raised points about ancient history and the explorer data that were in conflict with the then accepted biblical view, one finds that the members of the academic and theological establishment did little about them beyond burning or killing the worst offenders such as Bruno, Vanini and perhaps Marlowe. In England some of the radical Bible questioners were arrested and punished. Matters might have gone on that way were it not for the forceful presentation of the pre-Adamite theory by La Peyrère. Unlike his predecessors who presented the clash of data, La Peyrère offered his pre-Adamite theory as a system based on the Bible, producing a new Messianic theology. He entitled his book 'A Theological Systeme upon the Presupposition that Men were before Adam.' The first evidence used for his pre-Adamite theory was a passage in St. Paul's Romans. After this he reinforced his theory by the Renaissance developments. With all of this, he was able to offer within the Judeo-Christian world view, a theory that would encompass the new historical and anthropological data, but would do so at a tremendous price.

CHAPTER FOUR

BIBLICAL CRITICISM AND INTERPRETATION
IN LA PEYRÈRE

If we consider La Peyrère's theory that there were men before Adam as the culmination of Renaissance speculations concerning the conflict between exploration data and classical data on the one hand, and the biblical view on the other, I think we should also consider what La Peyrère said about his source; from his dead brother (who of course, could not be punished for it); from his pastor (who he may have thought deserved punishment), or from his own reading of the Bible.[1] The latter seems most plausible in the light of the way he structured his case. La Peyrère was not a genuine Renaissance scholar. We know from Richard Simon that he could read neither Hebrew nor Greek.[2] He cited comparatively few sources. He knew the pre-Adamite text in Maimonides. He seems to have known about Postel's Messianic theory, and perhaps about Judah Halevi's views. (Of course the works of both Maimonides and Halevi were available in Latin.) La Peyrère did not seem to know the work of previous biblical scholars, except for those he had met personally. He did cite a good many works of classical Greek and Roman authors, as well as some of the late Renaissance experts on these writers.[3] However, the account which seems to explain the genesis of his pre-Adamism is that of the published version, where he said he developed the theory first as a consequence of a passage in St. Paul's Romans, then buttressed it by the material about pagan history and modern anthropology.[4]

La Peyrère's main work, *Prae-Adamitae*, consists of two parts. The first, in the English translation, is *Men before Adam, or a Discourse upon the twelfth, thirteenth and fourteenth Verses of the First Chapter of the Epistle of the Apostle Paul to the Romans. By which are prov'd that the first Men were created before Adam.* This contains a dedication to all of the synagogues on the earth.[5] Depending on the edition, the discourse runs to about fifty pages. Next there is *A Theological Systeme upon that Presupposition that Men were before Adam*, which begins with a short Proeme, and five books of the *Theological Systeme*. Although the whole text of both items was usually bound together as *Prae-Adamitae*, the holdings of various great libraries indicate that sometimes one or the other was bound separately.[6]

In the Proeme to his *Theological System*, La Peyrère started out saying that it is natural to question who was the first man. The pagan records of the Chaldeans, the Egyptians, the Ethiopians and the Scythians, plus parts of 'the frame of the world newly discovered,' as 'also from those unknown Countries, to which the *Hollanders* have sayled of late, the men of which, as is probable, did not descend from Adam.'[7] Then La Peyrère provided us with a biographical clue. He said that 'I had this suspition also being a Child, when I heard or read the History of Genesis: Where Cain goes forth: where he kills his brother when they were in the field; doing it warily, like a thief, least it should be discovered by any: Where he flies, where he fears punishment for the death of his Brother: Lastly, where he marries a wife far from his Ancestors, and builds a City. Yet, although I had this doubt in my mind, yet durst I not speak any thing of it, which did not rellish of that received opinion, concerning *Adam* created first of all men.'[8] So La Peyrère said that he did keep quiet until he came across verses 12-14 of chapter V of St. Paul's Epistle to the Romans.[9] Then he realized that his text proved that there were men before Adam. In the 'Proeme' he said he had brooded about this for about 20 years before the publication of the *Prae-Adamitae*. A further clue appears in an autobiographical passage in his final draft of the unpublished, *Rappel des Juifs*, presumably written in 1673. Here La Peyrère said that his pre-Adamite theory grew out of his Messianic theory.[10] In sum, we can see La Peyrère probably started out as a precocious youth, raising nasty questions such as 'Who was Cain's wife? Where did she come from?' As he started to draw possible heretical answers, he was forced back to conformity. Later on when he pondered the text in St. Paul's Romans, he saw what the implication had to be. There were men before Adam. This earth-shaking discovery only began to make sense when put in a Jewish Messianic setting. And finally it was this whole conception, the pre-Adamite theory and the Messianic theory together, that La Peyrère was trying to set forth throughout his lifetime.[11] But circumstances always prevented it from being done. So each successive presentation of his case was only a part of what he was trying to tell the world.

What are these verses in Romans that were so revealing to him? As they appear in the 1656 English edition they state,

> As by one man sin entered into the world, and by sin, death: so likewise death had power over all men, because in him all men sinned. For till the time of the Law sin was in the world, but sin was not imputed, when the Law was not. But death reigned from Adam into Moses, even upon those who had not sinned according to the similitude of the transgression of Adam, who is The Type of the future.[12]

La Peyrère quickly interpreted this to say that law came into the world with Adam. However, there was sin before Adam, but it only took on

moral significance with Adam. Therefore there must have been men
before Adam.[13] This idea, La Peyrère readily admitted, would be startling to almost everybody. But before showing what a wonderful explanatory hypothesis this is, its author tried to quiet the outraged reader.
He offered his usual comparison with the Copernican theory, and said
that these theories do not change reality. So he said, *'whether we think that
Adam was created alone, and that he was first of all men, or believe that other were
begotten before Adam, all Christian Religion shall still keep its own place and its
own mysteries.*'[14] So the crucial connection between Romans 5 and the pre-
Adamite theory is that if Adam sinned in a morally meaningful sense,
then there must have been an Adamic law according to which he sinned.
If law began with Adam, then there must have been a lawless world
before Adam, containing people. And if law only began with Moses, then
sin could not have started with Adam.

The passage in Romans that La Peyrère found puzzling led him to the
pre-Adamite theory. Immediately after stating his interpretation and insisting that there is nothing irreligious in his view, La Peyrère began
listing all of the great advantages of his theory. First, it clarifies the
history set forth in the first chapters of Genesis, and renders this account
consistent both with itself and also with the profane records, ancient or
new. La Peyrère listed the Chaldeans, the Egyptians, the Scythians, the
Chinese and the Mexicans as ones whose records would not square with
the Bible. Then he declared, 'Again, by this Position, Faith and right
Reason are reconciled, which suffers us not to believe that the world had
so late an infancy.'[15]

In analyzing this passage in Romans, La Peyrère was also led to one
of the bases of his biblical criticism. After showing that the clause 'sin was
not imputed' is ambiguous, and has been interpreted in different ways,
he offered his revolutionary explanation of the problem of understanding
the clause, namely that 'by the carelessness of the Transcribers' a
mistake was made.[16]

Because of that error the wrong word had crept into the Greek text.
Although, as has been pointed out, Richard Simon claimed La Peyrère
did not know Greek, he nonetheless devoted a page to rewriting the
clause so that it more clearly suggested the pre-Adamite reading.[17] Once
it had been shown or admitted that the biblical text as it now stands can
contain mistakes due to transcribers, then it seems likely that we do not
presently possess an accurate copy of the Bible. To find out what this
original text said, some kind of critical reconstruction of it would have
to be carried out.

Before doing that La Peyrère pursued the explication of the verses of
Romans. This led him to the interesting question of what was the state

of man before Adam. It was lawless, since law began with Adam. La Peyrère specifically calls it 'the state of Nature,' and describes it as a nasty, brutal condition. Everything could occur, and nothing was a crime.[18] Adam was the first person to live in a lawful society, and the first to be able to sin. Thus the sense in which Adam is the father of mankind is that it is from him that we are all sinners. But, as La Peyrère is careful to point out, this does not make him the actual ancestor of the entire human population. The sense in which we are all children of God is that we are all made from the same materials, but not from the same person. It is of great significance for La Peyrère's theology that Adam is the father of the Jews, but not the father of all mankind.[19]

Before going on, I should like to comment briefly on La Peyrère's state of nature theory. It sounds very much like that of Thomas Hobbes. It could well be the case that he borrowed it from Hobbes, or that it was somehow a joint effort. They must have known each other since they were both members of the same intellectual circle in Paris. Hobbes fled to France in 1640 and immediately became part of the avant garde scene. Hobbes, when he arrived in Paris, stayed with Jacques du Bosc, a member of the circle of Mersenne, Gassendi and Naudé, to which La Peyrère also belonged. Hobbes also became a close friend of Samuel Sorbière, who was also a friend of La Peyrère's. In the period, 1640-1651, when Hobbes lived in Paris and wrote *De Cive* (which was translated into French by Sorbière) and *Leviathan*, he must have encountered La Peyrère often since they were part of the same intellectual and social group.[20]

Regardless of the lines of influence, it is worth noting that Hobbes was attacked because he was not able to give a chronological date for the state of nature without imputing a lawless society to God's actions. Since Hobbes presumably accepted the biblical account, the world started with Adam, and law began then. Thereafter, some kind of a Divine Order prevailed up until this very moment. So, when could this state of nature have taken place? Hobbes was evasive in dealing with this point, avoiding placing his state of nature in historical time. La Peyrère, on the other hand, has a simple solution. There was an indefinite amount of time before Adam, during which there was no Divine Order. If Adam was created in 4004 B.C., then the state of nature could have existed from that date indefinitely backwards. During that period there was natural sin which 'depended upon no prohibition of the Law, but had its original from the meer ill disposition of humane nature.'[21]

Since La Peyrère held that natural sin predated Adam, then how could he explain how or why God made men so bad? To account for this, he developed his theory that there were actually two creations, the first when God made man out of corruptible matter which quickly degenerated.

People of this creation ended up in the Hobbesian state of nature. The second creation involved transforming men into gods, men who could be immortal. This creation was achieved through Election starting with Adam. What this involves is that everybody has the possibility of election. For some mysterious reason it pleased God to elect the Jews, and then later on to reject them and elect the Gentiles in their place, and finally to join the Gentiles and the Jews together in one election.[22]

Adam was the first Jew, and his election carried down to his posterity described in the Bible. The election of the Jews did not occur for any reason that we know of. It was simply arbitrary. Besides eschewing any explanation of the election of the Jews, La Peyrère also insisted that the Jews had no racial superiority. Considering how his theory was later to be used by European racists, it is good to remember that he said, 'For they [the Jews] were made up of the same flesh and bloud as the Gentiles and were temper'd with the same clay of which other men were fram'd.'[23] God just chose to make the Jews gods, and 'God became the God of the Jews, not only by Election and mind, but also by Covenant and paction often confirm'd and iterated.'[24] The Jews were set apart from all other peoples and were given an elected land, which on La Peyrère's account ran from the Nile to the Euphrates, and from the Mediterranean to the lower end of the Arabian peninsula.[25] (*Prae-Adamitae* comes with a map of Terra Sancta which would please the most expansionist Israelis, and would horrify even the most pacific Arabs. It even has the Holy Land, Eretz Israel, including much of what is now Saudi Arabia and Yemen.)

The Gentiles acquired their election second-hand through the Jews. Mysteriously the Gentiles were grafted onto the tree of the Jews, and thus became sanctified. This, however, did not change the Gentiles into Adamites. The Gentiles are more ancient than the Jews, but their entrance into Providential History is much later. Until they were adopted they were 'Those Gentiles which were called,' were 'Atheists and without a God,'...they 'were called wicked, foolish, corrupt, abominable in their iniquities.'[26]

Arguing his case entirely on interpretations of biblical texts so far, La Peyrère contended that Adam was made differently by God than were Gentiles. Adam was made of the dust of the earth. The Gentiles were made by the Word of God.[27] The Jews are the sons of Adam, and as such constitute a separate species of mankind. There are also many species of Gentiles, some of whom were unknown to the ancient Jews. As La Peyrère explored the implications of his polygenetic theory, he saw that he could account for some of the bewildering new discoveries, 'those of *America*, the Southern, and the *Greenlanders* and the rest, to which neither the Jew, nor the rest of the Gentiles as yet had accesse.'[28] Thus La Peyrère's interpretation of the Bible solves the problem of explaining the origin of the newly-discovered peoples, and of explaining why they seem to have no connection with the story in Scripture.

La Peyrère argued at great length and in great detail that item after item in Genesis proves that it is 'clearer than the Sun, That the men of the first Creation were created long before Adam.'[29] He kept contending that any reasonable reader would have to adopt the pre-Adamite hypothesis. He also argued for a pre-Eveite theory. She was not the first woman. She was the first Jewish woman, Jewish wife, and Jewish mother.[30] As La Peyrère produced case after case, he indicated that he had gotten some of his points from his friend, Claude Saumaise, some from another friend, Ishmael Bouillau, and some from Michel de Marolles, who later worked with La Peyrère on a French edition of the Bible that was suppressed. Josephus was also a source for some of his points.[31]

Having used data in the Bible to support his theory, he turned to his next level of evidence, the pagan accounts of the beginning and the development of the world. There is a truly amazing compilation of the ancient pagan material that indicates an independent and pre-Adamite view. Taking up the Egyptian, Greek, Babylonian and Chinese histories, as well as data about Mexico and about the Eskimos, on whom La Peyrère was the leading authority at the time, he built up a strong case. The Eskimos, of course, were also used to rebut Hugo Grotius, now deceased, who had attacked La Peyrère twelve years before his book came out. Grotius, as mentioned earlier, claimed that the American Indians were Norwegians left over from the Viking voyages to Iceland and Greenland. La Peyrère deftly pointed out that when the Vikings got to Greenland, they had found Eskimos there. So where did the Eskimos come from?[32] La Peyrère employed materials from a wide range of classical authors including Homer, Hermes Trismegistus, Plato, Cicero, Porphyry, Pomponius Mela, Claudian, Virgil, Lucan, Varro, Ausonius, Horace, Iamblichus, Josephus, Diodorus Siculus, and Herodotus.[33] It is hard to tell if he actually read all of these sources, since even when he quoted material, he gave no citations. However, he often referred to his friend, Claude Saumaise, and to Joseph Scaliger, who may have been his actual sources.

From all of this material, La Peyrère showed that the ancient chronologies, no matter how they are computed, go back to a time before Adam. Also, human events that must have occurred prior to Adam are described by the most reliable ancient authors, such as Plato, Herodotus, and Cicero. None of them would have believed that the world was of recent or Adamic origin. The Chinese and the Americans (probably Mexicans) both have accounts of the world that long predate Adam. And La Peyrère felt that the most convincing evidence that the pagan world existed long before Adam was the astronomical and astrological discoveries of the ancient Babylonians and Egyptians. (If he had known about the Mayans, his case would have been overwhelming.) For them to be able to do their sophisticated calculations and computations, to be able to develop their elaborate theories and interpretations, must have required ages of observation and intellectual development. This time span would have had to be much longer than that allowed for in the Bible.[34] This material and the argument based on it come from Claude Saumaise's book on the history of ancient astronomy and astrology, *De Annis Climactericus* of 1648. As mentioned earlier, La Peyrère later told a person who was working on a life of Saumaise (who is mainly remembered because of his controversy with John Milton) that when this great book came out, he had thanked the author on behalf of *'mes pre-Adamites.'* The wealth of learning that Saumaise had shown was known by the Egyptians and the Chaldeans convinced La Peyrère that it could not have been acquired in the short period of time between Adam and Abraham, or Adam and Moses. La Peyrère regarded it as ridiculous that Adam could have arrived on the earth with all possible scientific knowledge.[35]

Having made a plausible case for the pre-Adamite theory from the internal data in the Bible, from the material in the ancient pagan writers, and from the current anthropological findings, La Peyrère went on to the development of a second revolutionary thesis that he had only briefly introduced before, namely that the Bible we possess may be an inaccurate document. How do we know that the text we have is the original? There are several passages in Joshua, Chronicles and Kings that indicate they are taken from works that are now lost. Moving from the possibility that the Bible we possess is a truncated version of the original, we can ask a much more basic question. Is Moses the author of the first five books of the Bible we possess? 'It is so reported, but not believed by all. These Reasons make me believe, that those Five Books are not the Originals, but copies out by another.'[36] There was the problem that Moses's death and events thereafter are discussed in the fifth book. La Peyrère used this plus other Scriptural texts to indicate that Moses could not have written them. He was willing to consider that Moses might have made a diary which was copied into the Bible. And the evidence he considered became the basis for modern biblical criticism. After discussing various discrepancies and inconsistencies in the text, he enunciated his revolutionary theory about the Bible in this passage previously cited, 'I need not trouble the Reader much further to prove a thing in itself sufficiently evident, that the first five books of the Bible were not written by Moses, as is thought. Nor need any one wonder after this, when he reads many things confus'd and out of order, obscure, deficient, many things omitted and misplaced, when they shall consider with themselves that they are a heap of Copie confusedly taken.'[37]

La Peyrère next developed what has been a major aspect of biblical criticism over the last three centuries. From various textual examples, he showed that there seemed to be different authors of different portions of Scripture 'these things were diversely written, being taken out of several authors.'[38] La Peyrère insisted that he believed in the Calvinist view that the Holy Spirit of God is in Scripture. However, he asserted, that what has come down to us is a product of Divine and human history, Revelation transmitted through fallible human copiers and transcribers. Because of the human element we now have an inaccurate text. Therefore, La Peyrère proposed in outline one of the tasks of future biblical criticism, that of separating what in the text has resulted from the copiers, and what was in the original text.[39] Subsequently, his younger contemporary, Father Richard Simon, tried valiantly to complete the undertaking delineated by La Peyrère.

La Peyrère was definitely not the first person to notice problems about the text of Scripture that raised questions about whether we presently possess a complete and accurate text and whether Moses wrote the entire Pentateuch. Hobbes in 1651 published his questioning of whether Moses could have written the part of Deuteronomy about Moses's death. Whether Hobbes got this from La Peyrère or vice-versa, we do not know. Various English radicals in the Puritan Revolution questioned the source and accuracy of the Bible. The problem of the Mosaic authorship was known and discussed by Jewish commentators much earlier.

Jewish scholars, in their efforts to find every level of divine message in Scripture, studied the text from the Hellenistic period all through the Middle Ages, with a seriousness and thoroughness that defies belief. They did not miss what became obvious to the Enlightenment readers, but they saw it within a context that led to explicating the text as God's message to man. One Medieval account of the passage about the death of Moses, is that Moses wrote it, as God dictated it to him, with tears pouring out of his eyes as he learned of his own approaching demise, and that he would not live to set foot upon the Promised Land. This reading accounts for how Moses could know the events of his death and thereafter.[40] Another account, used also as an answer to La Peyrère, was that Moses was given by God the ability to know the entire prior history of mankind as well as its future.[41] And this would explain how he could write about everything from the beginning of the world to events after his own lifetime.

The medieval commentator Abraham Ibn (or Aben) Ezra 1092/3-1167 brought the achievements of biblical scholarship from Islamic Spain into Christian Europe. One of his greatest works was his commentary on the Pentateuch. In it he advanced a new theory about the lines dealing with Moses's death and the events thereafter, namely that they were not by Moses. In view of this, he suggested that they had special significance and mysterious import. His view was the beginning of the questioning of the Mosaic authorship, though in his case he was not intending to raise doubts, but to find reassurance. His commentary was printed first in 1488, and reissued many times, giving wide dispersion to his views.[42]

The attempt to find the exact, accurate text of Scripture in Hebrew and Greek from the late fifteenth century through the Reformation, led scholars to study the available manuscripts, to search for the oldest ones, and to compare Greek, Aramaic, Coptic, Arabic, and other Near Eastern language versions. This led people from Erasmus onward to note variants. By La Peyrère's time, the French Protestant scholar, Louis Cappel, whom La Peyrère had consulted, had counted up eighteen hundred variants, amongst the various versions of the Hebrew Scriptures that had come down to his time.[43]

Internally, within the text, readers from ancient times onward had noted passages that seemed to be inconsistent with others. All kinds of exegetical techniques were offered by the Talmudic rabbis, the Church Fathers, commentators, Jewish and Christian, to show that the apparently conflicting text could be harmonized. In La Peyrère's day, the Amsterdam rabbi, Menasseh ben Israel, had published his famous *Conciliador* (first volume in 1632, second in 1651). He took apparently conflicting passages in Scripture, and showed ways by which these passages could be reconciled without questioning the truth or accuracy of Scripture itself.[44] Only the wildest radical enthusiasts of the Puritan Revolution and La Peyrère were willing to conclude that Moses was not the author of it all, and the text now available is 'a heep of copie confusedly taken' that may not be accurate. La Peyrère believed a more accurate text could be reconstructed by 'reasonable analysis,' and did not turn as the Levellers, Diggers, Ranters, and Quakers did, to private inspiration as the source of God's message to mankind.

The point of La Peyrère's biblical criticism, he made quite clear in *Prae-Adamitae*, was first to convince people that the text we possess of Scripture is deficient. If this is so, people will realize that the Bible does not really discuss the whole history of the world, or of the human race. Then it will not be surprising that the Bible makes no mention of men before Adam, since it does not discuss everything. The fact that there is no such discussion should not lead to the conclusion that there were no pre-Adamites. One should now recognize, from all that La Peyrère has said, that the design of the Mosaic books is to discuss the history of the Jews, not the history of all mankind.[45]

With this assumption, La Peyrère showed how to interpret all sorts of passages in Scripture so that they would only deal with what happened to the Jews, and to Palestine, and not to all mankind, and to the whole world. So, miracles such as Joshua's commanding the sun to stand still, are interpreted as dealing with local events; that is, the sun stood still just where Joshua was, and in no other place. Such an interpretation, La Peyrère pointed out, does not conflict too much with the scientific evidence. However, he apparently knew he might be accused of going too far in rationalizing miracles. He pointed out that other people are trying to make religion incredible, whereas 'I Ingenuously confesse, I do not give in my name amongst those enormous upholders of miracles, who put all reason out of square. I am reasonable, and any thing that is belonging to reason I pretend an interest in it. I believe those miracles of *Iosua* and *Isaiah*, and doe very magnifie God in them, but think them not greater than they were, nor as is agreeable to reason, therefore I have contained them within their own limits.'[46] However, La Peyrère's way of making religion more reasonable is to interpret miracles as local events rather than natural events.

The particular case that aroused the most opposition was La Peyrère's explanation of what happened during Noah's Flood. For La Peyrère a local interpretation of this is necessary so that the entire present population of the world are not descendants of Noah and his family. Thus he insisted that the Flood was a local event in Palestine directed against the sinful Jews of the time. Using some of the geological and geographical items in the biblical account, La Peyrère argued that the waters only covered the area around Palestine. Further, he argued, it was just implausible that all the people of the earth could descend from the seven survivors. The Bible indicates that the survivors produced all of the Nations on earth in five generations. But could they really have produced the inhabitants of China, America, the Southland and Greenland, among others? Could this even account for the population of Europe?[47] And, if one examines the matter, was there enough time between Noah and Abraham to account for what the world was like in Abraham's time, assuming that the Flood was universal, and only seven people survived? Also, La Peyrère was one of the first to take cognizance of the fact that many cultures, such as the Greek, Egyptian, Chinese and American, have flood stories. This does not mean that they are all talking about the same flood. Rather they may each describe a local flood. So, 'why should we not grant to *Palestine* their particular deluge'?[48] And, besides, he pointed out, there are cultures with very ancient records that make no mention of a flood. It is interesting that Sir Walter Ralegh in his *History of the World* used almost the same data to come to the conclusion that the floods in pagan countries were local and natural, but that Noah's flood was universal and miraculous.[49]

Accepting the Flood as universal leaves too little time to account for what has gone on in history. Nonetheless, even when La Peyrère was circulating his theory in manuscript, the denial of the universality of the Flood was one of the major things that shocked people. Only Saumaise seemed to have agreed with La Peyrère, and said that he had a demonstration as good as that for $2 + 2 = 4$ that the Flood was local.[50] Unfortunately, we do not learn what the demonstration was. The view of the opposition is indicated by the English divine and jurist, Sir Matthew Hale. He pointed out in his *The Primitive Origination of Mankind* that if one believed La Peyrère's interpretations of the Bible were true, this 'would necessarily not only weaken but overthrow the Authority and Infallibility of the Sacred Scripture.'[51] Bishop Stillingfleet tried to answer La Peyrère about the Flood in his *Origines Sacrae*. In so doing Stillingfleet made the Flood a bit less than universal to overcome some of the difficulties involved.[52] Thomas Burnet, in his *Telluris theoria sacra*, and in his *The Theory of the Earth*, advanced a geological theory to meet La Peyrère's view and to show that the Flood was not a localized event. Burnet's theory, even though it was more orthodox than La Peyrère's, was sufficiently novel to cause a lengthy controversy on the subject, a controversy that played an important role in the development of geology.[53]

La Peyrère passed from his heretical theory about the Flood to a more heretical theory, namely that the world is eternal. He declared that 'the foundations of the World were laid from eternal times, or from eternity, in regard to us, or from times and ages to us unknown, or from that beginning, of which there is no certain knowledge.'[54] Since it is possible to calculate from the time of Adam to the present, (as people like Archbishop Ussher had done), then creation could not have occurred in Adam's time, if creation were from eternity. Also, various ancient accounts indicate that the world has been going on endlessly.

The radical doctrines that La Peyrère set forth in the fourth book of *Prae-Adamitae*, namely his critique of the Bible, his interpretation of the events in the Bible as local and Jewish, and his theory of the eternity of the world, are all outgrowths of his Messianic vision. The pre-Adamite theory was developed in order to separate Jewish from Gentile history, so that only the former is strictly Providential. If the *real* Divine drama concerning human history is taking place only within Jewish history (whose culmination is imminent), then Gentile history must have different roots and must not be part of the same development. This state of affairs is not rational. There is no logical reason why Jewish history is at the center of the world stage. God just chose mysteriously to save mankind in this way. When one reads the Bible correctly, one gets an idea of part of what God is doing, in the course of Jewish history from Adam to Jesus. The force of God's plan becomes clearer when one is able to see it as solely about one select group, the Jews. Then one comprehends that the whole drama will end in the forthcoming events of Jewish history when the Jews are recalled.

Once it is seen that it is through Jewish history that the Divine Plan of salvation unfolds, then the rest of humanity is to be accounted for not as an offshoot of Jewish history, but as independent pre-Adamic groups, participating vicariously in the course of Providential history. It might be asked, why does not the Bible, which is the crucial document for telling us what is going on in the world, present the full picture as La Peyrère has portrayed it? His answer is simply, first, that the Bible is a Judeocentric document. Second, as has been pointed out, the Bible, as we possess it, is a defective document. From what we know of it, it was written by ancient Jews to tell the story of Jewish history. The Bible itself is also part of Jewish history, both as a Providential message, and a document transmitted by Jewish authors and copiers. Therefore, we need biblical criticism to reconstruct the accurate Bible, which can then be evaluated and interpreted.

When that is done, we will realize that Jewish history goes on in finite time in a fixed Divine Plan. On the other hand, Gentile history, which we can now see plays no role in the Providential scheme of things, goes on from eternity. Gentile history has no beginning and it has no end or goal. It is just the human comedy. But it is through the forthcoming culminating events of Jewish history that the whole world will be transformed.

Thus, those aspects of La Peyrère's theory that created the greatest impact in generating biblical criticism and the secular study of history, resulted from his attempt to buttress his visionary picture of what he thought was about to happen—the Recall of the Jews and the Coming of the Jewish Messiah. From this vision the rest followed. There were men before Adam, namely the Gentiles. The Bible was the accurate account of human history. However, our copies were defective. And the Bible had to be interpreted in a localized Jewish way. And, finally, the world was eternal, and the Jewish part of it just a small finite portion. However, through what is about to happen as the conclusion of Jewish history, everybody, pre-Adamite, Adamite and post-Adamite, will be saved.

La Peyrère's earlier work, *Du Rappel des Juifs* deals mainly with what will be involved in the future for the Jews who are about to be recalled to Divine History. Originally, the Jews were the sole actors in the Divine Drama. Then when they rejected Jesus, the Jews were cast aside, and the Gentiles were grafted onto the stock, and replaced the Jews as the Divine agents in History. Now, however, the Jews are about to be recalled when they join with the Christians, especially in France. La Peyrère claimed that the Jews would come to France from all over the rest of the world, because France was the land of liberty (it had no slaves). And then, as the triumphant next step, the King of France would lead these converted Jews back to Palestine.[55]

When God rejected the Jews, He dispersed them, He made Palestine an ecological mess, and He darkened the skin of the Jews. Now when they return to their homeland, and their long awaited Messiah arrives, Jerusalem will be rebuilt, and it will be the center of the universe. The Messiah, plus 'le roi universel,' the King of France, plus the Jews who have been recalled, will govern the world together. All of humanity will benefit and all will be saved. All of nature and mankind will be renewed.[56]

Since this lovely picture was what La Peyrère believed was about to happen, he devoted the bulk of *Du Rappel* to presenting a political action program that would help prepare for these great events. Most of his program deals with the central issue of getting the Christians and the Jews to unite. The first step in accomplishing this is to convince the Christians to treat Jews decently, and to give up their anti-Semitic activities and attitudes, even though the Christians may find Jews repulsive. The Christians should realize what ingrates they are when they treat the Jews badly. They should consider all of the benefits Christians have gained from Jews.[57]

Following this, La Peyrère carried on an amazing attack on anti-Semitism, considering what were the normal views on this subject at the time. He first challenged one of the principal reasons then offered by the Gentiles for rejecting, and hating Jews, namely that the Jews had killed Jesus Christ, and had thereby committed the most horrendous crime possible, that of deicide.[58] La Peyrère did not try to explain this away as many twentieth century liberal Christians and Jews do by asserting that it was the Roman officials and not the Jews who did the terrible deed. This assertion is sometimes joined with the view that if Christians have any complaints about the Crucifixion, they should take them up with the Roman authorities. Since they no longer exist, the matter perhaps should be taken up with the Italian authorities who are the successor regime. Instead, La Peyrère took it as fact that the Jews of the first century were responsible for the death of Jesus. This being the case, Christians have every right to be angry about it. However, God has already punished the Jews on this score. He does not need any assistance from the Christian world in order to wreak His Vengeance. At this point La Peyrère helpfully suggested that the Jews could reply to this charge of deicide by claiming that they did the Gentile world a very great favor by crucifying Jesus. Were it not for the fact that Jesus died on the cross, He would not have died for the sins of all mankind. Hence, everybody has profited from His death.[59]

La Peyrère next compounded his answer to anti-Semitism by asserting that the deicide committed by the Jews is almost the same crime as the anti-Semitism practised by the Christians. Both of these activities are wrong. Both the Jews and the Christians should ask for God's forgiveness. What is basically involved in both cases is ingratitude and excessive pride. The Jews in the first century did not appreciate that God was giving them a new Law. Their overwhelming pride led them to prefer their old Law to the new Dispensation. The Christians, on the other hand, do not appreciate that the Jews have given them their Messiah and the very possibility of salvation. Operating completely blindly, the Jews had killed the Son of God. But the Christians are also actively persecuting and killing the sons of God.[60]

However, La Peyrère claimed, if anti-Semitism could be eradicated, then possibly the Jews would be ready to convert to Christianity. Those Jews whom God will recall are the converts. And here La Peyrère uses the Spanish term, 'Christianos nuevos,' which at the time was used to designate Iberians forced to convert to Christianity, who were probably secret Jews, Marranos. Another group that would be recalled was the secret elect of Jews, spoken of by Saint Paul, numbering seven thousand, and known only to God.[61]. This elect has the true faith. They possess the spirit of Christianity even though they do not know of the Incarnation. They are able to be saved in the faith of Abraham, because in spirit they actually believe the same things that Christians do. La Peyrère declared that before the coming of Jesus, the good Jews such as the Patriarchs and the Prophets, could have had the spirit of Jesus without actually knowing Him, since information about the Incarnation was not available. These good Jews of antiquity had to deal with shadowy and confused images of a Messiah for whom they were waiting.[62] Jews living after the coming of Jesus are able to have this same belief in a Messiah who will rescue them from their present plight, and re-establish them in the Holy Land. La Peyrère further contended that this Jewish Messianic view was what was believed by John the Baptist, the Apostles and Mary when Jesus was alive. All of them saw Jesus as a temporal redeemer. Thus, La Peyrère said that the Messianic view held to by the Jews of his day was the same as the view that was held by the Patriarchs, the Apostles, and the Disciples. However, the Apostles and the Disciples gained added knowledge after the Resurrection had taken place.[63]

What La Peyrère was trying to establish in developing this point was the claim that seventeenth century Jews could have the spirit of Jesus without knowledge of the mystery of the Incarnation. The elect who possess this spirit, have Jesus within themselves even though they have not actually had a clear revelation of Jesus Christ Incarnate. However, God alone knows which Jews possess this spirit. On this basis, La Peyrère argued strongly against anti-Semitism. If the Christian world persecuted all of the Jews, they would also be persecuting this group of God's elect. The persecution of this group amounts to the same thing as persecuting Jesus, since it is His spirit that is within them. We cannot expect God to put up with that, La Peyrère warned his Christian readers: Just look at what God did to the Jews for persecuting Jesus. Then what can we think God will do for persecuting His elect who have the spirit of Jesus within them![64]

Seeing what is at stake, Christians ought to give up their natural revulsion towards Jews, and instead should treat all of them with hospitality and courtesy, since each Jew may be one of the elect.[65] La Peyrère did not suggest any particular way that his Christian contemporaries should go about extending their hospitality and courtesy. However, to make it easier for them to do so, he pointed out that Christians have only a minimal spiritual advantage over the good Jews. Christians know Jesus, while Jews have the power to know Him. And these good Jews hope also that soon He will be manifested to them. Therefore, the difference between the Christian and Jewish situation is very slight, and is not, La Peyrère asserted, worth making a fuss about. Instead Christians should try to teach the Jews about the Incarnation, but they should do it with kindness, patience, and charity.[66]

The method La Peyrère proposed for accomplishing this was to minimize the difference between Judaism and Christianity. The only significant difference is in the role of Jesus. Apart from that, Christians and Jews believe in the same God. Although the Christians say He is God the Father and God the Son, nonetheless this does not prevent Him from being the same as Jehovah. The central Christian concepts, 'Son of God' and 'God-Man' are both in the Old Testament. Thus, in terms of what is in the Old Testament, the Incarnation and salvation are plausible, even if they are not comprehensible.[67] The point that has always bothered the Jews, namely how is it possible that God-Man could be killed, can be ignored. All that has to be said is that God wanted it to happen as it did. It was prophesied in Isaiah 53 that this is what would occur. And, since the Jews accept the message of the book of Isaiah, they are therefore almost Christians, for the text of Isaiah 53 is pure Christianity.[68]

In the seventeenth century, Jewish polemicists such as Elijah Montalto and Isaac Orobio de Castro contended that Isaiah 53 had nothing to do with Jesus, and they also contended that the expected Messiah had not yet come. These polemicists were trying to get the New Christians to return to Judaism.[69] La Peyrère, on the other hand, seems to have been trying to get the Jewish converts and the Jews to exist inside Christianity, by showing that Judaism is almost the same as Christianity. In order to make this more acceptable to the Jews, La Peyrère next offered an extremely heretical interpretation of Messianism. He announced that, happily, Jewish Messianism is one view and Christian Messianism is another. The book of Isaiah sets forth Jewish Messianism. St. Paul's Epistles sets forth the Christian view. These two views describe two different forms of Jesus' role. According to the Christians, Jesus came in the first century in order to expiate the sins of both the Gentiles and the Jews. But according to the Jews, the Messiah will come in a different guise, that of political Messiah in order to redeem the Jews. These two views are compatible as long as they are understood to deal with separate and distinct visitations of Jesus on earth. In this light, La Peyrère claimed that the Jews should realize that their version actually depends upon an assumption of a prior visitation by the Messiah, since expiation must precede sanctification.[70]

So, if Jewish and Christian Messianism are compatible, there should be no great difficulty in converting the Jews. Both groups already worship the same God. They both accept the same Scripture. They have almost the same beliefs, except for what La Peyrère regarded as a minor difference concerning the role of the Messiah. Historically, the Jews provoked the Gentiles to gain knowledge of their Messianic movement. Now the Christians can return the favor by provoking the Jews to realize that Jesus will be their Messiah and Redeemer.[71]

The final book of *Du Rappel des Juifs* deals with the techniques that should be employed in order to convert the Jews. La Peyrère's method was to create a special Jewish Christian church which would adhere to a minimal Christian belief that would at the same time be acceptable to Jews. Such a church, he envisaged, would have no doctrines, dogmas or creeds except for belief in Jesus and belief in the resurrection of the dead. This church would have no rational theology (because that breeds scepticism). The ceremonies would be reduced to just two, baptism and the Eucharist. Obviously, La Peyrère noted, this would make life simpler for the Jewish Christians than if they continued following the Mosaic Law. In this Church, baptism would replace circumcision. The Eucharist would be the basis for making people live virtuous lives. The effect of all of this would be, according to La Peyrère, the re-creation of primitive Christianity, which was, after all, Jewish Christianity. The liturgy of this Church would be simplified. It would stress the Old Testament basis for Jewish Christianity. All of the myriad theological points that have been developed since the first century would be dropped. Thus Jewish Christianity would be Christianity developed strictly from Judaism.[72]

La Peyrère apparently believed that his proposed reform of Christianity would be easily acceptable to Jews, since all of the non-Jewish elements had been left out. Therefore, the Jews would become Jewish Christians. At the same time he envisaged that all of the Gentiles would become Christians, and all the different groups of Christians would reunite. Then the reunited Christians would be recalled by God, and the Jews would also be recalled. This would lead to the fulfillment of the aspirations of the Gentiles in the form of the reunion of the whole of the human race in the Messianic Age. In this wondrous time the world would be ruled by Jesus and by his earthly ally, the King of France. The Jewish Christians would be the central governing figures, directing the world's activities during the Messianic Age from the now redeemed and rebuilt Holy Land.[73]

La Peyrère had entitled his later work 'a system of theology based on the theory that there were men before Adam.' His theological system, an amazing combination of Jewish Messianism and French nationalism was developed out of his critical transformation of the import of the Bible. Later evidence offered was to be of great significance in biblical scholarship, anthropology, racist ideology, later Messianism, etc.

The system La Peyrère built up culminates in a marvelous vision of the coming of the Jewish Messiah, His alliance with the King of France and the converted Jews, producing the Messianic Age in which there will be universal salvation regardless of one's race or creed. Given the intolerance that prevailed in the early seventeenth century, it is wonderful to see a theologian, albeit an odd one, advancing such a completely universalistic theory. The march to redemption might only go through Jewish history. Nonetheless, it was not just those elected to play parts in the Divine Drama who would be rewarded. All mankind would be rewarded thus. By separating Providential history from secular history, Providential history becomes the drama of salvation not only for the actors, but also for the audience. In this, La Peyrère is much more Jewish than Christian in his conception. The Jewish view, expressed in its classical form by the Medieval Spanish poet-philosopher, Judah Halevi, is that Jewish history is the inner core of world history, and that all of mankind participates and profits from its fulfillment. In this view Jewish history goes on in its narrow, exclusive way, but its purpose is to complete a Divine plan in which everyone, the participants in Jewish history as well as the rest of mankind, takes part and reaps the rewards. Perhaps, because La Peyrère put Christianity back into Jewish history, he was able to be so universalist, unlike almost all of his Christian contemporaries. And, again unlike his Christian contemporaries, he could see Adam's sin not as a cosmic disaster, but as a genuine benefit for all mankind, since it started Jewish history.

La Peyrère dedicated *Prae-Adamitae* 'To all the Synagogues of the Jews dispersed over the face of the Earth.' Presumably, since the critical events in the near future would come from the world of the Synagogue, the Jews should be the first to know. On the other hand, the elaborate exploration of the Bible, of ancient history and of anthropology, would lead the Gentiles to become Christians. La Peyrère states the case as follows:

> That *Genesis* and the Gospel, and the Astronomy of the Antients is reconcil'd and the History and Philosophy of the most ancient Nations: So that if the *Chaldeans* themselves should come, those most antient Astronomers, who had calculated the course of the stars, as they say, many hundred thousand years ago; or the most ancient *Egyptian* Chronologers, with those most antient Dynasties of their Kings; if *Aristotle* himself come; if with Aristotle those of *China* come, Wise men that we may perchance henceforth find amongst the Southern and Northern people, as yet unknown, who have their ages receiv'd and known downward many Myriads of years. They will willingly receive this History of Genesis and more willingly become Christians.[74]

So La Peyrère's pre-Adamite theory will lead the Gentiles to become Christians. His theory of the Recall of the Jews will unite the Jews and the Christians. The Jewish Messiah will come and with the aid of the King of France redeem everyone.

For La Peyrère it all seemed so simple, so obvious and so marvelous. Alas, as we shall see, his theological system and his universalistic redemption were rejected by all the major religious movements. They felt that the price to be paid for all of the alleged benefits was much too high. The positive effect was greater on the scholars of religion, like Spinoza and Simon, than on the exponents of it. To La Peyrère's alleged surprise, neither the Jews, the Catholics, nor the Protestants liked his theory.

CHAPTER FIVE

FRENCH NATIONALIST MESSIANISM UP TO LA PEYRÈRE

The role La Peyrère assigned to the King of France in his universalistic picture of human salvation may seem a bit odd and provincial, as well as arbitrary. With his insistence on discovering the right meaning of Scripture, seeing it solely as Jewish history, the French element might seem quite out of place. France as a country, as a kingdom, arose long after the Jewish events described in the Bible. To present day readers French history from late Roman times down to the present is a national regional history developing from the activities of the Gauls, the Franks, the Romans, none of whom were, as far as we know, God's chosen people. Before indicating some of the antecedents to La Peyrère's French nationalist Messianism, I think that one has to remember that he developed the theory at the same time that the English Puritans saw England as the New Israel, and were proclaiming that the actions of the Parliament of Saints would usher in the Millenium. The sermons given from 1640 onward, the pamphlets of Dury and Hartlib among others, say that England, as a political entity, acting through its political government, is fulfilling the prophecies of Jewish history, and preparing the conditions for the Thousand Year Reign of Jesus on earth.[1]

Some European Protestants, like Joseph Mede in England, Abraham von Frankenberg in Germany, Peter Serrarius in Holland and Johann Amos Comenius in exile from Bohemia, saw the political events of the Thirty Years War, the Puritan Revolution, the rise of Swedish power, the weakening of Spanish power, etc. as part of the prophesied events in Daniel and Revelation that would precede Jesus's Second Coming.[2] They saw various political figures, like Gustavus Adolphus, or Oliver Cromwell, as agents of God in overthrowing the Anti-Christ. This was not just local pride, but rather a conviction that the Reformation had unleashed the forces that would bring about the 'end of days' and these forces were reaching their climactic activities in the 1640s and 1650s. Many Millenarians wrote of their expectation that in 1655 or 1656, the Conversion of the Jews would occur and the onset of the Millenium would soon follow.[3] The English Puritans saw England as having a special historical role in this, in that they had established a political land in which pure Christianity flourished. The Jews, seeing what pure Christianity was like, would of course convert. Up to now they had been put off by idolatrous and superstitious 'Christianity' of the Anti-Christ's Church of Rome.[4]

Thus, from the Protestant side, political, nationalist developments were seen as part of the fulfillment of the events in the Bible. Puritan England especially saw itself as the continuation of biblical Israel in a quite literal sense.

On the Catholic side, two major Catholic countries, Spain and Portugal also saw their histories in eschatological terms. Spain, after all, was the land where the Jews had converted, from 1391-1492. St. Vincent Ferrar's internal crusade to bring this about was described by him and his followers, in Millenial terms. Leading converts saw their own conversion as the prelude to monumental events. By the mid-sixteenth century, Spanish history was being described as Divine History with 1492 as the *annus mirabilis*—the Jews all converted or expelled, the country reconquered from the infidels, and the discovery of the New World, where the Gospel could be propagated to the gentiles.[5]

Portugal, up to quite recently, saw its role in Divine History as that of Christianizing the world. It was the Portuguese explorers who spread the Christian message to Africa, India, Indonesia, China, Japan, the Philippines, Brazil, etc. This broadcasting of the Gospel throughout the world would prepare it for Christ's final triumph.[6]

Portugal also had a theory about the role of its king in Divine History. The loss of its sovereignty to Spain in the mid-sixteenth century, spawned a view—Sebastianism. King Sebastian disappeared in a battle in Africa. His body was never found. Prophecies began appearing about his impending return, which would herald the final age of Divine History.[7]

Then Menasseh ben Israel, in 1650, published his Messianic work, *The Hope of Israel*, which showed that the fulfillment of Jewish Messianic expectations was at hand and needed only the return of the Jews to England to set the stage for the coming of the Messiah. At this time, the Portuguese Jesuit, Antonio de Vieira, who had been spreading the Gospel in Brazil and had returned to Europe in the 1640s to confer with Menasseh ben Israel, with English Millenarians and probably also with La Peyrère, wrote a work entitled *The Hopes of Portugal*, in which he wished for the recall of the Jews to Portugal, their conversion, and the coming of Jesus to Portugal to take the Jews to rebuild Palestine.[8]

Thus at the time La Peyrère wrote *Du Rappel des Juifs* with its French nationalist orientation, there were seriously written and seriously received competing nationalist eschatologies being published and acted upon in both the Protestant and Catholic worlds. La Peyrère's emphasis on France and the French King, however, is not just local pride, but is based on a long prior tradition that had developed in France during the Middle Ages and the Renaissance about France's connection with the biblical world, its special role in Christian history, and its religious mission at the present juncture of Divine History.

Each European group had a tradition of how it originated as linear descendants of the survivors of Noah's Ark, and how Christianity was brought to the group. Noah and his children and their wives had to be the source of all the peoples of the world. The French people traced their origins to Gomer, the oldest son of Japhet, the oldest son of Noah. Poliakov points out in his *Le Mythe Aryen* that in the Middle Ages the French developed a double theory of their origins, from one of the sons of Hector of the Trojan War, and from one of the sons of Noah, Japhet. The biblical genealogy was that the French were the descendants of the eldest son (Gomer) of the oldest son (Japhet) of the Patriarch Noah. Thus the French had seniority in descendance from all the rest of mankind.[9]

Further claims of France's importance in the scenario following from the Bible began to appear in the fourteenth century from followers of Joachim of Fiore, who had flourished in the twelfth century. Prophecies attributed to him had sought to identify the final emperor and the angelic Pope, who would overcome the Anti-Christ and bring about the *renovatio mundi* forecast by Joachim. Many had looked in Germany for these expected leaders, with France hardly mentioned. In the early fourteenth century, one Pierre Dubois claimed that the King of France would play a cosmic role in liberating the Holy Land. This king would become the world emperor, and rule a federation of nations from Jerusalem.[10]

Jean de Roquetaillade, in a work written in 1345-49, foresaw the King of France as leading the final battle against the Anti-Christ, to be followed by the Millenium. Roquetaillade saw all of this happening in the near future, with the forces of Anti-Christ, the Ghibellines in Italy, the Kings of Spain, the tyrants of Germany, the King of England, opposed by the true Pope, the King of France and Charles IV of Bohemia. The wars would last until 1415 when the Millenium would begin. In a later work, Roquetaillade predicted the King of France would be elected as Roman Emperor, and the whole world would submit to him. He and the Angelic Pope would bring about the reform of the world.[11]

In some fifteenth century prophecies, France's role was seen in terms of its being the lily of the Bible.[12] In the mid-sixteenth century, when Charles V was being heralded as the expected emperor who would overcome all opposition and prepare for the Second Coming of Christ, counter-claims were offered in France. The most thorough and most important was that presented by Guillaume Postel, 1510-1581. Postel was one of the first professors of Hebrew in the Academy of Francis I and a leading scholar of Hebrew, Arabic and other Middle Eastern languages, who translated the great Kabbalistic work, the *Zohar* into Latin. He had a stormy career, and after joining and being dropped by the Jesuits, worked in a hospital in Venice, where he claimed a woman, Joanna, taught him the way to read the secrets of the Kabbala. After her death, he wrote a series of prophetic works on the restitution of the world. Part of Postel's message, in works published from 1548 onward, was that the King of France had a divine mission, and a crucial role in the coming transformation of the world.[13]

In the restitution of all things, Postel foresaw the coming of the Messiah. The Messiah ben Joseph, after the Messiah ben David had been crucified in the flesh in Jerusalem, and in the spirit in Rome, will come in spirit alone, awaken men in their hearts, and bring about this restitution. The French people and the King of France will play leading roles in these Divine developments if the French king restores himself, his court, and his kingdom. For Postel, the French, the *Galli*, included the present French, German, Italians and Spaniards. The Galli are those who were saved from the Flood, the descendants of Noah. The present French and their King, have a special responsibility, but the kings and princes of Europe also have to play their roles in the restitution.[13a] The restitution will take place first in France and then, through the efforts of the French people and the French King, will be spread through the world.[14] William Bouwsma, in his book on Postel, observed that 'Taken as a whole, his argument may well constitute the most comprehensive, if not necessarily the most convincing, justification for French world leadership in the sixteenth century, if not in the entire history of French thought.'[15] Postel went far beyond in detail, and in justification, what had appeared in the earlier and then current Joachimist teachings about the role of France. And it is most likely that if La Peyrère drew his views from earlier sources, it would have been some of Postel's views that were still reverberating in the European scene in the early seventeenth century.

Postel argued that the unification of Christianity could only be accomplished by a monarch who is 'tres chrestian' and who is the eldest representative of the Divine scheme of things. The King of France, by primogeniture, is such a monarch, since he and his people are descended from Gomer, the oldest son of Japhet, the oldest son of Noah and are the 'half-Jewish race.' Gomer had inherited the temporal monarchy of the world from his father, and so, by primogeniture, the Salic law, the temporal rule of the world has passed down to each successive French ruler. Gomer after the Flood settled down in France, and the French are his descendants. Therefore they have the right of empire over the rest of mankind. So, the other European groups, being descended from junior lines from Noah, should pay respect to the French. Postel asserted, 'Ainsi

par Droict Divin de Humain, soit de Primogeniture, soit d'institution
Divine, Profetique Paternelle ou Humaine, soit par Droict d'occupation
ou de toute gens, tout le Droict du monde, & principallemant celuy de
toute l'Europe est du Peuple & Prince de Gauloys.'[16]

Postel added to this strong claim some astrological data, and then some
material from Christian legends, and from French medieval history. The
French, he said, have preserved and conserved true Christianity, and
that is why the King of France is called the 'tres chrestian' monarch.
France has been in the lead in developing good theology and humanistic
studies. From the beginning of Christianity, Postel proclaimed, France
had played a critical role. When Jesus knew he was about to be crucified,
he told Mary Magdalene, Martha and Lazarus to take refuge in France,
and so Christianity was brought directly from Jesus to France. Later on,
Constantine was converted to Christianity in France, and then converted
the entire Roman Empire to Christianity. A few centuries later it was in
France that the Moslem conquest was stopped by Charles Martel. In the
Middle Ages, St. Louis, King of France, brought the Crown of Thorns
to France, and built the magnificent Sainte Chapelle to house it. A bit
later Joan of Arc defended Christianity in France and saved the country.
All of this, Postel declaimed, 'se voyt donc comment par Droict
d'Aisnesse, per Droict d'Institution, par Droict Divin, & de Prophetique
Benediction, par Droict de toutes gens ou de Naturelle Occupation, par
Raison de Celeste influence & par Raison de merite souvrain meritant
souvraine & Premiere election, la Monarchye apparient aux Princes par
les peuples Gaulloys efluez & approuvez.'[17]

In addition Postel contended, as had some of the Joachimites, that
'l'huile Celeste pour Royalle unction' was only sent to the leader of the
Gauls. The Holy Lily, which appears in so many Scriptural prophecies,
'obviously' refers to France, and predicts the role of France and its King
in Divine History. Further, Postel said, the King of France has special
powers that enable him to cure illness, like scrofula, just by touch. Postel
claimed he had even seen this happen.[18] Postel believed that only the
King of France, because of his special status, would be able to free and
restore the Holy Land.[19] The French people, though always loyal to their
King, were always zealous for liberty. Poliakov points out the French
have embodied this in their name—Frank, enfranchise, etc. We will see
this point raised by La Peyrère.[20]

In Postel's more Kabbalistic writings, he gave a more theosophical explanation of the role of France and its monarch. Both earthly ruling and
religious priesthood come from ancient biblical sources. This derivation
is both historical and symbolic, and provides the basis for primogeniture.
From Judaic roots a tree has grown up. The Gentiles have been engrafted

on to it. From this growth a community of Israel, a universal monarchy, will appear. The French, as the sons of Japhet, are a half Jewish race which now has to fulfill its role by establishing the universal monarchy, or the Kingdom of Israel on earth. This Kingdom, in which there will be a restitution of all of the children of God in a theocracy, will be the Kingdom of the lily, which represents the marriage of God and His people, Israel.'[21] Postel equated the description in the Song of Songs with the French kingdom that maintains God's ancient law of primogeniture. And it is the law by which God's rule on earth is carried out. The lily, the rose of Sharon, is then interpreted as referring to a specific French King as well as to the redeemed Israel. Postel used much Jewish literature about the significance of the lily to apply it to France, and to give the theological significance of the lily to France and its king.[22]

Postel was not a quiet prophet. He not only poured out his view about France and its destiny in tracts and tomes, he also tried to convince the various French monarchs of his time to play their appointed role in the Divine Drama. He actually *walked* from Paris to Fontainebleau to induce François I to begin the events that would lead to the restitution of all things. He also cried out to Henri II and Francois II without any evident success.[23]

Postel was the most active advocate of a French oriented Messianism before La Peyrère. He wrote extensively on the matter, and was widely known for his views, even if he was treated as a crank, a madman, and a heretic.[24] Just before La Peyrère presented his views, another proponent of the French view appeared on the scene. The Italian priest, Tommaso Campanella, who defended Galileo, was offering the theory that there would be a universal monarch who would rule the world with the Messiah.[25] In his *De Monarchia Hispanica* he had presented a case for the role of the Spanish monarch based on Jewish history. However, when Campanella left Italy for France in 1634, he made out a case that Spain was just the Fourth Monarchy prophesied in Daniel, which must be destroyed before the end of the Anti-Christ. Then the fifth Monarchy would arise, that of the tres christian King of France who would help bring about the new world. Campanella 'like Postel was read and attended to by many in high places.'[26] He was received as a great figure in Mersenne's circle in Paris. Only Gassendi found his views outlandish.[27] It is possible La Peyrère might have met him, if La Peyrère had made a trip to Paris at the time. He certainly would have heard of him and his views.

All of this indicates that there was a significant tradition from some followers of Joachim de Fiore to Postel to Campanella, advocating a crucial role for France and the King of France in the Divine Drama before La Peyrère. In *Du Rappel des Juifs*, written in 1640-41, there is no mention of any source material other than Scripture, and no attempt to buttress his views by appealing to any predecessors, or to appeal to any of the Millenarian literature on the recall of the Jews coming out of Holland and England. When one examines La Peyrère's presentation, I think some of it seems to be like the view of Postel, and some the author's own vision. La Peyrère began his exposition in *Du Rappel des Juifs* by saying that soon the Jews would be brought to knowledge of the Gospels and everyone in the world would be converted to Christianity. These great spiritual developments would be accompanied by the temporal recall of the Jews, and their reestablishment in the Holy Land. This will be accomplished by a temporal king, who will bring about the conversion of the Jews, and who will be the universal monarch predicted by the prophets.[28]

In the second book of *Du Rappel des Juifs*, La Peyrère dealt with identifying who will be the universal king. Before offering his evidence, La Peyrère set himself apart from previous tradition on this matter by saying that he himself is not a prophet, and he can only offer 'coniectures [qui] sont si piussantes & si claires, qu'elles peuvent passer pour des Veritez connues.'[29] What king, he asked, can be this universal monarch who can reconcile the Jews and Gentiles, and make the Gentiles see the Jews as their brothers, in fact, their older brothers? What king can undertake to make Jews Christians? It would have to be, La Peyrère said, 'un Roy Tres Chrestian.' To make everyone see the right of priority of the Jews, the king himself would have to be the senior of all of the Christian kings. This would have to be the King of France, who is both 'Tres Chrestian' and the oldest son of the Christian Church. No other king, La Peyrère claimed, would dispute this.[30]

However, La Peyrère did not use Postel's points about primogeniture to justify the special status of the King of France. This is probably due to the fact that for La Peyrère, the Flood was only a local event in Palestine. Noah and his descendants are the actual Jews. The French and their monarch have no direct genetic relationship to Noah, Japhet or Gomer, who are all Adamites, whereas the French are pre-Adamites. So, the special status of the King of France in the Divine Drama is due to other factors.

These factors are (a) the King of France can cure the worst maladies the Jews have, like scrofula. With such curative power he should also be able to cure their souls of incredulity.[31] (b) The King of France is the embodiment of the lily. La Peyrère devoted over fifteen pages to interpreting biblical references to the lily, the rose of Sharon and the oil of the lily, as symbols relating to France. The fleur de lys is the symbol of

France. God, La Peyrère reported, chose the lily over all other flowers, to be 'un Roy de France, un Roy eleu, & choisi de Dieu d'entre tous les Roys de la terre pour la deliverance de son Peuple, & pour la Felicité de tous les hommes.'[32] La Peyrère did not seem to know most of the Kabbalistic interpretations of the lily. He did however connect the oil of the lily with France as the symbol of freedom and liberty, as the medieval Franks had done.[33]

Because France is the land of liberty, it is the place where the Jews will first be brought to be converted. At the time it was illegal for Jews to reside in France, though groups did live in Bordeaux, Narbonne, and other southwestern cities. La Peyrère said the Jews will come to France to avoid persecutions (as Spanish and Portuguese Jews were doing at the time). They will come because France is 'une Terre de Franchise' and does not permit slavery. Whoever reaches France is free. The Jews therefore will seek asylum in France where they will regain their liberty and escape persecution.[34]

The Jews will be restored to Divine History in France; when they accept Christianity (at least in the form La Peyrère watered it down to for their benefit) then the Jews will leave France to reconquer and rebuild the Holy Land. Jerusalem will become 'Ville princesse des villes de la Terre Saincte Et Ville Maitresse de toutes les villes du monde.'[35] The temple will be rebuilt, and Jesus will live there forever and ever. The universal monarch will govern the world, and everything will be wonderful. Jerusalem will be the heart of the Holy Land, and the Holy Land the heart of the world. The Jews will be restored to their land, the Gentiles will receive plenitude and happiness in the rest of the world. Everyone will be redeemed and restored through the conversion of the Jews. There will be a New Heaven and New Earth.[36]

La Peyrère provided much more literal detail in his views than did Postel. As a result, long before the state of Israel came into being, La Peyrère, rather than Postel, was already portrayed as one of the very first Zionists.[37]

La Peyrère's French oriented Messianism has some elements in common with Postel's views, and some traces of Joachimite prophecies. La Peyrère exhibited far less learning on the subject than Postel, and referred to practically no Jewish literature beyond the Bible. On the other hand, La Peyrère's presentation is different from his predecessors in some important respects. One of the main ones is that his picture is devoid of the apocalyptic elements that pervade previous and contemporary Millenarianism and Messianism. No Anti-Christ is mentioned who has to be overcome. No great battles and wars are to be waged before the Millenium. The only mention of conflict is that the Jews will leave France to conquer the Holy land. But nothing is said about a struggle—just the rebuilding of the Holy Land follows. La Peyrère relied on practically none of the texts in Daniel or Revelation for his picture. He appealed to the prophecies in Joel as his chief justification. And, although these contain some blood and thunder, they do emphasize how wonderful things will be when the Jews are restored to Zion.[38] La Peyrère also stressed that one has to distinguish carefully between the renewing of all things and the consummation of all things, thus distancing his picture from the finale in Revelation. Also La Peyrère did not describe the world run by Jesus and the universal king as the Fifth Monarchy.

In fact La Peyrère's Messianism is described apart from all of the events taking place around him, the Thirty Years War, the Puritan Revolution, the Turkish incursions in central Europe, etc. He made no effort to fit his picture into any time frame. Instead he offered an account in Books I - II of *Du Rappel des Juifs* of how it would all end, and in Books III - V, a social reform program to make the Jews happy and prepare them for what was to come, La Peyrère indicated no sources of his ideas. Whether he knew Postel's works or those of the Joachimites directly we cannot tell. There are certainly more echoes of Postel than other possible sources. His ideas may have still been discussed in circles in which La Peyrère moved.[39]

It was only later on, as his views gained him notoriety, and caused him troubles, that he gave actual historical people roles in his scenario.[40] Pope Alexander VII, Louis XIV and the Prince of Condé were given heroic parts to play if they would accept La Peyrère's vision.

La Peyrère's French oriented Messianism ends in a marvelous picture of how everyone will be saved: Adamites, pre-Adamites, post-Adamites. His is probably the most universalistic view being offered at the time (but we'll soon see how it was used to buttress racism). It is a most peaceful picture of how the Millenium will arrive through the benign efforts of the King of France. As far as we know, La Peyrère did nothing about it. He did not preach. He did not organize philosemitic activities. However in a later chapter we will see some influence his Messianism had, and how it may have actually led figures like Queen Christina, the Prince of Condé, and Menasseh ben Israel to play the roles they did.

CHAPTER SIX

LA PEYRÈRE'S HERETICAL THEOLOGICAL THEORIES

The two major heretical theories of Isaac La Peyrère that were to have such forceful effect on the intellectual and religious world were the pre-Adamite theory, and the denial of the Mosaic authorship of the Pentateuch. Each of these views constituted a challenge to the accepted view of Jews and Christians about the content and origin of the Bible.

The contention that there were men before Adam strikes at a fundamental interpretation of believers concerning Scripture. For Jews and Christians the Bible was presumed to explain the nature and destiny of man. Its historical account about the origin and development of the human race had been taken as an essential component for understanding world history. Almost all theologians of La Peyrère's day would have taken it for granted that the history of Adam and his descendants was the history of the human race. Both Jewish and Christian theologians from ancient times down to the seventeenth century had developed a way of rebutting any pagan claims to the contrary. The theologians simply insisted that the pagans did not possess divine revelation, and, therefore, they did not know what they were talking about. In view of the accepted account of man's origins and development one can appreciate that just the title of La Peyrère's book, *Men before Adam*, without any supporting evidence, could be a direct and a major assault on the Judeo-Christian religion.

Why should the view that there were men before Adam make so much difference? One of the possibilities this view suggests, which was included in La Peyrère's theory, is that the Bible does not present the history of all mankind, but only the history of one small group. Why should the destiny of this small group be of major importance to everyone else? La Peyrère used the pre-Adamite theory to justify his contention that the Bible dealt only with the history of the Jews. Only the Jews were descendants of Adam and the Noachides. Everyone else came from other sources. While this might appear to denigrate the importance of the biblical picture of the world, La Peyrère claimed that two major virtues of his theory would show that it was better than the accepted orthodox theory. The first is that it really does not seem plausible that the ancient pagan groups like the Egyptians, the Babylonians, the Greeks, and others were biological and cultural descendants of the ancient Hebrews. It also does not seem plausible that the Eskimos, the American Indians, the Mexicans, the Chinese, the South Sea Islanders, and others are descendants of the survivors of Noah's ark. If one adopts the pre-Adamite theory, there is no great difficulty in accounting for the varieties of mankind and their diverse locations. If one does not adopt this theory, one has to make all sorts of ad hoc assumptions to explain the matter.[1]

The second great advantage La Peyrère suggested for his theory is that it would make clear the direction in which the Divine Drama was being worked out. If the Bible is just about Jewish history, then one does not have to worry that any other human histories have religious purport. In a stronger sense, one could say that for La Peyrère, only Jewish history matters. Every other history is just the milling around of people, and their passing away and being followed by other peoples. Nevertheless, La Peyrère as universal humanitarian, insisted that everyone, pre-Adamites, Adamites and post-Adamites, would be saved when the Messianic fulfillment of Jewish history took place.[2]

If the pre-Adamite theory had the virtues which its author claimed for it, why was there such clamor and uproar about it? Why was it considered such a great heresy? First, I believe, because it suggested, or indicated that the biblical picture of man's place in the cosmos, was grossly overstated. The overwhelming number of people in the world consists of those whose origin and ancestry are outside of the Adamic world. Then, why take the biblical picture more seriously than the Mexican, Babylonian, or Chinese accounts? As historical accounts they are now on the same level. And, as such, all of the pre-Adamite (non-biblical) accounts show that the Bible is not the history of mankind, but is simply the history of one small group of people, the Jews.

La Peyrère would insist that it is correct to say that the Bible presents just the history of the Jews. However, people might draw the wrong inference from this. They might suppose that the history of the Jews is just another ordinary history. Instead, it is that history upon which the salvation of the human race depends. And, naturally, it turns out that La Peyrère's account of how this is possible involved him in an interpretation of Christianity that made it not significantly different from Judaism. However, to crown his heresies, La Peyrère claimed that it would be the long awaited Jewish Messiah (also named Jesus) who would soon appear to redeem all of mankind.

A leading French scholar, A. Dupront, has said that La Peyrère's work posed 'un double problème, celui de la valeur historique de l'Ecriture, et d'autre part, celui de sa valeur divine, ou pour mieux dire, de la révélation.'[3] Regarding the first problem, La Peyrère posed two possibilities: Either one admits that biblical history is in conflict with ancient pagan history and contemporary anthropology, or one reduces the range of biblical history so that it describes only the career of one group of human beings. As we will see in subsequent chapters, it was getting harder and harder in La Peyrère's time to reconcile biblical chronology with Babylonian, Mexican or Chinese chronology. It was also becoming more difficult to account for the origins of groups like the American Indians from a biblical point of view. Hence, the appeal of Pre-Adamism was evident. But so was the great danger that was seen as soon as the theory was presented. The Bible had lost its universality, and possibly also its historical accuracy. But, even more, as Dupront suggested, it had lost some (or all) of its revelatory value. Is the Revelation just to the people the Bible talks about, the Jews? Or, maybe the Bible only presents one per cent of the Revelation, since it only deals with a small sub-group of the world population.

Pushing some of these problems further, is the Bible actually a book that contains statements of Revelation? Until La Peyrère, practically every theologian would have answered positively. When asked for the basis of their assurance, the usual answer would be that the revelatory material was transmitted by God Himself to Moses, and that Moses wrote the Pentateuch on the basis of what God revealed to him.

La Peyrère, approaching the problem from a different perspective, denying the accuracy of certain claims in the Bible, raised the question of whether Moses did in fact write the first five books of the Bible. How do we know that Moses was the author? 'I know not by what author it is found out, that the Pentateuch is *Moses* his own copy. It is so reported, but not believed by all. These Reasons make one believe, that those Five Books are not the Originals, but copied out by another. Because *Moses* is there read to have died. For how could *Moses* write after his death?'[4] The evidence La Peyrère offered to support so drastic a claim was to become the basis for modern biblical criticism. He pointed out the conflicts and repetitions that occur in the text. The most striking of these appears in the section of *Exodus*, supposedly written by Moses, that describes the death of Moses.[5] Rabbi Ibn Ezra saw no reason to draw any sceptical inference from it. He instead advised especially careful study of the verses in the Books of Moses that are not by Moses.[6] As we have seen, La Peyrère concluded from his examination of the Bible that 'I need not trouble the Reader much further, to prove a thing in itself sufficiently evident, that the five first Books of the Bible were not written by Moses, as is thought. Nor need any one wonder after this, when he reads many things confus'd and out of order, obscure, deficient, many things omitted and misplaced, when they shall consider with themselves that they are a heap of Copie confusedly taken.'[7]

In the literature dealing with the history of modern biblical criticism, Thomas Hobbes is usually given credit for being the first person to deny that Moses was the author of the Pentateuch. In the sixteenth century, some theologians who saw difficulties in maintaining that Moses was the author of the entire Pentateuch offered theories to the effect that Ezra wrote some or maybe all of it.[8] Hobbes, in the third part of *Leviathan*, published in 1651, asserted that 'But though Moses did not compile these books entirely, and in the form that we have them; yet he wrote all that which he is there said to have written.[9] Hobbes's contention is certainly more modest and less sweeping than La Peyrère's. And, although La Peyrère's claim was not published until four years after Hobbes's, it was written years earlier, probably in 1641, and was known to a lot of people in the same circle as Hobbes. The latter may well have heard of, or seen, La Peyrère's version, and have proposed his own view as a modification. Certainly La Peyrère's biblical criticism had a strong effect on the next generation of Bible scholars, especially on Spinoza and Richard Simon.

Why is the denial of the Mosaic authorship so significant? If taken seriously, it strikes at the very basis for ascertaining the veracity of Scripture, and so is of tremendous importance. At the end of the seventeenth century, the French Catholic theologian, Louis Ellies Du Pin, in his *Nouvelle Bibliotheque des Auteurs Ecclesiastiques*, declared that, 'de tous les Paradoxes, que l'on a avancez en nôtre siècle, il n'y en à point à mon avis de plus temeraire, ni de plus dangereux, que l'opinion de ceux, qui ont osé nier que Moise fut Auteur de Pentateuque.'[10] This view, he said, would destroy the authority of the Bible as the basis for Judeo-Christianity. Ellies Du Pin then blamed this horrible view on the medieval Jewish thinker, Ibn Ezra, and on the claims of Hobbes, La Peyrère, and Spinoza.[11] If the ultimate guarantee of revealed information was that it comes from Moses who received it from God Himself, then, if or when the link with Moses is broken, a most serious doubt about religious knowledge may result. Once there is the possibility that Moses was not the biblical author, then who was? On whose authority did he write what he did? What, if anything, would assure us that what this author reported was true?

Also one can see that once one passage in Scripture has been challenged as unauthentic, a problem is raised about what possible criterion can be employed to justify accepting other passages: Having raised such doubts, La Peyrère could then proceed to maintain that it was the case that the Bible was simply inaccurate in claiming that Adam was the first man, and that all the people now on earth are descendants of the seven survivors of Noah's Flood.

As biblical scholarship developed in the seventeenth and eighteenth centuries, it became clear to the parties involved in defending or attacking the merits of the Bible that the question of the Mosaic authorship was central to belief or disbelief. The English jurist and theologian Sir Matthew Hale asserted that the belief that La Peyrère's interpretations of the Bible 'were true would necessarily not only weaken but overthrow the Authority and Infallibility of Sacred Scriptures.'[12] From the other side a leading Enlightenment anti-religionist, Tom Paine, could survey the damage done over a century and a half by those casting doubt on the Mosaic authorship. Paine asserted, 'Take away from Genesis the belief that Moses was the author, on which only the strange belief that it is the word of God has stood, and there remains nothing of Genesis, but an anonymous book of stories, fables and traditionary or invented absurdities or downright lies.'[13] The consequence Tom Paine saw is, of course, what has happened to a great many modern unbelievers, for whom the Pentateuch has become a collection of early Hebrew literature, containing just such myths or folk-tales. The question of the true value of this collection is not even considered.

From the opposite side, a religious opponent of Paine's, the London Jewish writer, David Levi, who was carrying on a dispute with Joseph Priestley, said in his second answer to Priestley that 'if a Jew once calls in question the authenticity of *any part* of the Pentateuch, by observing that one part is authentic, i.e., was delivered by God to Moses, and that another part is not authentic, he is no longer accounted a Jew, i.e., a true believer.' Levi continued by pointing out that all Jews are obliged, according to the eighth article of the thirteen principles of Maimonides, 'to believe that the whole law of five books ... is from God,' and was delivered by Him to Moses. Levi indicated that Christians ought to be under the same constraints about belief in the veracity of the Bible, because, 'if any part is but once proved spurious, a door will be opened for another and another without end.'[14]

Whether La Peyrère realized it or not, when he developed his critique of Scripture in order to buttress his case for the pre-Adamite theory, he also began a chain of analyses that would end up transforming the evaluation of Scripture from a holy to a profane work. The Bible, for many, would no longer be looked upon as Revelation from God, but as tales and beliefs of the primitive Hebrews, to be compared with the tales and beliefs of other Near Eastern groups. This rather drastic consequence grew out of La Peyrère's need, for the sake of his theory, to be able to rewrite, eliminate, or ignore, passages in Scripture.

Thus, the force of La Peyrère's challenge was two-fold, one outside the confines of the Bible, taking pagan history and the new information of the explorers seriously, and the other, inside the Bible, showing that one did not have to take everything in the biblical text at face value since Moses did not write it. Hence, biblical texts which disagreed with the pre-Adamite theory could be accounted for as the result of human errors in transcribing or writing the texts. Of course, in discussing this, one has to keep in mind that no matter what doubts he raised, La Peyrère still seemed to have maintained his firm belief in the Kabbalistic reading he offered of the Messianic message of Scripture. The critique of the Bible by La Peyrère, regardless of his reasons for offering it, was a very important step in the development of modern biblical criticism. Some of his spirit and method were taken over by Spinoza and Richard Simon.[15] Later, the important eighteenth century biblical critic, Jean Astruc, sought a way of accepting La Peyrère's data, without having to accept so negative a conclusion.[16]

The other direction in which La Peyrère's efforts pointed was towards the consideration of man apart from Scripture, the pre-Adamites, who constitute most of the human race. Such a study was one of the first efforts in what is now designated as anthropology. In one of the earliest histories of anthropology, that of Thomas Bendysche, the vice president of the Anthropological Society of London in 1864, La Peyrère played a sizeable role.[17] Much more recently, in James Slotkin's enormous compendium, *Readings in Early Anthropology*, which was completed in 1946 and published in 1965, La Peyrère plays a very significant role both in separating religious and scientific questions, and in proposing a polygenetic explanation of human origins based, at least to some degree, on what would be classified as anthropological considerations, that is the physical, cultural and geographical differences among groups of men.[18] The controversy that La Peyrère engendered over whether or not the differences among human beings can best be accounted for by a monogenetic or polygenetic explanation was to be a dominant issue from the mid-seventeenth century down even to the present day. Initially it was partly religious and partly scientific. In spite of La Peyrère's idiosyncratic reading of Scripture, practically everybody else took it for granted that the Bible presented a monogenetic view, and that a polygenetic view would have to be heretical. The central issue became whether a monogenetic theory is able to account for all of the human differences. Can it explain why some people are white, and some black, or brown, or red? More and more complex monogenetic explanations have been developed over the centuries since La Peyrère. More and more factors have been pointed out that can or may cause serious differences among peoples. Yet, in the literature from *Men Before Adam* onward, there is a continuous pull of the polygenetic theory. If one would set aside the Bible, many believe this view would seem to provide the simplest and easiest explanation of human differences.

By now there seem to be two quite different lines of argument against polygenesis, one scientific and the other social and political. La Peyrère's opponents had pointed out that his pre-Adamism would destroy Judaism and Christianity, and that it was possible to explain the data he had introduced by offering a more and more elaborate monogenetic explanation. Now, after the work of Darwin, and the development of modern genetics, many anthropologists and biologists seem to think that the weight of the scientific evidence is in favor of a monogenetic, evolutionary explanation. Louis Leakey and Jacques Monod are among many luminaries who hold this view.[19] Today the question of how two or more distinct groups could evolve through mutations to become beings as complicated as humans seems to make polygenesis less plausible. Nonetheless there are still such staunch advocates of polygenesis as Carleton Coons of Harvard.[20]

Another factor that has put polygenetic explanations under a cloud is the use they have been put to in justifying racism. Before the seventeenth century was over, American slave owners were using La Peyrère's pre-Adamite theory to justify what they were doing. First of all, blacks are obviously different from whites. Then, in a serious shift from La Peyrère's version of polygenesis, whites were seen as Adamites; blacks, American Indians, and other people of color as pre-Adamites. Finally, in what became a central racist view, whites were considered superior to blacks and other colored groups. All sorts of evidence was introduced in the eighteenth and nineteenth centuries to try to prove this. Cranial capacity, brain size, hair characteristics, among other features, were measured to establish that whites are, and always were, more intelligent. Prior to the Civil War in America, a polygenetic theory of human origins and development, that traced its ancestry directly back to La Peyrère, was the dominant view of the day. It provided a justification of the racial situation in America by claiming to present scientific evidence of permanent white superiority and of permanent black inferiority.[21]

With the development of genetics in the twentieth century, the continuation of this racist view based on a polygenetic theory of human origins, has tended to ignore the polygenetic/monogenetic issue. Instead the more recent type of theory has tried to show that there is a basic genetic difference between whites and blacks, and because of this difference it is naturally the case that whites are intellectually superior to blacks, a situation that cannot be overcome by any kind of social engineering. Nonetheless, even though present day theories of biological or anthropological racism are not usually polygenetic, one finds that al-

most any revival of polygenesis is greeted by fears that it will lead to a
new kind of racism.

As has been indicated thus far in this chapter, two of the central parts
of La Peyrère's theory, his pre-Adamism and his biblical criticism,
played vital roles in the intellectual world of his time and among subsequent generations. For La Peyrère, it all may have seemed simple and
acceptable. If one accepted his view, the Bible would be rightly
understood (including the all-important news that the coming of the
Messiah was imminent); the historical data from ancient times and the
recent data from the voyages of exploration would now be reconciled
with what is said in the Bible; and, now that it was clear how the Divine
Drama is working out, Jews, Christians, and Pagans could all become
united, and take part in the Messianic Age. La Peyrère seems to have
seen it all as a neat and wonderful picture of man's prospects. However,
just about everyone else who read or heard of his theory realized that the
price to be paid for all of these benefits was catastrophically high. The
first concept that had to be accepted was that the biblical text was not
necessarily accurate. And the second was that biblical history was no
longer world history!

Accepting La Peyrère's theses was extremely damaging to the Judeo-
Christian religious perspective. Even entertaining the very possibility of
La Peyrère's theses opened the door to biblical criticism and to various
aspects of social sciences. Once one could consider people apart from
their supposed Adamic-Noachic origin, then such peoples and their
cultures and their histories could be studied apart from the providential
context of Judaism and Christianity. At this point the secular,
naturalistic examination of most of human society, namely of the pre-
Adamites, was now possible. Included in this now secular study would
be the religion or religions of the pre-Adamites. These could be examined
from an anthropological point of view. La Peyrère, in his study of the
Eskimos, was one of the first to employ anthropological evidence in order
to interpret aspects of religion.[22] Finally, by raising certain questions
from a new perspective, La Peyrère was able to make some people see
that the Bible as we possess it is a document that has had a history.
Hence, the Bible is to be studied not just for its Message, but also for
what it represents. In fact, to ascertain the best present day hypothesis
as to what the real Bible (not just any copy) actually says; to find out the
genuine Divine Message, one has to uncover layers and layers of human
accretions before one really sees the Divine element. So, to find religious
truth a new method is needed, that of the biblical critics. This method
involves, in part, recognizing that what we presently have to deal with
is a historical document embedded in human history. From this situa-

tion, we have to try to find what transcends history—God's Message, but we can only do this when we have first understood the historical elements.

The secularization of human history and of the Bible's history launched major investigations in anthropology and biblical criticism. And, as we have suggested, and shall try to prove in the rest of this volume, these challenges of La Peyrère were extremely important in developing aspects of the intellectual world in which we live. As we noted above, they were also of serious significance in providing a so-called scientific basis for racism, especially in the United States before the Civil War. La Peyrère's challenges derive from his pre-Adamite theory. This theory in turn derives from his strange Jewish Messianism with its still stranger French component. This component, putting France and its ruler, in a central and crucial place in the great Divine Drama that was about to occur, was perhaps less revolutionary than either the pre-Adamite theory, or the denial of the Mosaic authorship of the Pentateuch. However it also played an important part in discussions and Millenarian analyses of the time, and encouraged a kind of French national Messianism at least up to the Revolution and the Napoleonic era.

For La Peyrère, this central position of France in Christian history was not accidental. Following out elements formulated by Joachim de Fiore and his followers, and by Guillaume Postel in the sixteenth century, France was seen as the land of Divine destiny. It is given this role in Holy Scripture itself, where the celestial lily, the symbol of France, the fleur de lys, is given such prominence in the redemptive prophecies about what is to come. Both Postel and La Peyrère appeal to the fact that France, Sarpeta in Hebrew, is named in the Bible. And finally, the French saw themselves as the senior line of descent from the survivors of the Flood. From way back the French claimed to have descended from Gomer, the oldest son of Japhet, the oldest son of Noah. Thus, they had inherited the original divine mission, and all other nations had a lesser claim upon it. So, La Peyrère contended that God not only chose the lily over all the other flowers of the world, but would also choose 'un Roy Eleu et choisi de Dieu 'entre tous les Roys de la terre pour la deliverance de son Peuple, le pour la Felicité de tous les hommes.'[23]

The French nationalist element had led some followers of Joachim de Fiore to look for the Third Age of the World to emerge in France. Postel cried out to the different French kings who reigned during his adult life to begin the process that would lead to the restitution of all things. La Peyrère saw in the emerging nationalist rivalries of the day, the special role of France in commencing and running the Millenium. This was certainly a challenge to the theological pretensions of the Puritans, setting

up their New Israel in the British Isles and in New England, to the
Counter-Reformation theologians claiming Spain or Portugal was to
play a crucial role in the Divine events to come.

La Peyrère's view influenced Menasseh ben Israel, and it was debated
in England, and changed to the Portuguese version by the Apostle to
Brazil, Antonio de Vieira. It may have played a role in the strange activities of the grand Condé, of Queen Christina, and Menassah ben
Israel in the 1650s. La Peyrère's French nationalist Messianism was his
basic message. The transformation of the world was at hand. The recall
of the Jews, which would be a key element of this transformation, would
take place in France, and then the King of France would rule the world
with the Jewish Messiah. For France to play this role, it had to make
some drastic changes in its laws and attitudes about Jews. France as the
key stage in the Messianic or Millenarian drama recurs into the nineteenth century, and La Peyrère's views are revived by some of the advocates of apocalyptic change, at least up to Napoleon's time. La
Peyrère's French nationalistic Messianism does not seem to have played
a role in the French-centered or oriented theological dramas of La Men-
nais or Mickiewicz, who saw France as the Christ of nations, undergoing
crucifixion in the Revolution, and then re-emerging post-Napoleon with
a Divine leader.

La Peyrère offered his revolutionary theological theses, pre-Adamism
and the denial of the Mosaic authorship of the Pentateuch, in order to
justify his Messianic vision. The revolutionary thesis of La Peyrère attempts to isolate Jewish history from everyone else's history, so that the
Bible can be seen strictly and only, as the Divine Drama constituted by
the history of the Jews from Adam onward to their recall in seventeenth-
century France. Whatever the author's intentions, and whatever degree
of sincerity he had about them, the effect of his pre-Adamism and biblical
criticism was enormous, because for the first time such basic assumptions
of the accepted religious framework of the Western world were being
questioned. The attempt to deal with these challenges brought about pro-
found changes in the modern intellectual world. The nationalist Messianism had some impact, and may have played some role in politics
from 1650-1815.

Father Eusebius Renaudot, in his *A Dissertation on the Chinese Learning*,
said that the author of the Preadamite System, having been informed of
the great antiquity of the Chinese, saw this as a proof of his view.
Similarly the information he gained about the antiquity of the Assyrians,
Babylonians, and Egyptians reinforced his questions about the authenticity of the Bible. This, Father Renaudot reported, did not lead people
to become Preadamites, but rather 'to harbor other Notions equally

subversive of Religion' namely that the Bible is not the original true Revelation.[24] La Peyrère's theory, offered as a Messianic appeal, was to have drastic effects on western religious thought, and to have influenced among others, young Baruch de Spinoza and Father Richard Simon, and to have opened the way to a secular consideration of human history (as well, unfortunately, as offering a basic theory to justify modern racism).

CHAPTER SEVEN

THE INFLUENCE OF LA PEYRÈRE'S BIBLICAL CRITICISM

La Peyrère said that when *Prae-Adamitae* was published, his views were rejected by Jews, Catholics and Protestants alike.[1] Not only was the author arrested, his views condemned from pulpits and by a government, his book was banned, and in several cities it was burned. There followed a stream of printed refutations by Protestant and Catholic authors. However, La Peyrère's statement notwithstanding, there is no record of a published refutation by a Jewish author. We do know of an unpublished one by Menasseh ben Israel, which is mentioned in a list given in 1656 of Menasseh's works ready for the press.[2] It is possible that La Peyrère may have met Menasseh in Amsterdam in 1655, and at that time heard that he was going to refute his theory.[3] Among Christian opponents at least twelve refutations appeared in 1656. From then on La Peyrère was constantly being refuted. To my knowledge there is no complete list of all the refutations. In the late seventeenth century many works that dealt with the Bible also dealt with some of La Peyrère's heresies. Thus, there are probably hundreds of answers in print. Also, in various scientific and/or theological works of the period, some pages were usually devoted to some claim of La Peyrère's.

The first published refutation was that of Grotius in 1643; twelve years before the book was published. Grotius had underlined how dangerous La Peyrère's views were to religion. He also presented a way of avoiding a polygenetic explanation of the inhabitants of North and South America, by claiming they were descendants of Viking explorers.[4] Grotius's two points are part of the pattern of those trying to refute La Peyrère. First they contend that his theory is a menace to religion. Then they try to offer monogenetic explanations, especially of the recently discovered peoples of the New World. An even stronger note in many of the refutations is to point out that La Peyrère's views are in disagreement with all of the authorities—the Church Fathers, the Doctors of Theology, the Protestant pastors of all denominations, and all of the Rabbis from Talmudic times down to the present. Among the dozen refutations published in 1656 were works by Eusebius Romanus, a pseudonym for a French Catholic, Philippe le Prieur;[5] Michael Colabus, a German;[6] Johann Christian Dannhauer from Strasbourg;[7] J. Hilpert, also a German;[8] Ant.Hulsius;[9] Samuel Desmarets of Groningen, The Netherlands;[10] J. Micraelius, another German theologian,[11] Jean-

Baptiste Morin, a French mathematician and astrologer;[12] J. Pythius from the Lowlands;[13] J. H. Ursinus from Germany,[14] and B. Morange from France.[15] One should also include the answer by the Bohemian mystic and Millenarian, Paul Felgenhauer, which was written then, but could not be published until 1659 because the author was in jail.[16] Felgenhauer's answer was that the only possible pre-Adamite was Jesus, because He was before all men.

Refutations continued for the next fifty years or so. Among the works in which some or all of the text is devoted to refuting La Peyrère are writings by Thomas Bangius, 1657;[17] a priest, F.D. Dormay, 1657;[18] Isaac Vossius, 1659;[19] Georg Horn, 1659;[20] Louis Cappel, the great Bible scholar (who had conferred with La Peyrère about his biblical criticism), 1660;[21] Bishop Edward Stillingfleet, 1661;[22] Martin Schook of Groningen (who had earlier written against Descartes and against scepticism) 1662;[23] Johann Heinrich Heidegger, 1667;[24] Johann Conrad Dietrich, 1671;[25] A. B. Hempel, 1673;[26] Matthew Hale, 1677;[27] Christopher P. de Waldenfels;[28] Theophile Spitzel, 1680;[29] Barthold Goldbach, 1682;[30] Willem Salden, 1684;[31] M. G. Vockerodt, 1687;[32] J. Vake, 1696;[33] J. Fecht, 1696;[34] Gottfried Arnold, 1700;[35] Friedrich Spanheim, 1703, Leiden;[36] Herman C. Engelcken, 1707;[37] Noel Alexandre, 1714; [38] J. Ant. Schmid, 1716;[39] Vincent Rumpf, 1721;[40] Jacob Friedrich Reimann, 1725;[41] and J. Hermansson, 1730.[42]

Of all these many refutations the only one that was usually cited was that of Samuel Desmarets of Groningen. He claimed he had heard a couple of years before the publication of *Prae-Adamitae* that La Peyrère was preparing a work with such heretical theses. Then he received letters from some French Protestants about how awful and dangerous La Peyrère's views were. Desmarets said that when *Prae-Adamitae* came out, a sect of pre-Adamites was formed in Amsterdam. It's hard to tell if this means a group that agreed with La Peyrère, or a group that saw themselves as Pre-Adamites. So, Desmarets entered the fray.[43] His refutation seems to be the only one that went through two editions in 1656. He went over La Peyrère's claims quite thoroughly; denied them and traced the pre-Adamite theory back to Maimonides and Paracelsus.[44]

It was La Peyrère's opinion that all of his critics simply pointed out at length that all of the Jewish, Catholic and Protestant authorities from ancient times to the present had disagreed with him, but that they had failed to show that he was wrong. In some of the material written around the time of his conversion, La Peyrère said that he was surprised at the Jewish rejection of his views, since he was trying to be so helpful to the Jews, and to show them their role in present and future history.[45] He was also hurt by the French Reformed Church's rejection, since he was one of their members, and had grown up and lived in their community.[46] What really hurt in the case of someone like Desmarets was how nasty he was about the whole matter. Desmarets had printed a letter from a French Calvinist minister at Charenton, J. Mestrezat, which said, 'L'autheur du livre des Preadamites s'est fait grand tort à nos Eglises, de mettre en lumiere un livre qui merite le feu comme taschant d'anéantir l'histoire de Moyse et de la creation. Il n'y a aucun de nous qui ne le deteste, bien que l'autheur ait vescu jusqui'ici en la Profession de la Religion et que nous estimassions sa personne. Je luy ai refuté ses fondements et luy ai fait voir que son livre combattoit la pieté. Depuis ce temps-là, il ne nous a plus veu, ayant reconnu qu'il ne trouvoit pas son compte avec nous. S'il se donne nostre approbation, je ne scai sur quel fondement il le fait; nous n'accordons pas les tenebres avec la lumiere, et Belial avec Christ. Je prie dieu qu'il benisse votre labeur contre cette impieté....'[47] Thus La Peyrère was abandoned by his coreligionists, even though he was a prisoner of the Inquisition.

When La Peyrère had decided to abjure his views while all these refutations were appearing, he could not also defend them. The only defense he did write was against Desmarets. It was written after his return to Paris and probably after he retired to Aubervilliers. There is no evidence that he ever tried to publish it. It exists in two manuscript copies.[48] In it La Peyrère challenged some of Desmarets' insults, as well as Desmarets' charges against the Church of Rome for having accepted La Peyrère and for protecting him. As La Peyrère asked, what did you want the Pope to do after I abjured the pre-Adamite theory?[49] Besides, as La Peyrère said in all of his apologetic works, he was a believer in the pre-Adamite view (and La Peyrère expressed this as 'estant Preadamite'), because he adhered to the Calvinist theory of religious knowledge, that is, studying Scripture according to one's sense and reason. 'Donc si j'estois Calviniste, je serois Preadamite'. In giving up pre-Adamism, La Peyrère surrendered his reason to the Catholic Church.[50]

In the ensuing answer, La Peyrère, of course, did not directly defend his old views. Instead he tried to show that Desmarets was wrong in some of the ways he had attacked him. Some of these answers subtly reinforce the original pre-Adamite theory. For instance, Desmarets insulted La Peyrère for being the author of this terrible heretical theory. La Peyrère, in turn, calmly pointed out that he did not invent the theory. All the ancient pagans believed the view.[51] All La Peyrère claimed to have contributed was a reconciliation of the history and philosophy of the past, with the account given in Genesis and with Christian theology.[52] Further, La Peyrère refused to grant that his former opinions were impious. He insisted he abjured them because they were contrary to the views of the Catholic Church, of the Church Fathers and Councils, and the Apostolic tradition. He had not abjured them because they were impious. Then he repeated the formula of abjuration to which he insisted he still adhered.[53] After this he took up various detailed items in the pre-Adamite theory that Desmarets had either misunderstood, or offered inadequate counter-arguments against. Without arguing for the pre-Adamite theory, La Peyrère showed repeatedly that the theory did not conflict with various Christian doctrines and that it did not have all sorts of awful consequences. La Peyrère insisted that, 'Mon dessein n'est pas, en refutant ce livre [that of Desmarets] de defandre l'opinion que j'ay retracte, et que ie retracte de nouveau.' Instead his intention was to answer the charges of atheism and blasphemy that Desmarets had made against him.[54] La Peyrère's critique of the Bible emerged from talks he had had with pious men, Louis Cappel and Isaac Vossius, but he had now rejected this anyway.[55] But, however, 'Je me suis contante de dire, qu'il y a dans les Saintes Ecritures, des choses obscures, ecrites sans ordre, et quelquefois oposees les unes aux autres.'[56] La Peyrère immediately defused this critical claim by saying that the obscure and confused matters do not involve those concerning our salvation. He went on to give examples of obscurity and confusion in the text of Scripture that even Desmarets would accept.[57] Then he indicated portions of Scripture that suggest there were men before Adam. But, he said cautiously, he did not hold this view because it was contrary to the view of the Catholic Church. However, a Calvinist like Desmarets could hold it since it seems to be the way Scripture reads. La Peyrère proceeded to develop a case for why Church authority should outrank Scriptural authority. After that he showed that Desmarets was unable to explain the specific problems in the Bible, such as those involved in the Cain story, and the story of Noah's Flood,[58] and also that Desmarets misunderstood lots of things in *Prae-Adamitae*.[59] La Peyrère's single direct answer to a critic ended by strongly suggesting that Desmarets ought to go back to school.[60]

La Peyrère made no effort to defend his heretical views from all of the attacks of every variety of theologian. Of course, he could not in view of the abjuration he had made. However, as appears in the response to Desmarets, he managed to find an indirect way of defending his original views by criticizing his opponent's attack on them. (And, as noted earlier, there is no evidence that he tried to publish this defense.)

In spite of the fact that La Peyrère had been forced to give way, and to abjure his views, portions of them were taken up by some of the avant-garde thinkers of the time. The first of them may have actually been influenced by La Peyrère directly prior to the publication of *Prae-Adamitae* and the arrest of the author. La Peyrère spent six months in Amsterdam in 1655. During this time young Baruch de Spinoza was apparently developing the heretical views that would lead to his excommunication in the next year. One of the teachers in Spinoza's school was Menasseh ben Israel, who had admired La Peyrère's *Du Rappel des Juifs*, and who had read, and disliked, *Prae-Adamitae* before it was published. There are some strong reasons to believe Menasseh either met La Peyrère when he went to visit Queen Christina in Brussels in late 1654, or in Amsterdam a few months later.[61] At any rate this would indicate that La Peyrère's revolutionary views were known to a leading intellectual in the Amsterdam Jewish community, who may have conveyed information about these views to students, such as Spinoza.

So far, no evidence has been discovered that Spinoza ever met La Peyrère. There is ample evidence that he knew his theories. A copy of *Prae-Adamitae* was in Spinoza's library.[62] Of course, one cannot ascertain when he acquired it. Material from La Peyrère's book was used by Spinoza in the *Tractatus-Theologico-Politicus*, which was not published until 1670, but was based on Spinoza's unpublished answer to the rabbis who excommunicated him.[63] Some relatively recently discovered material about the group of people Spinoza was associated with at the time of his excommunication makes it seem that La Peyrère's ideas were circulating at the time. And, one would expect in the ordinary course of events that such a critical, intelligent youth as Baruch de Spinoza would have been alerted to the fact that there were interesting ideas in La Peyrère's book by its condemnation in Holland, in late 1655, as a scandalous work, the arrest of the author the next February, and finally by the author's amazing recantation. It seems likely that a rebel like the young Spinoza would have been intensely curious about this controversy.

These suppositions become more probable in the light of some material that the late I. S. Révah discovered about Spinoza's excommunication. Révah found out that there had been three expulsions from the Synagogue during the same week in Amsterdam in 1656. These were those of Spinoza and two friends, Juan de Prado and Daniel Ribera. Prado had apparently become a freethinker before he left Spain for Holland. He had been captured by the Inquisition, and then fled the country. The leading philosopher of the Amsterdam Jewish community, Isaac Orobio de Castro, knew Prado in Spain, and knew that he had already become irreligious at that time. At some point Prado wrote a book claiming that the law of nature takes precedence over the law of Moses. Unfortunately, no copy of this work has been found, but two refutations of it by Orobio de Castro exist. From these it is possible to reconstruct what Prado had maintained. For our purposes here, it is also important that the records of the charges against Prado and Ribera, and their investigation have survived, and been located by Révah.[64] (On the other hand, notwithstanding intense researches in the Amsterdam city archives and the archives of the Synagogue, no information has yet turned up about Spinoza's case.) From this data, one learns that Prado and Ribera were critical of the Bible, and sometimes satirized portions of it. Prado was accused of holding various views that were similar to those which had just been published by La Peyrère. Prado was supposed to have held at the time of his excommunication that the world is eternal, and that human history is older than Jewish history. This latter view looks virtually the same as the pre-Adamite theory. Prado's evidence for this claim was that Chinese history is at least ten thousand years old. La Peyrère, of course, had used the antiquity of China as one of his chief points.) Also, according to Orobio de Castro, Prado suffered from the madness of those who assert that although it is the case that God created the universe, it is also the case that this creation occurred thousands and thousands of years ago, and not at the time usually estimated on the basis of the Bible. The madness being described here is definitely a major feature of La Peyrère's pre-Adamite theory.[65]

Thus, it would seem that Juan de Prado, who was the senior member of this little rebellious group in 1656, had adopted some of the heretical views of La Peyrère. Using them he had developed a minor level of biblical criticism. But Spinoza went on from the critiques of La Peyrère and Prado to develop a really full-fledged biblical criticism, based on a thorough-going analysis of the kinds of knowledge-claims made for the Bible and in the Bible. It would seem that La Peyrère's attack on the Bible may have played a role in triggering off a small rebellion in the Synagogue. The charges against Prado and Ribera amount to saying they indulged in a kind of biblical criticism and made fun of the Bible. Spinoza, according to the proclamation of excommunication (the *Herem*) was accused of holding atrocious views, and of engaging in atrocious practices.[66]

We have very little information about what happened to these rebels. Prado eventually returned to the Synagogue. We know from the content of the *Tractatus*, that Spinoza over the years worked out a much more philosophical form of biblical criticism as well as a naturalistic metaphysics which did away with any supernatural dimension. Spinoza took some of the bases of his biblical criticism from La Peyrère, but he certainly ignored his Messianic views. And Spinoza completely secularized religion, Jewish or otherwise, and transformed religious history into an effect of fear and superstition.

La Peyrère had been offering a 'theological hypothesis.' We learn that
Spinoza, by 1658-59, had given up such a venture. According to a
Spanish spy's report, Spinoza and Prado attended a theological discussion club in Amsterdam where they held the view that God exists, but
only philosophically.[67] The rest of Spinoza's intellectual career was
devoted to working out the implications of this principle, a principle
which probably would not have made sense to a Messianist like La
Peyrère.

Spinoza was thus, if anything, only a very partial disciple of La
Peyrère, for he was a much more original thinker who created a basic
metaphysical framework for a non-biblical world. (Spinoza, as we shall
see, apparently accepted the pre-Adamite theory, as historical.)
Nonetheless, it is of interest that some of Spinoza's contemporaries saw
La Peyrère in the background behind Spinoza. Jacob Thomasius said in
1670 that Spinoza might have been influenced by La Peyrère.[68] Orobio
de Castro, who wrote an answer to Spinoza as well as to Prado, said that
there were three kinds of enemies of the Bible—Praeadamitae, Athei,
and Theologi politici. (This was said in 1687.) The last on the list is, of
course, Spinoza; the first is La Peyrère. And the second may be Juan de
Prado.[69]

Another figure who may have been influenced by La Peyrère, and who
probably also influenced Spinoza is the Quaker bible critic, Samuel
Fisher, (1605-1665).[70] Christopher Hill has called him the most radical
biblical critic of the time.[71] Fisher developed a powerful set of arguments
to undermine Calvinist assurance that Scripture is the Word of God.
Fisher argued historically and epistemologically that Scripture, as we
know it, is a man-made artifact, that has gone through many changes
from Moses' time to the present. The Word of God is eternal, existing
before Moses, and is available to all mankind whether they have a human
printed Bible or a human Torah scroll or not. Fisher laid out his case in
a very long work, *The Rustick's Alarm to the Rabbis*, first published in
1660.[72] La Peyrère is not mentioned or cited in it. But many of the same
arguments about the transmission of the text appear as well as many of
the points about the Hebrew text that Spinoza raised in the *Tractatus*. A
careful comparison of material used by each needs to be carried out.
Historically Fisher could have met La Peyrère in England in 1654, or
later on, possibly in Rome when Fisher was there trying to convert the
Pope. Fisher was the only early Quaker who was a university graduate
and knew Hebrew and Greek. He became a Quaker in 1654-55. After
being arrested, he went to Holland, where he was the chief arguer for the
Quaker mission trying to convert the Jews there. Fisher attended
Synagogue services and argued with members of the community.[73] An

exhortation of his in Hebrew to the Jews was published along with a Hebrew translation of a Quaker pamphlet, apparently done by the recently excommunicated Spinoza.[74] I will examine Fisher's ideological and perhaps his personal relations with Spinoza in a future paper.

If Spinoza and his friends took La Peyrère seriously in 1656, and they may have constituted the sect of Preadamites that Desmarets and others were so worried about, another major figure in seventeenth century biblical studies developed his views in connection with the work of both La Peyrère and Spinoza. The great French Bible critic, already referred to, Father Richard Simon (1638-1712), who is often called the Father of Higher Criticism, was strongly influenced by both La Peyrère and Spinoza.[75] Simon was an Oratorian, and he came to know La Peyrère well when the latter took up residence with the Oratorians. There are six known letters of Simon to La Peyrère in the 1670s, and there is a later letter of Simon's giving a biography of the deceased La Peyrère.[76] No letters of La Peyrère to Simon exist. We know that Simon burned up his papers at one point when he was being accused of heresy.[77] The extant material indicates that they were quite close but that they did not agree on very much. They disagreed about the pre-Adamites, about the new evidence La Peyrère had unearthed, and about there being two Messiahs, among other matters. When Simon read over La Peyrère's last manuscript on the *Rappel des Juifs*, he strongly advised against its publication. Although Simon did not take La Peyrère's Messianism seriously, and even told La Peyrère that it would destroy the foundations of Christianity,[78] he nonetheless tried to interest his friend in the Messianic movement of Sabbatai Zevi. For example, Simon had a Jewish friend who believed in Sabbatai Zevi so he tried to get La Peyrère to talk to him, knowing La Peyrère was such a great Philosemite.[79] Simon's letter giving La Peyrère's biography states that they often disagreed. To Simon's irritation La Peyrère persisted in discussing his Jewish Messianic theories. And, on his death bed he would not give up either these views or his pre-Adamite theory.[80]

Although Simon indicated he had no great respect for La Peyrère as a scholar, since he knew neither Greek nor Hebrew, while Simon knew practically every Near Eastern language, they were not only personal friends, but also intellectual ones. Simon developed his own biblical criticism, in his *Histoire critique du Vieux Testament* of 1678, from elements that had appeared in the work of La Peyrère and of Spinoza. Though for good prudential reasons, he denied being influenced by either of them, he did admit, at least in Spinoza's case, that he accepted many of his claims, but he rejected the irreligious conclusions of the Dutch philosopher.[81] One reason, said Simon, that Spinoza came to such bad conclusions was that 'il ne parôit pas même qu'il ait fait beaucoup de reflexion sur la matiere qu'il traitoit, s'étant contenté' souvent de suivre le Systeme mal digeré de la Peyrère auteur des Préadamites'.[82]

Simon was the greatest biblical scholar of his time. He knew all of the relevant languages. He had studied all of the available manuscripts. He had studied everything he could find about the history of the Jews, about the nature of the early Church, and about the beliefs of other Near Eastern sects. Simon argued against the Calvinist claim that one could find the truth by reading Scripture. He sought to show that there were inordinate difficulties in establishing what the Bible said or meant at any given place. Using points raised by La Peyrère and Spinoza, he showed that in order to tell what a biblical text said, one would first have to establish an accurate text, not only of the present Bible, but of the actual message of God. He went on to argue that the present text contained all sorts of extremely difficult problems. To solve them we would have to get back to the original text. But, as La Peyrère and Spinoza had shown, the text we have cannot be by Moses. It must have been written over at least an eight hundred year time-span. Since then it has been copied and has been added to. In the course of this, all kinds of errors, glosses, variants, and so on, have gotten into the text. Because of that, the task of critical scholarship is to try to separate the divine message from the human accretions and variations. Simon's work revealed the overwhelming epistemological and historical difficulties involved in disentangling the human from the Divine dimension.[83]

Simon did not share either La Peyrère's Messianism or Spinoza's naturalism. However, he did really seem to believe that there actually was a Divine message. Nonetheless, regardless of his actual beliefs, his efforts greatly aided in the transformation of the study of religion into a secular subject. Simon's biblical scholarship not only launched the scientific study of the Bible, as was done by Astruc and Reimarus, but also the Enlightenment rejection of religion (when Simon's scholarship was combined with philosophical scepticism and Spinozistic naturalism).

Something should be said here about Jean Astruc's views about his predecessors as biblical scholars. In his famous work, *Conjectures sur les Memoires originaux dont il parôit que Moyse s'est servi pour composer le livre de Génèse* of 1753, Astruc offered the theory that Moses used two major earlier sources to compose Genesis. He appealed to Simon's work to buttress his case. On the other hand, he claimed to be rebutting 'le vain triomphe de Spinosa,' and of Hobbes. Regarding La Peyrère, Astruc contended that in order to maintain his view that there were men before Adam, he had to weaken the authority of Genesis. To do that, La Peyrère denied the Mosaic authorship. This denial, Astruc asserted, seems to have been the malady of the previous century. He then accused the liberal Protestant, Jean Leclerc, of having done the same by putting together the most outrageous portions of Hobbes, La Peyrère, and Spinoza. So, almost a century after they were published, the views of La Peyrère continued to reverberate among avant-garde scholars of the Bible.[84]

In contrast to the reactions of the early biblical critics, the leading English theologian, Bishop Edward Stillingfleet, repeatedly insisted that the denial that Adam was the first man, or that Moses wrote the Pentateuch, was unreasonable, contrary to commonsense, and ridiculous. In his *Origines Sacrae*, Stillingfleet insisted that it was essential to believe in the Adamic origin of mankind in order to believe in the truth of the Scriptures and the universal effects of the fall.[85] It is inconceivable, he asserted, 'how the account of things given in Scripture should be true, if there were Persons existent in the World long before *Adam* was.'[86] To claim, as the author of the *Pre-Adamites* does, that Moses was only trying to explain the origin and history of the Jewish Nation, and that Adam was just the first Jew 'is manifestly ridiculous.' Stillingfleet challenged La Peyrère's view by ridicule, by insisting that any reasonable person would accept Scripture at its word, and by arguing that it is more commonsensical to accept Scripture, than to accept La Peyrère's interpretation.[87] This type of rejection of pre-Adamism continued in the Anglican tradition to the second half of the seventeenth century.

Other indications of La Peyrère's influence appear in the views of two Italian thinkers, Rabbi Isaac Vita Cantarini, and Giambattista Vico. The material concerning Rabbi Cantarini's views on La Peyrère's theories comes to us a bit indirectly, but there seems to be no reason to question it. Count d'Oxenstirn, the grand nephew of the leader of the Swedish government in the middle of the seventeenth century, was traveling in Italy later in the century. He came down with gout between Venice and Padua and had to spend a month in the latter city. Lonely and bored, he asked his host if there was anyone interesting in town who might visit him. A Jewish doctor, Rabbi Cantarini, was sent for. According to Oxenstirn, after they discussed gout for a few minutes, they turned to other subjects, and finally to the Old Testament. At this point in the count's relation of the episode, he said that he took the occasion to ask the rabbi what his view was about the pre-Adamites.[88] (One wonders how often this must have come up in learned conversations of the time). The rabbi replied that he did not think it was impossible, since our world is only about 6,000 years old. God could well have created other worlds before this, without there being any contradiction. But the Count said nothing is mentioned about this in the Old Testament, while Genesis does tell us that in the beginning God created heaven and earth, and He made Adam, the first father of men. The rabbi answered that the word 'beginning' ought to be understood in terms of the works that Moses had any knowledge of. There could be all sorts of works of God that the Lord had not made known to Moses. Then, turning to his own view, Cantarini said that if you understood the Kabbala, you would not have difficulty understanding this mystery, as well as many others that you do not yet know about. The Count asserted that he knew nothing about all of this, and that he personally kept to the sense of Holy Scripture. But the rabbi replied that is just what you cannot do without the help of the Kabbala. Cantarini went on to explain why he did not believe that the sun stood still when Joshua commanded it to do so. He did not offer La Peyrère's explanation, that the sun stood still only where Joshua was. Instead the rabbi insisted that what is said about the sun in that passage is just a figure of speech, indicating that Joshua did something extraordinary.[89]

A bit later on in the conversation Oxenstirn asked him if the Old Testament was the oldest book ever written. Of course, Cantarini said no, and named some earlier ones. There was no touch of pre-Adamism in this, since he named works that are mentioned in the Bible.[90] As they went on to different topics, and at each one the rabbi turned out to have surprising views, Oxenstirn decided that that is what happens if a person is deprived of the illumination of the Holy Spirit and of Divine Grace. A person then tried to measure the judgments of God according to his own meager conceptions. Oxenstirn had just about decided that Cantarini had the views of an atheist. But the rabbi went still further and gave the Count an outline of the Kabbalistic conception of human life, in which one of the Count's favorite doctrines about sin and hell disappeared.[91] As a closing comment on this strange encounter, Oxenstirn reported that the unfortunate rabbi some time later broke his leg, and died. All of this happened when the Count was in Venice.[92]

Rabbi Cantarini seemed to have no difficulty in integrating the pre-Adamite theory into his Kabbalistic reading of Scripture. One wonders if he was unique in this or if many other orthodox Jews found it easy to add the pre-Adamite view to their other beliefs. La Peyrère himself had said that he was deeply saddened that the Jews completely rejected him. This would suggest that he never had the good fortune to meet such a rabbi as Cantarini.

One also wonders how common Oxenstirn's quest for opinions about the pre-Adamite theory were. Might there have been hundreds or thousands of Oxenstirns moving through all parts of the European intellectual world asking each scholar they met—what do you think of the pre-Adamite theory? Even if there were fairly few like Count d'Oxenstirn, his interest would indicate a nervousness about the problem, and about the widespread implications if the theory were true. Perhaps people like Oxenstirn were worried enough about La Peyrère's views that they needed constant reassurance from learned men.

Rabbi Cantarini, (1644-1723) was a fairly important figure in both Jewish and Italian intellectual circles. He was a graduate in medicine from the University of Padua, and had remained in Padua practicing medicine for the rest of his life. He published some important Hebrew works as well as a Latin one, and was a popular preacher whose sermons attracted non-Jews as well as Jews. He corresponded with non-Jewish intellectuals. It is possible that his knowledge of, and interest in, the pre-Adamite theory helped diffuse it in Italy.[93]

A kind of pre-Adamite view, somewhat like that of Rabbi Cantarini, appears in the writing of Lady Anne Conway, *The Principles of the Most Ancient and Modern Philosophy*, published posthumously in 1690. Lady Anne Conway (1631-1679) was a student and collaborator of Henry More, the Cambridge Platonist. Drawing heavily on the Kabbalistic texts assembled in Von Rosenroth's *Kabbala Denudata*, Anne Conway considered whether the world is 6,000 years old, or that 'before this World, there was another invisible World, from whence this visible World proceeded.' This earlier world could have lasted 60,000 years, or any number of years, since God has the power to make it such. God could have created the world of creatures before 6,000 years, before 60,000 years, or 600,000 years. The world is both of infinite duration and created. In its infinite duration its first person is the ultimate Adam, Adam Kadmon, followed in time by the historical Adam. Lady Anne Conway's Kabbalistic account probably parallels that of various Jewish and Christian Kabbalists of the period who saw no real challenge in the pre-Adamite theory when placed in a Kabbalistic understanding of God, as Infinite Creator creating necessarily in infinite time.[94]

Around 1690, Giambattista Vico in Naples was a friend of some 'epicureans' who were indicted by the Holy Office for their belief that there had been men in the world before Adam. At the time that Vico was working on the *Scienza Nuova*, people in the circle around Giannone knew of La Peyrère's work, and saw that it raised serious problems for the Christian believer.[95] And, what is most interesting regarding Vico and La Peyrère is that the latter is specifically mentioned in the beginning of the *Scienza Nuova*. Momigliano has shown that Vico did, in fact, develop a theory in his work that was intended to refute La Peyrère, among others.[96] Vico defended the historical reliability of Scripture, by carefully separating profane and sacred history. The latter, he insisted, was literally true, whereas the other is not. In Book I of the *Scienza Nuova*, Vico started examining the problem raised by La Peyrère, among others, namely that of the apparent conflict of the chronologies of Egypt, China and other ancient societies with that of the Bible. Vico quickly decided that 'the Hebrews were the first people of the world' and that Adam was their prince. Hebrew chronology, as the divine one, is strictly accurate.[97] The chronologies of other peoples are expressed as fables or mythology, and are to be studied by analyzing this basically irrational material. Like La Peyrère, Vico completely separated Jewish from Gentile history. Vico then declared the first to be completely accurate, and the other to be analyzed by the new science of history. Momigliano has declared that for Vico, 'There cannot be a real conflict between the language of unreason which characterizes the heroic ages of profane history and the language of reason which is the very essence of the biblical text. Vico's famous theory of the heroic ages is primarily an answer to La Peyrère and Spinoza.'[98] As an answer to La Peyrère, Vico's theory really builds upon one of his basic contentions—the separation of Jewish history from everybody else's history. The first is true history. The others have to be studied indirectly through their myths, legends, poetry, etc. in a secular scientific fashion. Since Vico refused to follow La Peyrère in a heretical direction he did not go on to claim only biblical history counts. Instead the new science of history was only possible if the one case of Providential History were omitted from the range of what could be studied scientifically.

Having considered several major figures of the seventeenth and eighteenth centuries who were influenced by La Peyrère's views, we should, before turning to the enlightenment theories about pre-Adamism, briefly mention the reactions of Blaise Pascal and Bishop Pierre-Daniel Huet to pre-Adamism.

Pascal's sole comment appears to be a reference in one of the *pensées* to 'extravagances des Apocalyptiques et preadamites, millenaristes.'[99] It seems probable that Pascal was using these categories as synonymous. In that case he simply rejected both La Peyrère's theology and his anthropology as extravagant. It would seem likely that Pascal and La Peyrère were part of the scientific circle around Mersenne in the 1640s. Yet so far, there has been no indication that they were at all influenced by each other's work or views.

Bishop Huet, a genuine philosophical sceptic and one of the most learned scholars of the time, tried to trivialize La Peyrère's main point. The Bibliothèque Nationale in Paris has Huet's copy of *Prae-Adamitae* which shows that he examined the work fairly carefully.[100] In Huet's major apologetic work, *Demonstration Evangelica* (which was written in answer to Menasseh ben Israel after the two had had a discussion in Amsterdam), the author sought to show that various cultures had independent origins and careers. Nonetheless, he contended they all expressed the same religious truth. Through the comparative study of religion one could find the same central figures, a Moses-type, a Mary-type, a Jesus-type, and so on. However, only the Christians have the names given correctly. La Peyrère's data, therefore, does not prove diverse origins of cultures, if there is a genuine cross-cultural unity. Each culture is independent, but mirrors the same basic religious truth which is properly given and stated in Christianity.[101]

If La Peyrère's views did not fare too well in the second half of the seventeenth century, what was their fortune during the Enlightenment? We will examine this after considering the fate of his French-oriented Messianism.

CHAPTER VIII

THE INFLUENCE OF LA PEYRÈRE'S FRENCH ORIENTED MESSIANISM

As indicated in Chapter II, La Peyrère's theology may have been designed as especially suitable for Marranos, that is Jewish Christians, forced converts from Spain and Portugal and their descendants who were living in various parts of Europe, including southern France, Rome, Holland, Belgium, northern Germany, Italy and elsewhere. The Spanish and Portuguese inquisitors claimed the Marranos were fake Christians, who were secretly Jewish, and would revert to Judaism if allowed to move to Italy, Holland and the Ottoman Empire. A long series of Inquisition trials produced plenty of evidence to support this view. People all over the Spanish and Portuguese empire, when sufficiently tortured, confessed to secret Jewish practices. Escapees in Holland and Italy, who joined Jewish communities there, reinforced this view by their practices and their pictures of what life in Iberia was like.[1]

There has been debate over the last few decades about the actual religious beliefs of the Marranos, whether they were secret Jews, converted Jews who were now Christians, or potential Jews, if they could move out of Iberia. If the term Marrano is applied to all the New Christians in Spain and Portugal, it no doubt includes a range of possibilities from secret Jews, potential Jews to genuine converts. However, people from this genealogically defined group (having a Jewish ancestor in the last few generations) were regarded with suspicion by Christians, and rejected by Jews if they did not revert to Judaism when they had the opportunity to do so. Some Marranos who had escaped from Iberia found themselves unable to decide whether to remain outwardly Christian or join the Jewish communities in Holland and Italy. The choice was not simple since it involved a great change of life, as well as some genuine suffering by going through adult circumcision. So some people wavered. Some who joined Jewish communities found they really did not fit in them, and reverted to Christianity. Some even returned to Spain or Portugal.[2]

In view of this range of behavior, it seems to me that there were probably some people who were genuinely Marranos, that is Jewish Christians. Since their conversion or their families' conversions had been such a dramatic turn of events, since they and their brethren suffered so much from the dire events in Spain and Portugal, they no doubt looked for some way of understanding their situation. Some looked for a way of giving significance to their situation, especially in theological terms. If people can write so much now about where was God when people were sent off to Auschwitz to be tormented and killed, it seems only too easy to imagine people asking where was God when the Spanish Inquisition began. There is in fact a masterpiece of Portuguese literature by Samuel Usque, *Consolations for the Tribulations of Israel*, written in the mid-sixteenth century, trying to cope with what had happened, and to put it in the perspective of Jewish Messianic expectations.[3]

I think various Spanish and Portuguese theologies, written by *conversos*, can be seen as attempts to deal with the novel situation, the Conversion of the Jews, and to place the converts in a unique position as far as the future unfolding of the Divine Drama. One of the first great converts, Pablo de Santa Maria, the Bishop of Burgos, né Solomon Halevi, Rabbi of Burgos, and his son, Alonso de Cartegena, also Bishop of Burgos, claimed that they were descended from the family of the mother of Jesus, and as such close relatives of the Messiah they would be in the inner circle of the faithful when Jesus returned. Luis de Leon insisted on the theological importance of the conversion of the Iberian Jews, and placed them in the center of what was to come in the Divine Drama.[4]

On the other hand, some Marranos saw their tragic life as a suffering needed before the coming of the Messiah. The fall of Spanish Judaism, the expulsion from Spain in 1492, fell on the same day as that commemorated in the Jewish calendar as the sad day upon which the first and second temples were destroyed. The ninth of the month of Ab became a super-fast day, a memorial for the three greatest tragedies in Jewish history. Additional prayers were added to Jewish services because of the tragedy of the Marranos. Kabbalistic rabbis in the mystical city of Safed in the Holy land tried to understand what was happening. Some developed the theory that this latest catastrophe was a necessary prelude to the coming of the Messiah. When Sabbatai Zevi appeared, proclaimed himself the Messiah (and said he was born on the ninth of Ab) and then converted to Islam, a theology offered by Abraham Cardoso insisted that Sabbatai Zevi came to save Marranos. In order to do so, he himself had to become a Marrano, hence his conversion![5]

La Peyrère's version is somewhere between the Marrano theologies of the *converso* theologians in Spain and Portugal, and the Sabbatean ones in the Ottoman empire. For La Peyrère, the Recall of the Jews will take place through making the Jews into Marranos in France. They will become Jewish Christians, neither plain Jews, nor ordinary Gentile Christians. They will have the religion of the first Christians, Mary, John the Baptist, and the Apostles, who knew and believed in Jesus as a *Jewish* redeemer. They will be able to see the faith through Jewish eyes, realizing that it is just the completion of what is said in Isaiah and other prophetic works. Their religion will be spared the dogmas, the theological formulations, and added practices developed for those who came to Christianity from paganism.[6]

Not only will Jewish Christianity be the original and purest version, its adherents, who, in the nature of the case can only be Jews converted to Christianity, will be the central figures in the Messianic Age about to begin. The King of France will lead them back to the Holy Land, where they will rebuild Jerusalem and its Temple, where their Messiah, Jesus in the flesh, will reside. The Jewish Christians will be the courtiers for the Messiah and the universal monarch, and will spread happiness and joy to everyone, bringing about the plenitude of the Gentiles.

La Peyrère's version should have made Jews want to become Marranos, and Marranos happy (especially Marranos residing in France) to be ready to play their role in the great events to come. Perhaps this is why La Peyrère, in his dedication of *Prae-Adamitae* to the Jews all over the world, wished he could be one of them, so that he could pass through all the stages of the Recall of the Jews—people happy and elect. He allowed a super-special role for the seven thousand secretly elected Jews who would be the most important figures in the Messianic Age.[7]

If I am right that La Peyrère was offering a Marrano theology, still there is no evidence that any Marranos took it seriously, and tried to form a Jewish Christian church. We will see, however, that La Peyrère's formulation of what Judeo-Christianity would be like did play an important role in the thought of Rabbi Menasseh ben Israel, of Father Antonio de Vieira, S. J., and perhaps other Millenarians of the time. We will also see that the French orientation of La Peyrère played some role in the seventeenth century, and was later revived at the time of the French Revolution and by Napoleon.

La Peyrère's views were set forth at a time of enormous interest and concern with Messianic and Millenarian theories. On the Jewish side, there had been growing conviction that the long hoped for Messiah was about to come. From the time of the Spanish Expulsion in 1492, to the revolutionary new interpretation of the Kabbala in the late sixteenth century, to the studies of Menasseh ben Israel, these convictions became stronger and stronger. Jewish Messianism in the seventeenth century reached its high point, of course, with the acceptance of Sabbatai Zevi as the Messiah by many of the Jewish communities.[8]

Protestant Millenarians, from the time of the Reformation, foresaw the imminent commencement of the Millenium. They wrote a great deal about the need to restore the Jews in Palestine and the need to convert them. These Millenarians saw the victories of England and Holland over Catholic Spain and the victories of the Protestants in England and Holland over the Catholics as sure signs of the coming Millennium. Perhaps more importantly they interpreted the Puritan Revolution as a key step on the road to a new age. Some Catholic thinkers, such as Father Antonio de Vieira of Portugal, constructed Millenarian scenarios out of the events going on in Iberia and Latin America.

A figure who played a most significant role in the theorizing about the events to come was Rabbi Menasseh ben Israel. He was well known in the republic of letters. He corresponded with many Christian scholars known to La Peyrère, such as Mersenne, Bochart, Vossius, and Grotius.[9] He was the leading expositor of Judaism to the Christian world through his many books in Latin and Spanish.[10] Important scholars and nobility came to meet him in Amsterdam, and to hear him preach.[11] He was often referred to as '*the* Jewish philosopher,' and to the non-Jewish world he was probably *the* Jewish thinker who could best explain and relate his views to those of the non-Jews.[12] Jewish scholars have tended to ignore his writings, except for the curiosity, *The Hope of Israel*, which claims some of the American Indians are part of the Lost Tribes. They have found much of what he did to be outside of the Jewish tradition. Recent interest has found that Menasseh was first and foremost a Messianist, steeped in the contemporary developments in Messianic thinking from Don Isaac Abarbenel to Isaac Luria and his disciples, and he made this material available to the non-Jewish world. Menasseh was a victim of the Iberian Jewish tragedy. He was born in La Rochelle, where his parents had fled after being severely punished by the Inquisition for being secret Jews. [12A] Menasseh became a teacher and publisher in the free atmosphere of Holland. In his writings, he saw the tragedy of the Marranos in Spain and Portugal as the prelude of the Messianic Redemption. The Marranos, like the Lost Tribes, would be brought back when the Messiah came.

If the redemption was imminent, one had to watch for signs. After the vast pogroms that occurred in Poland in 1648-1649, many Jewish Messianic thinkers might have given up hope.[13] Just at this point of despair, Menasseh received an all important sign. A Portuguese explorer, Antonio de Montezinos, had arrived from South America in Amsterdam in 1644, and reported that he had come across a tribe of Indians in the Andes mountains which was practicing Judaism. Menasseh had Montezinos repeat his story before a notary. Menasseh did not realize the full importance of this information until the English Millenarians, John Dury and Nathaniel Homes, used it to buttress Thomas Thorowgood's *Jewes in America, or Probabilities that the Americans are of that*

Race,[14] published in 1650. In the preface by Dury, he included the discussion he and Homes had had with Menasseh about the significance of discovering the Jewish Indians. They might be part of the Lost Tribes of Israel who were supposed to reappear just before the Millenium and return to the Holy Land. Dury asked Menasseh to send him an account of the Jewish view about the role of the Lost Tribes. Instead Menasseh sat down and wrote his most famous work, *The Hope of Israel*, which appeared in Latin, Spanish, Hebrew, English, and later in Dutch.[15] In this work, besides reporting the Jewish Indian theory, Menasseh moved from interpreting that sign to connecting Messianic expectations with the revolutionary events taking place in England. The book is dedicated to the revolutionary government of England. And in it Menasseh indicated that he thought the Redemption was close at hand, though he was not prepared to give a date. There were three English editions of his book (in 1650, 1651, and 1652), all promoted by leading Millenarians.[16] One result of this success was that Menasseh was officially contacted by the British government to discuss the readmission of the Jews to England (they had been banned in 1290) Unofficially he was contacted by various Millenarians as to whether this had Messianic significance. As Menasseh saw it, the Redemption would not come until the Jews were totally dispersed over the globe. Now that it was known that there were Jews in America, the next crucial step was to have Jews in England.[17] There were some there but they weren't officially recognized. Their official presence apparently was required in order for the Redemption process to unfold. Menasseh wrote Cromwell that 'the opinion of many Christians and mine concurre herein, that we both believe that the restoring time of our Nation in their Native Country, is very near at hand.'[18] He went on to explain to Cromwell that the only step that remained before the Messiah would come was the resettling of the Jews in England.[19] From 1653-1655 Menasseh negotiated about whether he should go to England, and discussed it with leading English Millenarians. The Amsterdam Jewish community was opposed to his going, since they feared that if he negotiated with the British government, the Dutch government might regard this as trading with the enemy.

At the end of 1654, Menasseh went to visit Queen Christina of Sweden, who had just abdicated her throne, and was living in Brussels, preparing for her official conversion to the Roman Catholic Church. Various reasons have been offered for Menasseh's visit: one that she owed him money for some Hebrew books he had sent her, another that he wanted to offer his services to become her Jewish Descartes. No matter why he made the visit, it seems to have been a turning point in his career, for it was in Brussels that Menasseh apparently became acquainted with La Peyrère's French oriented Messianic ideas. La Peyrère was living next door to Christina, who was living in the home of a leading Marrano, Garcia d'Yllan, one of the richest persons in the Spanish Netherlands because of his chocolate monopoly. La Peyrère was the intermediary between the Prince of Condé and Christina, who could not agree on the protocol of who should pay the first visit to whom.[20]

Menasseh never indicated that he had met or talked to La Peyrère, but he seems to have been shown and given a copy of *Du Rappel des Juifs* (a book which is included in the inventory of volumes Christina had shipped to Belgium). Something must have happened to the Queen during the visit because when Menasseh returned to Amsterdam in December 1654, he told people at the home of the leading Millenarian, Peter Serrarius, that the Messiah's coming was imminent. Serrarius, a free-floating Millenarian who had earlier been a minister of the French Reformed Church, had become a central figure in the off-beat theological world in Amsterdam. A couple of years later he aided young Spinoza. Later he became the leader of the Christian followers of Sabbatai Zevi).[21] One of those present, Paul Felgenhauer, a Lutheran Millenarian from Bohemia, had had a fervent discussion with Menasseh about the advent of the Messiah. Inspired, Felgenhauer rapidly wrote *Good News for the Jews*, telling of the coming of the Redeemer, a work Cecil Roth has called 'one of the maddest rhapsodies ever written.'[22] The book is dedicated to Menasseh and is really a joint effort. A letter of Menasseh's is included that is dated February 1, 1655. In this document Menasseh listed the people who were in contact with him who knew that the Messiah was coming. The list consisted of Abraham Von Frankenburg, Johann Mochinger, two English Millenarians, Nathaniel Holmes and Henry Jessey, plus 'ex Gallia Autorem Libelli Gallico Idiomate edite, *Du Rappel des Juifs*.'[23] Along with this document, Menasseh had included some of his correspondence with the four persons named, all dating from 1636-1649, but there were no letters to or from La Peyrère. Although Menasseh's letter states that he possessed letters from all the 'noble and learned' people named, the supporting evidence indicates that he possessed La Peyrère's *Du Rappel des Juifs* or had copied parts of it, but was not in correspondence with the author.[24] *Du Rappel des Juifs* is not mentioned in any previous writing of Menasseh's, even though he was extremely interested in Messianic and Millenarian works. Looking at *Du Rappel* seems to have convinced Menasseh of the imminence of the Messianic Age. The material in the letters from Von Frankenburg, Mochinger, Holmes and Jessey had been known to Menasseh for at least five years and had not led him to exciting conclusions about the imminence of the coming of the Messiah. So it would appear that his reading La Peyrère's *Du Rappel des Juifs* made a radical difference in his thinking. Given the sequence of events, it would seem likely that he first saw the book at Queen Christina's, either her copy or the author's. And, as a result of seeing the work, he decided to go to England. Before he left he wrote his most Messianic work, *La Piedra Gloriosa*, which was magnificently illustrated by Rembrandt.[25]

It may be the case that La Peyrère and Menasseh met through their common acquaintance, Queen Christina. If they had not met in Belgium one would expect that they came across each other in Amsterdam. Felgenhauer, in his refutation of *Prae-Adamitae* published in 1659, said that the unknown author of the *Prae-Adamitae* was in Amsterdam from the fall of 1654 to the spring of 1655. At some time after early February 1655 the author of *Prae-Adamitae* was asked if he wanted to take part in a disputation with Felgenhauer, probably at Serrarius' home, but he refused. We learn further that Felgenhauer received his copy of *Prae-Adamitae* from Menasseh, before the book was officially published, who apparently suggested he refute it. All of this indicates that Menasseh and Felgenhauer were interested in La Peyrère's views, and they could easily have met him.[26] Yet neither of them ever mentioned meeting La Peyrère. Menasseh apparently wrote a refutation of the pre-Adamite theory. In a list of works he said were ready for the press in 1656 was one entitled *Refutatio libri qui titulus Praeadamitae*. This volume never appeared, nor has any manuscript been found.[27] Before Menasseh left Holland, like La Peyrère, he wrote a letter to all the Synagogues in the world (in Portuguese). Unlike La Peyrère, he actually sent it to at least three Synagogues in Italy and Germany. In it he announced his impending trip to England to negotiate with the British government, appointed himself agent for the entire Jewish world, and asked if anyone had any business they wanted him to transact, to send him a letter in England. (He did present at least one letter, from Rabbi Nathan Shapira of Jerusalem to Cromwell.)[28]

One of the first persons to meet Menasseh in England in September 1655 was a strange Welsh Millenarian, named Arise Evans, who had been jailed for claiming to be the Messiah. When the Puritans overthrew Charles I and executed him, Evans had a vision that Charles Stuart, the son of the beheaded King or his resurrected father was the universal ruler who would rule the world with the Messiah. In his *A Voice from Heaven to the Commonwealth of England* of 1652, Evans contended that Charles Stuart is from the seed of Japhet. He had found in Menasseh's *Hope of Israel* passages to justify his view that the Messiah would come in England, that he would be slain and rise again, and that the triumphant finale would occur in the British Isles. He was so excited with this discovery he petitioned Parliament and gave his news to Oliver Cromwell and predicted the Jews would be converted in England in 1652 by Charles Stuart. Evans's next work, *An Eccho to the Voice from Heaven*, also of 1652, gives an account of all the efforts he had made from 1633 onward to get his prophetic messages to the government. He tried to save the King.[29] When that failed he went to see Cromwell's lieutenant, Hugh Peter. In July 1652, Evans reported he saw a book in Peter's chamber claiming to be an answer to Menasseh's *Hope of Israel*. In looking it over, Evans saw Menasseh's 'opinion so consonant to what I had set down by God's providence in my Book, and so agreeable to the promise both in the old and new Testaments...I came to know rightly what the *Jews* hope and look for.'[30]

Since Evans saw Menasseh as a potential ally, he rushed to meet him in London. The account of their meeting is most amazing, and indicates that Menasseh arrived in England a convinced follower of La Peyrère's French oriented Messianism. Evans had written a letter to Menasseh on March 16, 1655 arguing that on Menasseh's terms, Charles Stuart is the universal monarch embodying the spirit of the Messiah, and is the Deliverer Menasseh mentioned in sec. 26 of the *Hope of Israel*. The letter was delivered in person. Evans and Menasseh had no common language and so spoke to each other through an interpreter. Evans gave the content of the discussion, apparently verbatim, in his *Light for the Jews, or the Means to convert them, in Answer to a Book of theirs, called the Hope of Israel, written and Printed by Manasseth Ben-Israel, Chief Agent for the Jews here.* (This text has been used by Christopher Hill and David Katz to show how crazy Arise Evans was. They did not take note of what Menasseh was saying.)[31]

After Evans told Menasseh his view, we are told 'Menasseh said, 'That the time wherein their Messiah should appear was come, but that King *Charles Steeward* was he, that he could not believe, for he could not believe that ever King *Charles* should rise again and be restored to his Empire; *but said he*, Oliver, Protector, or the King of Swedland is more liken to do it than he, and specially the King of *France* is the most likest to be our Messiah. If he be a Gentile, and be in this part of the world; for he had, *as he said*, a great deal of confidence in the words of an Ancient French Author, that declares much to that purpose.'[32] Assuming that 'Ancient' is a mistranslation of 'venerable' or something like that, Menasseh was advancing La Peyrère's theory in answer to Evans's English oriented Messianism. In the conversation that followed Evans pointed out that under all sorts of medieval treatises the King of England *is* the King of France. He also sought to show, from materials in *The Hope of Israel* that Charles Stuart could be the Viceroy of the Messiah ben

David. He would not have to be a natural (i.e. genetic) Jew.[33] It is claimed that some rabbis who accompanied Menasseh checked on whether Cromwell was of Jewish ancestry.[34]

Menasseh offered La Peyrère's French oriented Messianism as the answer to Evans' views. One finds another occasion during Menasseh's stay in England when he advanced La Peyrère's theory. After the negotiations for the readmission of the Jews had broken down, Menasseh stayed on (and even applied for legal residence in England). He wrote and published one book in England, in English, the *Vindiciae Judaeorum*. It is an answer to a lot of anti-Jewish charges that had been made during the government's considerations about re-admitting the Jews.[35]

In replying to the charges that the Jews reject Christianity, Menasseh offered a strange view from La Peyrère's *Du Rappel des Juifs* as a means of settling the competing Messianic claims of Judaism and Christianity. 'For, as a most learned Christian of our time hath written, in a French book, which he calleth the *Rappel of the Iewes* (in which he makes the King of *France* to be their leader, when they shall return to their country), the Iewes, saith he, shall be saved, for yet we expect a *second* coming of the same Messiah; and the *Iewes*, believe that that coming is the *first* and not the second, and by that faith they shall be saved; for the difference consists onely in the circumstance of time.'[36] So Menasseh found in the French oriented Messianic views of 'a most learned Christian of our time' a way of minimizing the difference between Judaism and Christianity. La Peyrère's theory that there were two Messiahs, asserting that it did not matter which you believed in, the first or the second, made it appear that Christian Millenarianism and Jewish Messianism became almost the same view. The Jews could fulfill their Messianic role without becoming Christians, and the Christians could accept their *second* coming as the Jews' *first*. Hence, the apologetic for a Jewish Messianism without the need for conversion to Christianity, offered by one of the foremost Messianists of the mid-seventeenth century clearly developed from La Peyrère's ideas.[37]

Several matters about this are of interest. First, Menasseh felt it desirable to mention the French aspect of La Peyrère's theory, even though it was not really relevant to the general point he was making. This suggests that Menasseh may have pushed the French side of the story among the English Millenarians, who would hardly have appreciated it. It remains a mystery why, after all of the initial enthusiasm of the Millenarians to bring the Jews back to England, and watch them become Christians there, they dropped the matter after late December 1655, and did not bring up the re-admission issue again. Maybe one thing that dampened their enthusiasm was Menasseh's French oriented view. In the Evans conversations Menasseh is quoted as saying of the King of France, 'If he be a Gentile and be in this part of the World,' then Menasseh is confident of La Peyrère's view concerning the role of the King of France. This looks like gibberish unless Menasseh had heard through Christina or La Peyrère, some predictions about the King of France going to England. It may be, and this is just speculation, that the Prince of Condé expected soon to be the King of France . He had sent La Peyrère to England in 1653, and was carrying on all sorts of negotiations with Cromwell, allying him to French interests. So, the royalty who patronized La Peyrère, the Prince of Condé and Queen Christina, may have developed a scenario about the roles they were to play in La Peyrère's picture of what was to come. Menasseh, who apparently took La Peyrère's scenario seriously, may have expected to see the King of France arrive in England, the Jews be re-admitted, and then the Messianic Age begin.[38] Perhaps something about this may be found in Christina's papers.[39] It is also mysterious why, when Christina was preparing for the great religious step in her life, her official conversion to Catholicism, she would invite Rabbi Menasseh ben Israel to visit her, and make him aware of La Peyrère's French oriented Messianism and then finance La Peyrère's publication of his *Prae-Adamitae*.

Possibly more interesting is Menasseh's formulation of a peace treaty between the Jews and the Christians, where they could each describe the past without hurting each other's feelings, or having to convert to the others' view. They could each expect the Coming of the Messiah, and be saved thereby. The only difference is whether it is the first or second coming, which is just 'the circumstance of time,' and has no relevance to salvation.

This peace treaty, based on La Peyrère's formulation, seems to have emerged after much discussion amongst Millenarians. Dury, Jessey, Homes and Hartlib were all trying to make Christianity less offensive to the Jews, and sought to formulate what we might call Judeo-Christianity, in which the Jewish element is part of the statement of the true religion. They still envisaged the conversion of the Jews as a requisite step to the completion of the religious drama. They envisaged an important role for Menasseh in their work, and in their proposed college of Jewish studies. But there is no evidence they tried to convert Menasseh. He, on his side, did not argue against Christianity, except when forced to. He usually just explained the Jewish view on various matters, and explained it so that it did not necessarily or obviously contradict basic Christian claims.[40] A letter of Henry Oldenburg's indicates that in London Menasseh exposited his peace treaty with Christianity to Robert Boyle, Adam Boreel and others.[41]

The leading Portuguese Jesuit, (Antonio de Vieira (1608-1698), the Apostle to the Indians in Brazil, made two trips to Amsterdam in the 1640s. He wanted to discuss the differences between the Jews and the Christians. Chief Rabbi Saul Levi Morteira refused to deal with him, but Menasseh did.[42] We possess Vieira's version of their conversations when he was arrested by the Inquisition and had to explain his dealings with Jews. Basically Vieira sought a way of reconciling Judaism and Christianity. He found that Menasseh and he could formulate what happened in the first century so that they did not have to disagree. The Christian Messiah had come. The Jewish one was yet to come. They could formulate the future so that the anticipated Millenial-Messianic events would be the same. After working this out, Vieira went to England and then to Paris. He may have talked to English Millenarians. He arrived in Paris shortly after La Peyrère's return from Scandinavia, and may have met the author or learned of his ideas. A leading expert on Vieira's thought, A. J. Saraiva, has said, 'il existe une extraordinaire coincidence entre les idées de La Peyrère et celles de Vieira, à tel point que nous sommes obligés d'admettre que le jésuite portugais...a connu le *Du Rappel des Juifs*, sinon son auteur, pendant ses deux séjours à Paris.'[43] In Vieira's version, which is much like both Menasseh's and La Peyrère's view of what will happen, the major difference is that the King of Portugal will play the crucial political role. Vieira tried very hard to get the actual King of Portugal to end the ban on the practice of Judaism and to recall the Portuguese New Christians from all over the world (and this presumably would have included Menasseh ben Israel and Baruch de Spinoza) to prepare for Portugal's role in the imminent Millenium.[44]

One last point regarding the influence of La Peyrère on Menasseh should be noted. When Menasseh returned from the visit to Christina, apparently overwhelmed by the ideas in *Du Rappel des Juifs*, he made his announcement to the Dutch Millenarians that the Coming of the Messiah was imminent. He worked with Paul Felgenhauer in getting out the book, *Good News for the Jews*. Nobody reads Felgenhauer because he has such a bad reputation as a wild Millenarian fanatic. However, in the *Bonum Nunciam* he presented a view much like that of La Peyrère's *Du Rappel des Juifs* about how the Jews are the oldest sons of God, and the Gentiles came to know Him through being grafted on to the tree of the Jews. Then the Jews and Gentiles parted but will be reunited by the spirit of the Messiah, which is in both the Old and New Testaments. The Jews will return to the Holy Land, and mankind will be reunited in the Millenial world.[45] Menasseh did not endorse all of Felgenhauer's version, but both Menasseh and Felgenhauer seem to have found a way of reconciling Judaism and Christianity, or of avoiding the conflicts between them, in La Peyrère's formulation. Hence they could join together in awaiting the Good News for the Jews, which would be good news for everyone. In their formulations, and those of Vieira, Dury, and others, there may be a genuine presentation of something that deserves to be called Judeo-Christianity rather than toned down Judaism or Christianity.

So far I have found no further use of La Peyrère's theories among Jews (except the possible indications in Rabbi Cantarini's views). He is usually mentioned as an early advocate of Zionism.[46] But he seems to have had no further influence in the Jewish world. No connection has been found between his kind of Messianism and the Messianic movement of Sabbatai Zevi. Sabbatai Zevi and his followers apparently never heard of La Peyrère.[47] La Peyrère was told about the Sabbataean movement by Richard Simon, who offered to have a Jewish friend of his explain it all to La Peyrère. Simon even offered to give him a book of special prayers to say if he was going to Turkey to see the new Messiah. But La Peyrère apparently ignored the whole topic.[48]

La Peyrère's Messianism was basically political, involving political leaders such as the King of France. Political Messianism, as we have seen, was very common in England, Holland and Germany, especially during the Puritan Revolution. But in France it was much rarer. The only French contemporary who seems to have taken La Peyrère seriously as a Messianic thinker is the strange figure, Nicolas Charpy de Sainte-Croix. His life, as portrayed in the *Biographie universelle* (Michaud), started out as one of crime and libertinage. He was constantly hiding out from the authorities. Fairly suddenly he changed his conduct and became extremely devout, claiming to have visions. He published two religious books, *Le Hérault de la des fin des temps* and *Ancienne nouveauté de l'Ecriture Sainte, ou l'Eglise triomphante en terre* (1657).[49] Although he did not cite La Peyrère, or any other theologian, Charpy de Sainte-Croix had taken over many of La Peyrère's ideas. In Charpy's version the Anti-Christ (who does not appear in La Peyrère's theory) will be born in the seventeenth century. His power will be destroyed by a Jewish leader, a lieutenant of Jesus. Then under the reign of this Jewish King the rest of the Jews will rebuild Jerusalem and will become masters of the whole earth. Finally, 2,080 years later, after Jesus ascends to Heaven, everyone will be redeemed.[50] Charpy submitted his work to the great Jansenist theologian, Antoine Arnauld, who published an extremely sharp attack on it. Later Charpy is supposed to have renounced his errors, taken ecclesiastical orders and to have died in 1670 'in good faith.'[51]

Arnauld, who had no patience or tolerance for deviation in theology, published a long and nasty reply to what he regarded as a very pernicious theory. The answer was called *Remarques sur les principales erreurs d'un livre intitulé l'ancienne nouveauté de l'Ecriture Sainte, ou l'Eglise triomphante en Terre.* In this work, after Arnauld had strongly attacked Charpy de Sainte-Croix's Messianic vision, he then digressed to discuss La Peyrère's theory (which he knew only from the *Prae-Adamitae*). Arnauld was apparently impressed by La Peyrère's conversion to Catholicism, which he said 'a edifié toute l'Eglise.'[52] In spite of Arnauld's horror at any form of unorthodoxy, he calmly said of La Peyrère, 'On dira peut-être que quoique cette personne fût hérétique lorsqu'elle composa son livre des Préadamites, néanmoins toute ce que les hérétiques publient n'est pas hérétique, ni meme faux.'[53] Arnauld endorsed this view, but then strongly rejected the political or terrestrial Messianism of both La Peyrère and Charpy de Sainte-Croix. (There is also an unpublished answer to Charpy by Jean Desmarets de Saint-Sorlin, one of the first members of the Académie française, who had a quite different religious vision from Charpy's. Desmarets de Saint-Sorlin wanted to form a Millenarian army to stamp out all heresy. The King of France should lead the army, which would conquer the Turks and extend the kingdom of Jesus Christ over the whole earth.)[54]

In the eighteenth century, there are signs that La Peyrère's political Messianism was frequently revived by various French authors. Although *Du Rappel des juifs* was not reprinted, and had become very rare, Jean Pierre Nicéron, in his *Mémoires pour servir à l'histoire des hommes illustres* of 1730, published a three page detailed summary of La Peyrère's work.[55] The Protestant leader, Pierre Jurieu, devoted a chapter of his well known work, *Histoire critique des dogmes et des cultes*, of 1704, to a detailed summary of the *Prae-Adamitae*. It is strange that Jurieu, who was a fanatical enemy of all possible heresies, and who described the pre-Adamite theory as 'la reverie du Juif la Peyrère,' nonetheless gave a pretty objective presentation, which, he said, was for the benefit of those of his readers who might not have heard of it.[56]

If Nicéron and Jurieu provided direct sources from which to learn of La Peyrère's theories, a serious issue in French theology kept making his theories relevant. There is a great deal of literature, much by Jansenists, in the eighteenth century on the Recall of the Jews as the beginning of the Millenium. After the middle of the eighteenth century it became more intense. Among the titles that appeared were Jules Deschamps, *Rappel futur des Juifs*, 1760; Laurent Etienne Rondet, *Dissertation sur le rappel des Juifs*, 1777; François Malot, *Dissertation sur l'epoque du rappel des Juifs* (1776), and Charles François Desfours de la Génetière, *Avis aux catholiques sur le caractère et les signes des temps où nous vivions, ou De la conversion des Juifs, de l'avenèment intermédiare de Jesus— Christ et de son regne visible sur la terre*, (1794).[57]

One of those who was extremely interested in this theme was the abbé Henri Grégoire, a Jansenist Millenarian priest from Alsace, the area in France which had the most Jews. Grégoire first became known prior to the Revolution for the essay he submitted to the Academy of Metz on the subject, 'How to make the Jews happy and useful in France?' Grégoire's prize winning essay entitled, *Essai sur la régéneration physique, morale et politique des Juifs* was published just before the outbreak of the Revolution in 1789.[58] The abbé contended that the present unfortunate state of the Jews was mainly the result of Christian anti-Semitism and Christian maltreatment of Jews, forcing them to live in unhealthy ghettoes and to engage in unworthy marginal occupations. Grégoire's enlightened solution was to make the Jews citizens, and to abolish the anti-Semitic regulations that prevented the Jews from living healthy, decent French lives. This, the abbé claimed would bring about a regeneration of the Jews, and make them capable of enlightenment. In such a state, God could convert them, and thus usher in the Millennium. Grégoire's social action plan, achieved over the next two decades, was not just intended to bring about the secular emancipation of the Jews, but more importantly was envisioned as a key antecedent stage in the march to the Millennium.[59]

In setting forth his theory, Grégoire used a wide range of Jewish and Christian sources, including La Peyrère's *Prae-Adamitae*. Grégoire, in his *Essai* ignored La Peyrère's pre-Adamite heresy, and his denial of the Mosaic authorship of the Bible; instead he stressed his French Messianic views. He discussed the conversion of the Jews, the return of the Jews to Jerusalem, and the rebuilding of the temple; his material came from a summary of *Du Rappel des Juifs*. Regarding the French Messianic element, the abbé who was shortly to play a major role in the Revolution, said 'Les preuves de l'auteur sont convaincantes.'[60]

Grégoire took La Peyrère's heretical French Messianism seriously prior to the Revolution. The abbé's actions during the Revolution can be seen as a secularized version of La Peyrère's grand scheme. It was part of La Peyrère's program to bring the Jews to France because France is the land of liberty (so he said in 1641); to eliminate anti-Semitism, to create a Jewish Christian church with no doctrines or dogmas, or practices that are offensive to the Jews, and then to await the moment when God would recall the Jews and usher in the Messianic Age. Grégoire, once the Revolution started, fought for a Jewish-Christian, egalitarian, republican state in France. The Church would be regenerated by being put under state control. The state would be regenerated by removing the king and all vestiges of privilege. The Jews would be regenerated by living in such a wonderful state as equal citizens. The regeneration of the Church, the State and the Jews, and their union in Revolutionary

France, would set the stage for God's further intervention in history, first by making the Jews want to join with the Christians, and then by producing the Millennium.[61]

Grégoire happily saw signs that his scenario was being enacted, first under the Revolutionary government and then under Napoleon. The Revolutionary government created the constitutional Church. It made the Jews citizens. The King was deposed. Under Napoleon, the Pope (who Grégoire identified as the Anti-Christ) was overthrown. In 1799, a proclamation was issued in Napoleon's name, addressed to the Jews of Africa and Asia, urging them to join Napoleon in rebuilding the temple in Jerusalem. Although Grégoire kept seeing signs of the unfolding of the events he so fervently hoped for, Napoleon in many ways was frustrating them. He restored the old Church, and he failed to enforce the law about Jewish citizenship among other things. Grégoire was becoming vehemently anti-Napoleon, when in 1806 there was a sudden change. Napoleon won a string of victories, deposing the kings of the earth (and replacing them with his relatives). In the midst of all of this military activity, the Emperor suddenly announced he was calling the Grand Sanhedrin into session. The Sanhedrin was the governing body of the Jewish world. It had last met just before Titus conquered Jerusalem and destroyed the Temple in A.D. 70 Only the Sanhedrin could change Jewish law. And the Sanhedrin could only be reconstituted by the Messiah when He came.[62]

The Napoleonic Sanhedrin is usually considered a joke by Jewish historians.[63] In the last decade much more has been learned about the views of the participants and the interpretations of the actions of the Sanhedrin by various outside groups. Roman and Orthodox Catholics saw it as an attempt by Napoleon to proclaim himself the Jewish Messiah of the Jews, when, as they knew, he was really the Anti-Christ.[64] Some English and German millenarians saw what was happening as the sign that the Messiah had come back to earth.[65] As far afield as Richmond, Virginia, in the U.S.A., the *Impartial Observer* in 1806 debated whether or not Napoleon was the Jewish Messiah.[66] A sermon by Rabbi Gershom Mendes Seixas of New York, delivered on January 11, 1807, was devoted to considering the import of the convening of the Paris Sanhedrin. Rabbi Seixas was both cautious and optimistic. He hoped that his brethren in France 'May find favor in the sight of their Emperor, that he under the influence of divine grace, may be a means to accomplish our reestablishment if not as a nation in our former territory, let it only be as a particular society, with equal rights and privileges of all other religious societies.'[67]

With all of the excitement, plus the actual discussions that were being carried on by the Jewish leaders (to whom Grégoire was an adviser) and Napoleon's officials, another odd element suddenly entered in the picture. Two Paris newspapers, both controlled by the government, the *Gazette de France*, August 28, 1806, and the *Journal de Paris*, August 19, 1806, announced the discovery of 'un livre aussi rare que singulier,' namely Isaac La Peyrère's *Du Rappel des Juifs*. The newspaper accounts said that everyone was talking about the meeting of the Jewish assembly. Then they gave a summary of La Peyrère's opus of 1643 that predicted that the Jews and the Christians would be reunited in France, forming the basis for the New Age which would be run politically by 'un roi universel,' the King of France.[68] The reader should realize that indeed it was all happening under the aegis of that universal monarch, the Emperor Napoleon Bonaparte. To commemorate this historic moment, Napoleon issued a handsome coin showing himself giving the Ten Commandments to a kneeling Moses.[69]

I have found no information about how or when Napoleon or his advisors discovered La Peyrère. The details about the meetings of the Sanhedrin show that Napoleon had assistants studying the Jewish material in the national library. No further use of La Peyrère's views was, as far as I know, made by Napoleon or his assistants.

On the other hand, the abbé Grégoire appears to have been stunned. He was, at the time, an adviser and consultant to the Jewish leaders, and seems to have been happy about the assimilation of the Jews that appeared to be taking place. The information about La Peyrère seems to have aroused Grégoire's curiosity. There are two pamphlets of notes by his secretary about La Peyrère's book. The first set contains the newspaper accounts, and a detailed summary of *Du Rappel des Juifs*. On page six we learn that on September 11, 1806, the abbé Grégoire held this very book in his hands. Next, he satisfied himself that there was no doubt that the work was by Isaac La Peyrère. The articles on La Peyrère in various dictionaries and encyclopedias were carefully copied, as was the 'Advis au Lecteur' that appears at the close of *Du Rappel des Juifs*, which gives a summary of the author's entire Messianic theory. Grégoire seemed concerned that the *Rappel* was not listed as a work of La Peyrère's, except by Niceron. Simon's brief biography indicated that the work was never published. But now Grégoire knew the work had appeared and existed. After fifteen pages of notes in a notebook entitled 'Recueil de Pieces sur Le Rappel des juifs,'[70] the contents suddenly shifted to a supposedly verbatim report of the answers of the Jewish leaders to Napoleon's questions about Judaism. The notes cover the sessions of the Jewish assembly from August 4, 1806 to August 7, 1806, and

August 12, 1806. These notes have not been checked, as far as I know, with the transactions of the Sanhedrin that were published at the time.[71] A second Grégoire notebook that dates from 1806 is entitled, 'Analyse de l'Ouvrage intitulé *Du Rappel des Juifs*, 1643 dont Isaac La Peyrère est auteur.' It remarks that the work is 'très rare.' Then, in the hand of Grégoire's secretary, a quite detailed summary of the book is given, covering the entire text.[72]

Following the wave of excitement that seems to have been aroused in some quarters about the rediscovery of La Peyrère's French nationalist Messianism, the subject died down quickly. Napoleon, who had gone through the motions of fulfilling some of the Jewish Messianic prophecies, suddenly dropped the whole matter. The Jews pretty much agreed to his terms for them to become French citizens. He officially declared them citizens. The Sanhedrin, acting as if it were a permanent body, invited Jewish communities to send delegations to join it in Paris. It reported to the Jewish world at large that it was in business, and ready to settle everybody's problems. Then suddenly, with no explanation, Napoleon early in 1807, ordered it to dissolve. At the final meeting, Rabbi Zinzheim, the leader of the Sanhedrin, proclaimed, 'O Napoleon, our Redeemer, Consoler of the human race, father of all mankind, Israel will build a Temple to you in its heart.'[73] Nevertheless, Napoleon issued some decrees a year later which took away a good many of the benefits the Jews had earlier received.[74] From then on the Emperor pretty much ignored both the Jewish problem and Jewish Messianism.

There are some indications that the Sanhedrin held a glimmer of its former importance after 1807. Various members (and these included Karl Marx's uncle and his grandfather) used their titles, such as 'secretary to the Grand Sanhedrin.' Some Jewish groups, such as those in Holland, were urged to modernize their views and practices, because of the decisions of the Sanhedrin.[75] As late as 1840, the French government was condemning degenerate practices by the Jews and telling them to live up to the Sanhedrin's rulings. In fact, late in Louis Philippe's reign, the decisions of the Paris Sanhedrin were reissued so that Jewish communities would know what they were.[76]

As the Sanhedrin disappeared, so also one might expect did interest in the views of La Peyrère. However, for no particular reason, an article by M. Bernadau, 'Notice sur Isaac Lapeyrère, *auteur Bordelais, extraite du* Pantheon littéraire d'Aquitaine, ou histoire des hommes illustres né dans l'ancienne province de Guienne,' appeared in the *Bulletin polymathique du Museum d'Instruction publique de Bordeaux* in 1810. It is more detailed than the usual encyclopedia articles, but is full of mistakes, especially about dates. It covers both La Peyrère's career and his views. His first work,

Du Rappel des Juifs, is summarized, and its French Messianist aspect is mentioned. We are told, as the Paris newspapers of 1806 said, that the book is 'aussi singulier que rare.'[77] La Peyrère's pre-Adamism is treated as a novelty, but not as a serious theory. The author himself is portrayed as a lovable character. 'La douceur, la simplicité, la tolérance formaient le fonds de son caractère.'[78] There is nothing in Bernadau's article which links La Peyrère to the revival of interest in his views a few years earlier at the time of the Paris Sanhedrin. Instead we are told in conclusion that 'Les ouvrage de Lapeyrère sont aujourd'hui complètement oubliés, même celui qui donna à cet auteur une sorte de célèbrité éphémère. Cet ouvrage n'a d'autre merite que celui d'avoir donne naissance aux mots *préadamite* et *préadamisme*, que servent à conserver le souvenir de l'inventeur d'un bisarre système théologique.'[79]

The local archivist, Bernadau, was hardly correct about La Peyrère's being completely forgotten. The chapter on anthropology and on racist theories of the period will show that he was still an important figure. There are several more items that show that La Peyrère's ideas were influential around the time of the Paris Sanhedrin. First, there was an exchange of views between one Father Lambert and an anonymous author (apparently the abbé Saillant) on the present importance of the Recall of the Jews. In 1806, Father Bernard Lambert published a work entitled *Exposition des Prédictions et des Promesses faits à l'Eglise pour les derniers temps de la Gentilité*. Chapters six through ten deal with the conversion of the Jews, when it will take place, that it will be universal, that the Jews will return to Israel, and Jerusalem will be rebuilt and will be the center of the religious world. Lambert presented the drastic changes involved as likely to occur in the immediate future. No reference though was made to current events. He concluded, 'Venez donc, peuple destiné à changer la face du monde. Sortez vos tombeaux, enfans de Judea. Venez apprendre à toute la tene à louer, à aimer le Seigneur, comme il mérite de l'estre.'[80]

This work was answered by the abbé Charles-Jacques Saillant in his *Les Véritables Promesses faite au Peuple juif et à toute l'Eglise, ... precédées d'un examen impartial de l'ouvrage intitulé Exposition des Prédictions et des Promesses faites à l'Eglise*. (Paris 1807). This book is heavily based on Jansenist theology, and is very critical of the Millenarian views of the time. The author saw that the topic had great relevance to the immediate present. He began 'Le peuple Juif attire aujourd'hui les regards de tout l'univers par l'heureuse révolutions qui parôit commencer à s'operer en leur faveur.'[81] Then he leisurely examined the theological errors of millenarianism, and considered Antoine Arnauld's critique of them. In considering Arnauld's answer to Charpy de Saint-Croix, Saillant quoted the entire text in Arnauld's work. Just before Arnauld got to his statement of his own views about La Peyrère's theory, he said that he had heard about a priest who had published the claim that there will be a king who will be the lieutenant general of Jesus Christ, and who will reestablish the empire of the Jews in Judea. The author, Arnauld went on, imagined himself to be this king, and he went completely mad. Immediately after telling this sad story, Arnauld summarized La Peyrère's Messianic theory.[82] At this point Saillant wrote a lengthy footnote giving an exegesis of what he took to be La Peyrère's excellent theory about the king who will aid the Messiah, 'un roi temporel qui sera l'executeur temporel des actions miraculeuses, dont le roi spirituel est le principe, l'auteur et le promoteur éternel.'[83]

It is curious that a Jansenist author, Saillant, was pointing out the relevance of La Peyrère's views in connection with what was occurring to the Jews of the time, and made no reference to the Napoleonic government's use of the same material. But this does show that La Peyrère's ideas were being studied for theological reasons at the very time that Napoleon was apparently using them for propaganda and self-aggrandizement.

A small item concerning the Napoleonic use of La Peyrère's ideas turns up in a footnote in Cecil Roth's *A Life of Menasseh ben Israel* where it is said that 'Interest in the *Du Rappel des Juifs* was revived 1806, at the period of the Napoleonic Sanhedrin.'[84] Roth cited a letter from 'Christianus' that appeared in *Gentleman's Magazine* in 1812.[85] 'Christianus' declared that the abbé Grégoire and others have been mistaken in claiming that the singular book, *Du Rappel des Juifs*, was printed during La Peyrère's lifetime. Using material from Richard Simon's account, he insisted that the book was suppressed, and it 'only appeared in print at Paris, after it became the pleasure of the head of the French government to assemble a Jewish Sanhedrin in May 1806 for reasons that are obvious.'[86] 'Christianus' summarized La Peyrère's messianic views with their special political character from what Grégoire said about them in his essay on the Jews.[87] The next year, 1813, 'Christianus' wrote again to *Gentleman's Magazine*, citing a letter of Richard Simon's which seemed to justify his claim that *Du Rappel des Juifs* had not been published until Napoleon set up the Paris Sanhedrin.[88] (Actually Simon was talking about La Peyrère's last manuscript, which was never published, and not his first book, which Simon had never heard of.) The convening of the Sanhedrin amounted to the reestablishment of Judaism, which 'was carried into execution, of assembling a Jewish Sanhedrin by the present French Emperor in May 1806. It is no uncommon thing with Monarchs to call in the aid of ancient traditions to accomplish their purposes.'[89] This is probably a good diagnosis of what Napoleon was about, and it shows that there were at least some repercussions from the revival of La

Peyrère's Messianism in England. (There is a good deal of English Millenarian literature about the Sanhedrin, ranging from William Blake's claim that it was the Sanhedrin of Satan, to Thomas Bicheno's that it was a marvelous Millenarian sign, the crisis of our time.)[90] A German comment by Friedrich Adolf Ebert from 1830 indicates some cynicism. 'Dieses seltne, aber wertlose Bucher (*Du Rappel des Juifs*) erhielt bei der von Napoleon 1806 geschehenen Zusammenberufung des Sanhedrin ein nur augenblickliches Interesse, weil man in demselben eine Prophezeihung dieses Ereignisses zu finden glaubte.'[91]

Grégoire remained a steadfast Millenarian up to his death in 1831. He sought to effect preconditions of the age to come through political events in the Jewish world, in the world of the enslaved Africans, in the revolutionary world of Haiti, and, at the end of his life, in the struggle for Greek freedom. As an indication that he continued to build on his earlier views, Grégoire was favorably impressed by the American Jewish politician Mordecai Noah, who is usually considered an amusing but inconsequential figure in American Jewish history. Noah is remembered, if at all, for trying to establish a Jewish National Homeland near Buffalo, on Grand Island.[92] Grégoire met Noah in Paris, where Noah made his project the continuation of the Paris Sanhedrin. Noah appointed himself Chief Judge of Israel, and then appointed two leaders of the Sanhedrin as his agents. One of them, Rabbi Cologna, immediately disowned Noah in a declaration in the Paris press.[93] Noah also was convinced that the Indians were Jews, the Lost Tribes, and that his Jewish state would prepare the way for the events in Palestine that would herald the coming of the Messianic age. These elements may explain why the abbé Grégoire might have thought well of Noah and his projects, in spite of Rabbi Cologna's denunciation.

Grégoire also kept up his interest in La Peyrère. In his six volume *Histoire des Sectes religeuses*, he started volume two with a section called 'Preadamites.' The section describes La Peyrère's views, without any reference to their Messianic import. The views are described rather negatively, and some refutations are referred to. Then, Grégoire turned to the current revival of La Peyrère's pre-Adamism, not his Messianism, and discussed Edward King, who, he said, was known for his penchant for paradoxical ideas. Grégoire claimed that, fortunately, the renewal of La Peyrère's paradoxes had not interested many people.[94] However, he reported that there was a professor of astronomy and mathematics at Brunswick, a Professor Grolpker, who in 1820 revived the pre-Adamite system. He claimed that a race of men before Adam died in a catastrophe that was neither a flood, nor a volcano, but rather the falling of a celestial body on the earth.[95]

No longer did Grégoire seem to find any Millenarian support in La Peyrère. Instead he saw his ideas as dangerous. After Grégoire, La Peyrère appears to have vanished completely as a source of inspiration for political Messianic ideas. There were quite a lot of new Millenarian theories developed after the French Revolution, some involving the roles of Napoleon, of the restored Bourbon monarchy, of the bourgeois monarch, Louis Phillippe, and finally of Louis Napoleon. Some of the theories were expounded by important figures like Felicité Lamennais, Adam Mickiewicz, and Victor Hugo. In none of this post-Napoleonic Millenarianism have I been able to find any sign of La Peyrère's ideas even though France and its travails play crucial roles in their scenarios. So, he seems to have vanished as an inspirer of a French oriented Messianism by the mid-nineteenth century. But as this happened he became more significant as an influence on theories about the nature of man.

CHAPTER NINE

THE PRE-ADAMITE THEORY IN THE ENLIGHTENMENT, AND THE SCIENTIFIC CONFLICTS OF POLYGENETIC AND MONOGENETIC THEORIES

Practically nobody in the seventeenth century was willing, publicly, to accept the pre-Adamite theory or any form of polygenesis. The irreligious implications were too great for the theory to be given much credence prior to the Enlightenment. Some hardy souls, like Spinoza, wrote as if they assumed that Adam was not the first man and that human history had multiple sources.[1] The explanatory value of a polygenetic theory was great, but the danger of holding to it was, perhaps, greater.

As one might expect, in the Enlightenment there was a less bigoted or raucous response to La Peyrère's theory. There were also some signs that the polygenetic theory was being adopted by some brave souls who were freeing themselves from tradition. The stream of refutations continued, but some are no longer either vituperative or religiously oriented. Some of La Peyrère's ideas were even adopted by avant-garde thinkers. And, perhaps more important, from many sides data were accumulating that seemed to cry out for a pre-Adamite or polygenetic explanation of the origin of mankind.[2]

In contrast to the large number of works 'refuting' the pre-Adamite theory, there is a strange work which came out towards the end of the 17th century that strongly advocated the theory, and brought up evidence, unknown to La Peyrère, that was to be important in discussions a century later. This work, *L'Espion Turc*, or in its full English version, *Letters Writ by a Turkish Spy, who lived five and forty years undiscover'd at Paris*, began to appear in French in 1684, and was completed in eight volumes in English in 1692.[3] The author of the original part was apparently a Genoese, Giovanni Paolo Marana, who was in France from 1682-89.[4] There is no agreement about the authorship of the rest of the text.[5] Various minor English authors have been considered, and the most recent study, attributes the entire text to Marana.[6]

The work is the first of the genre of having a non-European critically evaluate European religion, philosophy, politics and manners. The Spy wrote to a range of Ottoman officials, Moslem dignitaries, a Christian monk, and the Sultan's agent in Vienna, an orthodox Jew. The work was so successful that the full text, eight volumes, was reissued at least thirty times in English up to 1801, several times in French, in Dutch, German and even Russian in 1778. The original seems to have been in Italian. And a ninth volume, a continuation was apparently published by David Defoe in 1718.[7]

Hence the work was widely diffused in Europe, but has been almost completely forgotten. It was not cited at the time, but was obviously widely read if so many editions in various languages appeared.

One of the themes through much of the book is the evidence for the pre-Adamite theory. This is often broached to Nathan, the Sultan's Jewish agent in Vienna, as a reason for not taking Judaism as the unique religion. The spy's brother made a trip to China and India and came back with information indicating that Chinese and Indian cultures predated the Biblical world (information which only entered the scholarly discussions, as we shall see, when the Hindu Scriptures were translated into European languages late in the 18th century). The Spy gradually developed a case for pre-Adamism, and for a view that the world is eternal. In developing the case, no European authors are cited. So there are no direct references to La Peyrère, Spinoza, or Richard Simon, to support some of the general themes.

The 'General Preface' to the first volume points out that the Spy 'loves Antiquities, but tis only such as draw the Veil from off the Infancy of Time, and uncover The Cradle of the World. This makes him insist with so much Zeal and Passion, on the Records of the Chinese and the Indians.'[8] His information on this, we are told came from the unpublished journal of his brother, Pesteli Hali, a great traveller in Asia, which contained a great deal of information about the religions of countries there.[9]

In the letters, the pre-Adamite possibility is raised in a letter dated 19th of the 4th Moon, 1648, to Abdel Melec Muli Omar, Superintendent of the College of Sciences at Fez. The Spy asks the learned Moslem theologian, 'Whether this mighty Fabrick be but of Yesterday, that is, of five or six Thousand Years standing, as the Jews and Christians say; or Whether the Years of its Duration be not pass a Calcule.'[10]

An Arabic text is then cited, giving a vision of a world of a million ages.[11] The Spy then pointed out it would better fit with divine munificence if the visible Emanations of his divinity were 'without either beginning or Ending of Time.'[12] He asked, 'Tell me, great Light of Africk, Is it repugnant to Reason of [or] Faith, to believe, That the Earth has been inhabited from Eternity; since our holy Doctors teach us, that it was peopled long before the Creation of Adam?'[13] He then went over the Moslem version of the Adam and Eve story, in which the Earth was inhabited by angels, who turned into devils and were then expelled from the Earth. Alileth [Lileth], Adam's first wife was of this demonic group, and lived and quarreled with Adam for 500 years and had many children during this period. She abandoned Adam, and then God gave him another wife, Eve.[14]

The Spy pointed out that from this Moslem tradition, 'we need not doubt, that the Earth was inhabited before Adam's time.[15] And if so, why could it not 'be peopled for Millions of Ages?'[16] The Spy said he had discussed this with several Jewish rabbis and Christian theologians, and he was able to find but a few, who are emancipated from the Prejudices of a superstitious Education, to entertain the pre-Adamite possibility, and the eternal world one.[17] Since no one is named, we do not know if La Peyrère was one of the emancipated ones. The others 'rather than believe the indefinite Antiquity of the World, they contradicted their own Sense and Reason, invalidate the Testimony of a Prophet, deny their Father, and appear unmask'd Infidels'[18] The Christians and Jews have corrupted the truth with errors, but 'The Illuminated of God (!) have always taught, That the Earth was inhabited long before The Appearance of Adam. And all the Eastern Sages believe a Series of Generations to have dwelt on this Globe for indeterminate Ages.'[19]

The Spy then reported on what his brother had found in the books of the 'Brahmans' which are written in a language which only their priests understand. (This is a century before any European could read Sanskrit). 'These Books contain a History of the World, which they say, is above Thirty Millions of Years old.'[20] (As we shall see, when Nathaniel Brassey Halhed reported this a century later, it caused a great shock among European thinkers until Sir William Jones resolved the apparent conflicts between Hindu and Biblical chronology.)[21] After summarizing the Hindu chronological claims, the Spy asked who wrote these books and when, and where was this special language spoken? We know about the history of Latin and Greek, but the Brahman's language is not mentioned in any other record, save their own. And their own record says their books and language are as old as the world. If this is an imposture, it would have quickly been exposed by other learned sages of the east. If it has some truth, then the Spy said there is 'something extraordinary in the Pretension of these Indian Philosophers,' which makes him hope it is true. It gives 'an Illustrious Idea of the Divine Perfections, when one conceives all this vast and endless Concatenation of Beings, to flow from the Eternal Nature.'[22] Mosaic history can be reconciled with Brahman history, if a Mosaic day can be a thousand or millions of years. 'And it will be more congruous and agreeable to believe, that after the Birth of the First Matter, there elapsed many Ages, before it wrought into such an infinite Variety of Appearances, as we now behold; and that the five Days which Moses computes, before the Production of Adam, might be some Millions of Years; In which Time, the divine Architect gradually drew from the Abyss of Matter, the Sun, Moon, Stars, Plants and Animals...'[23]

Much of the pre-Adamite view of the Spy is in this initial statement, put forth as a plausible view in terms of Moslem and Hindu accounts, and a theology of Divine Perfection and Omnipotence. In a letter to his brother, Pesteli Hali, the Spy said he was constantly studying his brother's journal, 'because it treats of the most ancient Kingdoms and Governments in the World,' [24] and is not full of fables. The Spy said he was especially impressed with the material about China, the most ancient government in the world. He cited material from his brother's journal that indicated Chinese chronology 'takes in many thousands of Years before Noah's Flood.'[25]

In a letter from 1651, to Endel Al'Zadi Jaaf, Beglerbeg of Dierbekir, the Spy used some of the Chinese and Indian materials to criticize some Jewish legends. The Chinese and Indians, the Spy said, laugh at these legends 'as a Romance of later Date than their Chronicles, which makes those Extremities of the East to be the Stage of the first Mortals.' For them the human race began millions of years earlier. The parents of all mankind were Panzon and Panzona.[26]

In a letter early in 1652, to the Kaimachan, the Spy described the view of Isouf Eb'n Hadrill, an Arabian Philosopher, who 'gave no Credit to the Writings of Moses...; neither could any arguments persuade him to believe, That all Mortals descended from Adam.'[27] According to Isouf, men were formed from the slime of the earth. In another letter of this period, the Spy began to consider the possibility that there may be a plurality of worlds.[28]

Each of the possibilities and the consideration of Indian, Chinese, and later on of Egyptian historical evidence, and various mythologies, is put forth for consideration, without claiming they are true. They have the effect of making the pre-Adamite theory plausible without advocating it as definitely true. The myriad possible explanations lead to a kind of scepticism. 'Man's Senses are too weak, his Imagination too frail, and all his Faculties too short to comprehend the Works of the Omnipotent, who alone is wise and perfect in Science.'[29]

The various pre-Adamite possibilities are tried out on the Sultan's Jewish agent in Vienna, Nathan ben Saddi, as part of a campaign to get him to give up his rigid orthodoxy. In letters from 1653 onward the Spy tried to convince Nathan that Judaism is not unique, and that God created all of the nations on the earth as well.[30] The Spy followed out two lines of argument that occur in La Peyrère's work, denying the accuracy of the Jewish documents, and denying the Bible's account of the history of mankind. He also spent a good deal of time attacking the special status of the Talmud and the relevance of its laws. This latter aspect is peculiar, since, presumably the general European audience would know next to nothing about the content of the Talmud. La Peyrère did not discuss it, nor did Spinoza. So, one wonders who the volumes of letters were addressed to. The Spy made clear he was not trying to convert Nathan, but rather to make him become a rational Jew, who would give up rabbinical Judaism, and adopt something like what is now called reformed Judaism.[31]

The Spy pointed out that although the Jews believe their records to be of divine origin, their manuscripts are full of variants, and the text that has come down to us is full of inconsistencies.[32] The Jewish chronology, as well as the Assyrian and Egyptian records, do not approach the immense chronologies of the Chinese and Indians. So, what should we believe—that the world is five or six thousand years old, or 'of a more indefinite Antiquity'? The Jewish belief is based on the Mosaic account, but most of what God told Moses was lost during the Israelite captivities. 'So that what remains now, is only a Collection of Fragments patch'd up by Esdras, and other industrious Scribes, to which they gave the specious Title of the Law of Moses, that so they might fasten the wavering People in Obedience to something, though of their own devising.'[33]

When one examines human artifacts, the Spy insisted, one is convinced of pre-Biblical civilizations.[34] The Pyramids in Egypt were probably built before the Flood, hence before Jewish history began. Egyptian history, according to non-Jewish sources, goes back before Scripture and pre-dates other known civilizations except that of the Assyrians, the Chinese and the Indians.[35] So, 'Doubtless, there were many Nations establish'd on Earth before the Israelites.'[36] The Jews greatly overrate their lineages, since there were many groups before them.[37]

In a letter to his brother, Pesteli Hali in 1664, he was still overwhelmed by the data in his journal about the antiquity of China and India. He was developing a theory of the eternity of the world from what his brother had sent him, and hoped this view could be substantiated by further study of the Indian records.[38]

The climax of the pre-Adamite speculation in *Letters of a Turkish Spy* appears late in the last volume in a letter dated 1681 'To the Wisest of the Wise, the Key of the Treasures of Knowledge, the Venerable Mufti,'[39] where the Spy summed up his thoughts on the matter. The Jews and Christians 'have curtailed the Age of the World' to increase their own importance. The Jews wanted to possess fame as the nation of the greatest antiquity, and thus give themselves special status. The Christians adopted the Jewish view, restricting the world to just six thousand years. Other chronologies suggest it is at least six hundred thousand years. The Spy summarized Egyptian and Assyrian evidence, and then added, 'But the Chinese and Indians exceed all the rest of the World in the prodigious Antiquity of their Records. And among the latter, their Brachmans assert the Age of the World to be little less than infinite or eternal.' The Spy suspected the Indian documents were in the first language of the world. And he recommended that these writings be translated.[40]

The Christians, the Spy observed, try to get rid of the force of the Indian documents by treating 'the Indians as Fools, easily imposed on by their crafty Priests.' The Indian records are treated as fables or poetic fancies. But, the Spy urged, why should Moslems follow this Christian way of dealing with the evidence, since 'we are taught from our Cradles, That all Wisdom comes out of the East.'[41]

Next the Christians may say, how could these ancient Indian records have survived the Flood. The Spy, in response, offered a view like that of La Peyrère, namely that the Flood was only a local event in Palestine, not a universal deluge. So, Egypt, China and India could have survived with their documents of their chronologies intact. Once one realized this, 'The whole Firmament of Chronology would become clear and serene; and we should walk in the Light of the primitive Ages, without being dazzled, or forc'd to wink.'[42] We would 'see the Splendour of Historical Truth rising from the Orient, and gilding the Tops of those Mountains, which the Ignorance and Superstition of some, the Pride and Ambition of others, have raised to hinder our Prospect of the far-extended Ages of the primitive World. And without Rapture, or Hyperbole, I dare be bold to presage, That a little more knowledge in the Indian Language and Histories, will bring those Things to Light, which have been hid for many thousands of Years, from the greatest Part of Mankind.'[43]

He urged the Mufti, 'thou sacred Patron of History' to send messengers to India, to court the Brachmans, to get their books, and set them forth to the world'[44] of Islam against Judaism and Christianity.[45] Since it is claimed to be by a Moslem, it would not be heretical to European Christian authorities. The *Turkish Spy* was not banned, or censored, as far as we know, in any of its different editions in several languages from 1684 to the last known English edition of 1801.

The number of editions and translations would indicate wide dispersion of the work. However, strangely, it is not cited or discussed, or considered dangerous or avant-garde. Its format was adopted by libertin writers, using a non-European outsider to criticize European philosophy, religion and culture. But the *Turkish Spy* itself does not seem to have played any role, or any significant role, in discussions of pre-Adamism in the Enlightenment. It contains a wealth of material especially about the Indian documents that became part of the European discussion later on when the British took over India. If we knew more about the author or authors, we might be able to tell how such information became available in the late 17th century.

As the eighteenth century began, attacks on the pre-Adamite theory continued; first a learned German attack *Dissertatio de Praeadamitis* appeared in Helmstadt in 1714.[46] Two years later there was another one from Helmstadt by a Joh. Ant. Schmid, *Pentas Dissertationum I. de Praeadamitis exorbe proscriptis.*[47] In 1730 one J. Hermansson published a dissertation, *De Praeadamitis*[48] at Upsala in Sweden. The very important Spanish Enlightenment scholar, Father Benito Jeronimo Feijóo y Montenegro published an essay in the 1730s on the as yet unsolved problem of the source of the inhabitants of America. Feijóo, in the course of his essay, denounced polygenicism as a possible explanation, and denounced Isaac La Peyrère as one who 'vomito tam pernicioso error.'[49] Later in the century when information reached the Western Europeans about Behring's expedition in the area between Siberia and Alaska, suddenly a non-hypothetical land-bridge theory emerged. A Mexican clergyman wrote, apparently gleefully, a work entitled, *Solution to the Great Problem of the Population of the Americas, in Which on the Basis of the Holy Books there is Discovered an Easy Path for the Transmigration of Men from One Continent to the Other; and How There Could Pass to the New World, not only Beasts of Service, but Also the Wild and Harmful Animals; and by This Occasion One Completely Settles the Ravings of the Pre-Adamites, Which Relied on This Difficult Objection until Now Not Properly solved* The author of this, Father Francisco Xavier Alexo de Orrio, must have thought that what had been the strongest point of the polygenicist, namely explaining the population of the New World, had been put to rest.[50]

The Millenarian-abolitionist, Charles Crawford, also claimed that the Indians, whom he was sure were part of the Lost Tribes of Israel, got to America over the Behring Straits. Further, he happily said, 'it is probable when the time arrives, foretold by the prophets, that the Jews will be gathered from their dispersion among all nations, many of the Indians will pass over at Behring's or Cooks Straits into Asia.'[51] The stream of material that poured forth during the eighteenth century usually dealt negatively with La Peyrère. Ephraim Chambers, in his *Cyclopaedia; Or, An Universal Dictionary of the Arts and Sciences* has an article 'Preadamite.' A brief summary of La Peyrère's theory is given followed by the information that when his book came out, he gained a considerable number of proselytes. (None are named.) Then, fortunately, 'the answer of Desmarets, professor of theology at Groningen, put a stop to its progress.'[52] In the *Dictionnaire Universel* of Trévoux there is an article

'Préadamite,' which briefly mentions that when *Pre-Adamitae* appeared a sect of believers developed, but quickly became extinct. The article goes over La Peyrère's evidence from ancient history, and simply states that the Bible says otherwise. The article in this Jesuit dictionary is at pains to make clear that La Peyrère repented, blamed it all on his Calvinist upbringing, and died a true Catholic.[53] Father Dom Augustin Calmet, one of the best known biblical scholars in the eighteenth century, started his article 'Préadamites' in his *Dictionnaire historique, critique, chronologique, géographique et littéral de la Bible* with learned news about pre-Adamic views of St. Clement of Alexandria and of Julian the Apostate. He also cited some indications of the theory amongst Moslems and Jews in the Middle Ages. Finally, he explained that La Peyrère had renewed this view in the last century, summarized the theory, concluding, 'Nous ne nous étendons point ici à réfuter ce systeme errone, & monstreux.'[54]

Mosheim's *Ecclesiastical History* has a short, neutral article just giving the facts in La Peyrère's case.[55] Richelet's *Dictionnaire* has a lengthy (two folio column) article, quoting a good deal from La Peyrère's apology. The judgment about the theory consists mainly in reporting that pre-Adamism has been condemned by the Church.[56] Perhaps the two most interesting Enlightenment presentations are the articles in Diderot's *Encyclopédie* and in the *Encyclopaedia Britannica*. It is not known who wrote the article 'Préadamites,' but it is no longer accepted in the canon of Diderot's writings.[57] The article begins like most of the others, defining 'pre-Adamite,' and telling the story of La Peyrère and how he was refuted by Desmarais (sic), professor of theology at Groningen, and how this terminated the sect of pre-Adamites. After giving a neutral account of the theory, the author returned to the text in Romans. He carefully analyzed what each verse said in order to show that La Peyrère had misrendered the text so that it would suggest there were men before Adam. This philological disproof is not accompanied by any indication of the effect of the theory on Judaism or Christianity. Lastly the author challenged La Peyrère's reputation as an innovator. He went over the same material as Calmet had, material which apparently came from D'Herbelot's *Bibliotheque orientale*.[58]

In the third edition of the *Encyclopaedia Britannica*, which came out in 1797, the article on 'Pre-Adamite' is similar to most of those already discussed. In fact, it is just about word for word what is in some of the others,[59] (which shows that the present method of compiling encyclopedias by copying from previous ones is a well-established tradition). However, the article 'Peyrère, (Isaac la)' gives a detailed account of his life. It even suggests that La Peyrère wanted to found a sect, presumably made up of Jews. What led him astray, we are told, was 'His having no fixed sentiments of religion.' That state of affairs apparently resulted 'more from a peculiar turn of mind, than a corruption of the heart.' La Peyrère's scholarship and his style are discussed. Next a quite detailed summary of *Du Rappel des juifs* is set forth. The work is described as 'as singular as it is scarce.'[60] It is odd that the author of the article even had access to it for Richard Simon, for example, did not know that the work existed. As we have seen there was a controversy about whether there ever really was such a work, a controversy involved with the rediscovery of the work under Napoleon, where it was again described as being as singular as it is rare.[61] La Peyrère's reduction of Christianity in order to please the Jews is described without criticism. Mention is made of his works on Greenland and Iceland, plus his apology.[62] This article contains more detail than any other of the period and would indicate that La Peyrère was still an important figure at the close of the Enlightenment.

If La Peyrère was, for eighteenth century audiences, a significant historical figure who was often maligned, and usually assumed to have been refuted by the professor from Groningen, he was at the same time being taken seriously by some avant-garde thinkers, who adopted some of his ideas even if they did not attribute them to him. One of the first of the English Deists, Charles Blount, in *The Oracles of Reason* of 1693, raised La Peyrère's point about whether Moses was the author of the Pentateuch. Much of La Peyrère's data was used. Later on, again without citing La Peyrère, Blount claimed that it is plain from the Bible that there were two creations.[63] One of the first persons in the twentieth century to study La Peyrère, David R. McKee, claimed not only that La Peyrère was an important source for Blount, but also that he was a basic source for the whole movement of critical Deists.[64] A text edited by McKee, Simon Tyssot de Patot's, *The Travels and Adventures of James Massey*, contains a section contrasting the evidence that the world is very old with the evidence for the Mosaic account. The Chinese and Egyptian evidence, which is much like La Peyrère's, is shown to be quite strong. But, the author, unlike La Peyrère, does not decide that the world existed before Adam. Instead his conclusion is that one cannot determine the age of the world.[65]

An area in which La Peyrère's polygenetic view kept reappearing is in discussions about the origins of the inhabitants of Africa and America. An English doctor came back from Africa and reported in his account of the physical characteristics of blacks that 'From the Whole, I imagine that White and Black must have descended of different Protoplasts; and that there is no other Way of accounting for it.'[66] The doctor, John Atkins, having said that, drew no further implications. A French work by Lom D'Arce, reporting the conversations of Baron de Lahontan in South America at the end of the seventeenth century, showed how the polygenetic theory arose there, and what it implied for the Christian religion. We are told that there was a dispute with a Portuguese doctor who had made many trips to Angola, Brazil and Goa. From what he saw the doctor had come to the opinion that the peoples of America, Asia and Africa each had different fathers. His evidence was their cultural and physical differences. Then he pointed out that America was just too far away for people to have come to it. Considering all of the evidence, the doctor decided that Africans and Americans cannot be descendants of Adam.[67] The Baron answered him by saying that if his faith were not strong enough to disprove this polygenetic view, he still would not find the doctor's theory convincing, because there could be other explanations of the phenomena. Differences in people could be due to air or climate,[68] theories that were to be explored during the eighteenth century. The doctor denied this, pointing out that black people have black children anywhere on the globe. And to this it was responded that the doctor's principles were completely false and entirely absurd 'puis qu'il n'est pas permis de douter, sans etre depourvu de foi, de bons sens & de jugemens, qu'Adam est le seul Père de tous les hommes.'[69]

Soon enough people would be sufficiently deprived of faith to see the advantages of a pre-Adamite explanation. A French author, La Douceur, in his *Observations curieuses* claimed that Negroes and Kalmucks were not descended from Adam. Contrary to claims of various explorers and commentators, La Douceur insisted that the savages of America, the Kalmucks and the Negroes are not degenerate. They have not fallen and have no original sin and have not been redeemed by Christ. Their condition is that of 'Nature in its infancy.'[70] Those interested in justifying the enslavement of Africans and the elimination of the Indians would find the theory much to their advantage. We will show soon how it was used by various European and American thinkers to justify the slave trade and the slave plantations.

Others tried to modify La Peyrère's theory so that they could use its explanatory power without having to accept its heretical consequences. One effort of this sort was an anonymous work published in London in 1732 called *Co-Adamitae, or an Essay to prove the two following paradoxes, viz. I. That there were other men created at the same time with Adam, and II. That the angels did not fall.* There is not much evidence offered, but it is clear that the first paradox does not require that one accept La Peyrère's claim that there were men before Adam, but only that there were other men besides Adam. Though it is claimed that Scripture gives clear evidence that Adam was the first man, why would God create a whole world of flora and fauna that one man could never use. So there must have been more men that Adam.[71] If Adam was Lord of the Earth, he 'should have some of his own Species to command.'[72] The whole case in *Co-Adamitae* is based on internal arguments in the Bible like the Cain story. Some of the material was taken from Blount.

Later in the eighteenth century a more scientific and less theological form of co-Adamism, or double-Adamism was developed by the Scottish thinker, Henry Home, Lord Kames. In his well known *Sketches of the History of Man*, Kames began with a preliminary discourse on the origins of man and of languages. Building on a suggestion of Count Buffon (who remained a monogenicist), Kames theorized that the New World emerged from the sea later than the Old World, and that there was a separate and later Adam who was the father of the inhabitants of America. This would make the first Adam the father of mankind then existent, before America began, sometime after Moses (which accounts for why it is not mentioned in the Bible). Kames, after examining the differences among men, came to the conclusion that these differences were so great that men could not all belong to the same race. Buffon, on the contrary, contended they were all members of the same race if they could mate and produce fertile offspring. Kames felt that people had different shapes, different kinds of skin and hair, and different kinds of basic moral qualities.[73] To explain these differences Kames developed a multiple Adamism, namely 'that God created many pairs of the human race, differing from each other both externally and internally, and placed each pair in its proper climate, that the particularities of the original pairs were preserved entire in their descendants.' On the basis of geological and anthropological data he suggested his theory that the New World, both physical and biological, was created separately and later.[74]

It is interesting that Kames who was an important legal figure in Scotland and an active participant in the Scottish Enlightenment, could share in his distinguished relative, David Hume's, sallies against the Christian Church, yet he felt he had to back off when he saw the consequences of his multiple Adamism. 'This opinion, however plausible, we are not permitted to adopt; being taught a different lesson by revelation, viz. that God created but a single pair of the human species. Although we cannot doubt the authority of Moses yet his account of the creation of man is not a little puzzling, as it seems to contradict every one of the facts mentioned above.'[75] Many Scottish Calvinist ministers must have wondered if either Kames or Hume had learned any lesson at all from revelation. Kames, nonetheless, made the effort to put his theory in accord with the teachings of the Bible. He offered a post-Adamic explanation of the differences among men. God implanted these fixed

distinctions at the time of the Tower of Babel episode, so that each group
would be fit for the part of the world to which they were going to be
dispersed. Hence, before the Tower of Babel episode, a monogenetic account explained where all the people came from. After the Tower of
Babel episode, a polygenetic explanation was required. The way that
Kames treated biblical accounts would make one question how seriously
he took them. However, for the purposes of his theory he had to accept
the story of the Tower of Babel as fact and not as allegory. 'But that this
is real history, must necessarily be admitted, as the confusion of Babel
is the only known fact that can reconcile sacred and profane history.'[76]
This theory, unlike La Peyrère's, does not deny central Jewish and
Christian claims. But it is also able to use the explanatory power of La
Peyrère's hypothesis in dealing with the human world after the Dispersion. One of the most important criticisms of Kames's view was
developed by the Reverend Dr. Samuel Stanhope Smith, who became
the President of Princeton. Smith argued for the unity of the human
species and tried to show that scientifically all of the human differences
could be accounted for by environmental factors. He also insisted that
morality and religion required that one accept a monogenetic view.[77]

This view was reinforced by the work of James Adair, *The History of
the American Indians* (1775) presenting the 'strongest' evidence that the Indians were of Jewish origin. Adair set forth his case by first contending
that the differences in color between Indians and Europeans was not a
natural difference, but one due to customs and method of living. This,
Adair said, 'will entirely overturn Lord Kames's whole system of colour
and separate races of men.' Kames's view is contrary 'both to revelation
and facts.' And, Adair added, multiple creations would indicate a weakness on the part of infinite wisdom.[78] Further, he contended, his evidence
of the Jewish origin of the American Indians would 'sufficiently confute
the wild notion which some have espoused of the North American Indians being Prae-Adamites.'[79]

On the other hand, a Captain Bernard Romans, in *A Concise Natural
History of East and West Florida* (1785), rejected Adair's Jewish Indian
theory, and stressed the virtues of a multiple origin theory. Romans did
not want to challenge the Mosaic account as such, and instead offered a
view like La Peyrère's, namely that the *Pentateuch* is about the origins of
the Jews and their subsequent history—'why should this Historian's
[Moses] books be taken so universally, when he evidently has confined
himself to a kind of chronicle concerning one small part of the earth, and
in this to one nation only ... we do not at all derogate from God's
greatness nor in any ways dishonour the sacred evidence given us by his
servants, when we think that there were as many *Adams* and *Eves* (every-

body knows these names to have an allegorical sense) as we find different species of the human genus; is this not a more natural way, agreeing more with the proceedings of a God of order, than the silly suppositions that the variety is an effect of chance, much less a consequence of curses?'[80] So, on this account, polygenesis, or multiple Adamism is made more agreeable to Divine Wisdom or Order, than a monogenetic scheme of things.

These glimpses into the eighteenth century attitude towards pre-Adamism and polygenesis indicate the time was not yet ripe for publicly holding the theory. Voltaire seems to have been unique in saying in print that he believed the pre-Adamite theory.[81] Goethe for strange reasons said so too in his conversations with Eckermann.[82] Before turning to their views, I would like to explore some of the scientific developments of the time that seem to require a polygenetic explanation, and to see how they were handled.

The development of geology brought to light much material that suggested that the earth began earlier than 4004 B.C. Buffon had raised the amazing possibility that the earth was 500,000 years old, or maybe even older. As scholars got used to such large figures, they could entertain the possibility of a pre-Adamite earth of very great antiquity. But they were still unwilling to consider pre-Adamite people. Researches concerning fossils and sedimentation kept generating conflicts between Genesis and geology, conflicts that could easily be resolved by adopting La Peyrère's hypothesis.[83] An interesting example of what was happening appeared in the report of an English traveller, Brydone, who had gone to visit Sicily and Malta in 1773. Brydone was quite scientifically oriented, being a Fellow of the Royal Society. He went to see Mount Vesuvius with a priest named Recupero as his guide. The priest had told him that his researches indicated that lava had been flowing from the mountain for 14,000 years. 'Recupero tells me that he is exceedingly embarrassed, by these discoveries, in writing the history of the mountain... That Moses hangs like a dead weight upon him, and blunts all his zeal for inquiry; for that really he has not the conscience to make his mountain so young, as that prophet makes the world.—What do you think of these sentiments from a Roman Catholic divine? The bishop ... has already warned him to be upon his guard; and not to pretend to be a better natural historian than Moses; nor to presume to urge anything that may be in the smallest degree deemed contradictory to his sacred authority.'[84]

Studies like those of Father Recupero finally forced scientists to accept the idea of a pre-Adamite earth that had existed for a long, long time before there were any people. The days of creation as described by Genesis could be taken as eons. In this manner geology could be reconciled with Scripture. Adam could still be created in 4004 B.C., while the material world, the vegetable world and the non-human biological world could have been created much earlier.

Another source of pressure to adopt a pre-Adamite hypothesis came from the discovery of the Hindu Scriptures. The first man to translate them, Nathaniel Brassy Halhed, actually obtained a Persian translation and translated that into English. His work, *A Code of Gentoo Laws, or Ordinations of the Pundits, from a Persian Translation, made from the original, written in the Shanscrit Language* (sic) of 1776, contains a preface in which Halhed came to grips with the Indian claims about the great antiquity of their Scriptures. Twice in the preface Halhed went over the evidence of the age of these documents, and the claims of Indian chronology about their age, and lastly the claims of Indian chronology about the age of the world. Accepting these as genuine, he still insisted that by faith and revelation he knew they could not be the case. The evidence for the antiquity of the Hindu records Halhed put in the same class as Recupero's evidence about the age of Mount Vesuvius (which he quoted). Hindu chronology gives a figure for the age of the world of 7,205,000 years. 'To such Antiquity the Mosaic Creation is but as Yesterday.'[85] In one of the Hindu works the history of mankind covers several million years. In the face of this, what is one to believe? Halhed declared, 'Great surely and inexplicable must be the doubts of mere human Reason upon such a Dilemma when unassisted and uninformed by Divine Revelation; but while we admit the former in our Argument, we profess a most unshaken Reliance upon the latter, before which every Suspicion must subside, and Scepticism be absorbed in Conviction.'[86] Halhed was apparently so upset by the pre-Adamic implications of the Hindu Scriptures that he returned from the Orient and joined the wild Messianic sect of Richard Brothers.[87] He spent the remainder of his life announcing the imminent end of the world. And he wrote works such as *Testimony of the Authenticity of the Prophecies of Richard Brothers and of his Mission to Recall the Jews* (1795).[88] There is no evidence, however, of any reliance on La Peyrère's theory about the recall of the Jews. Richard Brothers was called 'The Elijah of the Present Day' and 'The Bright Star to Guide the Hebrews.'[89] Halhed's religious theory was about the imminence of the recall of the Jews and the end of the world. He even claimed he had found the secret and mysteries that explained all in the Hindu Scriptures.[90] Since he was a member of Parliament, he tried to introduce bills announcing apocalyptic developments to come.

Halhed's report of the evidence of the antiquity of the Hindu Scriptures was very worrisome to many intellectuals until the great Orientalist, Sir William Jones, published two papers showing how this data could be explained without questioning the Mosaic account of how the world began. Jones (1746-1794) was a great linguist, mastering many languages, including Arabic and Persian. He became a lawyer, and was appointed to judge of the high court at Calcutta in 1783. He there became the first European scholar of Sanskrit. His remark that there is a strong resemblance between Sanskrit and both Greek and Latin, led to the theory of an Indo-European language, and a common Aryan origin of Europeans and some Asians.[91] Jones himself was concerned to justify the biblical picture of the world in the face of the evidence in the literature of India. His two essays, 'On the God of Greece, Italy and India' (1784) and 'On The Chronology of the Hindus' (1788), provided the answer for the believers.

In the first essay Jones saw the problem raised by Indian data as that either the first eleven chapters of Genesis are true, 'or the whole fabrick of our national religion is false.' Jones insisted he was an objective truth-seeker, and 'if any cool unbiassed reasoner will clearly convince me that Moses drew his narrative through *Egyptian* conduits from the primieval fountains of Indian literature, I shall esteem him as a friend for having weeded my mind from a capital error, and promise to stand among the foremost in assisting to circulate the truth which he has ascertained.'[92]

After having examined the evidence, Jones was happy to report that Indian history was compatible with Mosaic history. He showed how this was the case in 'On the Chronology of the Hindus.' The great antiquity of the Hindus, he said, was believed so firmly by the Hindus and has caused a lot of concern among Europeans. The Indians have figures for the age of the world running into millions of years, and if true, Mosaic history would be erroneous. However, the accepted chronology of the Hindus begins with an absurdity 'so monstrous' that it overthrows the whole system.[93] By examining this absurdity, 'we may establish as indubitable the two following propositions; that the *three first* ages of the *Hindus* are chiefly mythological, whether their mythology was founded on the dark enigmas of their astronomers, or on the heroic fictions of their poets, and, that the *fourth*, or historical age cannot be carried farther back than about two thousand years before Christ.'[94] So, one did not have to go through the doubts Halhed had discerned and worried about. Instead, as had been said much earlier by Judah Halevi in the Islamic Middle Ages, the Indian dates are 'so much clouded by the fictions of the Brahmans, who, to aggrandize themselves, have designedly raised their antiquity beyond the truth.'[95] Jones then worked out a chronology on his theory that most of Hindu chronology was mythological and fictitious, and showed that the earlier figure in their history, Menu, is really Adam, 5,794 years ago. Menu II was Noah, Buddha was almost 1,000 years before Jesus.[96] So, 'what ever be the comparative antiquity of the *Hindu* scripture, we may safely conclude that the *Mosaik* and *Indian* chronologies are perfectly consistent.'[97]

Jones's scholarly authority satisfied most Europeans and Americans on the matter, and pleased the religious believers. One of the leading popularizers of information about India, Thomas Maurice, (1754-1824), assistant keeper of manuscripts for the British Museum, published three volumes of Indian Antiquities in 1794. He discussed Halhed's materials, and then, relying on Sir William Jones, debunked the claims about the antiquity of India, saying these were wild fables, mythology, blended with some authentic records, and some romantic dreams of astronomers.[98] However, since 'The daring assertions of certain sceptical French philosophers with respect to the Age of the World ... principally founded on the high assumptions of the Brahmins and other Eastern nations, in point of chronology and astronomy, could their extravagant claims be substantiated, have a direct tendency to overturn the Mosaic system, and with it, Christianity,' Maurice sought to invalidate these claims.[99] He was most probably answering Voltaire and his followers, though no one in particular is named. Using Jones's analysis, Maurice contended that the personages who are supposed to have flourished many thousands of years ago in Hindu accounts, 'were of celestial, not terrestial origin: that their empire was the empire of the imagination in the skies, not of real power on this globe of earth.' He claimed 'Adam' was actually a Sanskrit name, and means the first. So, real true history began with him.[100]

The soothing effect of Jones's researches and Maurice's popularization of them (which was largely underwritten by the India Company) can be seen in the comments of the American Revolutionary leader, Elias Boudinot, who in 1795 wrote *The Age of Revelation* in answer to Tom Paine's *Age of Reason*. Referring to Jones's and Maurice's texts, Boudinot announced that when all the facts about Hindu religion were studied, they, far from subverting the Mosaic account, and Christianity, reinforced its truth by showing that the pretended antiquity of the Hindus is not accurate.[101]

Sir William Jones may have eased the problem raised by Halhed's presentation of the Indian Scriptures, but, inadvertently, he created some other potentially worrisome difficulties. At the very end of his discussion of Hindu chronology, Jones appended a note about a claim by a Mr. Vansittart, to the effect that the Afghans are the Lost Tribes. Jones indicated that this seemed plausible, and that the Pushtu language 'has a manifest resemblance to the Chaldaick.' Jones strongly recommended further study of the literature and history of the Afghans.[102] With Jones's great authority, many Millenarians took him as having established the Jewish Afghan theory, thereby undoing the Jewish American Indian theory.[103] This would, of course, raise again the question of where the American Indians came from if they were not Jews or the Lost Tribes.

Further, Jones, the first European scholar of Sanskrit, mentioned in a letter that there was an astonishing resemblance between Sanskrit and Latin and Greek. This led very shortly to the theory that all three languages derived from an earlier language, Indo-European, and that the cultures of India, Greece and Rome had a common root. And, since Hebrew is not an Indo-European language, ancient Jewish culture was not a source of European culture. The nineteenth century use of Jones's finding of the similarity of Sanskrit, Greek, and Latin was to create the Aryan myth that removed any relation of the Mosaic account of human history from the account of the origin of European culture. Hence, while Jones thought he had saved the Mosaic account from the threat of the Hindu data, he provided the germ for a much greater challenge to the Bible as the history of the world.

Chinese chronology and documents had created similar problems to those raised by the Hindu Scriptures a century earlier, when contacts between Jesuit missionaries and the Chinese began. The conflicts which thus arose were resolved in part by contending that Noah ended up in China after the Flood, and that Noah actually was the source of Chinese civilization. The person who seems to have started this view was John Webb in his *An Historical Essay Endeavoring a Probability that the Language of the Empire of China is the Primitive Language* (1669). Webb contended, 'But in all probability, *China* was after the Flood first planted either by *Noah* himself, or some of the sons of Sem,' and that the Chinese 'retained the PRIMITIVE Tongue, as having received it from Noah.'[104]

Another and quite different kind of case in the literature about those who discuss pre-Adamism was an eccentric Irishman named Francis Dobbs, an M. P., who was supposed to have claimed that there was a race of men not descended from Adam. This race was created by an intrigue of Eve and the Devil.[105] (The heretical Dutch writer, Adrian Beverland, had cited La Peyrère as support of the view that the serpent was a penis and had copulated with Eve.)[106] However, this seems to have been a misreading of Dobbs's discussion of Genesis in his *Universal History*.[107] Dobbs, however, was very much like Halhed in his religious views. He wrote *A Concise View from History and Prophecy, of Great Predictions in the Sacred Writings that have been fulfilled, also of those that are now fulfilling, and that remain to be accomplished* in 1800. He was sure that what had taken place from the beginning of the French Revolution to his own time was the fulfillment of many key prophecies. Now to finish things off the Messiah would first go to Ireland and then to Palestine.[108]

Still another type of problem with pre-Adamite implications was one that pointed to some kind of pre-historic man. A Dutch scientist, Francis Xavier Burtin came to the conclusion in 1789, on the basis of fossil evidence, that there must have been intelligent beings before Adam. He also claimed that there had been a geological revolution in pre-Adamic times. Burtin won a prize for his work. Then he was accused of advocating pre-Adamism. However, Burtin insisted he was only claiming that there were rational or intelligent creatures before Adam, but not that there were human beings. The first human, he insisted, was of course, Adam.[109] Thus, the *Monthly Review* of the time said of Burtin, 'he promises that he will prove his theory to be strictly consonant to the words of Moses, and he insists on it that, provided he excepts the human species, he may believe rational animals to have existed on the earth before Adam, without being guilty of this terrible heresy, for which, about the middle of last century, poor Isaac de la Pereira was so roughly handled by the Inquisition.'[110] A page later the same *Monthly Review* reported that a Dr. Van Marum had found the jaws of a large animal. There is some suspicion, it said, that it was part of a pre-Adamite. Then mention is made of a pre-historic hatchet that may also have belonged to a pre-Adamite.[111]

One could go through many, many cases where the evidence suggested the pre-Adamite theory, yet religious orthodoxy would not permit such a theory to be espoused. Perhaps the fitting climax of the eighteenth century's struggle with this problem is the thesis set forth in the work of Edward King, Fellow of the Royal Society, entitled, 'Dissertation concerning the Creation of Man,' published in 1800. King said that starting from the Bible, 'There are many proofs and arguments that may be derived from the Holy Scriptures themselves, which tend to show, strange as the conclusion may appear, at first sight, to some persons, that *the commonly received opinion, that all mankind are the sons of Adam* (an opinion that has caused a great many stumbling blocks to be laid in the way of those who wish to understand the Sacred Writings), is so far from being really founded on Scripture or necessarily to be implied from the whole tenor of the Divine Mosaic Writings, that it is directly contrary to what is contained there.'[112] King then insisted that Genesis set forth two separate and distinct creation stories. The first one is about the creation of man in general, the species. The second is about Adam and Eve. Once this distinction has been recognized it is easy to account for the various groups of mankind, from the white Europeans, to the brown and black people, who can hardly have all had the same ancestors.[113] When one analyzes Genesis, it indicates that there must have been non-Adamites such as Cain's wife and the giants. And, after the Flood, many more people must have survived. Also many more species of plants and animals must have lived through it. The story as told in Genesis is implausible in that the number of species of flora and fauna known in 1800 could not have fitted in the Ark. So, King claimed, nothing except a polygenetic explanation could account for the diversity of the human species, and the stability of certain characteristics regardless of changes in the environment.

King worked out his case by combining biblical interpretations with scientific evidence. He also included in his account the racist element that was to be so predominant in nineteenth century pre-Adamism. Adam, he said, was the progenitor of the class or species of men who are endowed with the greatest and most useful abilities, such as language and science. The Noachides, Adam's sole surviving descendants after the Flood, were not the only race of men. However, they were the sacred race. Only the sons of Adam are the true sons of God, the elect. One almost hears La Peyrère rising from his grave.[114] The dominant kind of racist pre-Adamism was directed, as we shall see in the nineteenth century, to establishing the everlasting superiority of whites to people of color.

A positive kind of pre-Adamism that may have had far reaching effects is that offered by Voltaire and Goethe. Both of them stated in amusing ways that they adhered to some kind of pre-Adamism. Considering the pressure against such a view, both Voltaire and Goethe were quite brave in saying what they did. In the *Dictionnaire philosophique*, article 'Adam,' Voltaire poked fun at those who believed that Adam was the first man and gave some evidence, genuine or fictitious, that there were people before Adam. In the article 'Moses,' he showed why Moses could not be the author of the Scriptures that we have. In the dialogue with Monsieurs A, B, and C, Voltaire declared he was a pre-Adamite, a pre-Osirisite, a pre-Zeusite, etc. In sum, Voltaire was outspoken about his lack of belief in the Judeo-Christian worldview.[115] In his *Essai sur les moeurs et de l'esprit des nations*, Voltaire stated that whites, blacks and others must come from different races.[116] He presented much evidence for polygenicism. One of the uses to which he applied this theory was to claim only Jews were Adamites. Then the Jews are separate and different from the Europeans who belong to a pre-Adamite group. As Hertzberg and Poliakov (the historians of anti-Semitism) have argued, Voltaire was the father of secular anti-Semitism. He saw no place for the Jews in Europe and saw them as a permanently different race. As one of the founders of Aryanism, Voltaire saw the historical European Adam as coming from India and having nothing to do with the Semitic Adam of the Jews of Palestine. The Jewish Adam was a poor attempt to imitate the Aryan

Adam. It was not long before, at the end of the century, Voltaire's anti-Semitic polygenicism was being used to hold back the emancipation of the Jews in revolutionary France.[117]

Goethe gave some small indication that he might have held a similar view. In a discussion he had with the naturalist, von Martius, over whether all people were descended from Adam and Eve, the naturalist held to the biblical account. Goethe offered a theory much like those of Bruno and Vanini to the effect that men arose all over the world out of Nature, possibly a spontaneous generation theory. Then Goethe offered a novel version of pre-Adamism that had anti-Semitic implications.

> But we, as well as Negroes and Laplanders and slender men who are handsomer than any of us, had certainly different ancestors; and this worthy company must confess that we at present differ in a variety of particulars from the genuine descendants of Adam, and that they, especially where money is concerned, are superior to us all.[118]

Poliakov has pointed out that Goethe had taken La Peyrère's claim that only the Jews were true Adamites and transformed it from a glorification of the Jews to a condemnation of them. Both Voltaire and Goethe sought to derive European civilization from non-Jewish sources, Aryan and Hellenic, so that Europeans would no longer be descendants of the ancient Hebrews. This view, Poliakov says, led to the formation of the Aryan myth as a consequence of pre-Adamism, a myth that could deny any Hebraic basis of Western Civilization, and even transform the Jews into its age-old enemies.[119] Buttressed with the philological study of Indo-European, Semitic culture could be divorced from Hellenic and Roman and thus not basically related to true European civilization.

While Voltaire and Goethe transformed the pre-Adamite theory in a new direction, and Edward King saw its possibilities for separating people into superior and inferior species, La Peyrère's ideas had other sorts of influence in the Enlightenment and afterwards. We shall see how the pressure for a polygenetic explanation of human diversity combined with a decreasing acceptance of a biblical framework of explanation, led to a positive assertion of pre-Adamism as the best theory for explaining the origins and nature of mankind. As this occurred, La Peyrère himself was resurrected as a heroic martyr who had fought to throw important light on the human condition and was suppressed by the Inquisition and by all sorts of theologians of different persuasions.

What might be considered the modern study of anthropology began to appear in the eighteenth century. Among forms of polygenetic theories, the pre-Adamite theory of La Peyrère was one of the factors that forced a very serious reconsideration of the nature of human development. The problems involved in explaining the variations in human beings, and the origins of the human species intensified in the light of discoveries of different peoples during the sixteenth and seventeenth centuries. A polygenetic explanation, such as La Peyrère's, would offer a simple and neat basis for accounting for human differences and the various locations of human societies over the surface of the earth. But, as has been noted, this theory appeared to almost everyone except its author to be in direct violation of Scripture. Only some kind of monogenetic explanation was acceptable within the prevailing intellectual framework. But how could such an account explain how blacks became different from whites? The problem was neatly outlined by the anonymous author of a polygenetic tract written in 1695. (There were very few such documents at that time.) The tract, entitled *Two Essays, Sent in a Letter from Oxford to a Nobleman in London*,[120] starts with *'An Apology for writing the following Essays.'* Because the present age desires a rational religion, and because bigotry has been calmed and allayed, it should be possible to consider scientific objections to Scripture. After all *'Copernicus, Galileo, Campanella, Mersennus, Gassendus, Cartesius'* among others 'are not esteemed the worse Christians because they contradict the Scriptures in Physical or Mathematical Problems.'[121] After all the biblical authors did not write for people learned in the arts and sciences. Because of this 'The Philosophick History of the *Bible* is not always to be embraced.'[122] Examining it in the context of modern science should not in any way lead to atheism.[123]

The first essay deals with some errors about creation, the flood and the peopling of the world. The beginning deals with problems being raised by England's leading scientists, such as Thomas Burnet, John Ray, Robert Hooke and others about the nature of the earth, how it would be affected by a general flood, etc. The latter part, 'Concerning the Peopling and Planting the New World, and other remote Countries,' gets down to the issue of whether a monogenetic or polygenetic explanation better accounts for human origins and diversity. The author says, 'The Design of this second Part is not to calumniate, or diminish the Authority of *Moses*, who, without Dispute was one of the greatest and wisest Legislators that ever appeared in the World.'[124] Moses adapted his presentation of the origin and development of the human race to the capacity of his Jewish audience. 'Therefore, it can be no Crime in one, who is no *Jew*, to comment a little upon some Parts of it, with a Christian Plainness, and a philosophical Liberty, founded upon Nature herself.'[125] The anonymous author then outlined what gave rise to the problem, the discovery that, 'The *West Indies*, and the vast Regions lately discovered towards the South, abound with such Variety of Inhabitants, and new Animals, not known, or even seen in *Asia, Africa,* or *Europe*, that the Origin of them doth not appear so clear as some late Writers pretend.'[126]

The anonymous author contended that this was especially the case since there are no records or monuments describing the migrations of the flora, fauna and people before or after the Flood. If the origin of New World animals, plants and people is obscure, so 'their Differences from all the rest of the Globe in Manners, Languages, Habits, Religions, Diet, Arts and Customs, as well as in their Quadrupedes, Birds, Serpents, and Insects, render their Derivation very obscure, and their Origin uncertain, especially in the common Way, and according to the vulgar Opinions of planting all the Earth from one little spot.'[127] This 'common Way' is, of course, the monogenetic perspective of the Bible. The anonymous author had indicated that an explanation of the variety and of the origin of the different species then known would be extremely doubtful. What has happened is that 'The great Zeal to maintain a Jewish tradition, [has] put many learned Christians upon the Rack to make it out. Every Corner is searched to find out a Word, a Rite, or a Custom, in order to derive from thence many Millions of different People.'[128] If this could have been done, then the learned Christians would have been able to hold on to their biblical monotheism. The anonymous author, on the other hand, insisted that the cultural differences between the Old and New Worlds, the enormous geographical difficulties involved for a mass migration between the two, and the great differences between the flora and fauna in each, all indicate that a monogenetic explanation would not do. 'I see no Way at present to solve this new Face or Nature, by old Arguments fetched from Eastern Rubbish, or Rabbinical Weeds, unless some new Philosopher starts up with a fresh System; in the mean Time let them all be *Aborigines*.'[129] Thus, he suggested that the flora and fauna of the New World were the result of spontaneous generation.

The anonymous author, in dealing with the problem of explaining the causes of racial differences, pointed out the major religious and scientific matters that would have to be dealt with successfully to overcome a polygenetic view such as La Peyrère's. As we will see, some of the problems were basic to the struggle between the monogenicists and polygenicists in the eighteenth and nineteenth centuries. First, the biblical account of the origin of all species raises many questions. So, 'As many Difficulties lie against the *Mosaick* System of confining all Species of living terrestial Creatures within the *Asiatick* or *Primaeval Paradise*, and afterwards to *Noah's* Ark; so more seem to arise against the Propagation of all Mankind out of one single Male and Female, unless all Posterity, both Blacks and Whites, separated by vast Seas, were all included actually in Form within *Adam* and *Eve*.'[130] This case, that of accounting for white and black people, was to be the one that would get the most attention from later biologists and anthropologists. Could one account for the existence of black people on any monogenetic theory? The anonymous author went on to indicate that this did not seem possible.

First of all, 'The Origin of Negroes lies very obscure; [he did not consider the possibility that explaining the origin of whites might be just as obscure] for Time out of Mind there hath been Blacks with a wooly Substance on their Bodies instead of Hair; because they are mentioned in the most ancient Records now extant in the World. 'Tis plain, their Colour and Wool are innate, or seminal from their first Beginning, and seems to be a specifick Character, which neither the Sun, nor any Curse from *Cham* could imprint upon them.'[131] Second, the color of Negroes does not seem to be due to climate or heat. Even before all the eighteenth century climate theorists had a chance to offer their explanations of these facts, this anonymous polygenicist pointed out that some nations living under the same heat and climate are never black and that no child of whites ever became black even if he was born in Guinea, the Congo or Angola. Further no Negroes produce white offspring in New England or Virginia where the climate is much milder. When one turns to the Ham curse theory, the anonymous author pointed out that if this were a plausible explanation, a lot more Asiatics and Egyptians should be black, 'for they were curs'd more peculiarly then the Western remote coasts of *Africa.*' Lastly, he argued that the color of Negroes was not accidental, since accidental colors would not be reproduced in the offspring. Accidental colors also vary according to seasonal changes, diet, culture, etc. However, on the contrary, 'a Negroe will always be a Negroe, carry him to *Greenland*, give him Chalk, feed and manage him never so many Ways.'[132]

One John Harris, a Fellow of the Royal Society, wrote a very lengthy answer entitled, *Remarks on some late Papers relating to the Universal Deluge; And to the Natural History of the Earth* (1697).[133] Harris claimed that he would have ignored the anonymous pamphlet except that it 'was applauded generally by Men of loose Principles: such as make their small stock of Philosophy subservient only to Scepticism and Infidelity.'[134] Since it seemed to come out of the Deist intellectual world, a pious answer was needed. Harris said he knew the anonymous author well and saw his contribution as part of a larger controversy over the compatibility of Genesis and new geological findings. His own mission, however, was *'to shew the weakness and meanness of such Pretensions to Reason and Philosophy as oppose things Divine and Sacred.*'[135] He began by using material from the leading English scientists to justify a theory of the earth that accords with Scripture. Harris relied heavily on John Woodward of the Royal Society, whom he showed was the chief target of the anonymous author. When Harris came to the second essay, he simply pointed out that the

polygenetic theory conflicted with Scripture, and, therefore, could not be
set aside as Jewish nonsense. Without considering the data offered in the
pamphlet, he merely asserted that the wise scientist, Dr. Woodward,
would account for it all when he wrote his explanation of the peopling
of the New World after the Deluge. Then 'twill appear that the *Mosaick
History* is *very just* and *exactly conformable* to what *really* then *happened*.'[136]
The problem of why blacks differ from whites will also be solved by
Woodward, who will show that the black color is accidental and that the
Negroes are the descendants of Ham.[137] Unfortunately for Harris,
Woodward does not seem to have written the work that was to make
monogenesis a satisfactory explanation of all of the data. Woodward
wrote on fossils and on the theory of the earth, but there is no indication
that he ever published a work on the origins and development of peoples.
The major points at issue then became aspects of a major controversy
that lasted through all of the eighteenth and much of the nineteenth century as well.

Given the questions raised, the choice seemed to be, for the Enlightenment anthropologists to adopt some sort of pre-Adamism or some more
elaborated monogenetic theory. During the eighteenth century this was
really not a choice, since the public advocacy of a pre-Adamite theory
would probably have had dire effects for the author. Nonetheless, the
discoveries in geology, history, anthropology, archeology, and biblical
criticism produced many facts that did not seem to fit in with a historical
chronology that began only in 4004 b.c., or with a monogenetic theory
of human development. The leading biological and anthropological
theorists of the eighteenth century such as Linnaeus, Montesquieu, Buffon, or Blumenbach held to the thesis that the human race had a
monogenetic origin, and that differences present among peoples,
resulting in the superiority of whites and the inferiority of American Indians and blacks, could be accounted for in terms of environmental factors such as climate, diet and culture. (These had, as I have noted,
already been dismissed by the anonymous polygenecist.) From the late
seventeenth century into the nineteenth century, theories of this kind
were constantly being challenged because it was observed that there was
no noticeable alteration in racial characteristics among blacks living in
North America or Europe, or in Europeans living in Africa, or American
Indians living in Europe.

Throughout the eighteenth century, interest continued in the question
of why Negroes, American Indians, and others did not look and behave
like Christian Europeans. Scholars turned out an enormous literature on
why blacks are black, on why some peoples speak primitive and inferior
languages, and other related topics. Applying Sir Isaac Newton's ex-

perimental method of reasoning to these problems seemed to result either in a highly elaborated degeneracy theory or a polygenetic theory of fixed racial differences. And, obviously, part of what was involved in the dispute between these theories was whether there is a basic unity to the human race or a basic diversity.[138]

Those who assumed a basic unity of mankind usually went on to explain the observed differences as resulting from some kind or kinds of degenerative processes. Almost all of these monogenecists took it for granted that the natural, normal state of human beings is to be white. They were sure that Adam and Noah were both white. An exception was a Dr. John Mitchell who wrote in 1745 that 'white people who look on themselves as the primitive Race of Man, from a certain Superiority or Worth, either supposed or assumed, seem to have the least Pretensions to it of any, either from History or Philosophy; for they seem to have degenerated more from the primitive and original Complexion of Mankind, in Noah and his Sons, than even the *Indians* and Negroes.'[139] Except for Dr. Mitchell, one finds a great deal more effort to account for black skin color as degeneracy and to employ this explanation as an answer to the polygenetic menace. Thus, for example, Maupertius said in his *Vénus Physique* that blacks born from white parents are incomparably rarer than whites born from black parents. This he took to be a demonstration that white is the color of the first people and that it was an accident that black had become an inherited color of many peoples who live in the torrid zones. However, the original human color had not entirely disappeared in them. Maupertius claimed that his explanation of how blacks got to be black constitutes an answer to those who want to attack the history of Genesis denying that all people are descended from one mother and one father. He insisted that his theory was at least as probable as the polygenetic alternative.[140]

Montesquieu had made climate a crucial factor for explaining differences in cultures. This had been an important view in antiquity and Montesquieu sought to show in his *Esprit des Lois* how much in the current world could be accounted for in this way. Around the same time, Carl von Linné (Linnaeus), the founder of modern biology, presented the following classification of mankind (though he maintained the theory of the unity of mankind.) The differences, he claimed, were due to education, situation, climate, and social environment.

1. Wild Man, Four-footed, mute, hairy.
2. *American* [i.e. *Indian*] Copper-colored, choleric, erect, *Hair* black, straight, thick; *nostrils* wide; *face* harsh; beard scanty, obstinate, content free. Paints himself with fine red lines. *Regulated* by customs.

3. *European*. Fair, sanguine, brawny. *Hair* yellow brown, flowing; *eyes* blue; *gentle*, acute, inventive. *Covered* with close vestments. *Governed* by laws.

4. *Asiatic*. Sooty, melancholy, rigid. *Hair* black; *eyes* dark; *severe*, haughty, covetous. *Covered* with loose garments. *Governed* by opinions.

5. *African*. Black, phlegmatic, relaxed. *Hair* black, frizzled; *skin* silky; *nose* flat; *lips* tumid; *crafty*, indolent, negligent. Anoints himself with grease. *Governed* by caprice.[141]

In this biological classification it is obvious that white is best, and black is worst.

The purely climatic theory, that sought to explain all human differences in terms of climate, was constantly being attacked in the mid-eighteenth century. Enough evidence had accumulated to show that no significant changes were occurring as the result of changed climates among blacks in America and whites in Africa or South America. The greatest biologist of the eighteenth century, Count Buffon, tried to deal with this in his *Histoire naturelle*, by offering a more complete explanation in terms of a variety of environmental factors. He began with the premise that, 'White, then, appears to be the primitive color of Nature.' However, various peoples 'have undergone various changes by the influence of climate, food, mode of living, epidemic disease, and the mixture of dissimilar individuals.'[142] The changes that resulted from these factors have produced black, tawny, yellowish, brown and degenerate white groups (these are Laplanders and Eskimos.) These groups are fairly permanent and they have produced a fairly dismal picture of most of mankind. Buffon declared that the Eskimos 'are gross, superstitious and stupid,'[143] that the Tartars 'are gross, stupid and brutal;'[144] that the American Indians are 'stupid, ignorant and destitute of arts and of industry;'[145] and that the negroes of Sierra Leone are such that 'their indolence and stupidity make them insensible to every (useful) pleasure.'[146] On the other hand, Buffon claimed that the temperate climate between the fortieth and fiftieth degree of latitude 'produces the most handsome and beautiful men.' He went on, 'It is from this climate that the ideas of the genuine colour of man kind, and the various degrees of *beauty* ought to be derived.' He was speaking of the area from France and northern Spain across to the Caucasian mountains. 'The natives of those territories are the most handsome and the most beautiful people in the world.'[147]

Buffon's research, supposedly the best empirical investigation of the time, accounted for the variety of human beings in racial and racist terms. Whites were the best in terms of beauty, intelligence and civilization. All other kinds of humans suffered from some degeneration from the norm. Now that the factors causing degeneration were known it would be possible to take remedial action. If degenerate groups were moved to the proper geographical zone, were given a decent diet, and were given a European education and way of life, then Buffon apparently believed, everyone would become white and civilized.[148]

Buffon's theory accounting for human differences by degeneration from one species became the model used by theorists over the next century. Lord Kames, Oliver Goldsmith, J. F. Blumenbach and his successor James Cowles Prichard, all followed and tried to improve upon Buffon's views. Some of these thinkers tried to use their monogenetic theories as a basis for improving the conditions of non-whites. Most were also active in trying to abolish slavery, unlike those polygenecists whom we will consider in the next chapter who were working out a defense of slavery. Blumenbach referred to the Africans as 'his black brethren.'[149] He and the French Revolutionary leader, the abbé Henri Grégoire, diagnosed the causes of present Negro and Indian inferiority in terms of physical and environmental factors, and then tried to show that non-whites had the potential to achieve the same kind of civilization as whites. Both men wrote about cases where this had already happened, cases of black writers, scientists and artists.[150] Prichard, the leading English anthropologist before Darwin, had argued that Adam was black, and that whites are degenerate forms of the original human race. He had also argued that all of human diversity could be explained on a unitary origin theory. To account for the range of diversity he had to suppose that the earth had been inhabited for thousands of years, perhaps millions. Prichard admitted that in the present stage of human development blacks and Indians were inferior, but thought this could be changed by religion, education, etc. In his major work, *The Natural History of Man*, there are a great many illustrations. Those of non-whites are portrayed as idealized perfect Europeans, only of dark complexion.[151]

No matter how complicated the explanation of human variation as the result of degeneration, opponents constantly reiterated that this did not account for the known facts. For example, David Hume, whom we will deal with at length in the next chapter, had asserted, 'I am apt to suspect the negroes to be naturally inferior to the whites.'[152] Hume's statement leaves no room for remedial action or degeneration. Thomas Jefferson made a slightly more hesitant claim in his *Notes from Virginia*, 'I advance it herefore as a suspicion only, that the blacks, whether originally a distinct race, or made distinct by time and circumstances, are inferior to the whites in their endowments both of body and mind.'[153] Such a statement could be made to fit either a polygenetic or a monogenetic view.

It was early in the nineteenth century, that a full blown polygenetic theory started to be offered by some French biologists. In France, after the Revolution had dethroned the Church, a scientist did not have to be quite so concerned about opposing religious orthodoxy. The biologist, J. J. Virey, published his large *Histoire naturelle du genre humaine* in the year IX of the Revolutionary calendar. He put together a massive case using recent data in geology and anthropology to support a general polygenetic theory, appealing to a wide range of authorities including La Peyrère. The strongest part of his case for polygenecism was the great differences between Europeans, Africans and American Indians. He asked why people bothered trying to derive the American Indians from some group in the Old World. Why could not they be autochthanous?[154]

A stronger case for polygenesis was set forth in France by J. B. G. Bory de Saint-Vincent in his *L'Homme (Homo), Essai zoologique sur le genre humain*. In the section entitled, '*S'il existe une seule ou plusieurs espèces dans le genre Homme*, Bory de Saint-Vincent claimed that most scientists avoid this issue by talking about races instead of species. When one turns to the question of whether there is more than one human species, he said that it seemed to be a strange way of interpreting the Bible to read it as saying that the parents of all men are the same, and that the Papuan, the Hottentot, the Eskimo, and the descendants of King David are consanguine. Instead Bory de St. Vincent suggested that the reason Scripture reads as it does is that the early Jews knew only their own species. The divine ordinances deliberately separated them from everybody else. The biblical Jews would hardly have regarded the redskins or the blacks as their brothers. So, we are told, Adam was only the Father of the Jewish race. (La Peyrère is not cited as support for this idea.) The Jews would not have wanted the Chinese, the Negroes or the Botocudos for cousins. After all the whole of the Old Testament expresses a horror of mixing with strangers and mixing Jewish blood with theirs. The Jewish biblical text is not trying to establish that Adam, its first man, was the father of the human race. Instead it only wants to assert that Adam was the father of the Jews. Since the Scriptures deal only with the chosen people, the rest of human genealogies, that is those of the profane groups, are dealt with by secular historians. Hence, said Bory de St. Vincent, it cannot be impious to recognize that there are several species of men, each of which has its own Adam.[155]

Even though Bory de St. Vincent first carefully showed that his theory did not conflict with Scripture, and that it was not impious to assert that Adam was not the first man, the bulk of his evidence, as one might expect was biological and anthropological. He was not impressed by the claim that white and black people must be part of the same species because they meet Buffon's definition of a species, a group that can mate and produce fertile offspring. He pointed out that lots of hybrids are possible, but they do not all constitute the same species. If whites and blacks are members of the same species, then why are they different in complexion?[156] However, while Bory de St. Vincent was a thoroughgoing polygenecist, he did not combine this belief, as we shall see the American anthroplogists of the time did, with a justification for racism based on one species being superior or inferior to another. He rejected, on the one hand, the view that one has to be a monogenecist to avoid the immoral racist consequences that would result from admitting that one species of people is better than another. First, he insisted that in the search for truth, one cannot allow these considerations to intrude. Also, one cannot raise doubts about a conclusion by pointing out the sad results that would be involved. However, as a polygenecist, Bory de St. Vincent announced that he could not see why any person, no matter what species he belonged to should be mistreated, nor why, for that matter, any animal should be mistreated either. Hence, as he saw it, the polygenetic theory did not have to lead to any racist claims.[157]

In England, a physician, John Mason Good, presented a version of the polygenetic theory. Good was a linguist who knew Arabic, Hebrew, Persian, Russian, Sanskrit and Chinese. He was a Fellow of the Royal Society. A collection of his essays, originally given as lectures was published in 1826 under the title *The Book of Nature*. In one of the essays, Good employed his philological and scientific knowledge to criticize the Mosaic account of the origin of man. He insisted that the variety of human species must have had different sources. Further he claimed that even the biblical statement is open to a polygenetic interpretation and is not restricted to the claim that all people are descended from one pair of parents. 'This opinion was first stated, in modern times, by the celebrated Isaac Peyrère, librarian to the Prince of Condé; who about the middle of the last century, contended, in a book which was not long afterwards condemned to the flames, though for other errors in conjunction with the present one.'[158] Some of these errors were that the Bible included two separate and distinct creation stories, and that the problem of accounting for Cain's wife and his associates led to a pre-Adamite view. Good was unwilling to go along with La Peyrère on the first of these matters. But he saw La Peyrère as the founder of the polygenetic view that was just beginning to flourish [159] (though, of course, it was continuously challenged and rebutted by monogenecists such as James Cowles Prichard.)

A stronger version of Good's view appeared in William Frederick van Amringe's *An Investigation of the Theories of the Natural History of Man by*

Laurence, Prichard, and others (1848). He insisted that a polygenetic view was neither denied nor forbidden by Scripture. In fact, he contended, Mosaic history affords a very strong presumption that man was divided into several species by the Creator. Moses does not give us the history of any other species but he leaves us free to judge from various parts of Genesis that there were other people in the world, though not in Eden. Amringe then pointed out the implications of the Cain story. Next he turned to Good's book, reporting what he had to say about La Peyrère. Amringe was not definite that polygenesis was a better explanation of the facts but attempted to show that this alternative deserved consideration.[160]

When polygenesis finally became a strong scientific view in the first decades of the nineteenth century, and was no longer brushed under the rug as an unspeakable heresy, its modern founder, the French courtier, Isaac La Peyrère, became a scientific hero. He had dared to state the truth in the mid-seventeenth century, and had been persecuted for so doing. Like Galileo, he was a martyr to the development of modern thought. La Peyrère's status rose until an early twentieth century French anthropologist, P. G. Mahoudeau, saw him as almost personally the source of the French Enlightenment and modern rationalism, 'Ce precurseur du Polygenisme ne se montre-t-il pas aussi un peu celui de Montesquieu, de Voltaire, de Diderot et de Buffon? C'est qu'il appartenait à cette mentalité, si profondement française, qui répugne à tout ce qui est despotisme et mysticisme, c'est qu'il marchait dans la voie tracée par Rabelais et Montaigne et, alors, peu de temps auparavant, inaugurée par Descartes dans le domaine des sciences.'[161]

Of course, regardless of what was said about La Peyrère by nineteenth and twentieth-century enthusiasts, he had only a skimpy model of what a polygenetic theory would be like. The biologists and anthropologists of modern times have theories far more complex than La Peyrère's, based on a great deal more data, and concerned with a much larger number of factors. La Peyrère is appealed to as some kind of ancient heroic figure who had the courage to state the polygenetic theory under the most repressive circumstances.

The fight between the polygenecists and the monogenecists moved from a struggle between science and religion to a contest over which type of theory best described the facts. By the early nineteenth century, polygenesis had become a respectable theory, to be judged on its merits. Its advocates in England, France and Germany made a strong case for it. As we shall see in the next chapter, it was among the American ethnologists in the first half of the nineteenth century that the theory reached its highest development. However, this development became part of another that was hardly considered by the people we have discussed in this chapter—namely the use of the polygenetic theory as a justification of European and American racist ideas and as a justification for the continued enslavement of so-called inferior races. The racist aspect so colored the polygenetic theory that such leading humanitarian thinkers and scientists as Alexander von Humboldt and James Cowles Prichard felt that they were *morally* obliged to reject the polygenetic theory, regardless of the evidence, because of the terrible consequences of the application of the theory towards people of color. The original pre-Adamite theory of La Peyrère was certainly not racist in the modern sense. However, as we shall see, it took very little time before La Peyrère's theological system which had been based on the supposition that there were men before Adam was turned into a justification for treating groups of people as naturally and permanently inferior. This contrasted with the monogenetic view, whose account of how people came to differ as a result of some sort of degenerative process, usually also supplied a remedial process that would overcome present forms of superiority and inferiority. The conflict of theories involved here has continued to the present, taking on different forms as the fields of biology and anthropology have continued to develop.

CHAPTER TEN

PRE-ADAMISM AND RACISM

As I have pointed out, La Peyrère, in his formulation of the pre-Adamite theory, did not at all try to place one group of mankind above another. Despite his philosemitism, he still insisted that, biologically, Jews were made of the same stuff as everybody else. However, it was not long before interested parties found a way of using the theory to justify separating people into superior and inferior beings. The first instance I know of is mentioned by a minister, Morgan Godwyn, complaining in 1680 in his book, *Negro's and Indians Advocate*, that his opponents in the American colonies (he was in Virginia), denied that Negroes and Indians were men. Having first given the sort of evidence that Las Casas did (Negroes have bodies, voices, countenance, discourse, etc.), he considered the reasons being offered for denying the Negro's humanity. He took up biblical reasons, Ham's curse, or that Negroes are descended from Cain. Then he said his opponents were extremely fond of pre-Adamism as an explanation, 'But the Pre-Adamites whimsey, which is preferred above the *Curse* (because so exceeding useful to undermine the *Bible* and *Religion*, unto both which they have vowed never to be *reconciled*), they believe invincible.'[1] Godwyn saw the problem partly as an argumentative one, and partly as a way of justifying slavery. Pre-Adamism, he said, as a theory was thoroughly refuted by Matthew Hale's book on the origination of man.[2] And, if one rejects Moses' account of Creation, where is there a new and better one? All that is offered instead is conjecture.[3]

But, more importantly, Godwyn pointed out, pre-Adamism is not related to the questions of whether the Negroes are human, or what their origin or descent may have been. If there were men created before Adam, and they were really men, then their descendants will also be men.[4] As Frederick Douglass was later to point out, even if one admitted that whites and blacks do not have a common origin, they do have a common destiny. And, also, even though there were separate origin of species, what had that to do with whether one species is better than another.[5]

After Godwyn, there are occasional indications that some observers had come to the conclusion that, because of observed differences, whites, blacks, Indians, Asiatics could not all have the same origin. In the eighteenth century, as we have seen, there was a great deal of anthropological literature on why blacks are blacks, why peoples differ and so on. The pre-Adamite theory was continuously rejected as an explanation, partly because of religious pressure, partly because the leading biologists and anthropologists were believers in monogenesis. They thought they could explain human differences by cultural, climatic, and nutritional factors. Montesquieu, Buffon, Blumenbach and others developed more and more complicated monogenetic explanations (and James Cowles Prichard carried this on in the early nineteenth century). The monogenecists usually held that human beings were normally and naturally white, but that some had, unfortunately, become brown, yellow, red or black. These changes were chiefly explained as degenerations from the norm, brought about by too hot or too cold a climate or dietary deficiencies. The advocates of this explanation, though accepting white superiority as the present state of affairs, were usually reformers who felt that the lives and well-being of non-whites could be improved in some finite number of generations so that they could be brought up to the level of the whites. Often, the monogenecists were active abolitionists trying to remove one major impediment to black improvement—slavery.

A defender of slavery, Edward Long, fought back in his large *History of Jamaica* (1774), by proposing a polygenetic explanation both of the differences of whites and blacks, and of the superiority of whites over blacks. First Long started listing the leading differences between Negroes and whites, taken from the travel literature, the works of biologists and anthropologists, and his own observations. Starting from such bland observations as, 'In general, they [the Negroes] are void of genius, and seem almost incapable of making any progress in civility or science. They have no plan or system of morality among them. Their barbarity to their children debases their nature even below that of brutes. They have no moral sensations; no taste but for women;'[6] he went on to describe their savage characteristics. 'We find them [Negroes in America] marked with the same bestial manners, stupidity and vices, which debase their brethren on the continent, who seem to be distinguished from the rest of mankind, not in person only, but in possessing, in the abstract, every species of inherent turpitude that is to be found dispersed at large among the rest of the human creation, with scarce a single virtue to extenuate this shade of character, differing in this particular from all other men.'[7] Long advanced a great amount of detail about the differences between whites and blacks indicating that they are of different species. As his authority for his racist view, he cited the eminent Scottish philosopher, David Hume. 'Mr. Hume presumes, from his observations upon the native Africans, to conclude, that they are inferior to the rest of the species, and utterly incapable of the higher attainments of the human mind.'⁸ What Hume had actually said, in a footnote added to his essay, 'Of National Characters,' was,

> I am apt to suspect the negroes and in general all the other species of men (for there are four or five kinds) to be naturally inferior to the white. There never was a civilized nation of any other complexion than white, nor even any individual eminent either in action or speculation. No ingenious manufactures amongst them, no arts, no sciences. On the other hand, the most rude and barbarous of the whites, such as the ancient GERMANS, the present TARTARS, have still something eminent about them, in their valour, form of government, or some other particular. Such a uniform and constant difference could not happen in so many countries and ages, if nature had not made an original distinction betwixt these breeds of men. Not to mention our colonies, there are NEGROE slaves dispersed all over EUROPE, of which none ever discovered any symptoms of ingenuity, tho' low people without education will start up amongst us, and distinguish themselves in every profession. In JAMAICA indeed they talk of one negroe as a man of parts and learning; but 'tis likely he is admired for very slender accomplishments like a parrot, who speaks a few words plainly.⁹

Both Hume and Long set forth a position which seems to be based on an implicit polygenecism and an induction based on historical evidence about how different peoples developed and how they behave under present conditions. Various abolitionist thinkers, such as James Beattie, James Ramsay, the abbé Grégoire, and the Americans, Charles Crawford and Noah Webster, tried to answer this view.¹⁰ The issue between the monogenecists and the polygenecists was to become most severe in America, especially with its relation to the issue of slavery and the treatment of the American Indians. The constant contact in America with Indians and blacks made the problem of accounting for and evaluating racial differences a matter of immediate concern.

The accepted explanation around 1800, in America as well as Europe, was some kind of monogenetic one. In the United States, President Stanley Stanhope Smith of Princeton had offered the prevailing case for monogenesis in his answer to Hume's relative, Lord Kames.¹¹ However, new data, such as the discovery of the burial mounds in the Ohio River Valley, raised new questions about where such a high civilization could have come from in pre-Columbian America. With so much evidence of diversity in both the Indian and African cultures, some American scientists began questioning Stanhope Smith's environmentalist explanation. A Dr. John Augustine Smith challenged the climate thesis as an explanation of differences in skin color. Apparently this Dr. Smith did not go farther and offer a polygenetic account.¹² A Dr. Charles Caldwell took the next step and contended that neither climate nor culture was sufficient to account for the existing diversities. Further, he said, the matter should be dealt with solely on scientific grounds, and not in terms of religious consequences. Caldwell did not claim that there were diverse origins of peoples, but the only explanation he knew of, compatible with Scripture, was direct, miraculous Divine intervention in human affairs to create different races. People like Stanhope Smith, he contended, tell us 'you must either adopt the belief that all the varieties of complexion and figure which now prevail among the human race, are derived from the influence of climate, the state of society, and the manner of living, or you must admit that a plurality of races was originally created, and that more than Noah and his family escaped the deluge. There is no alternative; you must be either a philosopher or an infidel.' Caldwell did not make his choice.[13] However, the members of 'the American School' were willing to be infidels on the basis of their new scientific evidence.

The leader of the American ethnologists, Dr. Samuel G. Morton of Philadelphia, had patiently collected and studied skulls. In 1839, he published his masterpiece, *Crania Americana*, in which he set forth the evidence that was to provide the basis for the American version of the pre-Adamite theory. Instead of speculating about how mankind got to be so diverse, Dr. Morton presented the essential facts in the case, pointing to the most plausible hypothesis in terms of the then accepted assumptions about human history. Morton pointed out that as far back as we know about racial characteristics of the present diverse groups, they were the same as they are today. The evidence of Egyptian monuments that are three thousand years old is that even then Caucasians were as distinct from Negroes as they are right now. The pictures of Jews in sculptures at Luxor and Karnak look like present day Jews. The records of India and Arabia confirm this fixity of racial features for the last three millennia.[14]

According to the biblical chronology of Morton's time, the Flood was dated at 2348 b.c. This would have left a little over a thousand years for environmental factors to have wrought changes in racial types. Such developments, in so short a time, Morton asserted, were 'a physical impossibility.'[15] Thus, if Adam had been a Caucasian, as Buffon and Blumenbach claimed, or a black, as Prichard said, and if Noah and his family kept the original racial characteristics, then an environmentalist explanation could not account for the diverse situation that came into being so soon after the Flood. The possibility that this diversity could be the result of Divine Intervention in the cursing of Ham and Canaan was to be ruled out soon by Morton and his followers.

The second and most famous part of Morton's case was his evidence that there were fixed measurable differences between the races. Morton ascertained what these were by, apparently, careful measurements of skulls in terms of characteristics and cranial capacity. (He had the largest skull collection in the world, over 600). In his original work he filled the skulls with white pepper seed, and then computed the mean internal capacity for Caucasian skulls [87], for Mongolian [83], for Malay [81], for American Indian [80], and for Ethiopian (blacks in general) [78]. Later he used shot instead of pepper seed and obtained what he regarded as more precise data.[16] (A recent study of Morton's work shows that he consciously or unconsciously skewed the data to get the results he wanted.)[17] Further, Morton claimed that precise skull measurements established that the American Indians differ from all other races, and that all of the indigenous people of the Americas, with the exception of the Eskimos, were of one race. That race included the pesky, inexplicable, Mound Builders of the Ohio River Valley.[18]

Morton did not advance any more general theory about the source of human diversity in *Crania Americana* except to insist that the diversity was fixed by the time of the Dispersion after the Tower of Babel episode. His evidence made it very difficult to reconcile a belief in the unity of mankind and an environmentalist explanation of their present diversity. Morton also continued the normative evaluation of different races that had been accepted by previous anthropologists. Caucasians were the best and were highest in intellectual endowments while Indians and Blacks rated lowest. Morton claimed that he was basing his judgments not on prejudice but solely on brain size. The great monogenecist, Prichard, had insisted that brain size did not establish anything about intelligence. Nonetheless, many ethnologists were willing to accept that brain size did establish a crucial qualitative difference. In fact, some of the Mortonites even collected data by asking living people to measure their heads and by gathering statistics about hat sizes in various cultures.[19]

Morton's effort was almost universally acclaimed by anthropologists. He went on with his researches to press the evidence that the American Indian was the same throughout North and South America, and that he constituted a unique race. Morton's results were then joined to those of the amateur Egyptologist, George Robins Gliddon, who had been the U.S. vice consul in Egypt. Gliddon had gathered skulls for Morton in Egypt. He had also told Morton of the latest findings about the antiquity of Egyptian monuments, findings that did not square with the official biblical chronology of Archbishop Ussher. On the basis of the data, Morton published *Crania Aegyptiaca* in 1844. He reiterated his claim that the cranial characteristics of racial groups, in this case Egyptians and Negroes, had stayed constant from the time of the oldest records of the human species. Morton also added a new point, namely that the Negro had been a slave from ancient times in Egypt up to the nineteenth century in America. His new scientific effort was widely hailed by the learned world. Both Prichard and Alexander von Humboldt, Morton's two leading opponents, admired the careful, scientific work involved. Morton's work established the American school of ethnology as the leader in the world.[20]

Very soon the racist element that was implicit in Morton's researches began to emerge and play a role. The Southern leader, John C. Calhoun, was so impressed by Morton's evidence that Negroes had always been the slaves and servants of Caucasians that he used some of Morton's evidence to justify retaining slavery lest the Negro be left without guidance in his naturally fixed inferior status.[21] On the other hand, von Humboldt, while admiring Morton's scientific achievement, saw the 'désolante' conclusion that would result from accepting the implied polygenesis of his view. At the end of the first volume of *Kosmos*, published in 1844, von Humboldt insisted upon the unity of the human species as the sole means of avoiding classifying people as superior and inferior and as the means of avoiding justifying slavery *ad perpetuam*.[22]

Although Morton tended to minimize the racist implications of his work in his published views, his associates, Gliddon and a Dr. Josiah Nott, from Mobile, Alabama, tended to maximize the political and irreligious social results of this new anthropology. Nott added another dimension to the overall theory in a series of articles on the danger of racial intermixture, hybridization, especially between whites and blacks. Using the very unreliable data of the 1840 census, plus surveys of his own, Nott argued that mulattoes had a higher death rate than blacks. His first anthropological article was entitled, 'The Mulatto, a Hybrid-Probable Extermination of the Two Races if the Whites and Blacks are allowed to Intermarry.'[23] Nott's aim was to establish the polygenetic claim that whites and blacks were separate species. Buffon's interfertility criterion for determining the membership in a species could be set aside, Nott believed, if he could show that the offspring of a white and a black, though fertile, were defective, and that the defects were due to the fact that the offspring were hybrid.[24]

In developing his case, Nott pressed the polygenetic aspect directly in the face of the biblical claim to the contrary. He maintained that Scripture was not a textbook on natural science. Also, Scripture was wrong or inconsistent on many details. Therefore, it did not have to be taken literally on the origins of mankind. The most plausible explanation of the diversity of man, Nott asserted, was the original and separate creation of different races. Morton's cranial researches showed the fixed features of different races over long periods of time. The results of recent Egyptological researches showed that as far back as the flood or earlier,

Negroes and Caucasians had the same features that they now possess. And now the study of the human hybrids further confirmed the polygenetic theory.[25]

Nott gave two learned lectures at Louisiana State University 'on the connection between the Biblical and physical history of man' in 1848. He called these his lectures on 'Niggerology.' In these he strongly attacked the accuracy of the Bible, and he even more strongly advocated polygenesis.[26]

At the same time an archeologist, Ephraim George Squier, published evidence based on geology and tree ring dating indicating that the Mound civilization of the Ohio River Valley was of immense antiquity. Morton's analysis of the skull remains showed that these people were American Indians. The archeological evidence indicated that these were a sedentary not migratory people. So, the obvious conclusion was that the Indians were aboriginal to America and constituted a separate species.[27]

Squier's work was very favorably received. Nott was delighted and wrote Squier that he expected him 'to give the *coup de grace* to that venerable *Hebrayist*, Moses.'[28] Morton declared that Squier's work was the most important American contribution to archeology and Von Humboldt said that it and Morton's researches represented 'the most valuable contribution ever made to the archeology and ethnology of America.'[29]

There were two further elements involved in developing the scientific core of a polygenecism that could be stated as a pre-Adamite theory completely justifying racism. The first of these was the results of the voyages of Charles Pickering, a botanist friend of Morton. Pickering travelled up and down North and South America, and through the South Pacific, coming back with evidence that there were eleven separate species of mankind. In view of the fact that his findings were published by the U.S. Government, he had to disguise his polygenetic view. Nonetheless his evidence reinforced the Mortonites. At this point Morton finally publicly asserted the polygenetic thesis as the explanation for the various findings of his friends and himself.[30]

Just as the polygenetic theory became a major matter of discussion in America, it gained a new and most important advocate, Louis Agassiz, the leading biologist of the time. In his native Switzerland he had held the theory of unity of the human species. However, he was gradually developing polygenetic views about the origins of plants and animals due to their limited local distributions in contrast to the global distribution of people. In 1848, Agassiz came to America to study fossil fishes in the New World. He went to see the celebrated Dr. Morton and his skull collection. He reported that 'Nothing else like it exists elsewhere. This collection alone is worth a journey to America.'[31] When he dined with Dr. Morton, Agassiz for the first time in his life encountered Negroes, the waiters at a restaurant. He wrote his mother that night telling her of his shock. Agassiz said that he was immediately convinced that the Negro belonged to a different species than the Caucasian, and that the Negro was naturally inferior.[32] Agassiz became a confirmed polygenecist. He stated his view in two articles in *The Christian Examiner* in 1850 on the 'Geographical Distribution of Animals' and 'The Diversity of Origin of the Human Species.' The first of these begins by stating that the common view of a monogenetic origin of all living creatures is the greatest stumbling block to investigating the laws about the distribution of organized beings on this planet. The monogenetic theory is supposed to gain its force from the Bible. 'We hope, however, to be able to show that there is no such statement in the book of Genesis; that this doctrine of a unique centre of origin and successive distribution of all animals is of very modern invention, and that it can be traced back for scarcely more than a century in the records of our science.'[33] The evidence of fossils and of geology clearly point to a polygenetic origin of plants and animals. The monogenetic view that is supposed to be in Genesis is only about those plants and animals living and growing in the proximity of Adam and Eve. Also, 'That Adam and Eve were neither the only nor the first human beings created is intimated in the statement of Moses himself.'[34] Agassiz offered the Cain story as evidence that there were other people in the world who were not descended from Adam and Eve. Thus monogenesis is not a correct interpretation of the Bible concerning the origin of plants, animals and people. It is not a sound scientific view either. The remainder of Agassiz's first article dealt with the scientific evidence for limited geographical distributions of plants and animals from early geological time to the present, and with why a polygenetic theory best explained this phenomenon. At the close he suggested that similar evidence and similar reasoning would lead to a polygenetic theory about people.[35]

The second article dealt with the human question. Agassiz insisted here, and in his talk to the American Association for the Advancement of Science later in the same year,[36] that he believed in the unity of the human race, in the sense that all people had the moral and intellectual powers that made them human, in the sense that all were in relation to the Deity, and in the sense that all had the hope of eternal life. However, unity of these types did not imply that all people had the same biological origin. The question of origin is a scientific one, and not a religious one. And, Scripture only deals with the origin of the white race, an historical race. Genesis does not discuss Asiatics, Melanesians, American Indians, and so on. It treats of whites, and of those principally the Jews. It is the task of science to explain the origins of all groups of people.[37]

Before taking up the scientific evidence for a polygenetic theory, Agassiz dealt with the charge then being made against the Mortonites, namely that a polygenetic theory tended to support slavery. Agassiz asserted that he was only interested in the scientific examination of the causes of human diversity—'let the politicians, let those who feel themselves called upon to regulate human society, see what they can do with the results.'[38] (Soon, however, we will see that Agassiz was willing to offer them advice, when he had developed the results.)

Most of Agassiz's article sets forth the case that the evidence that establishes a polygenetic theory of plants and animals also applies to people. American ethnology had proved that there were fixed human differences over recorded history. The monogenetic theory is insufficient to account for the fixed differences. Different races of men have different locations on the globe. The white race is spread over the broadest area (through exploration and colonialism). Only a polygenetic explanation is able to account for the known facts about racial characteristics and distribution.[39] Further, Agassiz asserted, there is not a single passage in the Mosaic account that states that the present human diversity comes from a primitively more uniform stock of men. The Bible, he insisted, does not describe the origins of the Chinese, the Micronesians, the Malays, the American Indians and the Negroes. The only data Agassiz could find in Scripture was the passage that said that the Ethiopian cannot change his skin, nor the leopard his spots—a line Agassiz saw as pointing to a separate origin and development of Negroes.[40]

Next Agassiz set forth the evidence for polygenesis in terms of the natural geographical distribution of races. If all of the races are different, yet all human, how do they rank? Physically Agassiz found little to choose from. However, he announced that it is obvious that the whites are superior. Agassiz said he would not discuss the political and social implications of his research. But he also declared, 'And it seems to us to be mock-philanthrophy and mock-philosophy to assume all races have the same abilities.'[41] All that one has to do is to look at the development of the various cultures. One would find, for example, that the Indian is superior to the 'submissive, obsequious, imitative negro.'[42] Agassiz ended with his opinions about Negro education. It should be adapted to their state of being rather than consisting in a training fit for whites. The Swiss biologist was definitely opposed to equality for Negroes on the grounds of his own polygenetic findings.[43]

As so many scientists in America and Europe were adopting the polygenetic theory (and usually the racism connected with it as well), many were also remembering its source, namely La Peyrère's polygenetic theory. A year after Agassiz's lectures were published, an N. L. Frothingham, who was a Unitarian minister, published a long essay in *The Christian Examiner*, entitled 'Men before Adam.' About half of the essay consisted of a defense of the views of Agassiz. The other half dealt with the story of Isaac La Peyrère's martyrdom for bringing up the pre-Adamite heresy and with an analysis of La Peyrère's *Men before Adam*. A major purpose of Frothingham's article was to remind people that the supposition that Adam was not the first man was not a new one, but rather went back to La Peyrère in the seventeenth century.[44] The point of recovering a past hero, La Peyrère, was not to claim that he had already advanced the theory of the Mortonites with its great detail in terms of skull measurements, analysis of hybrids, fixity of species, etc. Instead to point out that the polygenetic theory had already been presented in rudimentary form two hundred years earlier was to give the theory a significant history and a martyr-hero from almost the same epoch as Galileo. Also, by starting the consideration of the theory from its 'theological' form in La Peyrère's work, one could then portray how it developed into the wonderful 'scientific' theory of the American ethnologists.

A few years before Frothingham's essay, John Pye Smith, in *On the Relation Between the Holy Scriptures and some parts of Geological Science*, had quoted La Peyrère, and described how he was persecuted by the church for his views.[45] And, when the great Dr. Morton died, Dr. Henry S. Patterson wrote a memoir of him. When he came to the polygenetic theory, he said, 'The unity and common origin of mankind have, until recently, been considered undisputed points of doctrine....It is curious that the only attack made upon this dogma, until of late, was made from a theological, and not from a scientific statement.' Dr. Patterson then told the sad story of what had happened to La Peyrère and his book.[46] In both England and America scholars were making La Peyrère into the Galileo of anthropology.[47]

What was probably the high point in American polygenetic theorizing appeared in the memorial volume to Dr. Samuel Morton, *Types of Mankind*, put together by Nott and Gliddon. When Morton died in 1851, the *Charleston Medical Journal*, probably the leading contemporary medical journal in the South, carried an obituary by R. W. Gibbes. It started out, 'The death of this eminent man leaves a large void in the world of science ... Among the scientific men of our country, he was most prominent in the first rank ... we have the most distinguished authority for saying that abroad he was considered the first in Ethnology ... We mourn his loss as a National bereavement.'[48] The *New York Tribune* said, 'probably no scientific man in America enjoyed a higher reputation among scholars throughout the world than Dr. Morton.'[49]

Later on Gibbes made clear what he believed was Morton's major contribution. 'Of his labours in Ethnology, we trust an extended memoir will be published with the work upon which he has been for sometime engaged. For the present, we can only say that we of the South should consider him as our benefactor, for aiding most materially in giving the negro his true position as an inferior race. We believe the time is not far distant, when it will be universally admitted that neither can the leopard change his spots, nor the Ethiopian his skin.'[50]

In the memorial volume, *Types of Mankind*, the various scientific claims of the Mortonites were put together into a massive case for both polygenesis and for the ranking of the races. Cranial, archeological, geological and biblical research were all joined together. There was even a posthumous paper by Morton which strongly advocated a pre-Adamite, polygenetic point of view. The book contains the results of several lines of research justifying a polygenetic theory of the origins and development of the human species. The Bible is attacked for not being an adequate history of mankind. And lastly, the volume advocated, on the basis of the findings set forth, a thoroughgoing racism against Negroes.[51] In Dr. Patterson's memoir, which starts the volume, it is recounted how Morton changed from being a typical Bible-accepting monogenecist to becoming the leader of the American school of ethnology. A letter of Morton's to Gliddon in 1846 is cited. Both of them were disturbed that the great Alexander von Humboldt had called Morton's views 'désolante.' Morton commented to Gliddon,

> Humboldt's word *désolante* is true in sentiment and in morals—but, as you observe, it is wholly inapplicable to the physical reality. Nothing so humbles, so crushes my spirit, as to look into a mad-house, and behold the drivelling, brutal idiocy so conspicuous in such places; it conveys a terrific idea of the disparity of human intelligence. But there is the unyielding, insuperable reality. It is so *désolante* indeed to think, to *know*, that many of these poor mortals were born, were created so, but it appears to me to make little difference in the sentiment of the question whether they came into the world without their wits, or whether they lost them afterwards. And so, I would add, it makes little difference whether the mental inferiority of the Negro, the Samoiyede or the Indian, is natural or acquired; for if they ever possessed equal intelligence with the Caucasian, they have lost it; and if they never had it, they had nothing to lose. One party would arraign Providence for creating originally different, another for placing them in circumstances by which they inevitably became so. Let us search out the truth and reconcile it afterwards.[52]

The Southern magazine, *De Bow's Review*, contains many articles on the work of the Mortonites, almost always favorable. A political question that De Bow was concerned with was whether Negroes could be educated and whether they really could be members of the *polis*. De Bow's answer was no. He used the example of Haiti as a dreadful reminder of what happens when blacks try to run a country.[53] As Morton had pointed out it did not matter whether blacks were born inferior, or if they acquired this status. The issue was that on the basis of ethnological findings blacks were irremediably inferior.

From about 1840 onward, the Mortonites had been opposed by scientists like von Humboldt and Prichard. They both saw monogenecism as the only way of avoiding the racist conclusion of the Mortonites and the justification of slavery in the United States. Morton and his supporters dismissed this objection as a moral one rather than a scientific conclusion. Others, especially some Southern ministers, fought back. The Reverend John Bachman wrote *The Doctrine of the Unity of the Human Race Examined on the Principles of Science*.[54] The Reverend Thomas Smyth wrote *The Unity of the Human Race Proved to Be the Doctrine of Scripture, Reason and Sciences*. In this work, Smyth declared that the theory of human diversity, 'overthrows not only Moses, but the prophets and apostles also, and thus undermines the Scriptures as a divine record, both of doctrines and duties. It was for this purpose the theory was introduced by Voltaire, Rousseau, and Peyrère, and it is for this purpose it is wielded by Paine, Drake, Dr. Nott and others.'[55] The Reverend William T. Hamilton wrote, *The Friend of Moses, or A Defense of the Pentateuch*. But the ministers usually were overwhelmed by the enormous quantity of scientific data offered by their opponents. The Reverend Hamilton resorted to appealing to the fact that there are intelligent Negroes. In fact, he said, he had met one on a riverboat.[56] Frederick Douglass got into the argument and appealed to his own case. He was black. He wrote books, gave speeches, and seemed to be as rational as any white. Douglass, in a speech given at Western Reserve College in 1854, entitled 'The Claims of the Negro Ethnologically Considered,' attacked the findings and claims of Morton, Nott, Gliddon and Agassiz.[57] He made the following argument:

> Human rights stand upon a common basis; and by all the reason that they are supported, maintained and defended, for one variety of the human family, they are supported, maintained and defended for *all* the human family; because all mankind have the same wants, arising out of a common nature. A diverse origin does not disprove a common nature, nor does it disprove a united destiny. The essential characteristics of humanity are everywhere the same. In the language of the eloquent *Curran*, 'No matter what complexion, whether an Indian or an African sun has burnt upon him,' his title deed to freedom, his claim to life and to liberty, to knowledge and to civilization, to society and to Christianity, are just and perfect. It is registered in the Courts of Heaven, and is enforced by the eloquence of the God of all the earth.[58]

Regardless of the opposition, Morton and his followers would probably have won the argument if it had been only a scientific dispute. They
had a very elegant hypothesis that accounted for an enormous range of
data. However, their theory also had strong racist implications, as well
as rejecting some major scriptural doctrines. The latter point led to a
general rejection of pre-Adamism and polygenesis among intellectuals in
the southern parts of the United States. Apparently they wanted their
own racism consonant with the Bible. Thus, the explanation of black inferiority that was based on the curse of Ham was more satisfactory to
most literate Southerners and Mortonism was largely rejected in the
ante-bellum South.

While Mortonism was dying in America, some new polygenetic
theories emerged in England causing a row over the pre-Adamite theory
during the 1850s and 1860s among the English and French anthropologists and archeologists. In a book by Edward William Lane,
edited by his nephew, Reginald Stuart Poole, keeper of the Egyptology
section of the British Museum, entitled *The Genesis of the Earth and of Man:
A Critical Examination of Passages in the Hebrew and Greek Scriptures, chiefly
with a view to the Solution of the Question whether the Varieties of the Human
Species be of more than one Origin*, of 1856, a wide variety of kinds of data
from the Bible, from geology, from ethnology, zoology, botany,
philology and Egyptology was integrated to set forth a polygenetic view.[59]
Poole in the preface states:

> It is also important to notice, that if certain of the opinions expressed in the
> following work be correct, they remove one of the chief causes of modern
> skepticism, and lay a new foundation for primieval history.... The cause of
> skepticism to which I allude is the difficulty of reconciling the received
> explanation of Bible-history with the physical and historical evidences of the
> existence of more than one race of mankind, or of reconciling any Bible-
> chronology with the existence of one race during a period of enormous
> duration, which in this case is held to be required for the development of
> its varieties and their language. Hence, some persons who would regard the
> theory of a plurality of origins with a religious aversion have not scrupled
> to abandon a belief in the early history of Scriptures.[60]

Poole and Lane summarized previous evidence, and then used the latest
findings dating Egyptian monuments as decisive.

One Isabella Duncan published *Pre-Adamite Man, or the Story of our Planet
and its Inhabitants told by Scripture and Science*. The work went through three
editions by 1860. By then she felt it necessary to insist that her theory was
original, and was not taken from 'the theological lubrications of Isaac de
Peyrère.' She claimed his work was only brought to her notice after her
book was close to completion.[61] In the preface she wrote, 'Pre-Adamite
man! The idea suggested by this title would, till lately, only have excited

a smile; and on this, as on most subjects some ridiculous absurdities have been written. Isaac de Peyrère, about two hundred years ago, maintained with many arguments, that St. Paul affirms the existence of a pre-Adamite race.'[62] Duncan, however, developed her case by using some of the usual scientific evidence, plus what were to be the most important data in dealing with the subject, namely the data about pre-historic animals and people. Another contemporaneous work also stressed this theme. Pascal Beverly Randolph's *Pre-Adamite Man: The Story of the Human Race, from 35,000 to 100,000 years ago*, first published in 1863, had a frontispiece purporting to show a 'Sketch of an undoubted Pre-Adamite skull now in the possession of the London Geological Society.' The skull was supposed to be 100,000 years old. Randolph dedicated his book to 'Honest Abraham Lincoln, President of the United States, as a Testimonial of my Gratitude for his efforts to save the Nation and widen the area of Human Freedom,' and 'to the thinking men and women of our grand but distracted nation, East as well as South, North as well as West.'[63]

Remains of pre-historic animals had been coming to light from the mid-eighteenth century. In the first part of the nineteenth century a French abbé, Jacques Boucher de Perthes, began finding human remains embedded in chalk. By dating the pre-historic animal remains, he obtained ages for the human bones that were quite old. Throughout his life, he insisted that the bones he was finding, as well as the remains of early animals, were ante-deluvian rather than pre-Adamite. If the date of the Flood were moved backward, these findings could fit with the Bible. Naturally, both the religious and scientific authorities refused to accept the abbé's findings. It was only in the second half of the nineteenth century that Boucher de Perthes' work was taken seriously. Then his results suddenly led to finding older and older human remains, dating back hundred of thousands of years.[64]

An example of integrating these results with Scripture is a work by Nemo (W. Moore), entitled *Man: Palaelithic, Neolithic and Several other Races, not inconsistent with Scripture* (1876).[65] The author dated Palaelithic man at 350,000 250,000 years ago, Neolithic man at 50,000 years ago, and Adam at 6,000 years ago. He explained that 'The creations of pre-Adamite man were not unrevealed. They will be found distinctly stated in the first chapter of Genesis; their dominion allotted to them, and their authority prescribed.'[66]

Until recent geological, anthropological research the belief was almost universal that the earth and all its contents were created in six days and that all mankind was descended from Adam and Eve. Nemo, by changing days to eons, changed the time span. After five days, the pre-Adamite period began. This was the age of pre-historic man, as well as of the mammoth. This was the Palaelithic and Neolithic age. The sixth day in Genesis encompasses all of this, since it was 3,000,000 years long.[67] Then, in the chapter on 'Adam and his Dominion,' we are told that 'The Mosaic record thenceforward relates chiefly and almost exclusively to that family, and to their direct descendants, and is silent on the general subject of the other races of mankind—the Palaelithic and Neolithic man.'[68] This would not have been a problem, he thought, if the two biblical creation stories had been properly separated, so that one was about mankind in general and the other about the Adam and Eve family. Another indication of the way the polygenetic theory of the American School and the accumulating evidence about the age and nature of mankind were joined appears in the initial studies of the Anthropological Society of London. The Society was formed in 1863. The introductory address by its founder and president, James Hunt, took up as one of the matters to be considered the serious charge against the American School of Anthropology, namely 'that their interest in keeping up slavery in- duced the scientific men of that country to advocate a distinct origin for the African race.' Hunt said he believed the charge was 'gross calumny.' He went on to declare that even if it could be demonstrated that the Negro was descended from the ape a few generations back, this would not change the fact that the Negro is now a man and deserves to be treated as such. Then, Hunt said, 'I would therefore express a hope that the objects of this Society will never be prostituted to such an object as the support of the slave-trade, with all of its abuses; but at the same time we must not shrink from the candid avowal of what we believe to be the real place in nature, or in society, of the African or any other race.'[69]

In keeping with this closing remark, Hunt published his most famous work, 'On the Negro's Place in Nature,' in the first issue of the *Memoirs read before the Anthropological Society of London* in 1863. Using English and American data, Hunt concluded that the Negro was a separate species, and also an inferior one, unfit for civilization as we understand it. Hunt's racist evaluation of the status of Negroes was approximately the same as that of the Americans. He was a polygenecist who also saw that even if the African were shown to be inferior he could still have the normal social opportunities of the rest of us. However, since enslavement of Africans was over in England, Hunt, unlike the Americans, did not have to make political cause out of his finding.[70]

It is also of interest that the *Anthropological Review*, which Hunt ran with an iron-hand, had quite a few references to Isaac La Peyrère as the revered father of this new science of man. In an anonymous essay entitled 'Notes on the Antiquity of Man' (probably by Hunt), in Volume I, a couple of pages are devoted to recording La Peyrère's pre-Adamite theory, and to telling the sad story of his arrest and forced recantation.' 'There is no doubt that poor Peyrère was much in advance of his times, and therefore fair game for persecution.'[71] One of the vice-presidents of the Anthropological Society, Thomas Bendysche, presented a memoir to the Society on 'The History of Anthropology,' in which La Peyrère was discussed for two pages.[72] Bendysche had looked into a lot of the material discussing the reception and rejection of *Prae-Adamitae*. He showed how prejudiced the opposition was. Then, appended to his history, Bendysche included a translation of the Fabricius-Rumpf reply to La Peyrère and a reprinting of the anonymous polygenetic *Essays sent in a Letter from Oxford to a Nobleman in London.*[73] In the second volume of the *Anthropological Review* a really worshipful tribute to La Peyrère appeared. It is by 'Philalethes' and is entitled 'Peyrèreius, and Theological Criticism.' It begins, 'After two centuries of neglect and oblivion, the name of Isaac de la Peyrère is once more received and honoured, as that of the first scholar who broke through the meshes of groundless traditional preju- dice, and proved that even in Scripture there are no decisive evidences of man's descent from a single pair; nay more, that there are distinct in- dications of non-Adamite races.'[74]

Philalethes outlined La Peyrère's theory as based on his interpretation of St. Paul's Roman, 5: 12:14. Then he proclaimed:

> Peyrère was two centuries before his time; and whether we accept or reject his special theories; it is impossible not to admire his acumen, his candour, and his courage. Like all people who are wiser, fairer, and more keen- sighted than their contemporaries, he was of course persecuted and rendered as miserable as his theological adversaries, with their three favorite weapons—persecution, imprisonment, and fire—had it in their power to make him. He had dared to step out of the magic exegetical circle which theology had drawn around all the sciences, and his presumption was punished with prompt violence.[75]

Then Philalethes told the story of La Peyrère's martyrdom and com- pared him to Galileo. The attacks on La Peyrère were briefly surveyed.[76] With regard to one opponent, J. Heidegger, Philalethes said 'The name of Peyrère will be reverenced when that of Heidegger is reposing in venerable dust.'[77] Next Dr. Smyth was attacked for calling La Peyrère a free-thinker. Philalethes went so far as to declare 'For Peyrère was the most devout, the most earnest believer *in the inspiration of every word of Scripture.*'[78] Then the nasty way La Peyrère was treated was compared with how the opponents of Dr. Morton, namely Dr. Bachman and Dr. Smyth treated the great ethnologist in the middle of the nineteenth cen- tury. All of this is part of the warfare between religion and science. And it is still going on in the fight against Boucher de Perthes.[79] The article ends saying that, 'It is ever thus; the thought of the solitary thinker in his closet is stronger than priests and princes; is omnipotent even against the banded conspiracies of the whole world's prejudice and interest.'[80]

The only monogenecist that Philalethes spoke about positively was the leading French anthropologist, A. de Quatrefages, 'who is tolerant, because he is scientific, and courteous because he is not ignorant.'[81] Quatrefages, who became professor of anthropology at the Museum of Natural History in Paris, had surveyed the argument of the polygenecists in his essay, 'Histoire naturelle de l'homme. Unité de l'éspèce humaine' of 1860,[82] tracing the dispute back to La Peyrère and summarizing the seventeenth century pre-Adamite theory, including its Jewish Messianic element. Though one is struck by the similarity of La Peyrère's point with current opinions, he wrote, one has to remember that La Peyrère 'est un théologian, un croyant, qui admet comme vrai tout ce qui est dans la Bible et les miracles en particulier ... En un mot, on trouve partout chez La Peyrère un mélange de foi complete et de libre critique. Ce livre du reste ne convainquit personne, et la doctrine de l'auteur retomba bientôt dans l'oubli jusqu'à ces dernières années, époque où on l'a réproduite et accueillie avec une faveur assez inattendue, principalement en Amerique.'[83]

Quartrefages went on to say that the basic problem had changed from a theological one to an anthropological one in the eighteenth century, dealing, for example, with whether Hottentots, Laplanders and Blacks are separate species. In America a new form of pre-Adamism developed in order to justify slavery. He referred to Morton and Nott, and mentioned that John Calhoun had used their material in arguing for the slave owners' case. So it has come about, Quatrefages reported, that those who believe the unity of mankind are abolitionists, and the polygenecists, especially in America, are pro-slavery. And that is what has become of 'la doctrine de La Peyrère.'[84] These comments were used as part of the introduction to his *Unité de l'Espèce humaine*, published first in 1861, and often reprinted in French and English thereafter.

The last European work of the time that we will briefly mention is Dominick McCausland's, *Adam and the Adamite; or the Harmony of Scripture and Ethnology* (1868). In the book he contended that recent geology and paleontology require that the Mosaic chronology be extended. In so doing, he said, the assumption of a pre-Adamite race was not inconsistent with either the New or Old Testament. People could be of one blood without being of one ancestry. The Bible is just the history of one particular race, the Adamites. For all sorts of reasons, it is obvious the Negroes are non-Adamites. 'Thus, when Scriptures are sifted, nothing appears that directly or implicitly warrants the position that Adam was the first of created human beings on earth.' Adam was the last 'item of creation and the first Caucasian.' And so the distinction between pre-Adamite and Adamite again becomes a racist one.[85]

However, this racist pre-Adamism that the Mortonites had developed so strongly was swept aside by the emergence of Darwinism. Darwin was well versed in the writings of Morton, Nott and Gliddon, and, of course, Agassiz who was to be his life long opponent. His explanation of diversity among the species was far more comprehensive than theirs. His account denied Agassiz's theory of the existence of fixed primordial species. Darwin not only offered a more successful theory but one that was at greater variance with the traditionally held sense of Scripture. Yet the theory of Social Darwinism could supply a basis for a racist position. In terms of the survival of the fittest doctrine, the American Indians and Negro slaves were hardly fittest for they were being dominated and destroyed by the American Caucasians.

While Darwinism replaced pre-Adamism, the lasting legacy of La Peyrère's theory in its American form was the acceptance of pre-history as a legitimate classification. As a result of this, there were many by the late nineteenth century for whom Adam was not a real historical personage. As discoveries of prehistoric men 10,000 years old and 25,000 years old occurred, pre-Adamism became a tame view. So, in 1879, *Scribner's* magazine could publish a serious article giving both sides of the question, 'Was Adam the First Man?'[86]

The last American 'scientific' work on the subject I have come across is a very large volume by a Professor Alexander Winchell of the University of Michigan, entitled *Preadamites: or a Demonstration of the Existence of Men before Adam; together with a study of their condition, antiquity, racial affinities, and progressive dispersion over the earth. With Charts and other Illustrations* (1880). (There were five editions by 1890. The illustrations include photographs of some pre-Adamites—a Dravidian, a Mongol, a Negro, an Eskimo, a Hottentot, a Papuan, and an Australian aborigine.)[87]

Winchell employed the data of the Mortonites, of the English anthropologists, and of brain measurements. (A professor at Cornell, instead of measuring crania, had measured actual brains.)[88] Winchell came to the conclusion both that Negroes were inferior and that they were from a non-Adamic race that is closer to the chimpanzee.[89] (There is a book of the period that is far worse than Winchell's by a Professor Charles Carroll of St. Louis, called *'The Negro a Beast' or 'In the Image of God. ... The Negro and his Relation to the Human Family. The Negro a beast, but created with articulate speech and hands, that he may be of service to his master—the White Man. The Negro not the Son of Ham.*)[90] The Negro, Winchell concluded has 'the curiousity of the child: he has a feeble power of combining his perceptions and drawing conclusions. In abstract conceptions he is still more helpless; no American Negro has ever produced any original work in mathematics or philosophy; the imaginative and aesthetic powers are similarly dormant; poetry, sculpture, painting, owe almost nothing to Negro genius.' After saying this, Winchell cited President Thomas Jefferson to support his case.[91]

Winchell used the best results of 19th century anthropology and archeology in order to justify his racism. Nonetheless he saw that the original crucial core of his theory came from Isaac La Peyrère. In chapter xxix, La Peyrère is made the seminal founder of pre-Adamism. Winchell repeated the story of La Peyrère's publication of his book and of his martyrdom. (By then some of the basic facts were becoming garbled. The hero, Peyrerius, is now 'a Dutch ecclesiastic.') Because he was persecuted, 'the work of honest Peyrerius was left to be remembered and mentioned only as the impious madness of one of the enemies of religion.' 'Peyrerius, nevertheless, was less impious and mad than the bond slaves of dogma who silenced his tongue. His sagacity surpassed his age; and I have come not to bury him, but to honor him.'[92] After this Winchell went on to show the very important role that the pre-Adamite theory had played in nineteenth century thought.[93]

Although by the turn of the century most anthropologists and biologists were Darwinists and accepted a prehistorical theory about the development of the human species, there were nevertheless some twentieth century scientists who continued to try to establish the biological inferiority of Negroes and other people of color, if not on pre-Adamitic grounds, at least on genetic ones. A collection of writings by professors and politicians from 1890 to the 1930s defending segregation shows the combination of the kinds of explanations offered in the polygenetic-racist traditions in America.[94] Professor Edward M. East, a professor at Harvard, published *Heredity and Human Affairs* in 1935.[95] The work purports to be a simple presentation of modern genetics. In dealing with 'Some Specific Race Problems,' East discussed why the negro is mentally inferior to the white. He quoted at length from T. A. Joyce's article 'Negro' in the eleventh edition of the *Encyclopaedia Brittanica*. Joyce had offered two explanations of the so-called phenomenon, namely that Negro brain growth is 'arrested by the premature closing of the cranial sutures and lateral pressure of the frontal bone,' and two, 'that after puberty sexual matters take the first place in the negro's life and thoughts.'[96] The issue of the negro's brain was discussed by Dr. Robert Bennett Bean, 'Some Racial Peculiarities of the Negro Brain' published in 1906.[97] After analyzing all sorts of statistical data comparing white and black achievements, East stated that 'the negro as a social group has produced but one man who would be placed among the first 15,000 to 20,000 Great Ones on Earth, as judged by the usual standards.' The one person was Alexandre Dumas, who, East quickly pointed out, was at most one quarter black. He went on to admit generously that there were probably twenty-five persons who are black who have produced decent intellectual or artistic work which would rank on the fourth or fifth level below true greatness. East reported that as far as he could find out, all of these people were mixed bloods with one possible exception,[98] asserting, 'The obvious conclusion from these facts and figures, therefore, is that the gene-packets of African origin are not valuable supplements to the gene-packets of European origin. It is the white germ-plasm that counts.'[99] Even today, there are some researchers again attempting to show that there is a basic or genetic factor that makes black intellectual inferiority a fixed feature of the human scene.

Thus, as we have seen, the benign polygenetic theory of La Peyrère quickly was adopted to justify slavery in America. In the nineteenth century, under the leadership of Dr. Morton, an up-to-date, much more detailed, polygenetic theory became one of the bases for American racism. The advocates of this view saw La Peyrère as their noble, heroic ancestor who was martyred for telling the truth.

Many of the American polygenecists thought that their conclusions justified white supremacy. With the appearance of Darwinism the new pre-Adamism started to disappear. But, unfortunately, the use of the latest developments in biology and anthropology to provide a justification for racism still appears to be going on.[100]

CHAPTER ELEVEN

LA PEYRÈRE'S LEGACY IN THE TWENTIETH CENTURY

The intellectual drama that began with the publication of Isaac La Peyrère's pre-Adamite theory has gone on, as we believe the previous chapters have shown, for more than three centuries. La Peyrère's views, novel for his time, have had a striking influence, especially on theology and on anthropology. While claiming that he was only trying to buttress his contention that the Jewish Messiah was about to arrive, and accomplishing this by isolating the Bible as the history of the Jews and by questioning its authorship and authenticity, La Peyrère inaugurated some great challenges to the then accepted view of the origin of man and man's role on earth. Basic aspects of accepted religious dogma had to be reconsidered. And a wide ranging re-examination of the nature of man, as found in the four corners of the earth, had to take place.

We have traced how La Peyrère's views influenced the development of biblical criticism and how they played an important role in the rise of the science of anthropology. His views also had some impact on certain strange philosemitic, Messianic theories. However, now that some of what La Peyrère said has been absorbed into the accepted views of intelligent people in the twentieth century, and some has been replaced by more up-to-date theories about the nature of man and the nature of the Bible, he himself has pretty well passed into oblivion. He is remembered, if at all, as either a bizarre theologian or as a minor *libertin* or both. But, even if La Peyrère is practically forgotten, some of the issues he raised are still being debated, sometimes in a new context and sometimes in one that retains some of the original material.

A little over a century ago, a German theologian, Otto Zöchler, who had written a history of creation theories, published an article (in 1876) on 'Peyrère's (gest. 1676) Praadamitenhypothese nach ihren Beziehungen zu den anthropologischen Fragen den Gegenwart.' The article appeared in a Lutheran theological journal. It showed the concern that nineteenth century theologians in various countries had about dealing with La Peyrère's theory.[1] This was the period when Darwinism and the notion of prehistoric man had to be digested. A more striking version of the lingering problem of coming to terms with the legacy of La Peyrère appears in some of the Catholic encyclopedias in our century. The English language *Catholic Encyclopedia* of 1911 published an article by A. J. Maas on 'Preadamites.'[2] The term is defined as referring to 'the supposed inhabitants of the earth prior to Adam.' We are then told that the priority does not really matter. Coadamites are like pre-Adamites, if they are descended from a stock that is older than Adam. It is admissable for religious believers, Maas said, to accept that there were human beings prior to Adam, provided those human beings were extinct by the time that God created Adam. A couple of theologians are cited as saying that there is nothing wrong with believing in the past existence of such pre-Adamites and that it is even probable that there were such beings. However, the polygenetic pre-Adamite view, which holds that the people existing before Adam also went on and co-existed with Adam, is labelled as heretical. Maas next divides this heretical view into two types of pre-Adamism, scientific and scriptural.[3]

The scientific view is about prehistoric people. Maas insisted that 'There are no scientific arguments which prove directly that the progeny of a Preadamite race coexisted with the descendants of Adam.'[4] The possibility that *Scribner's Magazine* had earlier raised, namely whether Adam had ever really existed, was not considered here. Instead the focus was put on whether the scientific evidence of the great antiquity of the human species, or the multiplicity of the human species, indicated that pre-Adamites existed. The author insisted that such a conclusion depended on a non-scientific premise. The variety of human beings is no evidence that they do not come from a common stock. The evidence of paleontology does not actually show that the human race existed before biblical times. So, this sort of data is insufficient to establish either polygenesis or pre-Adamism.[5]

With regard to scriptural pre-Adamism, we are first told that it is doubtful if the Church Father, Origen, believed in it. (He believed in the pre-existence of souls.) However, there is no doubt that Julian the Apostate (who returned to paganism after the Emperor Constantine had made the Roman Empire officially Christian) was an adherent of pre-Adamism. These early cases are not particularly interesting. The important version of this view is that of Isaac La Peyrère. A detailed summary of La Peyrère's theory was presented starting from his analysis of biblical passages. Maas continued, 'But La Peyrère's proofs are not solid,' and, writing in 1911, took up La Peyrère's questions about Cain, Cain's wife, and Romans 5: 12-14, showing that La Peyrère could be successfully answered on each of these points. It was explained, for example, that Cain killed Abel one hundred and thirty years after Adam had been driven out of Paradise. In that time interval 'the progeny of Adam must have amounted to several thousand souls.' La Peyrère's appeal to ancient Jewish Kabbalistic stories about Adam or to Moslem ones had been rejected by Richard Simon. 'It is, therefore, not astonishing that La

Peyrère's Preadamism proved to be a nine days' wonder and did not survive its author.'⁶ Yet this, as we have seen, was not the case, even if the discussion was limited to just the biblical points raised by La Peyrère. Many of them became basic elements in biblical criticism.

The encyclopedia article went on to list some of La Peyrère's seventeenth-century opponents. Then the author turned to a political or social pre-Adamism which, he said, was introduced by Dominic McCausland and Reginald Stuart Poole, following the ethnological views of Morton, Nott, Gliddon and Agassiz. They changed the pre-Adamite theory, so that Adam became the first Caucasian. Every non-Caucasian was then a pre-Adamite. On this basis 'The pro-slavery sentiment prevalent in certain parts of America indirectly supported such Preadamite theories.' Since Winchell's book is listed in the bibliography, Maas clearly knew of the racist application of the theory, though writing 45 years after the Civil War.⁷

A much longer article by E. Amann, on 'Préadamites,' appears in the *Dictionnare de Théologie Catholique* of 1933, in which there is also a strictly biographical one on La Peyrère and a most interesting one on polygenesis. The article on the pre-Adamites gives a very detailed, lengthy summary of La Peyrère's views as the beginnings of 'La Preadamisme Scripturaire.' Then we are told of various Catholics and Protestants who rejected the theory and denounced the author. The final page of the article is devoted to what was still bothering people about the possibility that there were men before Adam, namely the recent scientific evidence. The discovery of pre-historic man posed serious problems.⁸ The article on polygenesis treats the subject from Isaac La Peyrère to Teilhard de Chardin and shows possible heretical interpretations. It then tries to show some views about the subject that are compatible with Catholicism, or that should be so considered.⁹ One of these, as we are told in the article on pre-Adamites, is to separate prehistoric man from Adamic man. This time it is stated that we cannot be sure that primitive man has disappeared. We also cannot be sure when our ancestor, homo sapiens, entered the world. On this dubious note, the author closed by saying, 'Et donc, s'il revenait au monde, Isaac de La Peyrère aurait bien des motifs de retoucher son *Systema theologianicum*, mais il aurait la satisfaction aussi de constater qu'il avait bien quelque raison, quoi qu'il en soit de la solution imaginée par lui, de poser le problème et d'y chercher une réponse.'¹⁰

The more recent Catholic encyclopedia, the *Enciclopedia Cattolica* of 1952, has no article on the pre-Adamites, and refers people instead to the article 'Poligenismo,' which starts with a lot of the historical material about La Peyrère taken over from the *Dictionnarie de Théologie Catholique*.

The article deals with recent material about polygenesis. A good deal of literature is cited showing that, as of about 1950, it was a very live issue among Catholic thinkers as to whether the unity of the human race could be sustained.[11]

To finish the story of the modern Catholic concern with issues raised by La Peyrère, the *New Catholic Encyclopedia* has a brief article on pre-Adamites. It is first indicated that current anthropological evidence shows that man arose on earth from forty thousand to perhaps a million years ago. Next a brief summary of La Peyrère's views is given. Then we are told that as a result of La Peyrère, theologians specified that the unity of the human race is genetic. Also, it is asserted that, 'Neither Scripture nor the teachings of the Church denies the possibility of preadamites' as long as the preadamites did not survive after Adam. 'Any preadamite hypothesis must allow in some way for the doctrine of original sin and the unity of the present human race.' This suggests that by the middle of the twentieth century, pre-Adamism was no longer regarded as much of a threat.[12] Probably the principal reason, as we learn from the article 'Polygenism,' by the same author is that Pope Pius XII in 1950 said 'that one is not bound to the biological pre-suppositions of the inspired writers.'[13] But, nonetheless, Pius XII insisted that polygenicism was not an acceptable Catholic view. He called polygenicism a conjectural view rather than a false or heretical one, however. He did not say anything about pre-Adamites. The article ends on an uncertain note to the effect that 'There does not seem to be a complete and definitive answer in the vexed problem of human origins on this earth.'[14]

The material in these twentieth century Catholic encyclopedias indicates that the question of whether pre-Adamism could be true or even possible is still disturbing theologians. Joined with the evidence discovered by recent anthropology, this has kept one portion of La Peyrère's views a live issue. Also the monogenetic stand the Church took in the sixteenth and seventeenth centuries in the face of the Spanish and Portuguese mistreatment of Indians and blacks has remained a very important view not only for combating racism but also for understanding the nature of man in biblical terms. Hence, it has been and continues to be a very serious hope on the part of the theologians that the best scientific opinion will support monogenesis, as seems to be the case at the present time.

If Catholic theology shows traces in the current world of still being haunted by La Peyrère's theses in a modern form (after all they do discuss pre-Adamism as a living issue), there is less overt sign of this among the Protestants. The large Hastings' *Encyclopedia of Religion* does not cover 'La Peyrère,' or 'pre-Adamism.' Polygenesis is briefly and neutrally discussed as a possible explanation of modern anthropological data. By extension one might say that some of the living issues for Protestant fundamentalism are versions of issues raised by La Peyrère. The fundamentalist insistence on the literal reading of Scripture grew in large measure from the kind of biblical criticism that La Peyrère started. Two centers of this view indicate a bit of his legacy. The official seminary of the Missouri Synod Lutheran Church, Concordia Seminary in St. Louis, Missouri broke apart in the early 1970s over whether teachers and students could use data and interpretative techniques to understand Scripture. The fundamentalists rejected all kinds of literary, metaphorical, allegorical, and historical methods. In so doing they won the fight politically and have forced the modernists out. The fight involved questions raised by La Peyrère such as whether Moses wrote the Pentateuch, whether we have an accurate copy, whether the Flood could have covered the whole earth, and so on.

In the last several years a fundamentalist group has arisen that is attempting to show that their view of the origin of man is at least as verifiable as the contemporary secular view of man and his place in the world that is taught as the theory of evolution. The Creation Research Center of El Cajon, California, one of the more vociferous fundamentalist groups, has been arguing against the scientific merits of the Darwinian theory of evolution and against prehistorical anthropology. (They do not seem to have heard of the pre-Adamite theory.) In trying to show that the evolutionists and prehistorians have not scientifically proven their case, they contend arguments for the creationists are as good or better than for the evolutionists. Presently the Creation Research Center is demanding that their theory, biblical creation, be taught co-equally with the biologists' and anthropologists' theory in the U. S. public school system. And in early 1983 a meeting was held at Hebrew University, sponsored by the Israeli Ministry of Education, and the Israel Academy of Sciences, at which the leaders of the Creation Research Center and a group of orthodox Jewish scientists joined in condemning Darwinism as scientifically inadequate, and advocating the teaching of the biblical creation story instead. The next step in the argument is to insist that the scales actually tip in the direction of the creationist case, because the Bible, their source, is constantly being shown to be true about various matters. A favorite point is that a large wooden object has been identified in a glacier on Mt. Ararat. Expeditions have tried and failed to reach it, aerial surveys have been made, reports of climbers correlated and analyzed, all in an attempt to establish that the wooden object is what is left of Noah's Ark (which the Bible says landed on Mount Ararat). If this could be done convincingly, then the credibility of the whole of the Bible would be greatly increased. Reasonable men, then, could accept the scriptural account as more likely than others.[15] At that point the intellectual world would be turned back to what it was like before Isaac La Peyrère. So the basic problems posed by La Peyrère still reverberate among fundamentalist Protestants though they may not have heard of him or his theory.

La Peyrère was, as we have seen, most concerned about how he was considered by the Jews. On one level he is an object of interest among Jewish scholars. Of the people who have written on him in this century, the largest group are Jews.[16] Some are fascinated by his philosemitism. Others believe that he was a secret Jew (a Marrano). Still others are struck by the apparent link between his Bible criticism and that of Spinoza. Still others see the relationship between La Peyrère and Menasseh ben Israel as of some significance. Some know of La Peyrère principally as one of the earliest advocates of Zionism. In his Messianic view the Jews would return to Palestine (after they had joined with the Christians in France), and would rebuild Jerusalem. An early major history of Zionism, written by one of the then prominent leaders of the movement, Nahum Sokolow, describes those elements of La Peyrère's theory that have been incorporated in modern Zionism; H. J. Schoeps also portrayed him as a precursor of Herzl's Zionist views.[17]

I have also encountered a fundamentalistic Jewish reaction to La Peyrère's pre-Adamism much like that of the Protestant fundamentalists. Some years ago I gave a talk on La Peyrère in Jerusalem. At the end of the talk, a rabbi who had been sitting directly in front of me, got up and said, 'I don't know who this Professor Popkin is, or who this La Peyrère was. But if there was such a person, and if he really said that Adam was not the first man and that Moses did not write the Pentateuch, then this La Peyrère should be forgotten and should never be mentioned again.' The rabbi proceeded to declare that if he did not believe that Adam was the first man and Moses was the author of the Torah, he, the rabbi, would have no reason for living. At that point, he walked out. Obviously for him and probably many others, the literal truth of Scripture is still the keystone of the edifice of belief.[18]

An elegant attempt to save the Pentateuch from the ravages of La Peyrere's views and those of the later Higher Critics of the Graf-Wellhausen school appeared in the work of the eminent Jewish scholar, A. S. Yahuda. In two works, *The Language of the Pentateuch in its Relation to Egyptian* and *The Accuracy of the Bible*, he sought to show that biblical Hebrew in the Pentateuch was heavily influenced by Egyptian, that the first five books had a unity and that they are historically accurate in describing events and things.[19] He did not deny that all sorts of sources were used by the biblical author (whom he did not identify), but insisted that the Bible leads the world in the right direction, by revealing the sources of evil and destruction, and pointing to the path of good, truth, and justice.[20] Yahuda did not insist on the literal accuracy, in the fundamentalist sense, but tried to put forth a scholarly case for the Pentateuch being written by one author, and being accurate about events in Egypt and during the Exodus at the time. His views have been ignored or rejected. It is interesting that Yahuda, one of the greatest manuscript collectors of this century, collected a majority of Sir Isaac Newton's religious papers, and found an affinity with Newton in the latter's attempt to justify biblical chronology over other ancient chronologies.[21]

Thus, one can find indications that La Peyrère's revolutionary ideas of three hundred and forty years ago are still having repercussions within the religious establishments. In some cases, like that of the Protestant fundamentalists, some of the issues raised by La Peyrère are still crucial concerns, though La Peyrère seems to be unknown. This may be due to the fact that the American fundamentalist movements grew up in the nineteenth century, in opposition to the ethical, non-historical kind of liberal Protestantism that was dominant in the established Christian movements. The Jews who know of La Peyrère are interested in his place in Jewish and philosemitic movements of the time, and in his place as precursor of later Zionism. Long before any officially Jewish author had advocated that Jews should return to Palestine to rebuild it, La Peyrère, along with some of the Christian Millenarians in England and Holland, and the remarkable Portuguese Jesuit, Antonio de Vieira, had advocated the return of the Jews to Zion and the rebuilding of Jerusalem.[22] (However, the people looking for historical antecedents to Zionism should note that all of the people referred to above made the conversion of the Jews a pre-condition to the Zionist events. Only La Peyrère reduced what was involved in the conversion of the Jews to a triviality.)[23] Among Catholic theologians the actual views of La Peyrère, identified as such, and discussed as 'Scriptural pre-Adamism' still are debated. As we have seen by looking at four twentieth century discussions in Catholic encyclopedias, there is a continuing concern to reconcile the latest finding in anthropology with a monogenetic view about the origin of man. Some form of pre-Adamism has been considered acceptable in order to account for the pre-historic remains of people. But such pre-Adamism cannot prevent the view from being accepted that all people living after Adam got their humanity, including their original sin from him. La Peyrère had tried to keep to this view by maintaining that the pre-Adamites participated in Adam's Fall by mystical imputation, rather than by biological inheritance.[24]

In the world of anthropological studies, La Peyrère's initial influence led people to consider human affairs in a time frame that extended far beyond the biblical one and in a situation in which a theory of multiple origins or polygenesis made the most sense. The evidence of different societies and different histories continued to make La Peyrère's theories seem like plausible explanations. And as his polygenetic view became endowed with apparently hard scientific evidence such as Dr. Samuel Morton's measurements of cranial capacity, La Peyrère appeared, from the point of view of the mid-nineteenth century, to be one of the founders of the science of anthropology who was martyred for his bravery in stating the truth about the origins of man.

Since Darwinism and modern genetics, a polygenetic explanation has become a minority view. The pre-historical findings along with the withering away of belief in the literal accuracy of the Bible have made pre-Adamism a somewhat meaningless theory for most people, especially for those who have their doubts that there ever was a historical personage corresponding to the biblical Adam. So for the anthropologists of today, La Peyrère appears a curious forerunner from the Dark Ages. He usually receives only a paragraph or a page in modern histories of anthropology.[25]

Ironically, the area where he has probably had the most influence is in racist theories. La Peyrère was a universal humanist who saw all people as constituted of the same biological material and who saw all people as about to be saved. Nonetheless some of the early anthropologists who were seeking a justification of white superiority and black and American Indian inferiority saw in La Peyrère's pre-Adamism an ideal theory to provide both the scientific and political bases of their position. La Peyrère's theory had been intended in part by its author to answer the vexing questions raised by the discoveries of human dispersion and human difference. But this was quickly turned into an explanation of why some humans are better than others and why some should dominate others. As these polygenecist racists redid the pre-Adamite theory in the early nineteenth century, Adamite became equal to Caucasian and pre-Adamite to people of color. Now the differences could be seen to be eternally fixed and the relationship of dominance of the Caucasians over the non-Caucasians was also fixed for all time. This position, as a scientific anthropological one, was pretty much overwhelmed by Darwinist theory. However, besides the writings of occasional figures, such as Professor Alexander Winchell, who still believed at the end of the nineteenth century that pre-Adamism was the best explanation, the main form in which polygenetic racism still appears in the modern world is in theories purporting to find significant genetic differences among the races.

The opponents of this present kind of scientific racism point out how very limited our knowledge of genetic factors involved in our intellectual and cultural life really is. We are also far from understanding many of the social and environmental factors that cause people to want to learn. Besides these points the actual data used has been seriously challenged. Quite recently grave doubt has been cast on the famous identical twin studies of Professor Cyril Burt of the University of London, doubt that the studies were actually made. Recent studies of his files have indicated, as the British say, that he fudged his data.[26]

No matter what genetic findings can be established, the fundamental moral problem will still remain, namely how should different groups of human beings be treated by one another. Frederick Douglass had pointed out that even if groups of people have different ancestries they still have a common humanity, a common set of human problems, and a common destiny. Hence all of the polygenetic research does not change the actual human situation. The abbé Henri Grégoire, who fought all his life for the rights of blacks, Jews, and other downtrodden minorities, was a committed monogenecist. All people were created by God and through this creation belong to one human family in which all are co-equal. As Grégoire said in one of his last works, *De la Noblesse de la peau* of 1828, the soul has neither color nor sex, and those who believe in 'the nobility of the skin will suffer the same fate as that of parchment,' namely they will crumble.[27]

Perhaps the strongest moral statements against pre-Adamite racism were made by the great German scientist, Alexander von Humboldt, and by his brother, Wilhelm. As we have seen, Alexander von Humboldt was interested in Dr. Morton's work. Not only did he correspond with him, he also closely followed the developments in American ethnology. When he saw the direction American polygenetic theory was taking towards providing a basis for color racism, Von Humboldt took a strong stand against this view. At the end of the first volume of his major work, *Kosmos* (published in 1844) he declared, 'Whilst we maintain the unity of the human species, we at the same time repel the depressing (désolante) assumption of superior and inferior races of men. There are nations more susceptible of cultivation, more highly civilized, more ennobled by mental cultivation than others. All are in like degree designed for freedom.'[28] Von Humboldt was a complete cultural relativist. Each culture was to be appreciated in its own terms. One might have bigger buildings, more books, more universities than another. This would only show how cultures differed. It would not show that one culture is nobler than another.

Wilhelm von Humboldt saw that the aim of human activity should be to find, or create, a unity of mankind in spite of all of the diversities. Our goal, he claimed, should be 'that of establishing our common humanity—of striving to remove the barriers that prejudice and limited views of every kind have erected amongst men, and to treat all mankind without reference to religion, nation, or colour, as one fraternity, one great community, fitted for the attainment of one great object, the unrestrained development of the psychical powers. This is the ultimate and highest aim of society...Thus deeply rooted in the innermost nature of man, and even enjoined upon him by his highest tendencies—the recognition of the bond of humanity becomes one of the noblest leading principles in the history of humanity.'[29]

One paradox in the story we have been telling is that La Peyrère who, through no fault of his own, spawned polygenetic racism, would most likely have supported the views of Grégoire, Frederick Douglass and the von Humboldt brothers. In generating a theology and a cosmology to place the Marranos in the center of world history, and to end the discrimination against them, La Peyrère developed a picture of the nature of man that, unfortunately, could too easily be used to justify discrimination against other groups. For La Peyrère the common element in all mankind was both the same biological makeup and the same spiritual destiny. When both of these features were ignored or forgotten, La Peyrère's universal humanism could be transformed into a basic theory of racism. Polygenesis could mean not only that people had different origins, but also that people were basically different in a way that made some forever superior and some inferior. Hence it could provide the intellectual justification for the situations that European expansion had created.

The history of La Peyrère's influence provides a case study of the effect of radical new religious ideas in their time, of the way some were adopted, some were changed and some were reversed over three hundred years. The dramatic effects of the pre-Adamite theory, from La Peyrère onward, are remarkable. A heretical theory being used to buttress a most humanitarian Messianic view had the effect first of challenging the accuracy of the biblical text, and second of challenging whether the Bible is the history of all mankind, or is just the history of the Jews. Through La Peyrère's influence on Spinoza and Richard Simon, this contributed to the development of modern biblical criticism. La Peyrère's influence on Vico and the English Deists contributed to the construction of non-Providential histories of most, and later, all of mankind. In the course of this development an important aspect of the modern intellectual interpretation of religion grew up which gradually accommodated to a separation of scriptural history from world history, and accepted the Bible as an element in that world history. The pre-Adamite theory also, and perhaps most important, had a striking influence on anthropology, in opening up important ways of explaining the new data about the diversity of human beings. But, as we have seen, such an explanation was not wanted simply to satisfy idle curiosity about why blacks are black. The explanation was unfortunately desired to justify the social, political and moral ways that the American Indians and the Africans were treated. La Peyrère's polygenetic theory became the basis of the new racism and he became the wise precursor of this racist science. Although La Peyrère by now is pretty well forgotten, or remembered in obscure footnotes, much of his legacy has been incorporated into our present intellectual framework and many of the issues he raised are still being considered, albeit in modern dress. One can hope that the racist transformation of his views will disappear before too long and the other fruitful aspects of his vision will go on aiding in the development of the modern mind.

NOTES

CHAPTER TWO

1. For example, Jean-François Niceron's *Mémoires pour servir à l'histoire des illustres*, Tome XX (Paris, 1732), p. 42, states that La Peyrère was 82 when he died in 1676. This information was carried over into later biographical dictionaries and encyclopedias. The recent monograph study by Dino Pastine, 'La Origini del poligenismo e Isaac La Peyrère,' *Miscellanea Seicento, Istituto di Filosofia della Facolta di Lettere e Filosofia dell'-Universita di Genova* (Firenze, 1971), I, pp. 7-234, repeats the 1594 birthdate that appears in many of the standard reference works (see p. 127).

2. Philippe Tamizey de Larroque et A. Communay, 'Isaac de la Peyrère et sa famille,' *Revue Critique d'histoire et de littérature*, XIX (1885), pp. 135-37. A portion of the article is separately entitled 'Notes généalogiques sur les Lapeyrère' by A. Communay. More details about La Peyrère's family appear in Jean-Paul Oddos, *Recherches sur la vie et l'oeuvre d'Isaac de Lapeyrère* (1596?-1676) (unpublished thèse de 3ème cycle, 1971-1974, Université des sciences sociales, Grenoble) II, chap. 1.

3. Oddos, *op. cit.*, pp. 11-12; and Communay, *op. cit.*, p. 137.

4. Communay, *op. cit.*, pp. 136-37; Oddos, *op. cit.*, pp. 31-32. Nothing further seems to be known about what happened to La Peyrère's wife.

5. Bibliothèque Nationale Ms. Fonds Français 15827, fols. 149 and 162. The latter item is Pastor Alba's letter. See also Oddos, *op. cit.*, pp. 41-42.

6. Oddos, *op. cit.*, chap. III; and René Pintard, *Le Libertinage érudit* (Paris, 1943), p. 358.

7. Duc d'Aumale, *Histoire des Princes de Condé*, Tome VI (Paris, 1892) p. 346n.

8. Naudé's letter to Cardinal Barberini, 1641, Biblioteca Vaticana, Barberini Coll. Latin 6471, fol. 22v. See also Pintard, *op. cit.*, p. 360.

9. Cf. R. H. Popkin, 'The Marrano Theology of Isaac La Peyrère,' *Studi Internazionali di Filosofia*, V (1973) p. 99; and Pintard, op. cit., p. 360.

10. Hugo Grotius, *Dissertatio altera de origine Gentium Americanarum adversus obiectatorem* (n.p., 1643), pp. 13-14. The translation is from the 1656 English edition of La Peyrère's *Men before Adam* (London, 1643), p. 275.

11. This is described in La Peyrère's *Prae-Adamitae*, Lib. IV, cap. xiv, p. 297; English edition, p. 275. (Since there are several different printings of *Prae-Adamitae*, it does no good to give page references to the original Latin. References will be given by book and chapter, and the pages in the English translation.)

12. Popkin, 'Marrano theology,' p. 99 and note 12; Pintard, *op. cit.*, p. 360; letters of André Rivet to Claude Sarrau, Aug. 24, 1643, and of Marin Mersenne to Rivet, Nov. 7, 1643, in *Correspondance du P. Marin Mersenne*, Tome XII (Paris, 1972), pp. 362-65; Rivet to Sarrau, April 4, 1644, Bibliothèque Nationale Ms. Fonds français 2390, Part I, fol. 26; Christian Du Puy to I. Boulliau, Jan. 5, 1646, Bibl. Nat. Ms. Fonds français 9778, fol. 33; Bibl. Nat. Coll. Dupuy 730, fol. 154; and also the letters of Guy Patin to Charles Spon, in *Lettres de Gui Patin*, ed. J-H. Reveillé-Parise (Paris, 1846), I, pp. 297-99. These letters of Sept. 14, 1643 and Oct. 26, 1643 contain the information Patin had at the time about La Peyrère and *Du Rappel des Juifs*. Mersenne also sent a copy of *Du Rappel des Juifs* and something about the pre-Adamite theory to Martin Ruar in eastern Europe. See Ruar's letter to Mersenne, June 20, 1644, in *Correspondance du P. Marin Mersenne*, Tome XIII (Paris, 1977), p. 157.

13. See Popkin, 'Marrano Theology,' pp. 103-4; Pintard, *op. cit.*, p. 360; and letters cited in note 12. There is also a letter of a Scottish scholar, Jacques Valois to Mersenne, Oct. 11, 1643. Mersenne had given Valois *Du Rappel des Juifs*. Valois found it 'forte docte en theologie et fort curieux.' He thought the Pope might want the author's help in reconciling all the religions. See Mersenne, *Correspondance*, Tome XII, p. 339.

14. On Finch and his theory about the Jews, see Nahum Sokolow, *The History of Zionism* (London, 1919), I, pp. 47-49; Peter Toon, ed., *The Millenium and the Future of Israel: Puritan Eschatology — 1600 to 1660* (Cambridge and London, 1970), pp. 32-34; and Mayir Vereté, 'The Restoration of the Jews in English Protestant Thought, 1790-1840,' *Middle Eastern Studies*, Jan. 1972, p. 16, and his lecture 'The Idea of the Restoration of the Jews,' Clark Library Lecture, May 1982, forthcoming. See also David S. Katz, *Philosemitism and the Readmission of the Jews to England 1603-1655* (Oxford, 1982), chap. 3, 'The Calling of the Jews,' pp. 89-126; and Christopher Hill, 'Till the Conversion of the Jews,' Clark Library Lecture, Oct. 1981, forthcoming, and his *The Antichrist in Seventeenth Century England* (Oxford, 1971).

15. See the views discussed in Norman Cohn, *The Pursuit of the Millennium* (New York, 1961); Ernest Tuveson, *Millenium and Utopia* (Gloucester, MA, 1972); Toon, *op. cit.*; Vereté, 'Restoration of the Jews,' pp. 13-20; Katz, op. cit.; Hill, *Antichrist*, and Katherine R. Firth, *The Apocalyptic Tradition in Reformation Britain, 1530-1645* (Oxford, 1979).

16. On Mede see 'The Life of the Reverend and most Learned Joseph Mede, D.D.,' in Joseph Mede, *The Works of the Pious and Profoundly-Learned Joseph Mede* (London, 1672), pp. I-XLV; Toon, *op. cit.*, pp. 56-65; Tuveson, *op. cit.*, pp. 76-85; and Firth, op. cit., pp. 213-28. On Mede and his influence on Sir Isaac Newton and the Newtonians, see Arthur Quinn, *The Confidence of British Philosophers* (Leiden, 1977), Part I; and R. H. Popkin, 'Divine Causality: Newton, the Newtonians and Hume,' in *Greene Centennial Studies, Essays Presented to Donald Greene*, ed. by Robert Allen and Paul Korshin, (Charlottesville, Virginia 1984), pp. 40-56, and 'The Third Force in 17th Century Philosophy: Scepticism, Millenarianism and Science,' *Nouvelles de la Republique des lettres*, III (1983), pp. 35-63.

17. See Gershom G. Scholem, *Major Trends in Jewish Mysticism* (New York, 1969), pp. 244-86.

18. See Joseph L. Blau, *The Christian Interpretation of the Cabbala in the Renaissance* (New York, 1944) and François Secret, *Le Zohar chez les Kabbalistes chrétiens de la Renaissance* (The Hague, 1964).

19. Discussions of these possible sources will be taken up in chapter V. More detail about the millenarian and messianic background will be discussed then.

20. The unpublished work entitled *Des Iuifs, Elus, Reietés et Rapelé*, was completed in 1673, three years before his death. It is in the Condé library at Chantilly, Ms. 191(698).

21. Isaac La Peyrère, *Du Rappel des Juifs* (n.p., 1643), Livres I-II, pp. 1-153. Postel's French Messianism appears in his *Les Raisons de la Monarchie, De Foenicium Literis*, and other works. On Postel, see Marion L. Kuntz, *Guillaume Postel* (The Hague, 1981); William Bouwsma, *Concordia mundi: The Career and Thought of William Postel* (Cambridge, MA 1957); and François Secret, 'Introduction' to Guillaume Postel, *Le Thresor des Propeties de l'Univers* (The Hague, 1969). On the possible relation of Postel's, and maybe La Peyrère's thought, to the tradition of Joachim de Fiore, see Marjorie Reeves, *The Influence of Prophecy in the Later Middle Ages* (Oxford, 1969), esp. pp. 381-84; and Ira Robinson, 'Isaac de la Peyrère and the Recall of the Jews, *Jewish Social Studies* XL (1978), pp. 123-24.

22. The notion of making Christianity less offensive to the Jews also appeared in a pamphlet by either John Dury or Samuel Hartlib (both leading millenarian figures in England at the time) in 1642. In the pamphlet, 'England's Thankfulnesse,' it is said, 'A care to make Christianity lesse offensive and more knowne unto the Jewes, than it is now.' This pamphlet is reprinted in Charles Webster, ed., *Samuel Hartlib and the Advancement of Learning* (Cambridge, 1970), pp. 90-97. The quotation is on p. 95. Hartlib and Dury did not propose dropping doctrines or dogmas, but rather stating them and explaining them, so that Jews could understand and accept them. See also R. H. Popkin, 'The First College of Jewish Studies,' *Revue des Etudes juives*, CXLIII (1984), pp. 351-364.

23. La Peyrère, *Du Rappel des Juifs*, Livres III-V.

24. Popkin, 'Marrano Theology,' pp. 100-103.

25. Oddos, *op. cit.*, pp. 50, 164, 192-94, and 266.

26. This will be discussed in chapter VIII.

27. However, as we shall see in Chapter VIII, some of these thinkers were influenced by La Peyrère.

28. Richard Simon wrote La Peyrère in 1670, and told him about the messianic claims of Sabbatai Zevi, and about the Jewish messianic movement this had inspired. As far as one can tell, La Peyrère did not react at all. See Richard Simon, *Lettres choisies de M. Simon* (Rotterdam, 1702), II, p. 14.

29. *Borboniana*, in François Bruys, *Mémoires historiques, critiques et littéraires* (Paris, 1751), II, p. 284.

30. Dean Brian Armstrong of Georgia State University has told me this, based on a study he is doing of manuscript letters of several of the leading French Protestants of the time.

31. This will be discussed in chapters V and VIII.

32. It is so reported in Claude Sarrau's letter to Claude Saumaise, November 1643, in Sarrau's *Epistolae* (Orange, 1654), p. 74. The Latin form of the title is *Somnium Nobilis Aquitani de Prae-Adamitae*. The Bibliothèque National has Bishop Pierre-Daniel Huet's copy of Sarrau's *Epistolae*. Huet marked the passage giving this title.

33. Oddos, *op. cit.*, pp. 55-56. André Rivet's letter to Claude Sarrau, April 4, 1644, Bibl. Nat. Fonds français Ms. 2390, Part I, fol 26; and Sarrau to Rivet, April 23, 1644, BUP Leiden, Ms BLP 289/2. These letters have been published in the *Correspondance Intégrale d'André Rivet et de Claude Sarrau*, publiée et annotée par Hans Bots et Pierre Leroy, Tome II (Amsterdam, 1980). Lettres CCXXVIII, CCXXXII, and CCXXXIV show that La Peyrère visited both Rivet and Sarrau, both of whom enjoyed him as a personality, but found his theories troubling.

34. Oddos, *op. cit.*, pp. 56-60.

35. La Peyrère, *Relation de l'Islande* (Paris, 1663), pp. eiii^r - eiiii^v.

36. *Ibid*, p. 63. La Peyrère dedicated his *La Bataille de Lents* (Paris, 1649) to Christina, and showed how impressed he was by her.

37. Ole Worm *Olai Wormii et ad eum Doctorum Virorum Epistolae*, 2 vols. (Copenhagen, 1751), esp. vol. II, pp. 916-57. A French translation of these letters appears in Oddos, *op. cit.*, pp. 210-76.

38. Worm, *Epistolae*, II, pp. 920-25; Oddos, *op. cit.*, pp. 216-23. La Peyrère's works on Iceland and Greenland were reprinted in various languages throughout the 18th century. The Hakluyt Society published the work on Greenland in its collection in 1855.

39. Worm, *Epistolae*, II, pp. 938-39; Oddos, *op. cit.*, pp. 240-41.

40. Thomas Bangius (1600-1661) was professor of Hebrew at Copenhagen. La Peyrère showed him the manuscript of his work on the pre-Adamites in 1645. Bangius offered a brief refutation in his *Coelum Orientes et Prisci Mundi Triade Exercitationum Literariarum Repraesentatum* (Copenhagen, 1657), pp. 132-34. On p. 136 he mentioned that he gave La Peyrère some information reported by Maimonides about claims that there were people before Adam. Bangius's work was reprinted at Krakow in 1691 under the title *Exercitationes Philologico-Philosophicae quibus Materia de Ortu et Progressu Literarum*.

41. Worm, *Epistolae*, II, pp. 945-46; Oddos, *op. cit.*, pp. 248-50.

42. La Peyrère, *Prae-Adamitae*, Lib. IV, chap. xiv; *Men Before Adam*, pp. 278-81.

43. La Peyrère, *Relation du Groenland* (Paris, 1647). In the preface La Peyrère acknowledged the help he got from Roberval, Naudé, Chapelain, and Gassendi. On pages 273-76, La Peyrère raised several points against the theory of Grotius that the Americans came from Greenland and the Greenlanders from Norway.

44. Oddos, *op. cit.*, pp. 70-74; and La Peyrère's letter to Philibert de la Mare, Sept. 9, 1661, where he said, 'Je puis dire qu'ils (the pre-Adamites) doivent la à Monsieur Saumaise qui a esté comme leur sage-femme.' La Peyrère also said he had intended to dedicate his book to Saumaise. This letter is in the Bibliothèque Publique de Dijon, Fonds Baudot no. 82. It appears in Oddos, *op. cit.*, pp. 287-91.

45. Mersenne's letter from Paris to Rivet, dated October 18, 1646, mentions that La Peyrère arrived a few days earlier and gave Mersenne a letter from Rivet. Mersenne, *Correspondance*, Tome XIV, p. 549.

46. Oddos, *op. cit.*, pp. 77-79; Saumaise's letter to Mersenne on *De annis climacteris*, Bibl. Nat. Fonds français 6204, fol. 85. The nine letters of La Peyrère to Philibert de la Mare of 1660-1663 that are given in Oddos, *op. cit.*, pp. 282-302 show how important Saumaise and his researchers were in La Peyrère's work. Saumaise died in 1653, thus before *Prae-Adamitae* appeared. Saumaise might have been able to help the heretical author. Philibert de la Mare was writing a biography of Saumaise, which accounts for La Peyrère's correspondence. It is interesting that in the 1660s, after recanting his advocacy of the pre-Adamite theory, La Peyrère kept referring to 'mes préadamites.' It is also interesting to note that it is reported that Saumaise said on his deathbed 'que si Dieu exigeait un culte, la religion juive était la veritable.' Espiard de la Cour, *Oeuvres Mêlées. . .* (Amsterdam, 1749), p. 22.

47. See note 36.

48. Oddos, *op. cit.*, pp. 80-87. The trip to Spain is described in La Peyrère's report to Condé, dated Namur, Oct. 8, 1655, Chantilly Papiers de Condé, p. XV, fols., 347-54. People in Spain said 'que je fusse quelque animal fantastique' because 'j'estois hugenot et preadamite.'

49. Oddos, *op. cit.*, pp. 86-87. Condé's correspondence of the period indicates that he was trying to make an alliance with Cromwell. Condé wanted Cromwell to invade France at Bordeaux. The French Protestants would rebel. Condé, plus an army supplied by Queen Christina, would attack France. This plan is discussed in the letters to and from Condé's agent in London at the end of volume VI of the Duc d'Aumale's *Histoire des Princes de Condé*, pp. 684-697. La Peyrère may have been involved in the negotiations.

49a. See David S. Katz, 'Menasseh ben Israel's Mission to Queen Christina of Sweden, 1651-1655,' *Jewish Social Studies*, XLV (1983-84), pp. 57-72; and R. H. Popkin, 'Menasseh Ben Israel and Isaac La Peyrère, II.', *Studia Rosenthaliana*, XVIII (1984), pp. 12-20.

50. Popkin, 'Marrano Theology,' p. 105; Oddos, op. cit., pp. 90-91; and Duc d'Aumale, *Histoire des Princes de Condé*, Tome VI, p. 699. Sven Stolpe, in *Christina of Sweden* (New York, 1966), p. 130, says that when the Queen read La Peyrère's manuscript 'she persuaded the author to have it printed without delay.' René Pintard, in *Le Libertinage érudit*, said that Christina was responsible for the publication of *Prae-Adamitae* (pp. 399 and 420). Pintard and Pastine (*op. cit.*, pp. 149-50) report Christina's concern to obtain a copy of *Les Trois Imposteurs*. The full history of this work remains to be written. All known copies of the French work, which is different from *De Tribus Impostoribus*, contain material from Hobbes' *Leviathan*, published in 1651. Oldenburg apparently saw or heard part of the text in 1656, and asked Adam Boreel, the leader of the Collegiants in Holland to write an answer. He did, but his response remains unpublished. The work as we know it surfaces in the libertine circle around Prince Eugene of Savoy in The Hague. It was printed in 1719 under the title, *La vie et l'esprit de M. Spinoza*, and later as *Les Trois Imposteurs*. See Margaret Jacob, *The Radical Enlightenment: Pantheists, Freemasons and Republicans* (London, 1981) and my review of this book in the *Journal of the History of Philosophy*, forthcoming. We hope to unravel what happened from 1650 onward to develop the text. *Les Trois Imposteurs* does not mention La Peyrère or pre-Adamism. (The 'Dissertation' by La Monnoye that often accompanies it does mention La Peyrère as an author who has been often refuted for his religious heresies.) Baron de Hohendorf, the agent of the Prince of Savoy, had manuscripts of *Les Trois Imposteurs* as well as a copy of La Peyrère's opus. Baron d'Holbach, who published an edition of *Les Trois Imposteurs* also owned La Peyrère's work. It is curious that the editors of clandestine literature in Holland and France did not reprint *Prae-Adamitae*, or excerpt the non-theological parts.

51. This version of what happened is humorously presented in the *Lettre de la Peyrère à Philotime* (Paris, 1658), pp. 114-18.

52. La Peyrère's letter to Ishmaël Boulliau, Feb. 16, 1661, published in Philippe Tamizey de Larroque, *Quelques Lettres inédites d'Isaac de la Peyrère à Boulliau* (*Plaquettes Gontaudaises*, No. 2), (Paris, 1878), p. 24. The letter also appears in Oddos, *op. cit.*, pp. 304-6.

53. Cf. R. H. Popkin, 'Menasseh ben Israel and Isaac La Peyrère,' *Studia Rosenthaliana*, VIII (1974), pp. 59-63. Felgenhauer described the attempt to organize a debate with La Peyrère in the 'Beschluss' to his *Anti-Prae-Adamita* (Amsterdam, 1659), pp. 89-90.

54. See Popkin, 'Menasseh ben Israel,' pp. 59-60. The original title of Felgenhauer's book is *Bonum Nunciam Israel quod offertur Populo Israel &e Judae in hisce temporibus novissimus de MESSIAH* ... (Amsterdam, 1655). On pp. 89-90, Menasseh ben Israel listed 'ex Gallia Autorem Libelli Gallico Idiomate edite, *Du rappel des juifs*' as one of the few who knew that the coming of the Messiah was imminent.

55. See La Peyrère's letter to Philibert de la Mare, May 30, 1662, where he said, 'Je ne courus aucun risque en Hollande, parce que mon livre n'y fut publié qu'après que j'en fus dehors. Et je demeuray six mois paisable à Namur, avant que Mons. l'Evesque n'ait censuré mon livre.' This letter appears in Oddos, *op. cit.*, pp. 293-94. In La Peyrère's *Lettre à Philotime*, he said that the Dutch printer had promised not to send a copy of the book to Belgium so that the Prince of Condé would not be embarrassed. And while the printing was going on, La Peyrère spent six months in Namur in peace.

56. This document states that the book is 'valsche, schadelicke, ende ergelicke Leeringen striidende tegens Godts Woort,' as well as being scandalous, Godless and against the States' interest. A copy of this Condemnation of the President and Council of Holland/Zeeland, dated November 26, 1655 is in the British Library.

57. La Peyrère, *Lettre à Philotime*, p. 123.

58. *Ibid.*, pp. 125-26.

59. La Peyrère, letter to Philibert de la Mare, May 30, 1662, in Oddos, *op. cit.*, p. 294. 'Ce qui me fit résoudre à me faire Catolique, fut l'injustice avec laquelle les Calvinistes me traitèrent en escrivant contre moy.' One of La Peyrère's bitterest critics, Samuel Desmarets, quoted two very nasty letters by Protestant leaders against La Peyrère. Cf. Desmarets, *Refutatio Fabulae Prae-Adamiticae* (Groningen, 1656), preface. On Condé's possible involvement, see Oddos, op. cit., pp. 93-95.

60. Cf. Bibl. Nat. Ms. Fonds français 6728, Papiers de Pierre Lenet, Documents divers, no. 20. (Lenet was one of Condé's advisers.) See also La Peyrère, *Lettre à Philotime, pp. 128-30;* and *Recueil de Lettres escrites à Monsieur le Comte de la Suze, pour l'obliger par raison à se faire Catholique* (Paris, 1661). When La Peyrère converted, it was said that hundreds of others would do so too. As a matter of fact, the only person we know of that La Peyrère tried to convert was le Comte de la Suze. Pope Alexander VII, who had just taken office in 1655, apparently had some apocalyptic leanings. One thing that he did was to commission a Hebrew translation of the works of St. Thomas Aquinas so that when the Jews converted they would be able to study the true theology. The history of the project appears in the first volume of the series, which was only partially completed.

61. This is reported by Richard Simon in his letter to M. Z. S., *Lettres choisies*, II, p. 24.

62. Cited in Louis Lafuma's note on La Peyrère in his edition of Pascal's *Oeuvres complètes* (New York and Paris, 1963), p. 657, from Huygens' *Journal* for Feb. 21, 1661. Pascal himself just dismissed the 'Extravagances de Apocalyptiques et préadamites, millenaristes, etc.' Lafuma ed., p. 582, Pensée 575-651.

63. Oddos, *op. cit.*, pp. 107-11. At the end of the *Lettre à Philotime*, of which the second half is a letter to Pope Alexander VII, La Peyrère announced that the Pope was to play a crucial role in bringing about the climactic events in human history.

64. La Peyrère presented this explanation in the *Lettre à Philotime, Recueil de Lettres escrites à Monsieur le Comte de la Suze* and *Apologie de la Peyrère* (Paris, 1663).

65. This picture of the Pope's role appears at the end of the letter to the Pope in *Lettre à Philotime*, pp. 157-67. The letter to the Pope was written while La Peyrère was in prison in Belgium. On the 'sincerity' of La Peyrère's abjuration, see Oddos, op. cit., pp. 107-9.

66. La Peyrère, *Lettre à Philotime*, pp. 100-113; *Recueil des Lettres à Comte de la Suze*, pp. 63-68 (pp. 67-68: 'Si j'etois Calviniste, je serois bon Preadamit'); *Apologie de la Peyrère*, Dedication and pp. 1-18.

67. The title of the main part of *Prae-Adamitae* is *Systema Theologicum ex Prae Adamitarum Hypothesi*.

68. La Peyrère, *Apologie*, pp. 19-20; and *Lettre à Philotime*, pp. 111-13.

69. La Peyrère, *Lettre à Philotime*, in the letter to Pope Alexander, pp. 130-40; *Recueil de Lettres escrites à M. le Comte de la Suze*, pp. 62-68; *Suite des Lettres escrites à Monsieur le Comte de la Suze* (Paris, 1662), pp. 122-26; and Apologie, pp. 40-45, 57-61.

70. La Peyrère, *Apologie*, pp. 21-22; and *Lettre à Philotime*, p. 109.

71. La Peyrère, *Lettre à Philotime*, pp. 142-53; *Apologie*, pp. 26-37.

72. La Peyrère, *Lettre à Philotime*, pp. 154-55; and *Apologie*, p. 38.

73. La Peyrère, *Lettre à Philotime*, pp. 156-68.

74. La Peyrère, *Recueil de Lettres escrites à Monsieur le Comte de la Suze*, p. 110. (The text of La Peyrère's abjuration is given on pp. 101-12.) See also Oddos, *op. cit.*, pp. 108-9.

75. See note 60.

76. Letter of the abbé Claude Nicaise to Carrel, in *Nouvelles de la Republique des Lettres*, Oct. 1703, pp. 390-91. Thomas White was a friend of Thomas Hobbes, who wrote a refutation of White's *Anima Mundi*. La Peyrère and White must have had many friends in common, since White lived in Paris for a while.

77. Her correspondence, which was looted from the Vatican Library by one of Napoleon's soldiers has not been examined. It is hoped that when it is some further data about the relationship between La Peyrère and Christina will be uncovered. So far I have found none. On this, see chap. 8, n. 39.

78. This is reported in Richard Simon's letter to M. Z. on 'Quelques particularités touchant l'Auteur & l'Ouvrage des Preadamites,' *Lettres choisies*, II, p. 25.

79. Letter of Patin to Spon, April 9, 1658, in *Lettres de Gui Patin*, III, p. 83.

80. Oddos, *op. cit.*, p. 114. La Peyrère seems to have formulated his view to avoid the difficulty Galileo got into. Thirty years earlier Galileo was condemned for maintaining that the Copernican theory was more than a hypothesis. His accusers said he held that it was an accurate picture of reality.

81. La Peyrère, *Recueil des Lettres à Monsieur le Comte de la Suze*, p. 75. This work begins with an anonymous attack on La Peyrère mainly for his views on Jews and Judaism. Then La Peyrère defended his philosemitism.

82. This is La Peyrère's work, *Suite des lettres escrites à Monsieur le Comte de la Suze, pour l'obliger par raison à se faire Catolique* (Paris, 1662).

83. In the advice to the readers in the *Suite des Lettres*, La Peyrère complained that orthography depends more on fantasy than reason. He hoped the Acádemie française would do something about it. In the *Relation de l'Islande*, La Peyrère outlined his own proposal, namely that words should be spelled as pronounced, at least until the dictionary of the Acádemie appears. The longest statement about his orthographic system appears in the unpublished manuscript, Chantilly, Ms. 191 (698). Regarding the important philosopher who had adopted La Peyrère's system, I consulted Prof. Louis Marin. Neither of us could find a plausible candidate.

84. All of this appears in chapters 1 and 2 of *Apologie de la Peyrère*.

85. *Ibid*, chaps. 3-5.

86. Approbations by Doctors Flavigny and Nicolas Petitpied.

87. Oddos, *op. cit.*, pp. 123-24, and 128.

88. Richard Simon's letters to La Peyrère, May 20, 1670-1671, in Simon's *Lettres choisies*, II, pp. 1-23 and IV, pp. 36-45. La Peyrère had already raised the subject of Adam's gout in *Prae-Adamitae*.

89. Pierre Bayle, art. 'Peyrère, Isaac la,' in *Dictionnaire historique et critique*, Rem. G. Bayle quoted from a letter sent him by one of La Peyrère's close friends, François Morin du Sandat.

90. Simon's letter to M. Z. S., 1688 in *Lettres choisies*, II, pp. 23-28.

91. Desmarets had written *Refutatio Fabulae Prae-Adamiticae* (Groningen, 1656), which had appeared in two editions. La Peyrère was strongly criticized for his heresies, his irreligion, etc. This refutation was highly regarded and was still being cited in the eighteenth century by people such as Diderot or whoever wrote the article on the pre-Adamites in the *Encyclopédie*. Desmarets called La Peyrère's views the 'confluence of all heresies.' La Peyrère wrote *Reponse de Lapeyrère aux Calomnies de Des Marais (sic), Ministre de Groningue*. There are two known manuscripts of this work, one at Chantilly, the other at Dôle.

92. Michel de Marolles, *Le Livre de Genese*, p. 2. There are copies of this work in the British Library and the Bibliothèque Nationale. Details about the suppression appear in

Niceron, *Memoires pour servir à l'histoire des hommes illustres*, XX, p. 43. Marolles, in his *Memoires* (Amsterdam, 1755), II, pp. 63-70 and 234-36 discussed his relations with La Peyrère. He had given the latter some data for *Prae-Adamitae*, but Marolles claimed he was always against the theory. He enjoyed reading the refutations, especially the one by Desmarets.

93. Simon, letter to La Peyrère, May 27, 1670, in *Lettres choisies*, II, pp. 16-17.

94. The details about the attempt to publish the work appear in Simon's letter to M. Z. S., *Lettres choisies*, II, p. 26.

95. La Peyrère, according to Simon, *loc. cit.*, was afraid that after his death the Fathers at the Oratory would sacrifice his work to Vulcan. Hence, it was placed in the Prince of Condé's library, where it still is.

96. La Peyrère, *Des Iuifs, Elus, Reietés et Rapelés*, 1st through 3rd pages.

97. On the role of the Anti-Christ, see Christopher Hill, *The Anti-Christ in Seventeenth Century England* (London and New York, 1971) and Arthur H. Williamson, *Scottish National Consciousness in the Age of James VI: The Apocalypse, the Union and the Shaping of Public Culture* (Edinburgh, 1979).

98. Simon told La Peyrère that a Jewish friend of his, one Jona Salvador, often spoke about a new Messiah of the Jews, Sabbatai Zevi. Simon was willing to introduce La Peyrère to Salvador, and to give La Peyrère prayers in Spanish that are said by Jews going to Adrianople to see their Messiah. There is no sign that La Peyrère showed any interest. Simon, *Lettres choisies*, II, p. 14. Also, although Menasseh ben Israel, a leading Messianist, was impressed by La Peyrère, there is no evidence that La Peyrère cared about Menasseh or his views. Menasseh's views were cited by a large number of seventeenth-century Millenarians.

99. Simon, Lettre à M. Z. S., *Lettres choisies*, II, p. 26.

100. All of this appears in Jean-François Morin du Sandat's letter of April 6, 1696 to Pierre Bayle. Most of the letter is published in remark G of the article 'Peyrère, Isaac la,' in Bayle's *Dictionaire*. Morin du Sandat had been with Condé, and was a close friend of La Peyrère's.

101. Oddos, *op. cit.*, p. 134.

102. Simon, Lettre a M. Z. S., *Lettres choisies*, II, pp. 26-27.

103. 'La Peyrère ici gît, ce bon Israelite, Hugenot, Catholique, enfin Pre-Adamite. Quatre Religions lui pleurent à la fois, Et son indifference étoit si peu commune, au'apres quatre-vingts ans qu'il eut à faire un choix, Le bon homme partit, & n'en choisit pas une.' This text is from Gilles Ménage, *Ménagiana*, II, p. 69. Pastine, *op. cit.*, who denies any possibility that La Peyrère was Jewish, calls this epitaph satirical (p. 127).

104. René Pintard, *Le Libertinage érudit*, pp. 355-61, 379, 399, 420-24; Don Cameron Allen, *The Legend of Noah* (Urbana, IL, 1963), pp. 86-90 and 130-37; and David McKee, 'Isaac de la Peyrère, a Precursor of the Eighteenth Century Deists,' *Publications of the Modern Language Association*, LIX (1944), pp. 456-85. Pastine sees La Peyrère as more than just a *libertin*, and sees him as having ecumenical ideals growing out of the religious world of the seventeenth century. See, *op. cit.*, pp. 200-202 and 225. I have not been able to consult A. Dini's 'La teoria preadamitica e il libertinismo di La Peyrère,' *Annali dell'Istituto di filosofia*, Universita di Firenze, 1979. The title would suggest that the author holds to an interpretation like that of Pintard.

105. Cecil Roth, *A Life of Menasseh ben Israel* (Philadelphia, 1934), p. 161; Leo Strauss, *Spinoza's Critique of Religion* (New York, 1965), p. 84; Hans Joachim Schoeps, *Philosemitismus im Barok* (Tübingen, 1952), pp. 14-18; *Barocke Juden Christen* (Bern and Munich, 1965), p. 24; and Léon Poliakov, *Le Mythe aryen* (Paris, 1971), pp. 127-29.

106. Patin wrote Spon, 'Le sieur de la Peyrère gentilhomme gascon et prétendu réformé (s'il n'est pas juif, car plusiers l'en soupconnent)'; *Lettres de Gui Patin*, II, p. 263. Simon told La Peyrère that Simon's Jewish friend, Jona Salvador, was sure that La Peyrère was a Marrano, because of what he had written, because of the gossip at l'Hotel de Condé, and because La Peyrère was from Bordeaux; Simon, *Lettres choisies*, II, p. 16. Christian Du Puy told Boulliau that La Peyrère's name sounded Spanish (Bibl. Nat. Ms. Fonds francais 9778, fol. 33v). Philippe Le Prieur, in his refutation of La Peyrère, also indicated he thought his opponent was Jewish.

107. Pierre Jurieu, *Histoire critique des dogmes et des cultes* (Amsterdam, 1704), described the pre-Adamite theory as 'la reverie du Juif la Peyrère.' Jurieu was certainly not hostile to Jews per se, so he was not using the term pejoratively.

108. Miriam Yardeni, 'La Religion de La Peyrère et 'Le Rappel des Juifs,'' *Revue d'Histoire et de Philosophie religieuse*, LI (1971), pp. 245-59.

109. Ira Robinson, *'Isaac de la Peyrère and the Recall of the Jews,'* esp. pp. 123-27. The quotation is on p. 125.

110. Oddos, *op. cit.*, pp. 16-18; and Pastine, *op. cit.*, pp. 127-28. Pastine was specifically attacking B. Mariani, who wrote the article on 'Poligenismo' in the *Enciclipedia Cattolica*, Vol. IX, col. 1676.

111. Oddos, *op. cit.*, pp. 185-204.

112. Pastine, *op. cit.*, pp. 128, 141.

113. As, for instance, in Philippe de Mornay, *De la Verité de la Religion Chrestienne contre les Athées, Epicureans, Payens, Juifs, Mahumedistes, et autres infideles* (Anvers, 1581); and *Advertissement aux Juifs sur la venue du Messie* (Saumur, 1607).

114. See the article on Nicholas Anthoine in Haag and Haag, *Anthoine's case*, *'Vie et Mort de Nicholas Anthoine'*, and Elisabeth Labrousse's study of Anthoine's case.

115. Even philosemites like John Dury showed some reluctance to counting Jews as equals, or treating them as such. See his *A Case of Conscience, Whether it be lawful to admit Jews into a Christian Commonwealth?* (London, 1656). Dury was in favor of admitting the Jews to England, but still insisted on some strong restrictions on their behavior.

116. See Popkin, 'Marrano Theology,' pp. 111-12; and 'Jewish Messianism and Christian Millenarianism,' William Andrews Clark lectures on *Culture and Politics from Puritanism to the Enlightenment*, edited by Perez Zagorin (Berkeley, Los Angeles and London, 1980), pp. 67-90. This will be discussed in chapter VIII.

117. La Peyrère, *Du Rappel des Juifs*, pp. 177-78.

118. Popkin, *'Marrano Theology,'* pp. 112-13.

CHAPTER THREE

1. *Theophilus to Autolycus*, in the *Ante-Nicene Christian Library*, vol. III (Book III, chap. XVI), p. 120.

2. See Paul H. Kocker, *Christopher Marlowe, A Study of his Thought, Learning and Character* (New York, 1962), p. 44 n. 11. Here various pagan figures for the length of human history are given, figures which far exceed biblical ones. The estimates of Herodotus, Diodorus Siculus, Pomponius Mela, Plato, Diogenes Laertius, Alexander Polyhistor, and Abydemus are presented. Ancient theories about the origins of the human race are treated at length in Arthur O. Lovejoy and George Boas, *Primitivism and Related Ideas in Antiquity* (New York, 1965). Diodorus Siculus began his history by saying that there are two theories of the generations of men offered by scholars—one that mankind had no beginning, but always existed, and the other that it emanated by some process.

3. Emperor Julian, 'Letter to a Priest,' in *Works* (Loeb Library edition), (London and New York, 1913), II, p. 307.

4. *Ibid*, loc. cit.

5. On Julian, see the recent works by G. W. Bowersock, *Julian the Apostate* (Cambridge, MA, 1978); and Robert Browning, *The Emperor Julian* (London, 1975). See also the article on Julian in the *Encyclopedia Judaica*.

6. This is the title in the Renaissance English edition, St. Augustine, *Of the Citie of God: with the Learned Comments of Io. Lod. Vives*, Englished by J. H. (n. p., 1610). The translator is identified in the British Museum catalogue as John Healey. The place of publication is given as London. The Latin text is in *De Civitate Dei*, Libri XI-XXII, Corpus Christianorum, Series Latina, vol. 48 (Turnhout, 1955), pp. 364-65.

7. St. Augustine, *Of the Citie of God*, p. 684; *De Civitate Dei*, p. 635.

8. St. Augustine, *Of the Citie of God*, p. 685; *De Civitate Dei*, p. 635.

9. Judah Halevi, *The Kuzari*, intro. by Henry Slonimsky (New York, 1964), Part I, sec. 60-61, p. 52.

10. I wish to thank Dr. G. A. Salinger, formerly of the University of California San Diego Library, for information about this work. The *Nabatean Agriculture* has never been published. Dr. Salinger has been preparing a translation of a large section of it. There is some dispute about the authorship and intent of the work. See following T. Fahd, 'Ibn Wahshiyya' in *The Encyclopedia of Islam, new edition* (Leiden and London, 1969), p. 964. Some have argued that the work was intended to criticize Mohammedamism and to glorify the Nabateans at the expense of the Arabs. Daniel Chwolson described a portion of the work in *Über die Überreste der Altbabylonishchen Literatur in Arabischen Ubersetzungen. Académie Imperiale des Sciences de St. Petersbourg, Mémoires des savantes étrangers*, Vol. VIII, no. 2, (reprinted Amsterdam, 1963), pp. 158-59 and 173-74. Chwolson indicated that there is a full blown pre-Adamic theory in the work, claiming that there were innumerable people before him. Adam was the first to bring civilization and agriculture to Babylonia, but he was not the first man.

11. In Moses Maimonides, *The Guide for the Perplexed*, translated with an introduction and notes by Schlomo Pines, with an introductory essay by Leo Strauss (Chicago, 1964), Book III, chap. 29. La Peyrère referred to this section in Maimonides in *Men before Adam*, Lib. 3, chap. III, p. 143. Thomas Bangius of Copenhagen apparently alerted him to this text. Simon explained the section to La Peyrère in his letter of June 4, 1670; Simon, *Lettres choisies*, II, pp. 18-19.

12. Halevi, *op. cit*, sections 61-67.

13. *Ibid.*, sec. 67, p. 54.

14. See Simon, letter to La Peyrère, May 20, 1670, *Lettres choisies*, II, p. 5.

15. These Jewish possibilities are discussed in Schoeps, *Philosemitismus im Barok*, pp. 15-16. Schoeps indicates how some of the views entered into seventeenth-century discussions. La Peyrère could have learned of some of them from Menasseh ben Israel's writings. Some of the Moslem versions of this kind of pre-Adamism are cited in Arno Borst, *Der Turmbau von Babel* I (Stuttgart, 1957), pp. 338-39. See also Léon Poliakov, *Le Mythe Aryen* (Paris, 1971), pp. 125-29.

16. See Origen, *Origines in Sacras Scriptura*, notes by Pierre Daniel Huet, (Rothomagi, 1668), p. 63.

17. Maimonides, *Guide*, p. 515.

18. This appears in Fahd's article in the new edition of *The Encyclopedia of Islam*.

19. See note 11 of this chapter.

19a. See Yves Marquet, 'Cycles de la Souveraineté chez les Ihwan Al-Safa,' *Studia Islamica*, XXXVI (1972), pp. 48-50.

20. Otto Zöckler, *Geschichte der Beziehungen zwischen Theologie und Naturwissenschaften* (Gutersloh, 1877), I, p. 340.

21. Otto Zöckler, 'Peyrère's (gest. 1676) Präadamiten-Hypothese nach ihren Beziehungen zu den anthropologischen Fragen den Gegenwart,' *Zeitschrift fur die gesammte Lutherische Theologie und Kirche*, XXXIX (1878), p. 38. The charges against Zaninus de Solcia are listed there in note 2. Pastine, op. cit., pp. 55-58, suggests that Zaninus de Solcia's theory derived from Averroist sources, and from a cyclical theory of history developed by Arabic thinkers. La Monnoye's 'Dissertation' which appears at the beginning of many manuscripts and printed versions of *Les Trois Imposteurs* in the eighteenth century, states that, according to a Vatican manuscript, 'Jeannin de Solcia' was condemned in 1459, (apparently the same person), for having maintained 'that Moses, Jesus Christ and Mahomet had ruled the world at their pleasure.' See *The Three Impostors* (Dundee, 1844), p. 10.

22. Marcelino Menendez Pelayo, *Historia de los Heterodoxos Españoles*, Vol. I (Madrid, 1956), p. 593; and *Historia de los Heterodoxes Españoles*, Vol. VII, ed. E. Sanchez Reyes (Santander, 1948), Appenice I, pp. 324-25, where extracts from Alvaro Pelagio's *Collyrium contra haereses* are given from the manuscript in the Bibliotheca San Marco, Venice. Menendez Pelayo was unable to find much information on Scoto beyond that he had been both a Dominican and a Franciscan, and that he had been imprisoned in Lisbon. According to La Monnoye, in his 'Dissertation' accompanying *The Three Impostors*, Scoto was supposed to have said 'that Moses, Jesus Christ and Mahomet were Three impostors' (p. 9).

23. Pastine, *op. cit.*, pp. 49-55.

24. The case is mentioned in Wilhelmus Schickard, *Tarich* (Tübingen, 1628), pp. 175-76. It is cited in James Sydney Slotkin's *Readings in Early Anthropology* (Chicago, 1965), p. 38, as an indication of an early polygenetic theory.

25. See Vives's commentary on St. Augustine, *Of the Citie of God*, Book XII, chap. 10, pp. 450-51. This text is discussed by Ernest A. Strathmann in his *Sir Walter Ralegh, A Study in Elizabethan Skepticism* (New York, 1951), p. 200.

26. On Vives's naturalism and his Jewish background, see Carlos G. Noreña, *Juan Luis Vives* (The Hague, 1970).

27. Jean Jacquot, "Thomas Harriot's Reputation for Impiety," *Notes and Records of the Royal Society of London*, IX (1952), p. 170.

28. Thomas Bendysche, "The History of Anthropology," in *Memoires read before the Anthropological Society of London*, Vol. I (1863-64), p. 353.

29. Cited in Lewis Hanke, *The Spanish Struggle for Justice in the Conquest of America* (Philadelphia, 1949), p. 73. The Papal Bull is dated June 9, 1537. There is a separate study of it in Hanke's article, "Pope Paul III and the American Indians," *Harvard Theological Review*, XXX (1937), pp. 65-102. See also Pastine, *op. cit.*, pp. 20-27.

30. Lee Eldridge Huddleston, *Origins of the American Indians, European Concepts, 1492-1729* (Austin and London, 1967). See also Don Cameron Allen, *The Legend of Noah*. See also Lynn Glaser's 'Indians or Jews,' An Introduction to a reprint of Menasseh ben Israel's *The Hope of Israel* (Gilroy, CA, 1973).

31. John Rastell, *A New Interlude and a mery, of the nature of the i i i i Elements*, published in London c. 1520, cited in Huddleston, op. cit., p. 8.

32. Theophrastus von Hohenheim, called Paracelsus, *Samtliche Werke*, Abt. I, Band 12, ed. Karl Sudhoff (Munich and Berlin, 1929), p. 35: 'also seind wir alle von Adam hie. Und so mag ich das nit underlessen, von denen ein kleine meld ung zu tun, die in verborgenen insulen gefunden siend worden und noch verborgen sind, das sie von Adam zu sein geglaubt mogen werden, mag sichs nit befinden, das Adams kinder seind komen in die verborgenen insulen, sonder wol zu bedenken, das dieselbigen leut von einem anderen Adam seind; dan dahin wird es schwerlich komen, das sie fleisch und bluts halben uns gefreunt sein.' The English translation is from Slotkin, *op. cit.*, p. 42. Other similar texts of Paracelsus are given there.

33. These citations are presented in Bendysche, *op. cit.*, p. 354 from the 1605 edition. I have not been able to locate such an edition, and I have not been able to find the passages in question. However, similar views are found in the *Astronomia magna* and the *Weiteres zum Astronomia magna*, as well as in *De nymphis, sylphis, pygmaeis et salamandris et de coeteris spiritibus*, in *Samtliche Werke*, Abt. I, Band 14, ed. Karl Sudhoff (Berlin, 1933), pp. 115-51.

34. Henry Home, Lord Kames, *Sketches of the History of Man* (Glasgow, 1819), II, pp. 236-40, where this view is developed from a conjecture of Buffon's.

35. Paracelsus's discussions make it evident that he was less concerned with the problem of the origins of the American Indians than with developing his own cosmology and theology, and then placing the Indians in it. Walter Pagel has written two basic studies on Paracelsus; *Paracelsus: An Introduction to Philosophical Medicine in the Era of the Renaissance* (Basel and New York, 1958), and *Das medizinische Weltbild des Paracelsus, sein Zusammenhange mit Neuplatonismus und Gnosis* (Wiesbaden, 1962). I am very grateful to the late Dr. Walter Pagel for his helpful discussions with me over several years concerning Paracelsus's role in the development of the pre-Adamite theory. On Paracelsus's role in the history of polygenetic theories, see also Pastine, *op. cit.*, pp. 31-38.

Paracelsus's non-Adamic possibility was discussed by Sir Thomas Browne in his *Pseudodoxia Epidemica*, book IV, chap. 11, where he said 'and wise men may think there is as much reality in the Pigmies of Paracelsus, that is, his non-Adamical men, or middle natures betwixt man and spirits.

'There being thus no sufficient confirmation of their verity, some doubt may arise concerning their possibility, wherein, since it is not defined in what dimensions the soul may exercise her faculties, we shall not conclude impossibility.' *Works of Sir Thomas Browne*, ed. by Geoffrey Keynes, Vol. II, (London 1928), pp. 51-52.

Charles Webster indicates in his *From Paracelsus to Newton. Magic and the Making of Modern Science*, (Cambridge, England 1982), that the possible existence of non-Adamical people was discussed during the seventeenth century. See, for instance pp. 84 and 93.

36. Samuel Desmarets, *Refutatio Fabulae Prae-Adamitae*. In answer to the question whether Adam was the first man and the parent of the whole race, Desmarets listed Maimonides, Crellius, Cesalpino, Paracelsus, and the Kabbala as giving negative answers. With regard to Paracelsus, his views were related to the problems of accounting for nymphs, mermaids, sirens, Tritons, Pygmies, sylphs, gnomes and salamanders (pp. 1-9).

37. Jordani Bruni Nolani, *Opera Latine Conscripta*, ed. F. Fiorentino et al. (Naples, 1879-91; rep. Stuttgart and Baden, 1962), I, part 2, p. 282: 'Quia multicolores sunt hominum, nec enim generatio nigra Aetheiopum, et qualem producit America fulva, Udaque Neptune vivens occulta sub antris, Pygmeique iugis ducentes saecula clausis, Cives venarum Telluris, quique minaerae, Adstant custodes, atque Austri monstra Gigaintes, Progeniem referunt similem, primique parentis Unius vires cunctorum progenitrices.'

38. See the text cited in Slotkin, *op. cit.*, p. 43.

39. See Arthur Imerti's note to his translation of Giordano Bruno, *The Expulsion of the Triumphant Beast* (New Brunswick, 1964), p. 307, n. 52.

40. Giordano Bruno, *Spaccio della Bestia trionfante*, in *Dialoghi italiani: Dialoghi metafisici e dialoghi morali*, with notes by Giovanni Gentile, 3rd ed., ed. by Giovanni Aquilecchia (Florence, 1958), pp. 797-98.

41. Bruno, *Cabala del cavallo pegaseo*, Dialogo Secundo, in *Dialoghi Italiani*, pp. 882-891. Also on Bruno, see Pastine, *op. cit.*, pp. 38-48.

42. Concerning the accusations against Ralegh at this time, see Pierre Lefranc, *Sir Walter Ralegh, écrivain, l'oeuvre et les idées* (Quebec, 1968), chap. XII.

43. Thomas Nashe, *Pierce Pennilesse* and *Christs Teares over Jerusalem*, ed. by R. B. McKerrow (London, 1910), I, p. 172 and II, p. 116.

44. This appears in the Cholmley report. It is published in F.-C. Danchin, 'Etudes critiques sur Christopher Marlowe,' *Revue germanique*, IX (1913), p. 576.

45. The text of this report by agent Baines appears in Kocher, *Christopher Marlowe*, pp. 34-36. See also Lefranc, *op. cit.*, pp. 375-77.

46. See Jacquot's 'Thomas Harriot's Reputation for Impiety,' pp. 164-87; and Lefranc, *op. cit.*, pp. 344-52. Bruno's possible influence on Harriot and the Ralegh Circle is also discussed in these works.

47. On this, see also R. H. Popkin, 'The Pre-Adamite Theory in the Renaissance,' in Edward P. Mahoney, editor, *Philosophy and Humanism, Renaissance Essays in Honor of Paul Oskar Kristeller* (Leiden, 1976), esp. pp. 61-62. See Pastine, *op. cit.*, p. 9.

48. Huddleston, *op. cit.*, chap. I.

49. Quoted in Huddleston, *op. cit.*, p. 50 from Acosta's *Historia Natural y moral de los Indias* (Mexico, 1940), pp. 75-76. Huddleston also quotes Juan de Castellanos, as saying in 1589 (a year before Acosta), 'Pues no son en estado de inocencia que hijoy son de Adan y descendientes' (p. 46).

50. Quoted in Huddleston, *op. cit.*, p. 61. In the second edition of Garcia's work, an attack against Paracelsus and La Peyrère was added. Many refutations of La Peyrère's pre-Adamite theory were mentioned. See Gregoria Garcia, *Origen de los Indios de el Nuevo Mundo e Indias Occidentales*, Sequanda Impresion (Madrid, 1729), Libro Quarto, chap. XXIV, p. 248.

51. Lucilio Vanini, *De admirandis naturae reginae deaeque mortalium arcanis* (Paris, 1616). This passage was apparently considered quite significant in the history of anthropology. It is quoted in Bendysche, *op. cit.*, p. 355 and Slotkin, *op. cit.*, p. 80.

52. Francis Bacon, 'Of vicissitude of things,' *Essays* (London 1958), p. 232.

53. The quotation is given in Slotkin, *op. cit.*, p. 81.

54. Cf. Oddos, *op. cit.*, p. 50.

55. Christopher Hill, *The World Turned Upside Down* (London, 1972), p. 210.

56. *Ibid.*, p. 211.

57. *Ibid.*, p. 211.
58. British Library, Sloane MS. 1022, or 1115, fols. 15-16. I am most grateful to Dr. David Kubrin for bringing this item to my attention.

CHAPTER FOUR

1. La Peyrère, *Apologie*, pp. 8-12 describes his discussion with ministers about the theory when he was young. Richard Simon in his letter to Z. S., *Lettres choisies*, said that La Peyrère attributed the theory to a brother who died in England (II, p. 24). La Peyrère, in the 'Proeme' of *Men before Adam*, first two pages, related his childish ruminations on the subject.
2. Simon, letter to Z. S., *Lettres choisies*, II, p. 27.
3. Cf. R. H. Popkin, "The Development of Religious Scepticism and the Influence of Isaac La Peyrère's Pre-Adamism and Bible Criticism," in R. R. Bolgar, *Classical Influences on European Culture, Ad 1500-1700* (Cambridge, 1976), pp. 275-77.
4. This is the view set forth in La Peyrère's "Proeme" to *Men before Adam*.
5. 'To all the Synagogues to the Jews, dispersed over the face of the EARTH. People holy and elect! Sons of *Adam*, who was the Son of God! Sons of God also your selves. One, I know not who, wishes you all happiness; and himself to be one of you' (p. A4).
6. A London bookseller has recently listed *Men before Adam* as a separate item. It is so listed in the Wing catalogue. See Donald Wing, *Short-Title Catalogue 1641-1700* (New York, 1948), II, entry 427 (La Peyrère, Isaac de), *Men before Adam* (1656) and 428 *A Theological systeme*, 1655.
7. La Peyrère, 'Proeme,' p. F.
8. *Ibid.*, F - F^v.
9. *Ibid.*, F^v.
10. La Peyrère, *Des Iuifs, Elus, Reietés et Rapelés,* Preface, first page.
11. Miriam Yardeni, in her 'La Religion de La Peyrère et 'Le Rappel des Juifs,'' *Revue d'Histoire et de Philosophie religieuse*, LI (1971), pp. 245-59 claims La Peyrère was developing two different presentations of his theory, one for Jews and one for French nationalists. I have tried to show the inadequacy of this account in my 'Marrano Theology of La Peyrère.'
12. La Peyrère, "Discourse upon the Twelfth, Thirteenth and Fourteenth Verses of the Fifth chapter of the Epistles of S. Paul to the Romans," pp. B-B^v in *Men before Adam*.
13. La Peyrère, "Discourse," p. 19.
14. *Ibid.*, p. 20.
15. *Ibid.*, p. 22. La Peyrère went on a couple of lines later to say, *"Lastly, by this Position these words of the Apostle which seem pugnant concerning original sin, are reconciled upon which all Christian Doctrine is built, which is our chief design."*
16. *Ibid.*, p. 25.
17. *Ibid.*, p. 25-26.
18. *Ibid.*, chap. XVIII, pp. 42-45.
19. *Ibid.*, chap. XXIII-XXV, pp. 54-59.
20. See Gaston Sortais, *La Philosophie moderne depuis Bacon jusqu' à Leibniz*, Tome II (Paris 1922), pp. 272-85 on Hobbes in Paris. See also Perez Zagorin, 'Thomas Hobbes' Departure from England in 1640: An Unpublished Letter,' *The Historical Journal*, XXI (1978), pp. 157-160; and R. H. Popkin, 'Hobbes and Skepticism' in Linus J. Thro, S. J. ed., *History of Philosophy in the Making, Essays in Honor of James D. Collins*, (Washington 1982), pp. 134-35.
21. La Peyrère, 'A System of Divinity,' Book I, chap. 1, p. 4, in *Men before Adam*.
22. *Ibid.*, Book I, and Book II, chap. 1.
23. *Ibid.*, p. 59.
24. *Ibid.*, p. 66.
25. *Ibid.*, Book II, chap. 2-4.

26. *Ibid.*, chap. 5-6. The quotation is on p. 92. La Peyrère went on, 'This was a lively portraiture of the Gentiles, because they are, and are simply called the sons of men, and have nothing in their Nature to seek or reach God.'

27. *Ibid.*, chap. 7-11. 'It is worth our taking notice, that the men of the first creation (who, according to my supposition, are Gentiles,) as also the whole world, were created *by the word*. The first chapter of *Genesis* hath this expressly; which is the Chapter of the creation. *And God said make man according to our own Image*. He said, *Let us make*. And by his word he made him. But not by his word, but of wrought clay, the Lord made *Adam* Gen. Chap. 2. Which Chapter peculiarly handles the creation of *Adam*; and the framing of the Jews in Adam. ...

'*And God made* Adam *of the dust of the earth*, saith Gen: Chap. 2. He did not create *Adam* by his word, but made him with his hand out of the dust of the earth.'

28. *Ibid.*, p. 124.

29. *Ibid.*, p. 130. pp. 129-30. 'I'll prove out of Genesis it self, that the Gentiles are different in stock from Jews, which being understood it shall appear clearer, than the Sun, That the men of the first Creation were created long before *Adam*, who according to my supposition is Author of the Linage of the Jews.'

30. *Ibid.*, Book III, chap. 2-3.

31. See the references La Peyrère gave in Book III.

32. La Peyrère, *Men before Adam* Book IV, chap. XIV.

33. *Ibid.*, Books III and IV.

34. These arguments are developed in *Ibid.*, Books III and IV.

35. On La Peyrère's relations with Saumaise, see chap. II, pp. 8-9, and La Peyrère's letters to Philibert de la Mare, which are given in Oddos, *op. cit.*, pp. 282-302. La Peyrère, in a letter of June 15, 1660, said that when he received a copy of the *Annis Climactericus* he thanked Saumaise 'au nom de mes Préadamites' (p. 284).

36. La Peyrère, *Men before Adam*, Book IV, chap. 1, pp. 204-5.

37. *Ibid.*, p. 208.

38. *Ibid.*, p. 210.

39. *Ibid.*, Book IV, chap. ii-iii.

40. This appears in the Talmud, Baba Bathra 15A.

41. See, for instance, Simon Patrick, *A Commentary upon the First Book of Moses called Genesis*, 2nd edition (London, 1698). On p. 36, Bishop Patrick specifically denied the Preadamite theory.

42. Ibn Ezra is discussed by most commentators up to the eighteenth century.

43. See La Peyrère's unpublished *Réponse de Lapeyrere aux calomnies de Des Marais*, Bibl. municipale de Dole, Ms. no. 107, fol 47.

44. Menasseh ben Israel's *Conciliador* was extremely widely read, and is one of his early works that gained him the reputation of '*the* Jewish philosopher.' In only one comment on a passage did Menasseh indicate that there might be something in Scripture that did not make sense.

45. This is the burden of most of the fourth book of *Men before Adam*.

46. *Ibid.*, Book IV, chap. v, p. 234.

47. *Ibid.*, Book IV, chap. v, p. 250.

48. *Ibid.*, Book IV, chap. ix, p. 255.

49. See Ralegh's *History of the World*, Book I, chap. vii.

50. So La Peyrère reported in his letter to Philibert de la Mare, Sept. 1661, which appears in Oddos, *op. cit.*, p. 290.

51. Matthew Hale, *The Primitive Origination of Mankind*, (London, 1677), p. 185.

52. Edward Stillingfleet, *Origines Sacrae* (London, 1662), Book III, chap. IV. In the Preface to the reader, Stillingfleet indicated that he hoped his work would 'salve the Authority of Scripture' so that '*we may hope to hear no more of Men before Adam.*'

53. Thomas Burnet, *Telluris theoria sacra* (London, 1681), and *The Theory of the Earth* (London, 1684). The debate about Noah's Flood in the seventeenth century is examined in Don Cameron Allen's *The Legend of Noah*. Pierre Bayle cited La Peyrère as the modern author who held that only Judea was inundated in the Flood; *Reponses aux Questions d'un Provincial*, Part IV, chap. V.

54. La Peyrère, *Men before Adam*, 'A System of Divinity,' Book IV, chap. X, p. 261.

55. La Peyrère, *Du Rappel des Juifs*, 'Au Lecteur,' and Livres I-II.

56. *Ibid.*, pp. 82-151.

57. *Ibid.*, Livre III, pp. 153-55.

58. *Ibid.*, pp. 156-60.

59. *Ibid.*, p. 162. La Peyrère stated the Jewish response as 'si nos Peres n'avoient pas Crucifié Iesus Christ: Iesus Christ ne seroit pas Mort pour toy. Et si Iesus Christ n'estoit pas Mort pour toy, tu serais mort en tes pechez & serois mort d'une Mort eternelle . . . Tu nous veux faire mourir pour ce que nos Peres ont peché. Tu ne le peux vouloir sans Ingratitude; par ce que tu nous poursuis pour un crime qui t'a esté profitable.' Views like this concerning the merits of the Jewish contribution to the Crucifixion had appeared in the Middle Ages. See Bernard Blumenkranz, *Juifs et Christiens dans le Monde Occidental, 430-1096* (The Hague, 1960), p. 271.

60. *Ibid.*, pp. 164-76.

61. *Ibid.*, pp. 177-78. At the time that La Peyrère was writing, the terms 'Cristianos nuevos,' 'conversos,' and 'Marranos' were often used interchangeably though 'Marrano' was pejorative, signifying a crypto-Jew or a subversive Christian. The seven thousand figure was attributed to St. Paul.

62. *Ibid.*, pp. 179-93.

63. *Ibid.*, pp. 194-202.

64. *Ibid.*, pp. 203-9.

65. *Ibid.*, pp. 213-15.

66. *Ibid.*, pp. 217-25. La Peyrère regarded the Recall of the Jews as so crucial that the Christians of the seventeenth century should do what they could 'pour accomplir un si haut Ouvrage' (pp. 227-28).

67. *Ibid.*, Livre IV, pp. 230-38.

68. *Ibid.*, pp. 243-46.

69. Elijah Montalto (who was Queen Marie de Medici's physician) wrote a treatise on Isaiah 53 which exists in manuscript copies all over Europe, as well as the libraries of Columbia University and Hebrew Union College in Cincinnati. The first part of it was published in English by 'Philo-Veritatas' in London in 1770. Cecil Roth, in *The History of the Jews in Venice* (Philadelphia, 1930), p. 243, said that Montalto's work 'remains a classic of Jewish polemics.' Orobio de Castro's writing on Isaiah 53 exists in manuscripts in many major libraries. A part of it was published in A. Neubauer, *The 53rd Chapter of Isaiah* (Oxford, 1876), pp. 21-118.

70. La Peyrère *Du Rappel des Juifs*, Livre IV, pp. 248-84. La Peyrère insisted that if one did not carefully distinguish Jesus Christ 'venu pour les Gentils' and Iesus Christ qui est le Redempteur à venir pour les Iuifs,' it would be impossible to reconcile many scriptural texts (pp. 248-49).

71. *Ibid.*, pp. 288-89.

72. *Ibid.*, Livre V, pp. 304-6 and 330-56. La Peyrère was in favor of omitting all canons, decrees, etc. that might disturb the Jews. Otherwise the Jews might say, 'Vos canons, ô Chrestians! & vos Articles de Foy sont plus difficiles à comprendre, que les Regles & les Ceremonies de Moyse ne sont difficiles à observer,' p. 331.

73. *Ibid.*, pp. 366-75.

74. La Peyrère, 'Discourse upon the Twelfth....,' *Men before Adam*, pp. 60-61.

CHAPTER FIVE

1. John Dury, *Israel's Call to March out of Babylon into Jerusalem* (London, 1646); Samuel Hartlib, *Englands Thankfulnesse* (London, 1642); Christopher Hill, *Puritanism and Revolution* (London, 1965); and Hugh Trevor-Roper, 'Three Foreigners: The Philosophers of the Puritan Revolution,' in *Religion, the Reformation and Social Change* (London, 1967).

2. See R. H. Popkin, 'The Third Force in Seventeenth Century Philosophy: Scepticism, Science and Biblical Prophecy,' *Nouvelles de la Republique des Lettres*, III (1983);

Peter Toon, (ed.), *Puritans, the Millenium and the Future of Israel* (Cambridge, 1970); Jan Van den Berg, 'Quaker and Chiliast: the contrary thoughts of William Ames and Peter Serrarius,' in R. Buick Knox, ed., *Reformation Conformity and Dissent. Essays in honour of Geoffrey Nuttall* (London, 1977); and E. G. E. van der Wall, 'De Hemelsche Tekenen en het rijk van Christus op Aarde. Chiliasme en Astrologie bij Petrus Serrarius, 1600-1669,' *Kerkhistorische Studien* (Leiden, 1982), pp. 45-62.

3. Christopher Hill, ''Till the Conversion of the Jews,' William Andrews Clark Lecture, Oct. 1981, forthcoming; Mayir Vereté, 'The Restoration of the Jews in English Protestant Thought, 1790-1840,' *Middle Eastern Studies*, VIII (1972), pp. 3-50, and 'The Idea of the Restoration of the Jews in England's Protestant Thought,' William Andrews Clark lecture, May 1982, forthcoming; and David S. Katz, *Philosemitism and the Readmission of the Jews to England, 1603-1655* (Oxford, 1982).

4. See Katz, *op. cit.*, chaps. 3 and 5. One of the main points made in the much published account of the supposed Great Council of the Jews in Hungary, October 12, 1650, was that the Jews rejected Catholic attempts to convert them, but welcomed concern from English Protestants. The account of the Council, by one, otherwise unidentified, Samuel Brett, first appeared in 1655. It also appears in the *Harleian Miscellany*, ed. W. Oldys (London, 1808-1813), I, pp. 379-85. On this work, see R. H. Popkin, 'The First College of Jewish Studies, *Revue des Etudes juives*, forthcoming.

5. Karl Kottman, *Law and Apocalypse. The Moral Thought of Luis de Leon* (The Hague, 1972), Introduction and references given there. See also Americo Castro, *La Realidad historia de España* (Mexico, 1966).

6. See Lucio d'Azevedo, *A Evolucao do Sebastinismo*, 2nd ed. (Lisbon, 1947); R. Cantel, *Prophetisme et Messianisme dans l'oeuvre du Père Vieira* (Paris, 1960); and A. J. Saraiva, 'Antonio Vieira, Menasseh ben Israel et le Cinquième Empire,' *Studia Rosenthaliana*, VI (1972), pp. 26-32.

7. H. V. Livermore, *A New History of Portugal* (Cambridge, 1967), pp. 165-67; and Saraiva, *op. cit.*, pp. 30-33.

8. Antonio de Vieira's most important work is entitled *Historia do Futuro, Esperancas de Portugal, Quinto Imperio do Mundo*, which was begun in 1649, but only published in 1718. Cf. Saraiva, op. cit., p. 50.

9. Poliakov, *Le Mythe Aryen* (Paris, 1971), p. 31.

10. Marjorie Reeves, *The Influence of Prophecy in the Later Middle Ages*, p. 320.

11. *Ibid.*, p. 323.

12. *Ibid.*, p. 339. There is some indication that the Italian expedition of King Charles VIII of France was seen by both Jews and Christians as having Messianic significance. See Ammon Linder, 'Expedition italienne des Charles VIII et les esperances messianiques des Juifs: Temoinage du manuscrit B.N. Lat. 5971A,' *Revue des Etudes juives*, CXXXVII (1978), pp. 179-86.

13. Marion L. Kuntz, *Guillaume Postel: Prophet of the Restitution of All Things* (The Hague, 1981).

13a. See M. L. Kuntz, 'Guillaume Postel and the World State: Restitution and the Universal Monarchy,' *History of European Ideas*, IV, (1983) Part II, pp. 445-465. Pp. 446-450 deal especially with Postel's concept of the Galli and their role.

14. See Kuntz *Guillaume Postel*, and 'Guillaume Postel and the Universal Monarchy,' *Proceedings of the Postel Congress, Avranches 1981*, forthcoming; and Claude-Gilbert Dubois, 'La Mythologie nationaliste de Guillaume Postel,' *Proceedings of the Postel Congress, Avranches 1981*, forthcoming.

15. William Bouwsma, *Concordia Mundi, The Career and Thought of Guillaume Postel (1510-1581)* (Cambridge, MA, 1957), p. 292.

16. Guillaume Postel, *Les Raisons de la Monarchie* (n.p., n.d.), p. xix. See also Kuntz, 'Guillaume Postel and the World State,' esp. pp. 446-50.

17. Postel, *op. cit.*, pp. xxvi-xxvii and xxx.

18. Guillaume Postel, *De Foenicium Literis* (Paris, 1552), no. 32.

19. Postel, *Les Raisons de la Monarchie*, p. xxxi.

20. Poliakov, *Le Mythe Aryen*, chap. 2.

21. See for instance, Postel's *Candelabri Typici in Mosis Tabernaculos* (Venice, 1548), edited by F. Secret (Nieuwkoop, 1966).

22. Kuntz, 'Guillaume Postel and the Universal Monarchy.' I have also drawn on a draft of part of Prof. Kuntz's work in preparation on Postel's philosophy.

23. See Kuntz, *Guillaume Postel*, and J. Dupèbe, 'Poursuites contre Postel en 1553,' in the *Proceedings of the Postel Congress, Avranches 1981*, forthcoming.

24. See, for instance, the attack on Postel in Philippe de Mornay, *Reponse pour le Traité de l'Eglise...aux Objections proposées en un livre nouvellement mis en lumière intitulé Les Trois Veritez*, Seconde edition (n.p., 1595). Pierre Charron defended Postel from this attack in his *La Replique de Maistre Pierre Charron sur la Responce faite à sa troisième Verité* (Lyon, 1595), p. 9. Gabriel Naudé, in his *Considerations politiques sur les Coups d'Etat* (n.p., 1752), II, pp. 37ff., put Postel in the same class as political crackpots like Savonarola and Campanella. Naudé wrote this in 1639.

25. See Reeves, *op. cit.*, p. 387.

26. *Ibid.*, p. 388.

27. Cf. Mersenne's correspondence for 1634.

28. La Peyrère, *Du Rappel des Juifs*, 'Au Lecteur,' and Livre I.

29. *Ibid.*, p. 115.

30. *Ibid.*, pp. 116-17.

31. *Ibid.*, pp. 117-18.

32. *Ibid.*, pp. 121-22.

33. *Ibid.*, p. 131.

34. *Ibid.*, pp. 135-36.

35. *Ibid.*, p. 141.

36. *Ibid.*, pp. 141-52.

37. Nahum Sokolow, *The History of Zionism* (London, 1919), I, pp. 41-42.

38. La Peyrère, *Du Rappel des Juifs*, 'Synopsis' at the end of the book.

39. Naudé, for instance, knew Postel's works, and possessed some of them. There is a copy of one of Postel's works *De Foenicum Literis* in the Olin Library of Washington University that belonged to Naudé. The Bibliothèque Nationale has a copy of Postel's *Panthenosia* that also belonged to Naudé. Cf. Kuntz, *Guillaume Postel*, p. 187.

40. In La Peyrère's preface to *Relation de l'Islande*, published in Paris in 1663, Louis XIV is cited in the dedication to the Prince of Condé as a universal king who, with Condé's help, will spread God's message and begin the conquest of the world. In La Peyrère's *Lettre à Philotime* (Paris, 1658), Pope Alexander VII is given the role of uniting the world, as Alexander the Conqueror tried to do (see pp. 157-62).

CHAPTER SIX

1. La Peyrère, *Men before Adam*, 'Discourse upon the twelfth, thirteenth and fourteenth Verses of the Fifth Chapter of the Epistle of the Apostle Paul to the Romans,' p. 22: 'The History of *Genesis* appears much clearer, and agrees with itself. And it is wonderfully reconciled with all profane records whether ancient or new to wit, those of the *Chaldeans, Egyptians, Scythians*, and *Chinensians*; that most ancient Creation which is set down in the first of *Genesis* is reconciled to those of *Mexico*, not long ago discovered by *Columbus*. It is likewise reconciled to those Northern and Southern Nations which are not known, All whom, as likewise those of the first and most ancient creation, were, it is, probable, created with the Earth itself in all parts thereof, and not propagated from Adam.

'Again, by this Position, Faith and right Reason are reconciled, which suffers us not to believe that the world had so late an infancy.'

See also, R. H. Popkin, 'The Development of Religious Scepticism and the Influence of Isaac La Peyrère's Pre-Adamism and Bible Criticism,' in R. R. Bolgar, *Classical Influences on European Culture, AD 1500-1700* (Cambridge, 1976), 278-79.

2. La Peyrère, *Du Rappel des Juifs*, Livre V; and *Men before Adam*, Book V. See also Popkin, 'Marrano Theology,' pp. 102-3, 110-12.

3. A. Dupront, *Pierre Daniel Huet et l'exégèse comparatiste au XVIIe siècle* (Paris, 1930), p. 270.

4. La Peyrère, *Men before Adam*, Book IV, chap. 1, pp. 204-5.

5. *Ibid.*, pp. 205-8.

6. See W. Bacher, 'Ibn Ezra, Abraham ben Meir (Aben Ezra),' *Jewish Encyclopedia*, VI, pp. 520-24; and Adolphe Lods, *Jean Astruc et la Critique biblique au XVIII siècle* (Strasbourg and Paris, 1924), p. 27. Spinoza said that Aben Ezra, 'a man of enlightened intelligence, and no small learning,' was the first to question the Mosaic authorship of the Pentateuch; *A Theological-Political Treatise* in *Works of Spinoza*, Elwes ed. (New York, 1955), I, chap. VIII, pp. 120-21.

7. La Peyrère, *Men before Adam*, Book IV, chap. 1, p. 208.

8. Adolphe Lods, 'Astruc et la critique biblique de son temps,' *Revue d'Histoire et de Philosophie religieuses* (1924), pp. 111-13.

9. Thomas Hobbes, *Leviathan*, Part III, chap. XXXIII, p. 369 in volume three of the Molesworth edition of the *English Works of Thomas Hobbes* (London, 1839).

10. Louis Ellies-Du Pin, *Nouvelle Bibliothèque des Autheurs Ecclesiastiques*, 2nd edition (Paris, 1690), I, p. 4.

11. *Ibid.*, p. 30. Richard Kidder, Bishop of Bath and Wells, also blamed Hobbes, 'the Author of the Book called the *Praeadamitae*' and Spinoza for boldly denying the Mosaic authorship, and thereby striking at the very root of Christianity. See *A Commentary on the Five Books of Moses: with a Dissertation concerning the Author or Writer of the said Books* (London, 1694), I, b 4v. La Peyrère's evidence is discussed at length on pp. LXXI-LXXIX. In Filleau de la Chaise, *An Excellent Discourse Proving the Divine Original and Authority of the Five Books of Moses* (London 1682), Part II, it is said that the view that Moses cannot be the author of the Books which are attributed to him was raised by Hobbes, La Peyrère, and Spinoza 'All Atheists or Infidels.' p. 62.

12. Matthew Hale, *The Primitive Origination of Mankind* (London, 1677), p. 185.

13. Thomas Paine, *The Age of Reason, Part the Second, being an Investigation of True and Fabulous Theology* (London, 1795), p. 4.

14. David Levi, *Letters to Dr. Priestley in answer to his Letters to the Jews, Part II, occasioned by Mr. David Levi's Reply to the Former Part* (London, 1789) pp. 14-15.

15. This is discussed in chap. V. Both Spinoza and Simon read La Peyrère. Simon knew him very well, and Spinoza may have met him prior to Spinoza's excommunication.

16. Jean Astruc, *Conjectures sur les Mémoires originaux dont il paroit que Moyses s'est servi pour composer le Livre de Genese* (Bruxelles, 1753), p. 454.

17. Thomas Bendysche, 'The History of Anthropology,' *Memoirs read before the Anthropological Society of London*, I (1863-64), pp. 335-420. La Peyrère was discussed on pp. 355-56. Answers to him are treated. Pp. 365-71 contain as an appendix a reprint of a polygenetic argument published in 1695 which will be dealt with in chap. VII. Pp. 372-420 are a translation of a learned discussion of the refutations of La Peyrère by Vincent Rumpf of Hamburg.

18. James S. Slotkin, *Readings in Early Anthropology* (Chicago, 1965), pp. 81-82, and 108.

19. Louis L. S. Leakey and V. M. Goodall, *Unveiling Man's Origins* (Cambridge, MA, 1960); and Jacques Monod, *La Hasard et la Nécessité* (Paris, 1970).

20. Carleton Coons, *The Origin of Races* (New York, 1962). On the present discussion of polygenesis and monogenesis, see Stephen Molnar, *Races, Types, and Ethnic Groups: The Problem of Human Variation* (Englewood Cliffs, NJ, 1975).

21. See chapter X; and also Popkin, 'The Philosophical Bases of Modern Racism,' *Philosophy and the Civilizing Arts, Essays Presented to Herbert W. Schneider*, ed. by Craig Walton and John P. Anton (Athens, OH., 1974), pp. 126-64; and 'Pre-Adamism in 19th Century American Thought: 'Speculative Biology and Racism,' *Philosophia*, VIII (1978), pp. 205-39.

22. See La Peyrère, *Relation du Groenland* and La Peyrère's correspondence with Ole Worm on this matter. Some similar views appear in the passages quoted by Slotkin, *op. cit.*, p. 108 on the evolution of religion from *Praeadamitae*.

23. Isaac La Peyrère, *Du Rappel des Juifs*, pp. 121-22.

24. Eusebius Renaudot, *A Dissertation on the Chinese Learning* (London, 1733), p. 255. I am grateful to Dr. Yuen-Ting Lai for this reference.

CHAPTER SEVEN

1. La Peyrère. *Lettre à Philotime*, p. 76; *Apologie*, p. 38; *Des Iuifs, elus, reietés et repelés*, first page of preface.

2. At the end of *Vindiciae Judaeorum, or a Letter in Answer to certain Questions propounded by a Noble and Learned Gentleman, touching the Reproaches cast on the Nation of the Jewes, wherein all objections are candidly, and yet fully cleared* (London, 1656), Menasseh ben Israel listed the works he had ready for publication. One of them is *Refutatio libri qui titulus Praeadamitae*. No trace of this work has been found.

3. See Popkin, 'Menasseh ben Israel and Isaac La Peyrère,' pp. 61-63.

4. Grotius, *Dissertatio Altera de origine Gentium Americanarum adversus obtractatorem*, esp. pp. 13-14.

5. Eusebius Romanus (Phillipe le Prieur, listed in Bibliothèque Nationale as le P. Jean Mabillon), *Animadversiones in librum de Prae-adamitis* (Paris, 1656, 2nd ed. 1658.)

6. Michael Colabus, *Disputationes ex capite V Epistolae ad Romanos contra Praeadamitae* (Rostock, 1656).

7. Johann Christian Dannhauer, *Praeadamitae Utis, sive fabula primorum hominum ante Adamum conditorum explosa* (Strasbourg, 1656).

8. J. Hilpert, *Disquisitio de Praeadamitis* (Utrecht, 1656). There were apparently two other editions in Helmstadt and Amsterdam.

9. Ant. Hulsuis, *Non ens praeadamiticum* (Leiden, 1656).

10. Samuel Desmarets, *Refutatis fabulae praeadamiticae* (Groningen, 1656). Interesting material on Desmarets' relations with Saumaise appears in Paul Dibon, 'Lettres de Samuel Des Marets à Claude Saumaise,' LIAS, I (1974), pp. 267-99.

11. J. L. Micraelius, *Monstrosae de Praeadamitis opinionis abominanda foeditas demonstrata* (Stettin, 1656).

12. Jean-Baptiste Morin, *Refutatis compendiosa erronai ac detestandi libri de Praeadamitis* (Paris, 1656).

13. J. Pythius, *Responsio exetastica ad tractatum incerto authore nuper editum cui titulus Praeadamitae* (Leiden, 1656).

14. J. H. Ursinus, *Novus Prometheus Praeadamitarum plastes ad Caucasum relegatus et religatus* (Frankfort, 1656).

15. B. Morange, *Libri de Praeadamitis brevis analysis, quae paveis totius libri fundamentum exponitur et evertitur* (Lyon, 1656).

16. Paul Felgenhauer, *Anti-Prae-Adamita. Prüfung über das Lateinische in Truck Aussgegangne Buch dessen Titul is Prae-Adamitae, Dass, vor Adam auch sollen Menschen gewesen seyn* (Amsterdam, 1659).

17. Thomas Bangius, *Coelum Orientes et Prisci Mundi Triade. Exercitationum Literarium Repraesentatum* (Copenhagen, 1657), pp. 132-34. This work was reprinted in Cracow in 1691 under the title *Exercitationes Philologico-Philosophicae quibus Materia de Ortu et Progressu Literarum.*

18. F. Dormay, *Animadversiones in Libros Prae-Adamitarum* (Paris, 1657).

19. Isaac Vossius, *Dissertatio de vera Aetate Mundi* (The Hague, 1659).

20. Georg Horn, *Dissertatio de vera aetate mundi qua sententia illorum refellitur qui statuent Natale Mundi tempis Annis minimum 1440 vulgarem aerem anticipare* (Leiden, 1659).

21. Louis Cappel, *The Hinge of Faith and Reason*, trans. by Philip Marinel (London, 1660).

22. Edward Stillingfleet, *Origines Sacrae* (London, 1661).

23. Martin Schook, *Diluvium Noachi Universale sive Vindicae Communis sententiae quod Diluvium Noachicum universae terrae incubuerit*, (Groningen, 1662).

24. Johann Heinrich Heidegger, *Historia sacra Patriarchum* (Amsterdam, 1667).

25. Johann Conrad Dietrich, *Antiquitates Biblicae* (Gissae-Hassorum, 1671).
26. A. B. Hempel, *Exercitatio de Praeadamitis* (Thorem, 1673).
27. Matthew Hale, *The Primitive Origination of Mankind* (London, 1677).
28. Christopher P. de Waldenfels, *Selectae Antiquitatis Libris XII. De Gestes primaevis, item Origine Gentium Nationumque migrationibus, atque praecipius nostratum dilocationibus, ex Sacre Scripturae* (Nuremberg, 1677).
29. Theophile (Gottlieb) Spitzel, *Infelix literatus ex infelicium periculis et casibus* (Augsburg, 1676).
30. Barthold Goldbach, *Dissertation Disp. de controversia celebri utrum ante Adamum alii fuerint homines* (Konigsberg, 1682).
31. Willem Salden, *Otio Theologica* (Amsterdam, 1684).
32. M. G. Vockerodt, *Historia Societatum et Rei Literariae ante Diluvium* (Jena, 1687).
33. J. Vake, *Beweisthun dass ein Gott sey, samt Vorbericht von der Praeadamiterey* (Hamburg, 1696). There is an earlier work by this author, *Disputatio physica de origine animal humane* (Leipzig, 1669).
34. J. Fecht, *Praeadamitismi recens incrustati examin* (Rostock, 1696).
35. Gottfried Arnold, *Kirchen und Ketzer Historie* (Frankfurt, 1700).
36. Friedrich Spanheim, *Disputatis Theologica de Statu Instituto Primi Hominis*, in *Opera*, Tomus III (Leiden, 1703).
37. Herman Christopher Engelcken, *Dissertatio Theologica Praeadamitiste recens incrustati examen complectens* (Rostock, 1707). Apparently there was an earlier edition in 1698.
38. Noel Alexandre, *Historia Ecclesiastica Veteris Novique Testamenti* (Paris, 1714).
39. J. Ant. Schmid, *Pentas Dissertationum. I. de Praeadamitis ex orbe proscriptis* (Hemsted, 1716).
40. Vincent Rumpf, *Dissertatio Critica de hominibus orbis nostri incolis, specie et ortu avito inter se non differentibus*, (Hamburg, 1721). This work was translated in the mid-nineteenth century, and appears as appendix III of Bendysche's 'History of Anthropology.'
41. Jacob Friedrich Reimann, *Historia Universalis Atheismi et Atheorum falso de merito suspectorum apud Judaeos, Ethnicos, Christianos, Muhamedanos* (Hildesiae, 1725).
42. J. Hermansson, *Dissertation de Prae-adamitis* (Upsala, 1730). There are several more refutations listed in Johann Anton Trinius, *Freydemker Lexicon* (Leipzig and Bernberg, 1759), art. 'Isaac Peyrerius,' pp. 389-93.
43. All of these points appear in Desmarets's preface to his *Refutatio*.
44. Desmarets, *op. cit.* On pp. 1-3 the author showed that the pre-Adamite theory went back to Book III, chap. 29 of Maimonides' *Guide*, and to Paracelsus's views.
45. See, for instance, La Peyrère, *Apologie*. See also the first page of the preface to the unpublished *Des Iuifs, Elus, Reietes et Rapeles*.
46. La Peyrère, *Recueil des Lettres escrites à Monsieur le Comte de la Suze*, pp. 66-68.
47. The letter appears on p. xxxix of the preface of Desmaret's *Refutatio*.
48. One is the manuscript at Chantilly and the other at Dôle. Both are entitled *Reponse de Lapeyrère aux calomnies de Des Marais, Ministre de Groninque*, and both are in La Peyrère's hand.
49. La Peyrère, *Reponse* (Chantilly ms), p. 6.
50. *Ibid.*, pp. 8-9.
51. *Ibid.*, p. 13.
52. *Ibid.*, p. 14.
53. *Ibid.*, p. 17.
54. *Ibid.*, p. 28. La Peyrère used some of his phonetic spelling in his work.
55. *Ibid.*, pp. 34-36.
56. *Ibid.*, p. 44.
57. *Ibid.*, p. 53.
58. *Ibid.*, pp. 98-99.
59. *Ibid.*, p. 110.
60. On the last page La Peyrère declared, 'A l'école Pedan Des Marais.'
61. See Popkin, 'Menasseh ben Israel and Isaac La Peyrère.' Menasseh's interest in La Peyrère's Messianic theories will be discussed in chap. VIII. As I shall show later on

Menasseh seems at least to have read *Du Rappel des Juifs* when he visited Queen Christina.

62. See the list of Spinoza's books in Jacob Freudenthal, *Die Lebensgeschichte Spinoza's* (Leipzig, 1899); item 54 is 'Prae-Adamitae 1655.'

63. A list of some of the borrowing is given in Leo Strauss, *Spinoza's Critique of the Bible*, pp. 264 and 327.

64. Cf. I. S. Révah, *Spinoza et Juan de Prado* (Paris and The Hague, 1959); and 'Aux Origines de la Rupture Spinozienne: Nouveaux documents sur l'incroyance dans la communauté judéo-portugaise d'Amsterdam à l'époque de l'excommunication de Spinoza,' *Revue des Études juives*, III, CXXIII (1964), pp. 357-431.

65. Révah, *Spinoza et Juan Prado*, pp. 43 and 84-153; and 'Aux Origines de la Rupture Spinozienne,' pp. 370-73, 378, and 391-408. See also Popkin, 'Spinoza and La Peyrère,' *The Southwestern Journal of Philosophy*, VIII (1977), p. 189; and *The History of Scepticism from Erasmus to Spinoza* (Berkeley, Los Angeles and London, 1979), pp. 227-28.

66. See Frederick Pollock, *Spinoza His Life and Philosophy*, 2nd ed. (London, 1899), pp. 17-18 for the full statement of the excommunication decree.

67. Révah, *Spinoza et Juan de Prado*, pp. 31-32 and 64.

68. Jacob Thomasius, *Dissertationes LXIII Varii Argumenti* (Halle, 1693), p. 574. I am grateful to Professor Asa Kasher of the University of Tel Aviv for bringing this item to my attention.

69. Philip van Limborch, *De Veritate Religiones Christianae, Amica collatio cum erudito Judaeo* (Gouda, 1687), p. 148. I should like to thank Dr. Joseph Kaplan of the Hebrew University of Jerusalem (who wrote a dissertation on Orobio de Castro) for bringing this text to my attention.

70. On Samuel Fisher's career, see the article on him in the *Dictionary of National Biography*; and William C. Braithwaite, *The Beginnings of Quakerism*, 2nd ed. revised by H. J. Cadbury (Cambridge, 1955), esp. pp. 288-94 and 426-28.

71. Christopher Hill, *The World Turned Upside Down*, pp. 213-15.

72. Fisher's *The Rustick Alarm to the Rabbies* of 1660 is over 900 pages long. It was printed again in the collection of Fisher's writings, *The Testimony of Truth Exalted* (n.p., 1679), where it is over 750 folio pages. Henry J. Cadbury, in his 'Early Quakerism and Un-canonical Lore,' *Harvard Theological Review*, XL (1947), p. 183, said that Fisher was known among his opponents as 'the best scholar that ever professed Quakerism.'

73. This appears from letters sent by members of the Quaker mission in Amsterdam. See R. H. Popkin, 'Spinoza, the Quakers and the Millenarians, 1656-1658,' *Manuscrito*, VI (1982), pp. 113-33.

74. The pamphlet is Margaret Fell's *A Loving Salutation, to the Seed of Abraham among the Jews* of 1657. Margaret Fell had asked Fisher to translate it, but he was unable to do it. He did, however, append his own Hebrew exhortation to the Jews to the Hebrew translation that was published in 1658. The evidence that it was probably done by Spinoza appears in my article referred to in footnote 73. The text with commentary, and with the original English, has been prepared for publication by Prof. Michael Signer of Hebrew Union College and myself, and should appear shortly. Two copies of the Hebrew translation are in the collection of the Friends Library of London.

75. On Simon see A. Bernus, *Richard Simon et son histoire critique du Vieux Testament* (Lausanne, 1869); Louis I. Bredvold, *The Intellectual Milieu of John Dryden* (Ann Arbor, 1959), esp. pp. 98-107; Paul Hazard, *La Crise de la conscience européenne* (Paris, 1935), Deuxième partie, Chap. III, pp. 184-202; Henri Margival, *Essai sur Richard Simon et la critique biblique en France au XVIIᵉ siecle* (Paris, 1900); and Jean Steinmann, *Richard Simon et les origines de l'exégèse biblique* (Paris, 1960).

76. These are letters 1, 2 and 3 of Simon's *Lettres Choisies*, Vol. II, and 7, 8 and 9 of Vol. III, and the letter to M. Z. S. Paris 1688, Vol. II, lettre 4.

77. See Steinmann, *Richard Simon*, Cinquième partie, chap. V.

78. All of this appears in Simon's letters cited above.

79. Simon, letter to La Peyrère, May 27, 1670, *Lettres choisies*, II, pp. 12-17.

80. Simon, letter to M. Z. S., *Lettres choisies*, II, pp. 25-28.

81. Simon's usual view about Spinoza was that, 'Spinoza a pû avancer dans son livre

plusieurs choses véritables, et qu'il aura même prises de nos Auteurs; mais il en aura tiré des consequences fausses et impies'; Richard Simon, *De 'l'Inspiration les Livres sacrés* (Rotterdam, 1687), p. 43.

82. *Ibid.*., p. 48. Regardless of Spinoza's conclusions, Simon asserted, 'Il faut condamner les consequences impies que Spinosa a tiré de certaines maximes il suppose. Mais ces maximes ne sont pas toujours fausses d'elles-memes, ni à rejetter'; *Lettres choisies* (Rotterdam, 1702), Letter to M. Dallo, 1682, Vol. IV, p. 81.

83. See Popkin, 'Scepticism, Theology and the Scientific Revolution in the Seventeenth Century,' in I. Lakatos and A. Musgrave, *Problems in the Philosophy of Science* (Amsterdam, 1968), pp. 23-25; and 'Bible Criticism and Social Science,' *Boston Studies in the Philosophy of Science* XIV (1974), pp. 347-50.

84. Jean Astruc, *Conjectures sur les Memoires Originaux dont il paroît que Moyse s'est servi pour composer le Livre de la Genese*, pp. 452-54.

85. Edward Stillingfleet, *Origines Sacrae*, 8th ed. (London, 1709), p. 334.

86. Ibid., p. 334.

87. Ibid., p. 335. On Stillingfleet's views and their influence see Robert T. Carroll, *The Common-Sense Philosophy of Religion of Bishop Edward Stillingfleet* (The Hague, 1975).

88. Gabriel, Count Oxenstirn, 'Relation d'un Entretien qu j'eus autrefois à Padoue avec un fameux rabin,' in *Pensées de Monsieur le Comte d'Oxenstirn sur divers sujets* (The Hague, 1742), II, pp. 142-44. Concerning Rabbi Isaac Vita Cantarini, see the article on him in the *Encyclopedia Judaica*, V, pp. 122-23.

89. Oxenstirn, *op. cit.*, pp. 144-45.

90. *Ibid.*, p. 146.

91. *Ibid.*, pp. 146-49.

92. *Ibid.*, p. 149.

93. 'Cantarini, Isaac Vita Ha-Kohen,' *Encyclopedia Judaica*, V, p. 122.

94. Anne Conway, *The Principles of the Most Ancient and Modern Philosophy* (The Hague), pp. 153-58. The quotation is on p. 153.

95. G. Ricuperati, 'Alla origine de Triregno: La Philosophia Adamito-Noetice di A. Constantino,' *Rivista Storica Italiana*, LXXVII (1965), pp. 602-38. Pastine, *op. cit.*, p. 189, indicates that La Peyrère's work was circulating in Italy by 1659.

96. Arnaldo Momigliano, 'Vico's Scienza Nuova: Roman 'Bestioni' and Roman 'Eroi,'' *History and Theory*, V (1966), pp. 3-23; and 'La Nuova Storia Romana di G. B. Vico,' *Rivista Storia Italiana*, LXXVII (1965), pp. 773-90 (pp. 780-81 deal with Vico's use of La Peyrère's ideas). See also, Pastine, *op. cit.*, p. 190.

97. Giambattista Vico, *Principi di Scienza Nuova*, in *Opere*, ed. F. Nicolini (Milan and Naples, 1953), Libro primo. La Peyrère is specifically mentioned on p. 402, as is Martin Schoock's refutation of La Peyrère.

98. A. Momigliano, comment in Popkin, 'Scepticism, Theology and the Scientific Revolution in the Seventeenth Century,' p. 34.

99. Blaise Pascal, *Pensées*, Lafuma edition, in *Oeuvres complètes* (Paris and New York, 1963), pensée 575-651.

100. Pierre-Daniel Huet's copy of *Prae Adamitae* is in the Bibliothèque Nationale, D^2. 5227. It has several markings of key passages. It is also bound with Eusebius Romanous *Animadversiones in Librum Praeadamitarum* of 1656.

101. Cf. Pierre-Daniel Huet, *Demonstratio Evangelica* (Paris, 1679). A. Dupront, in his work, *Pierre-Daniel Huet et l'exégèse comparatiste au xvii* siecle* (Paris, 1930), pp. 45-46, discussed Huet's view regarding La Peyrère's theory.

CHAPTER EIGHT

1. Cecil Roth, *The History of the Marranos* (Philadelphia, 1941); Americo Castro, *The Structure of Spanish History* (Princeton, 1954); I. S. Révah, 'Les Marranes,' *Revue des Études Juives*, CXVIII (1959-60), pp. 29-77; B. Netanyahu, *The Marranos of Spain* (New York, 1973); Joseph Hayim Yerushalmi, *From Spanish Court to Italian Ghetto, Isaac Cardoso* (New

York, 1971); Yosef Kaplan, 'The Portuguese Jews in Amsterdam. From Forced Conversion to a Return to Judaism,' *Studia Rosenthaliana*, XV (1981), pp. 37-51; and H. P. Salomon, 'The De Pinto Manuscript,' *Studia Rosenthaliana*, IX (1975), pp. 1-62, and his many articles and reviews in the *American Sephardi*.

2. Yosef Kaplan, 'R. Saul Levi Morteira en zijn geschrift 'Obstaculus y opociciones contra la religion Xptiana,'' *Studies on the History of Dutch Jewry*, I, (Jerusalem, 1975), pp. 9-31; and H. P. Salomon, 'Haham Saul Levi Morteira en de Portugese Nieuw-Christenen,' *Studia Rosenthaliana*, X(1976), pp. 127-41.

3. Samuel Usque, *Consolation for the Tribulations of Israel* (Philadelphia, 1965). See also R. H. Popkin, 'Jewish Values in the Post-Holocaust Future,' *Judaism* XVI (1967), pp. 273-76.

4. Kottman, *op. cit.*, chaps. 1 and 2.

5. Gershom Scholem, *Sabbatai Sevi, The Mystical Messiah* (Princeton, 1973), chap. 7, esp. pp. 814-20; and Yerushalmi, *op. cit.*, chap. vii, esp. pp. 303-6.

6. La Peyrère, *Du Rappel des Juifs*, Livre V.

7. See La Peyrère's dedication to all of the Jews and all of the Synagogues in the world, in *Prae-Adamitae*. The text appears usually at the beginning or the end of various editions. It is interesting that at just about the time this was being printed in Holland, Menasseh ben Israel sent a letter to all of the Synagogues of the world (actually apparently just three in Italy and Germany), in which he self-appointed himself as their agent before leaving for England.

8. See Scholem, *Sabbatai Sevi*, esp. chap. i, and his *Major Trends in Jewish Mysticism* (London, 1946), chaps. vii and viii. See also the introduction by Henri Méchoulan and Gerard Nahon to the French translation of Menasseh ben Israel, *L'ésperance d'Israel* (Paris, 1979).

9. On Menasseh's friends and contacts in the Christian world, see Cecil Roth, *A Life of Menasseh ben Israel*, chap. viii.

10. *Ibid.*, chap. vi; and Henri Méchoulan, 'Menasseh ben Israel au Centre des rapports Judeo-Chretiens en Hollande au XVII^c siècle dans un lettre inédite d'Isaac Coymans à Andre Colvius,' *Studia Rosenthaliana*, XVI (1982), pp. 21-24.

11. Queen Henrietta Maria, consort of Charles I of England, and the Prince of Orange came to see and hear him in 1642. The leading Portuguese Jesuit, Antonio de Vieira, went to hear him in 1640 and 1648. Pierre-Daniel Huet, the future Bishop of Avranches, heard him in 1652, as did many others. See Roth *Life of Menasseh*, p. 66 and 140-73.

12. Roth, *op. cit.*, indicates 'Menasseh was fond of describing himself as a 'Hebrew philosopher and Divine' though he really was not much of a philosopher.' Roth's fifth chapter surveys Menasseh's writings and shows how his Latin and Spanish works made certain Jewish ideas accessible to the Christian world. The introduction to the French edition of Menasseh shows how seriously he was taken by the Christians. In 1985 a conference was held in Israel on Menasseh's place in the intellectual world of his time.

12a. See H. P. Salomon, *Studia Rosenthaliana*, 'The Portuguese Background of Menasseh ben Israel's father as revealed through the Inquisitorial Archives at Lisbon,' XVII (1983), pp. 105-46. In a recent telephone conversation Professor Salomon has told me that he has discovered further information in the Portuguese Inquisition files that shows that Menasseh's parents returned to Lisbon a couple of months after his birth and that Menasseh spent his first several years in Portugal.

13. Sokolow, *History of Zionism*, claimed that the great pogrom of 1648-49 in Poland and the Ukraine, as well as the Marrano tragedy, gave rise to Menasseh's Messianism. See chaps. iv and vi of his work.

14. Montezinos's statement was appended to Thomas Thorowgood's *Jewes in America, or Probabilities that the Americans are of that Race* (London, 1650). This was added by John Dury who received the Montezinos document from Menasseh ben Israel.

15. Menasseh ben Israel, *Spes Israelis* (Amsterdam, 1650); *Esperança de Israel* (Amsterdam, 1650); *Mikve Israel* (Amsterdam, 1650); *The Hope of Israel*, translated by Moses Wall (London, 1650). Roth, *op. cit.*, pp. 301-3, also lists a Dutch translation, three printings of a German one, and Hebrew printings up to 1929. The French translation appeared

in 1979. On the work see Katz, *op. cit.*, chaps. 4-6; and the introduction to the French translation.

16. These are all the same translation, but some Christian conversionist material was added to show Jews why Menasseh's data should lead them to convert. The 1651 and 1652 editions have an exchange of letters between a reader, E. S., and the translator, Moses Wall, a friend of John Milton's, about the value of the work for understanding the Millenium and for converting Jews. Roth, *op. cit.*, p. 302, lists reprintings of the *Hope of Israel* in 1792, 1850, and 1901. It has also been reprinted in Lynn Glaser, *Indians or Jews* (Gilroy, CA, 1973) which indicates various eighteenth- and nineteenth-century works in which Menasseh's text is included in whole or part.

17. See Roth, *op. cit.*, pp. 207-24; and Roth, *A History of the Jews in England*, 3rd ed. (Oxford, 1964), pp. 154-58; and Popkin, 'Jewish Messianism and Christian Millenarianism.'

18. Menasseh ben Israel, *To His Highness, the Lord Protector of the Commonwealth of England, Scotland and Ireland. The Humble Addresses of Menasseh ben Israel, a Divine and Doctor of Physick, in behalf of the Jewish Nation* (probably Amsterdam, 1651), 2nd page.

19. The only place the Jews are missing is in England. So, Menasseh told Cromwell, 'Therefore this remains only in judgment, before the MESSIA come, and restore our Nation, that first we must have our seat here likewise'; *Humble Addresses*, 2nd page.

20. The data indicates that La Peyrère lived next door to Christina in Antwerp from August to late December 1654. La Peyrère was functioning as the Prince of Condé's agent in his affairs with Christina. During this period he read Christina *Praeadamitae* after which she sent him off to Amsterdam to have it printed at her expense. Menasseh ben Israel visited Christina late in 1654. See Roth, *Menasseh ben Israel*, pp. 174-75 and 225; Oddos, *op. cit.*, pp. 90-91; Stolpe, *Christina of Sweden*, pp. 178ff; Popkin, 'Marrano Theology,' p. 105 and note 55, and 'Menasseh ben Israel and La Peyrère,' p. 62. Katz in 'Menasseh ben Israel's Mission to Queen Christina of Sweden, 1652-1655' suggests that Menasseh had hopes of becoming Christina's Jewish Descartes.

21. On Serrarius, see my note 62* in the French edition of Meinsma, *Spinoza et son cercle*; (Paris 1983), pp. 277-279 and Van den Berg, 'Quaker and Chiliast,' pp. 186-93; and van der Wall, *op. cit.*

22. Paul Felgenhauer, *Bonum Nunciam Israeli quod offertur Populo Israel & in hisce temporibus novissimus de Messiah.* Roth, in *Menasseh ben Israel*, considered Felgenhauer the most bizarre member of Menasseh's circle (pp. 154-56). Felgenhauer's work is discussed and analyzed in Schoeps, *Philosemitismus im Barok*, pp. 18-45; and Saraiva, 'Antonio Vieira, Menasseh ben Israel,' pp. 36-39.

23. Felgenhauer, *op. cit.*, pp. 89-90.

24. Roth, *Menasseh*, p. 162, claimed that after Menasseh read *Du Rappel des Juifs*, he initiated a correspondence with La Peyrère, of which Menasseh was proud. However there is no evidence that they corresponded. See Popkin, 'Menasseh ben Israel and La Peyrère,' p. 60, and 'Menasseh ben Israel and La Peyrère, II,' *Studia Rosenthaliana*, XVIII (1984), pp. 12-20.

25. This work, which is rarely treated except for Rembrandt's magnificent illustrations, is about the prophecies in Daniel. Méchoulan and Nahon, in their introduction to their French edition of Menasseh, examine the more emphatic Messianism in this work when compared with Menasseh's previous writings. They are preparing a new edition and translation of *La Piedra Gloriosa*.

26. Paul Felgenhauer, *Anti-Prae-Adamita. Prufung über das Lateinische in Truck Aussgegangne Buch dessen Titul ist Prae-Adamatae. Dass, vor Adam auch sollen Menschen gewesen seyn* (Amsterdam, 1659), pp. 89-90.

27. Menasseh ben Israel, *Vindiciae Judaeorum, or a Letter in Answer to certain Questions propounded by a Noble and learned Gentleman touching the Reproaches cast on the Nation of the Jewes, wherein all objections are candidly, and yet fully cleared* (London, 1656), p. 41. I have found a Latin manuscript, not on this list, but on the Kabbala, by Menasseh. David Katz and I are preparing an edition of it.

28. This letter was published by Cecil Roth in the *Transactions of the Jewish Historical*

Society of England, XI (1928), p. 116. On this, see Katz, *op. cit.*, p. 198. The presentation of a letter from Rabbi Shapira is mentioned in Henry Jessey's account of Menasseh's negotiations in England; *A Narrative of the Late Proceeds at Whitehall Concerning the Jews* (London, 1656). On Rabbi Shapira's involvements with the Millenarians in Holland and England, see Popkin, 'Rabbi Shapira's Visit to Amsterdam,' *Dutch Jewish History, Proceedings of the Conference of the History of Dutch Jewry*, Israel, Dec. 1982, ed. by Joseph Michman and Tirtsah Levie (Jerusalem 1984), pp. 185-205.

29. Arise Evans, *A Voice from Heaven to the Common-Wealth of England* (London, 1652); and *An Eccho to the Voice from Heaven* (London, 1652-1653). On Evans, see Christopher Hill, *Change and Continuity in Seventeenth Century England* (London, 1974), chap. 2, pp. 48-77.

30. Evans, *An Eccho to the Voice from Heaven*, p. 106.

31. Evans, *Light for the Jews, or the Means to convert them, in answer to a Book of theirs, called the Hope of Israel, Written and Printed by Menasseth Ben-Israel, Chief Agent of the Jews here.* (London, 1664). See Hill, *Change and Continuity*, p. 58; Katz, *Philosemitism*, pp. 121-22.

32. Evans, *Light for the Jews*, pp. 4-5.

33. *Ibid.*, pp. 5-20.

34. Isaac De Larrey, *Histoire d'Angleterre, d'Ecosse et d'Irlande* (Rotterdam, 1713), IV, p. 341; Hannah Adams, *The History of the Jews from the Destruction of Jerusalem to the Present Time* (London, 1818), pp. 386-87; Charles Malo, *Histoire des Juifs* (Paris, 1826), pp. 402-3; and Popkin, 'Jewish Messianism and Christian Millenarianism,' pp. 75-76.

35. Roth, *Menasseh*, pp. 225-73; and *History of the Jews in England*, pp. 161-66.

36. Menasseh ben Israel, *Vindicae Judaeorum*, p. 18.

37. Menasseh's special brand of Messianism is treated in more detail in my 'Jewish Messianism and Christian Millenarianism,' pp. 76-77; and 'Menasseh ben Israel and La Peyrère, II.' See also the discussion of his Messianism in Méchoulan and Nahon, introduction to the French edition of *L'Esperance d'Israel*. A quite different interpretation appears in Sokolow's *History of Zionism*, chaps. iii-vi.

38. I have discussed whether such a scenario could have been believed by people like the Prince of Condé, Queen Christina, etc., with several seventeenth-century historians, who have told me that it is quite compatible with the behavior of these leaders.

39. As indicated previously, a large amount of Queen Christina's papers was stolen from the Vatican Library by one of Napoleon's soldiers. They are in the manuscript collection of the École de Médecine of Montpellier, Mss. 258, fifteen volumes, and 258 bis, two volumes. In January 1984 I briefly examined them. They seem to contain nothing relevant to these matters. All of the papers dated from 1660 onward, and the draft portions of an autobiography do not cover any events after Christina left Sweden in 1654. Her correspondence with French persons does not include any letters to or from La Peyrère. There are a few letters from Dr. Bourdelot, who was close to La Peyrère, and was with him in Scandinavia. These contain no references to La Peyrère or his theories. There are some stuffy letters to and from the Prince of Condé, mainly about Christina and Condé's rivalry in trying to become the monarch of Poland, and about the persecutions of the Protestants in France.

40. Menasseh's discussions with Christians rarely led to any controversies. He usually presented the Jewish views but did not challenge Christian ones. One of the rare indications of a dispute about the truth of Christianity is his discussion with Jean d'Espagne in London which appears in *Les Oeuvres de Jean Despagne*, (La Haye 1674), Tome I, pp. 470-77.

41. Letter of Henry Oldenburg to Menasseh ben Israel, 25 July 1657, in Oldenburg, *Correspondence*, I, pp. 123-27. Oldenburg described a book about the Second Coming of the Messiah 'equally desired by you and by us. I say the coming, meaning that you take to be the first and we are persuaded will be the second.' It will, of course, involve 'the glorious restitution of the Jews to their homeland' (p. 126).

42. Saraiva, 'Antonio Vieira, Menasseh ben Israel et le Cinquième Empire,' pp. 36ff.

43. *Ibid.*, p. 43.

44. *Ibid.*, pp. 46-50.

45. Felgenhauer, *Bonum Nunciam Israeli*. The content of this rare work is summarized in Saraiva, *op. cit.*, pp. 37-38; and in the introduction to the French translation of Menasseh's *Esperance*.

46. Sokolow, in his *History of Zionism*, I, pp. 41-42, listed La Peyrère (whom he said was 'probably of *marrano* Jewish blood') as one of the early advocates of Zionism.

47. The late Professor Gershom Scholem told me that he had found no evidence that La Peyrère's views were known to any of the Sabbateans. It is claimed in Johann Jacob Schudt's *Judische Merkwürdigkeiten*, (Frankfurt & Leipzig 1718), Vierter Teil, p. 548, that the Jews translated La Peyrère's dedication to them into Hebrew and passed it from hand to hand in Germany and elsewhere, and that they regarded La Peyrère almost as a prophet. I have come across nothing so far that would indicate there is any truth to these claims. And, as far as I know, no Hebrew manuscript text of La Peyrère's dedication has turned up in Germany or anywhere else.

48. Simon, Letter to La Peyrère, May 27, 1670, in *Lettres choisies*, II, pp. 14-16. See Gershom Scholem's discussion of the content of this letter in *Sabbatai Sevi, The Mystical Messiah*, pp. 827-28.

49. Art, 'Charpy de Sainte-Croix, Nicolas,' Michaud, *Biographie universelle*, VII, pp. 680-81. Charpy de Sainte-Croix, *Le Hérault de la fin des temps ou Histoire de l'Eglise triomphante* (Paris, n.d.); and *L'ancienne nouveauté de l'Ecriture Sainte, ou l'Eglise triomphante en terre* (n.p., 1657).

50. This is the plot of *L'ancienne nouveauté*.

51. Michaud, *Biog. universelle*, art. 'Charpy,' VII, p. 681.

52. Antoine Arnauld, *Remarques sur les principales erreurs d'un livre intitulé l'ancienne nouveauté de l'Ecriture Sainte, ou l'Eglise triomphante en Terre, Oeuvres de M. Antoine Arnauld* (Lausanne, 1775-1783), V, p. 337.

53. *Ibid.*, *op. cit.*

54. On Jean Desmarets de Sainte-Sorlin (1595-1676), see the article on him in Michaud, *Biographie universelle*, X, pp. 532-33. His unpublished work, *Examen d'un livre intitulé L'Ancienne Nouveauté de l'Escriture Sainte, ou l'Eglise Triomphante en Terre* is in the Colbert collection of the Bibliothèque Nationale. The ms. apparently dates from 1659. I am grateful to Prof. H. P. Salomon of the State University of New York at Albany for letting me use his copies of the works of Charpy and Desmarets de Sainte-Sorlin.

55. Jean-Pierre Nicéron, *Memoires pour servir à l'histoire des hommes illustres* (Paris, 1730), XII, pp. 72-75.

56. Pierre Jurieu, *Histoire critique des dogmas et des cultes* (Amsterdam, 1704), Preface 3rd page, and Part I, chap. xxv, pp. 175-81.

57. Jules Deschamps, *Rappel futur des Juifs* (Paris, 1760); Laurent Etienne Rondet, *Dissertation sur le rappel des Juifs* (Paris, 1777); François Malot, *Dissertation sur l'époque du rappel des Juifs* (Avignon?, 1776); and Charles Francois Desfours de la Génetière, *Avis aux catholiques sur le caractère et les signes de temps où nous vivions, ou De la conversion des Juifs, de l'avènement intermediare de Jesus-Christ et de son regne visible sur la terre* (Lyon, 1794), among many others.

58. On Grégoire's background and early career, see Ruth Necheles, *The Abbé Grégoire 1787-1831. The Odyssey of an Egalitarian* (Westport, CO, 1971), chaps. 1 and 2. Henri Grégoire's *Essai sur la régeneration physique, morale et politique des juifs* (Metz, 1789), was also published in English at London in 1791.

59. These themes are developed in Grégoire's *Essai*.

60. *Ibid.*, pp. 228-29.

61. Necheles, *op. cit.*, chap. 2; and R. H. Popkin, 'La Peyrère, the Abbé Grégoire, and the Jewish Question in the Eighteenth Century,' *Studies in Eighteenth-Century Culture*, IV (1975), pp. 211-12.

62. Popkin, 'La Peyrère, Grégoire,' pp. 212-14. Napoleon's proclamation about the rebuilding of the temple was published in the *Gazette National* ou *le Monsieur universal*, 3 Prairial, An 7, where it is stated that 'Bonaparte a fait publier une proclamation dans laquelle il invite tous des juifs de l'Asie et de l'Afrique à venir se ranger sous ses drapeaux pour rétablir l'ancienne Jerusalem.' My son, Prof. Jeremy Popkin, has pointed out that

there is no evidence that Napoleon himself was responsible for this proclamation. The original does not seem to exist in Napoleon's papers.

63. See for instance, the recent discussions of the episode in Raphael Mahler, *A History of Modern Jewry, 1780-1815* (New York, 1971), pp. 59-72; and in Norman Cohn's *Warrant for Genocide, The Myth of the Jewish World Conspiracy and the Protocols of the Elders of Zion* (London, 1970), p. 34. See also earlier discussions in Heinrich Graetz's *History of the Jews* (Philadelphia, 1895), V, pp. 479-500, and in Simon Dubnow, *History of the Jews,* (South Brunswick, 1971), IV, pp. 543-66. A recent volume edited by Edouard Privat, *Le Grand Sanhédrin de Napoléon* (Toulouse, 1979), has some interesting re-evaluations of the circumstances and achievements of the Sanhedrin.

64. See the references given in Cohn, *Warrant for Genocide*, pp. 34-35. In the French emigré journal published in London, *L'Ambigu*, a writer said, 'Does he hope to form, from these children of Jacob, a legion of tyranicides? . . . Time will show. It remains for us only to watch this Antichrist fight against the eternal decrees of God; that must be the last act of his diabolic existence.' See also Louis Gabriel Ambroise Bonald, 'Sur les Juifs,' *Mercure de France*, XXIII (1806), pp. 249-67.

65. See Baruch Mevorah, 'Napoleon Bonaparte,' *Encyclopedia Judaica*, XII, pp. 824-25; and Popkin, 'La Peyrère, Grégoire,' p. 214.

66. See Joseph J. Shulim, 'Napoleon I as the Jewish Messiah: Some Contemporary Conceptions in Virginia,' *Jewish Social Studies*, V (1945), pp. 275-80.

67. Rabbi Seixas was willing to settle either for the Messianic Restoration of the Jews in Palestine or for their new secular state in the United States, as co-equal members in a pluralistic society. See 'Minutes of the Spanish and Portuguese Congregation of New York—J. J. Lyons Collection,' Publications of the American Jewish Historical Society, II, no. 27 (1920), pp. 140ff. Some of the sermon also appears in Paul R. Mendes-Flohr and Jehuda Reinharz, *The Jew in the Modern World, A Documentary History* (New York and Oxford, 1980), pp. 124-25.

68. See Popkin, 'La Peyrère, Grégoire,' pp. 214-15; and *Journal de Paris*, 29 Août 1806, and the *Gazette de France* 28 Août 1806.

69. See Popkin, 'La Peyrère, Grégoire,' p. 215, for some of the ways Napoleon used the meeting of the Sanhedrin to bolster his Messianic image. The coin, of which I have a copy, was issued in 1806. The face shows a bust of Napoleon with the inscription, 'Napoleon, Emp. et Roi.' On the reverse side Napoleon, in Roman robes, is shown giving the tablets with the Ten Commandments to a kneeling Moses. The inscription is 'Grand Sanhedrin XXX Mai MDCCCVI.' The coin is still being issued by the Paris mint from the original die. It is reproduced in Ismar Elbogen, *History of the Jews after the Fall of the State of Jerusalem* (Cincinnati, 1926), facing p. 167. The reverse of the coin is there described as 'Napoleon receiving the Tablets of the Law,' which is hardly what the scene looks like.

70. This collection was in the hand of Grégoire's secretary, Rondeau. The manuscript is located at the Bibliothèque de Port-Royal in Paris. It has not yet been published. The original text of the Sanhedrin proceedings appears in Privat, *Le Grand Sanhédrin*, pp. 151-221.

71. There were French and English editions of the Transactions of the Assembly of Jewish Notables and of the Sanhedrin. A brief check indicates there are some variations in Grégoire's text from the printed ones. Grégoire's notes also indicate that he was talking to members of the Assembly of Jewish Notables and was giving them advice.

72. This pamphlet is also located at the manuscript collection of the Bibliothèque de Port-Royal in Paris. There is a third Grégoire manuscript on the Recall of the Jews about a contemporary Millenarian work that touched on such matters as whether the Jesuits were false prophets.

73. On the career of the Grand Sanhedrin, see Robert Anschel, *Napoléon et les Juifs* (Paris, 1928), chap. IV-VI; and Privat, *Le Grand Sanhedrin*. The text from Rabbi Zinzheim's closing statement is quoted with ringing condemnation in Bruno Bauer's *La Question Juive* in Karl Marx, *La Question juive*, ed. by Robert Mandrou (Paris, 1968), pp. 178-79. The text in the reproduction of the French text in Privat, *La Grand Sanhédrin*,

states, 'Et toi Napoleon, toi le bien-aimé, toi l'idole de la France et de l'Italie, toi la terreur des superbes, le consolateur du genre humain, le soutien des affligés, le père de tous les peuples, l'élu du Seigneur, Israel t'élève un temple dans son coeur' (p. 130 of the reproduction).

74. These decrees are known to the Jews as 'The Infamous Decrees.' On them see Anchel, *op. cit.*, chap. VIII.

75. The abbé Grégoire, in his discussion of the Dutch Jews in his *Histoire des Sectes religieuses* (Paris, 1828), III, pp. 391-401, showed how the embattled liberal and modern Jews were aided by the Sanhedrin. See also Joseph Michman, 'Les Juifs des Pays-Bas et le Grand Sanhédrin' in Privat, *Le Grand Sanhedrin*, pp. 86-100.

76. Henry Lucien-Brun, *La Condition des Juifs en France depuis 1789*, Deuxième edition (Lyon, n.d.), esp. Troisième Periode, chaps. i-iii, and Appendice on 'La condition des Juifs depuis l'Ordonnance de 1844 jusqu'a nos jours,' pp. 299-310. The decisions of the Sanhedrin were published in Theophile Hallez, *Des Juifs en France. De leur état moral et politique* (Paris, 1845), pp. 297-335.

77. M. Bernadau, 'Notice sur Isaac Lapeyrère, auteur Bordelais, extraite du Panthéon litteraire d'Aquitaine, ou Histoire des hommes illustres nés dans l'ancienne province de Guienne,' *Bulletin polymathique du Muséum d'Instruction publique de Bordeaux*, Annee 1810, p. 375.

78. *Ibid.*, p. 378.

79. *Ibid.*, p. 378.

80. Bernard Lambert, *Expositions des Prédictions et des Promesses faites à l'Église pour les derniers temps de la Gentilité*, Tome I (Paris, 1806), p. 399.

81. Charles-Jacques Saillant, *Les Véritables Promeses faites au Peuple juif et a toute l'Église....precédées d'un examen impartial de l'ouvrage intitulé: Exposition des Prédictions et des Promesses faites à l'églisè* (Paris, 1807), p. v.

82. *Ibid.*, pp. 86-87.

83. *Ibid.*, 87n.

84. Roth, *Menasseh ben Israel*, p. 327, n. 27.

85. 'Christianus,' letter in *Gentleman's Magazine*, LXXXII (1812), pp. 432-34.

86. *Ibid.*, p. 432.

87. *Ibid.*, p. 434.

88. 'Christianus,' letter in *Gentleman's Magazine*, LXXXIII (1813), pp. 614-16. The letter of Simon's is one to La Peyrère of May 27, 1670. It appears in Simon's *Lettres choisies*, II, pp. 12-17.

89. *Ibid.*, p. 616.

90. See David V. Erdman, *Blake: Prophet against Empire* (Garden City, NY, 1969), p. 419 and n. 9. Thomas Bicheno, *The Restoration of the Jews, The Crisis of All Nations to which is now prefixed, A Brief History of the Jews from their first Dispersion to the Calling of their Grand Sanhedrin at Paris*, October 6, 1806, 2nd. ed. (London, 1807).

91. Friedrich Adolf Ebert, *Allgemeines Bibliographisches Lexikon*, Zweiter band (Leipzig, 1830), p. 378, entry 16560, Peyrerius, 15 (anon), *Du Rappel des Juifs*.

92. See, for instance, Mordecai Manuel Noah, *Discourse on the Restoration of the Jews* (New York, 1845); and Noah, 'The American Indian and the Lost Tribes of Israel,' *Midstream*, May 1971, pp. 49-64.

93. This is described favorably to Noah in Grégoires *Histoire des Sectes religieuses*, III, pp. 376-79.

94. *Ibid.*, II, pp. 1-5.

95. *Ibid.*, II, p. 5. This sounds like an anticipation of Immanuel Velikovsky's theory. Thus far I have been unable to find any information about Professor Grolpker.

CHAPTER NINE

1. Spinoza, especially in the *Tractatus-Theologico-Politicus*, held that the Old Testament should be read as written for the understanding of the ancient Hebrews and not as the

history of the world. Although Spinoza did not explicitly state the pre-Adamite theory, his account of the Old Testament, and his analysis of it, imply that Adam was just the first figure in the Mosaic account but not in history in general.

2. Pastine, *op. cit*, p. 96, contended that the dispute of monogenesis versus polygenesis became more a scientific than a theological problem in the eighteenth century. We will see to what extent this is true in this and the next chapter.

3. The work first appeared as *L'Espion du Grand Seigneur* in 1684 and 1686. The full eight volume edition was published in London in 1692, and was then translated into French.

4. C. J. Betts, in *Early Deism in France*, (The Hague 1985) gives the evidence for Marana being the original author. p. 97. The original Italian manuscript of the first sixty-three letters exists in the Bibliothèque Nationale in Paris.

5. A bibliography of the discussions about the authorship is given in Giovanni P. Marana, *Letters Writ by a Turkish Spy*, selected and edited by Arthur J. Weitzman, (London 1970). More recent discussions of authorship appear in C. J. Betts, *Early Deism in France*, chap. 7, pp. 97-99.

6. See, Betts, *op. cit.*, p. 98.

7. A list of English and French editions is given in Weitzman's selections from Marana, *Letters Writ by a Turkish Spy*, p. 232. The London 1801 edition is listed as the last one. Other editions are listed in the catalogues of the British Library, the Bibliothèque Nationale, and the National Union Catalogue. UCLA has a microfilm of the Russian edition of 1778. The additional volume attributed to Daniel Defoe is *A Continuation of Letters Written by a Turkish Spy at Paris*, 1687-1693, (London 1718). The various editions are quite similar. I have used the 13th edition (London 1753), after comparing it with earlier French, and earlier and later English editions.

8. Marana, *Turkish Spy*, Vol. I, p. xix.

9. *Ibid.*, loc. cit.

10. *Ibid.*, Vol. III, p. 250.

11. *Ibid.*, Vol. III, p. 251.

12. *Ibid.*, Vol. III, p. 252.

13. *Ibid.*, loc. cit.

14. *Ibid.*, Vol. III, p. 253.

15. *Ibid.*, loc. cit

16. *Ibid.*, Vol. III, p. 254.

17. *Ibid.*, loc. cit.

18. *Ibid.*, loc. cit.

19. *Ibid.*, Vol. III, p. 254.

20. *Ibid.*, Vol. III, p. 255.

21. See later in this chapter, p. 410 ff.

22. Marana, *Letters of a Turkish Spy*, Vol. III, p. 255.

23. *Ibid.*, Vol. III, p. 256.

24. *Ibid.*, Vol. IV, p. 71.

25. *Ibid.*, *loc. cit.*

26. *Ibid.*, Vol. IV, p. 157.

27. *Ibid.*, Vol. IV, p. 166.

28. *Ibid.*, Vol. IV, p. 202.

29. *Ibid.*, *loc. cit.*

30. *Ibid.*, Vol. IV, p. 211.

31. *Ibid.*, Vol. IV, p. 251. In a forthcoming study, I will discuss the Spy's attempt to make Nathan a 'reformed' Jew.

32. *Ibid.*, Vol. IV, p. 286.

33. *Ibid.*, Vol. V, pp. 70-71.

34. *Ibid.*, Vol. V, p. 164.

35. *Ibid.*, Vol. V, p. 167.

36. *Ibid.*, Vol. VI, p. 30.

37. *Ibid.*, Vol. VI, p. 126.

38. *Ibid.*, Vol. VI, p. 149.
39. *Ibid.*, Vol. VIII, p. 253.
40. *Ibid.*, Vol. VIII, p. 254.
41. *Ibid.*, Vol. VIII, p. 255.
42. *Ibid.*, Vol. VIII, p. 257.
43. *Ibid.*, Vol. VIII, p. 257-258.
44. *Ibid.*, Vol. VIII, p. 258.
45. *Ibid.*, Vol. VIII, p. 265-266.
46. Andraes B. Hempel, *Dissertatio de Praeadamaitis* (Helmstadt, 1714). I have seen a 1673 edition of this work mentioned, but have not yet been able to locate it.
47. Joh. Ant. Schmid, *Pentas Dissertationum, I. de Praeadamaitis exorbe proscriptis* (Helmstadt, 1716).
48. J. Hermansson, *Diss. de Praeadamitis* (Upsala, 1730).
49. Benito Jeronimo Feijóo y Montenegro, 'Solucíon del gran problema historico sobre populacion de la America, y Revoluciones del Orbe Terraques,' in *Teatre Critico Universel*. This essay was published in *Dos Discursos de Feijoo sobre America* (Mexico, 1945). See esp. pp. 40-48. See also Pastine, *op. cit.*, pp. 28-30, on Feijóo's answer.
50. This pamphlet was published in Mexico in 1763. It is reproduced by Nicolas Leon, in *Bibliografia mexicana del siglo XVIII*, sección primera, (Mexico City, 1902), pp. 379-409. See Antonello Gerbi, *The Dispute of the New World* (Pittsburgh, 1973).
51. Charles Crawford, *An Essay on the Propagation of the Gospel, in which there are Numerous Facts and Arguments Adduced to prove that many of the Indians in America are Descended from the Ten Tribes* (Philadelphia, 1801), pp. 8 and 28 (the quotation is on p. 28).
52. Ephraim Chambers, *Cyclopedia; or An Universal Dictionary of Arts and Sciences* (London, 1786), III, art. 'Praeadamite.'
53. *Dictionnaire Universal françois et latin, vulgairement appellé Dictionnaire de Trévoux*, Tome V^e (Paris, 1743), pp. 452-53.
54. Dom Augustin Calmet, *Dictionnaire historique, critique, chronologique, geographique et littéral de la Bible* (Paris, 1722), II, p. 211.
55. John Laurence Mosheim, *An Ecclesiastical History, Ancient and Modern*, Vol. II, (New York, 1880), p. 221.
56. Pierre Richelet, *Dictionnaire de la langue françoise, ancienne et moderne*, Tome II (Lyon, 1750), entry, 'Pré-adamites,' pp. 237-38.
57. Cf. Leon Schwarz, *Diderot and the Jews* (Rutherford, New Jersey 1981), p. 42 and p. 163 note 18; and Jacques Proust, *Diderot et l'Encylopédie* (Paris, 1962), pp. 531-38.
58. Denis Diderot, art. 'Préadamite,' in *Oeuvres complètes* (Paris, 1876), 16, pp. 387-89.
59. *Encyclopaedia Britannica*, 3rd ed., art. 'Pre-Adamite', Vol. XV (Edinburgh, 1797), pp. 454-55.
60. *Encyclopaedia Britannica*, 3rd ed., art. 'Peyrère, (Isaac la),' Vol. XIV, pp. 258-59.
61. See chap. VIII, p. 111.
62. *Enc. Brit.* art. 'Peyrère,' p. 259. This article may derive from the one in *Bibliographia Gallica*, (London 1752), Vol. I, pp. 233-55, which is also quite favorable.
63. Charles Blount, *The Oracles of Reason* (London, 1693), pp. 16 and 218.
64. David R. McKee, *Simon Tyssot de Patot and the Seventeenth Century Background of Critical Deism*, Johns Hopkins Studies in Romance Literatures and Languages, Vol. XI (1941), n. 45.
65. Simon Tyssot de Patot, *The Travels and Adventures of James Massey* (London, 1733).
66. John Atkins, *The Navy Surgeon: Or a Practical System of Surgery* (London, 1734), p. 24.
67. Lom D'Arce, *Nouveaux Voyages de Mr. Le Baron de Lohontan dans l'Amérique septentrionale* (The Hague, 1703), letter dated May 10, 1693, pp. 249-50.
68. *Ibid.*, p. 250.
69. *Ibid.*, pp. 251-52. The quotation is on p. 252.
70. A. Gerbi, *op. cit.*, p. 105.
71. Anon., *Co-Adamitae, or an Essay to prove the two following paradoxes, viz. I. That there were other men created at the same time with Adam, and II. that the angels did not fall* (London, 1732), p. 2.

72. *Ibid.*, p. 5.

73. Henry Home, Lord Kames, *Six Sketches on the History of Man, Containing the Progress of Men as Individuals* (Philadelphia, 1776), pp. 13-14 and 29-30.

74. *Ibid.*, pp. 45-47. See also William Stanton, *The Leopard's Spots* (Chicago, 1960), pp. 15-16.

75. Henry Home, *Sketches of the History of Man* (Glasgow, 1819), I, p. 41.

76. Home, *Sketches*, 1819 ed., I, p. 42.

77. On Stanhope Smith, see Stanton, *op. cit.*, chaps. 1 and 2. Smith's work is entitled *An Essay on the Causes of the Variety of Complexion and Figure in the Human Species, to which are added Strictures on Lord Kames's Discourse on the Original Diversity of Mankind* (Philadelphia and Edinburgh, 1787).

78. James Adair, *The History of the American Indians* (London, 1775), pp. 2-3.

79. *Ibid.*, p. 11.

80. Bernard Romans, *A Concise Natural History of East and West Florida* (New York, 1785), pp. 54-55.

81. This comes up in various forms in Voltaire's *Essai sur les moeurs*, and in his article on the Bible in the *Dictionnaire philosophique*, as well as in the Appendices to the *Dictionnaire*. Léon Poliakov, in *Le Mythe Aryen* (Paris, 1971), pp. 174-75, gives many citations from various works of Voltaire of his avowed pre-Adamism or polygenicism. Patrick Girard in his mimeographed *Trois thèmes de recherches sur les origines des doctrines raciales de l'Occident moderne* (Paris, 1975), Maison des Sciences de l'Homme, Fascicule VIII, p. 14, calls Voltaire the 'polygéniste le plus connu.' See also Pastine, *op. cit.*, p. 99, on Voltaire's polygenetic views.

82. Johann Wolfgang von Goethe, *Conversations of Goethe with Eckermann*, trans. by John Oxenford (London, 1882), p. 322. See also Pastine, *op. cit.*, p. 104.

83. Charles C. Gillispie, *Genesis and Geology* (Cambridge, MA, 1951).

84. P. Brydone, *A Tour through Sicily and Malta in a series of letters to William Beckford* (London, 1773), I, pp. 131-32. Bishop George Berkeley, in *Alciphron*, had to guard against taking any of the historical evidence of Egyptian, Chinese or other cultures, as indicating that the Mosaic account might be wrong. His questioner had asked, 'Shall we reject the accounts and records of all other nations, the most famous, ancient and learned in the world, and preserve a blind reverence for the Legislator of the Jews?' Berkeley's spokesman replied, 'And pray if they deserve to be rejected, why should we not reject them? What if those monstrous Chronologies contain nothing but names without actions and manifest fables'; *Alciphron: Or, the Minute Philosopher* (London, 1732), Dialogue VI, sec. 21, Vol. II, p. 74.

85. Nathaniel Brassey Halhed, *A code of Gentoo Laws, or Ordinations of the Pundits, from a Persian Translation, made from the Original, written in the Shanscrit Language* (London, 1776), Preface. The quotation is on pp. xxxviii-xxxix.

86. *Ibid.*, pp. xliii-xliv.

87. On Richard Brothers, and Halhed's role in the Brothers movement, see Clarke Garrett, *Respectable Folly, Millenarians and the French Revolution in France and England* (Baltimore and London, 1975), chap. 8. See also John F. Harrison, *The Second Coming: Popular Millenarianism 1780-1850* (New Brunswick, 1979).

88. Nathanel Brassey Halhed, *Testimony of the Authenticity of the Prophecies of Richard Brothers and of his Mission to Recall the Jews* (London, 1795).

89. See the collection of pamphlets by Brothers and his followers in the British Library, BM3185.f.i (1-10).

90. Halhed, *Testimony*, pp. 10 and 36. On the latter page he declared, 'Now that all Scripture as well as all Tradition bears testimony to the certainty of the recall of the Jews in the latter ages of the world, no man who has a smattering of acquaintance with either can for a moment pretend to deny.'

91. On Jones's life and career and influence, see the article on him in the *Dictionary of National Biography*.

92. Sir William Jones, 'On the Gods of Greece, Italy and India,' in *The Works of Sir William Jones*, with the life of the author by Lord Teigmouth (London, 1807), III, p. 325.

93. Jones, 'On the Chronology of the Hindus,' in *Works*, IV, pp. 1-4.

94. *Ibid.*, p. 22.

95. *Ibid.*, p. 51.

96. *Ibid.*, p. 45.

97. *Ibid.*, p. 47.

98. Jones, 'A Supplement to the Essay on Indian Chronology,' in *Works*, IV, p. 65.

99. Thomas Maurice, *Indian Antiquities* (London, 1794), I, pp. 15-29.

100. *Ibid.*, pp. 29-30.

101. *Ibid.*, p. 31.

102. Elias Boudinot, *The Age of Revelation. Or the Age of Reason shown to be an Age of Infidelity* (Philadelphia, 1801), pp. 133-35. The work was written for his daughter in 1795. Boudinot was a leading Millenarian as well as an important early leader of the United States. At the time he published *The Age of Revelation*, he was director of the U. S. Mint. He retired in 1805 to devote himself to Millenial activities by spreading knowledge of the Bible, in preparing for the Conversion of the Jews and the Second Coming. His theology does not seem to have been studied. I hope to remedy this in the near future.

103. Jones, 'Note to Mr. Vansittart's Paper on the Afghans being descended from the Jews,' *Works*, IV, p. 70.

104. See the use made of Sir William Jones's researches concerning the Afghans in the work of the Millenarian, George Stanley Faber, in his *A General and Connected View of the Prophecies, relative to the Conversion, Restoration, Union and Future Glory of the Houses of Judah and Israel* (London, 1809), I, pp. 69-81. Boudinot, among others, rejected Jones's Afghan hypothesis.

105. John Webb, *An Historical Essay Endeavouring a Probability that the Language of the Empire of China is the Primitive Language* (London, 1669), pp. 31-32. This work is dedicated to Charles II.

106. This theory is attributed to Dobbs by William E. H. Lecky, *The History of the Rise and Influence of the Spirit of Rationalism in Europe* (New York, 1866), I, p. 301 n. 1. Joseph Mede, early in the seventeenth century, had claimed that the American Indians were children of the Devil. This would not make them pre-Adamites since he claimed they were spawned after the coming of Jesus.

107. Adrian Beverland, *Histoire d l'Etat de l'Homme dans le peché originel* (n. p., 1731), pp. 57-58. After citing a text from La Peyrère's *Prae-Adamitae*, Beverland remarked, 'Tout ce qui l'Auteur établit dans cet endroit & dans tout l'ouvrage, consiste en des réveries continuelles qu'il a tirées d'un petit livre imprime en 1561' (p. 58).

108. Francis Dobbs, *Universal History commencing with the Creation...in Letters to his Son* (London, 1787), did not suggest a separate non-Adamic race arose from Eve's meeting with the serpent.

109. Francis Dobbs, *A Concise View from History and Prophecy, of Great Predictions in the Sacred Writings that have been fulfilled, also of those that are now fulfilling, and that remain to be accomplished* (London, 1800). Dobbs claimed the second advent of the Messiah is imminent and 'that Ireland is to have the glorious pre-eminence of being the first kingdom that will receive him' (p. vi).

110. François Xavier Burtin, 'Réponse à la Question physique proposée par la societé de Teyler sur les Revolutions generales, qu'a subies la surface de la Terre, et sur l'ancienneté de notre globe,' in *Verhandelingen uitgegeeven door Teyler's Tweede Genootschap, zevende Stuk* (Haarlem, 1789), pp. 194-95.

111. *The Monthly Review*, III (1790), p. 543.

112. *Ibid.*, p. 544.

113. Edward King, 'Dissertation concerning the Creation of Man,' in *Morsels of Criticism, tending to illustrate some few passages in the Holy Scriptures upon philosophical principles and an enlarged view of things* (London, 1800), pp. 70-71.

114. *Ibid.*, pp. 73-78.

115. All of this is covered in the remainder of King's dissertation. 72. François-Marie Arouet Voltaire, *Dictionnaire philosophique*, ed. by Julien Benda, text established by Raymond Naves (Paris, 1954) arts. 'Adam' and 'Moses,' pp. 6-7, 320-25; and the seven-

teenth conversation between A, B, and C, appended to Peter Gay's edition of Voltaire's *Philosophical Dictionary* (New York, 1962), II, pp. 593-96.

116. Voltaire, *Essai sur les moeurs de l'esprit des nations,* in *Oeuvres complètes de Voltaire,* ed. Moland, Tome XI, p. 7. Diderot apparently also accepted the Pre-Adamite theory; see Schwarz, *Diderot and the Jews,* pp. 42ff.

117. Arthur Hertzberg, *The French Enlightenment and the Jews* (New York, 1968), pp. 280-313; and Léon Poliakov, *Histoire de l'antisémitisme de Voltaire à Wagner,* (Paris, 1968), pp. 103-17.

118. Goethe, *Conversations with Eckermann,* p. 322.

119. Poliakov, *Le Mythe aryen,* p. 129.

120. L. P., *Two Essays, Sent in a Letter from Oxford, to a nobleman in London* (1695). I have used the reprint that appeared in the *Somers Collection of Scarce and Valuable Tracts,* Third Series (London, 1751), III, pp. 291-308. It is also reprinted as an appendix to T. Bendysche's *History of Anthropology.*

121. *Ibid.,* p. 291.

122. *Ibid., loc. cit.*

123. *Ibid.,* p. 292.

124. *Ibid.,* p. 297.

125. *Ibid., loc. cit.*

126. *Ibid.,* pp. 297-98.

127. *Ibid.,* p. 298.

128. *Ibid., loc. cit.*

129. *Ibid.,* p. 300. Pastine, *op. cit.,* discusses the role of the spontaneous generation theory in the rise of polygenetic theories.

130. *Two Essays,* p. 301.

131. *Ibid., loc. cit..*

132. *Ibid.,* pp. 301-2.

133. John Harris, *Remarks on some late papers relating to the Universal Deluge: And to the Natural History of the Earth* (London, 1697).

134. *Ibid.,* Preface, p. A.

135. *Ibid.,* Preface, p. A 5.

136. *Ibid.,* p. 65.

137. *Ibid.,* p. 66.

138. See R. H. Popkin, 'The Philosophical Basis of Eighteenth-Century Racism,' *Studies in Eighteenth-Century Culture,* III (1973), pp. 245-62; and 'The Philosophical Basis of Modern Racism,' in Craig Walton and John P. Anton, editors, *Philosophy and the Civilizing Arts, Essays Presented to Herbert W. Schneider* (Athens, Ohio 1974), pp. 126-65.

139. John Mitchell, 'An Essay upon the Causes of the Different Colours of People in Different Climates,' *Royal Society of London Philosophical Transactions,* XLIII (1744-45), p. 146.

140. P. L. Moreau de Maupertius, *Venus physique;* in *Oeuvres de Maupertius* (Lyon, 1756), II, pp. 128-29.

141. Linnaeus, (Karl von Linné), *A General System of Nature Through the Three Grand Kingdoms of Animals, Vegetables, and Minerals,* (London, 1806), I, section 'Mammalia. Order I. Primates.'

142. Georges Louis Leclerc, Comte de Buffon, *Natural History, General and Particular,* trans. by William Smellie, 2nd ed. (London, 1785), Vol. III, *The Natural History of Man,* Sec. IX, 'Of the Varieties of the Human Species,' p. 207.

143. *Ibid.,* p. 60.

144. *Ibid.,* p. 65.

145. *Ibid.,* p. 170.

146. *Ibid.,* p. 146.

147. *Ibid.,* p. 205.

148. *Ibid.,* p. 207. This seems to be the implication of what Buffon said about how human differences are to be overcome.

149. Johann F. Blumenbach, *On the Natural Varieties of Mankind,* trans. by Thomas Bendysche (New York, 1969), p. 307.

150. Blumenbach, *op. cit.*, pp. 305-12; Henri Grégoire, *De la Littérature des Nègres* (Paris, 1808), chap. V-VIII.

151. James Cowles Prichard, *The Natural History of Man* (London, 1848).

152. David Hume, 'Of National Characters,' in *The Philosophical Works*, ed. by T. H. Green and T. H. Grose (London, 1882), III, p. 252n.

153. This work appeared in 1784. In Stanley Feldstein, *The Poisoned Tongue* (New York, 1972), Jefferson's discussion of the differences between blacks and whites is given (pp. 46-53). The quotation is on p. 52.

154. Julian J. Virey, *Histoire naturalle du genre humain, Tome II* (Paris, An IX).

155. J. B. G. Bory de Saint-Vincent, *L'Homme (Homo), Essai zoologique sur le genre human* (Paris, 1827), 2nd ed., II, pp. 61-66. Pastine, *op. cit.*, discusses Bory de St. Vincent (p. 186).

156. *Ibid.*, pp. 68-80.

157. *Ibid.*, pp. 67-68.

158. John Mason Good, *The Book of Nature* (London, 1826), II, p. 92.

159. *Ibid.*, pp. 92-93.

160. William Frederick Van Amringe, *An Investigation of the Theories of the Natural History of Man by Laurence, Prichard and Others* (New York, 1848), pp. 46-65.

161. P. G. Mahoudeau, *Revue anthropologique* 25ᵉ Année (1915), p. 26. On the other hand, the orthodox Catholic, Joseph de Maistre, shrugged off polygenesis as one more example of infidel nonsense. 'Tout le genre humain vient d'un couple. On a nié cette verité comme toutes les autres: eh! qu'est-ce que cela faire?'; *Les Soirées de Saint-Petersbourg* (Paris, 1821), I, p. 94.

CHAPTER TEN

1. Morgan Godwyn, *The Negro's & Indians Advocate, Suing for their Admission into the Church: or a Persuasive to the Instructing and Baptizing of the Negro's and Indians in our Plantations* (London, 1680), p. 15.

2. *Ibid.*, *loc.cit.*

3. *Ibid.*, p. 18.

4. *Ibid.*, pp. 18-19.

5. Frederick Douglass, 'The Claims of the Negro Ethnologically Considered,' reproduced in Louis Ruchames, ed., *Racial Thought in America*, Vol. I, (New York, 1970), pp. 478-92.

6. Edward Long, *History of Jamaica* (London, 1774), Vol. II, Book III, Chap. 1, p. 353.

7. *Ibid.*, p. 354.

8. *Ibid.*, p. 376.

9. David Hume, 'Of National Characters,' in The *Philosophical Works of David Hume*, ed. by T. H. Green and T. H. Grose (London, 1882), III, p. 252n. The person in Jamaica Hume was referring to was a graduate of the University of Cambridge, Francis Williams, who wrote Latin poetry, and ran a school where he taught mathematics and history.

10. Bartolemé de las Casas, *History of the Indies*, trans. by Andre Collard, (New York, 1971), insisted that if the Spanish and Portuguese priests and explorers 'admit to the world that the Indians descend from Adam our father,...this suffices for us to respect the divine principle of charity toward them...' (p. 66). See James Beattie, *Essay on the Origin and Immutability of Truth*, 2nd ed. (Edinburgh, 1776), pp. 310-13; James Ramsay, *An Essay on the Treatment and Conversion of African Slaves in the British Sugar Colonies* (Dublin, 1784), chaps. IV and V (which like Beattie's text is devoted to challenging Hume); Henri Grégoire, *De la Litterature des Négres*, chap. ii, where Hume and Jefferson are attacked; Charles Crawford, *Observations upon Slavery* (n.p., 1790), which supports Beattie against Hume; and Noah Webster, *Effects of Slavery* (Hartford, 1793), which rebuts Hume and Jefferson. See also Popkin, 'Hume's Racism,' *The Philosophical Forum*, IX (1977-78), pp. 211-26.

11. See Stanton, *The Leopard's Spots*, pp. 1-23.

12. Stanton, *op. cit.*, pp. 18-19.

13. *Ibid.*, pp. 19-23. The quotation is on p. 21. See also George M. Fredrickson, *The Black Image in the White Mind* (New York, 1971), pp. 73-74.

14. On Morton's background and early work see Stanton, *op. cit.*, pp. 25-44.

15. *Ibid.*, pp. 30-31.

16. *Ibid.*, pp. 28-32.

17. Stephen Jay Gould, 'Morton's Ranking of Races by Cranial Capacity. Unconscious manipulation of data may be a scientific norm,' *Science* 200 (1978), pp. 503-9.

18. Stanton, *op. cit.*, pp. 32-33. The mound builders of the Ohio River Valley remained a problem throughout the nineteenth century. A scholar in the field, J. W. Foster, in his *Pre-Historic Races of the United States of America* (Chicago, 1887), held that all attempts by anthropological means 'to establish a common centre of human creation' for the mound builders and the rest of the Americans 'are utterly futile' (p. 319). Further he asserted that 'all attempts to trace that origin to a common foundation of life, as with other races now inhabiting the earth, soon involve the investigator in the mazes of conjecture' (pp. 349-50).

19. Stanton, *op. cit.*, pp. 33-44.

20. *Ibid.*, pp. 45-54.

21. *Ibid.*, pp. 61-65.

22. Alexander von Humboldt, *Cosmos*, trans. by E. C. Otté (London, 1888), I, p. 368.

23. This article of Nott's appeared in the *American Journal of the Medical Sciences*, VI (1843), pp. 252-56.

24. Stanton, *op. cit.*, pp. 66-68.

25. *Ibid.*, pp. 68-81.

26. Josiah C. Nott, *Two Lectures on the Connection between the Biblical and Physical History of Man*, originally published in 1849, reprinted (New York, 1969). See also, Stanton *op. cit.*, p. 118.

27. Stanton, *op. cit.*, pp. 82-89.

28. Letter of Nott to Squier, quoted in Stanton, *op. cit.*, p. 87.

29. The citations of Morton and von Humboldt are given in Stanton, *op. cit.*, pp. 82-88.

30. Stanton, *op. cit.*, pp. 92-96.

31. Cited in Stanton, *op. cit.*, p. 103. On Agassiz on the races of man, see also Thomas Gossett, *Race, The History of an Idea in America* (New York, 1971), pp. 59-60; and Edward Lurie, 'Louis Agassiz and the Races of Man,' *Isis*, XLV (1954), pp. 227-42. 32. Stanton, *op. cit.*, p. 103.

33. Louis Agassiz, 'Geographical Distribution of Animals,' *The Christian Examiner and Religious Miscellany*, XLVIII (1850), p. 181.

34. *Ibid.*, pp. 184-85.

35. *Ibid.*, pp. 185-204.

36. Agassiz presented some remarks after Josiah Nott had read a paper on 'An Examination of the Physical History of the Jews, in its bearing on the Question of the Unity of the Races,' *Proceedings of the American Association for the Advancement of Science*, Vol. 3, March 15, 1850. See Lurie, *op. cit.*, pp. 236-37.

37. Agassiz, 'The Diversity of Origin of the Human Races,' *Christian Examiner*, XLIX (1850), pp. 110-12.

38. *Ibid.*, p. 112.

39. *Ibid.*, pp. 112-34.

40. *Ibid.*, pp. 134-35.

41. *Ibid.*, p. 142.

42. *Ibid.*, pp. 143-44.

43. *Ibid.*, pp. 144-45. As an example of how people were affected by Agassiz's views, the young Virginia student, Moncure Daniel Conway, was told about Agassiz's polygenetic theory by a professor at the Smithsonian Institute who had already accepted the view. Based on what Agassiz said at Harvard and published in the July 1850 *Christian*

Examiner, Conway quickly developed the theory 'that the negro was not a man within the meaning of the Declaration of Independence.' He then wrote an essay aimed at proving 'that the 'Caucasian' race is the highest species; and that this supreme race has the right of dominion over the lower species of his genus that he has over quadrupeds'; Moncure Daniel Conway, *Autobiography Memories and Experiences* (Boston and New York, 1904), I, pp. 89-90.

44. N. L. Frothingham, 'Men before Adam,' *Christian Examiner*, L (1851), pp. 79-96.

45. John Pye Smith, *On the Relation between the Holy Scriptures and some parts of Geological Science*, 3rd ed. (London, 1843), pp. 398-99. The first edition appeared in 1839. The author was a non-conformist divine. He was a friend of Samuel Coleridge. Smith apparently learned about La Peyrère from Edward King's *Morsels of Criticism*.

46. Henry S. Patterson, 'Memoir of the Life and Scientific Labors of Samuel George Morton,' in Josiah Nott and George A. Gliddon, *Types of Mankind* (Philadelphia, 1854), pp. xliii-xliv.

47. For instance, see what is said about La Peyrère in Thomas Bendysche, 'History of Anthropology,' *Memoirs read before the Anthropological Society of London 1863-64*, Vol. I, pp. 355-356.

48. R. W. Gibbes, 'Death of Samuel George Morton, M.D.' *Charleston Medical Journal*, VI (1851), p. 594.

49. Cited in Stanton, *op. cit.*, p. 144.

50. Gibbes, *op. cit.*, p. 597.

51. The full title of this work is *Types of Mankind: or Ethnological Researches, based upon the Ancient Monuments, Paintings, Sculptures, and Crania of Races, and upon their Natural, Geographical, Philological and Biblical History* (Philadelphia, 1854). The volume has some important unpublished papers of Morton, as well as essays by Nott, Gliddon, Agassiz, and W. Usher.

52. Quoted in Patterson's 'Memoirs of Morton,' in *Types of Mankind*, pp. li-lii.

53. J. D. B. De Bow, 'Ethnological Researches—Is the African and Caucasian of Common Origin?,' *De Bow's Review LX* (1850), pp. 243-5. De Bow used Morton and Agassiz to support his negative answer to the question.

54. John Bachman, D. D., *The Doctrine of the Unity of the Human Race Examined on the Principles of Science* (Charleston, 1850). Bachman and the campaign against the Mortonites are discussed in Stanton, *op. cit.*, pp. 123-36.

55. Thomas Smyth, D. D., *The Unity of the Human Races proved to be the Doctrine of Scripture, Reason and Science with a Review of the Present Position and Theory of Professor Agassiz* (New York, 1850). The quotation is on p. 337.

56. William T. Hamilton, D. D., *The 'Friend of Moses' or A Defence of the Pentateuch as the Production of Moses and an Inspired Document against the Objection of Modern Skepticism* (New York, 1852).

57. Douglass, 'The Claims of the Negro Ethnologically Considered' in Ruchames, *Racial Thought in America* I, pp. 478-92.

58. *Ibid.*, p. 490.

59. (Edward William Lane), *The Genesis of the Earth and of Man: A Critical Examination of Passages in the Hebrew and Greek Scriptures, chiefly with a view to the Solution of the Question whether the Varieties of the Human Species be more than one origin*, ed. by Reginald Stuart Poole (Edinburgh, 1856).

60. *Ibid.*, pp. ix-x.

61. Isabella Duncan, *Pre-Adamite Man or the Story of our Planet and its Inhabitants told by Scripture and Science*, 3rd edition (London, 1860), Preface to 3rd edition.

62. *Ibid.*, Preface, p. ix.

63. Pascal Beverly Randolph, *Pre-Adamite Man: The Story of the Human Race from 35,000 to 100,000 years ago* (New York, 1863), Frontispiece and Dedication. This work was published under the pseudonym Griffin Lee of Texas. There were six editions by 1888, the last being published in Toledo, Ohio.

64. On Boucher de Perthes, see Jacques Roger, 'Boucher de Crèvecoeur de Perthes, Jacques,' in *Dictionary of Scientific Biography*, ed. by C. G. Gillispie, (New York, 1978), Vol. XV, Supplement I, pp. 50-52.

65. Nemo (W. Moore), *Man: Palaelithic, Neolithic and Several other Races, not inconsistent with Scripture* (Dublin, 1876).

66. *Ibid.*, Preface.

67. *Ibid.*, pp. 1-59.

68. *Ibid.*, p. 75.

69. James Hunt, 'Introductory Address on the Study of Anthropology,' *Anthropological Review*, I (1863), pp. 3-4. This essay was also published separately as a book in London in 1863.

70. James Hunt, 'On the Negro's Place in Nature,' *Memoirs read before the Anthropological Society of London*, I (1863), pp. 1-63.

71. Anon., 'Notes on the Antiquity of Man,' *Anthropological Review*, I (1863), pp. 64-65.

72. Thomas Bendysche, 'The History of Anthropology,' *Memoirs read before the Anthropological Society of London*, Vol. I (1863-64), pp. 355-56.

73. *Ibid.*, Appendix II, 'L. P. *Essays sent in a Letter from Oxford to a Nobleman in London* (London, 1695),' pp. 365-71. This work was discussed in chap. 9. Appendix III, *Dissertatio Critica de hominibus orbis nostri incolis...Vincentius Rumpf* (Hamburg, 1721), pp. 372-81. (This lists a great many of the answers to La Peyrère.)

74. Philalethes, 'Peyrerius and Theological Criticism,' *Anthropological Review*, II (1864), p. 109.

75. *Ibid.*, pp. 109-10.

76. *Ibid.*, pp. 110-11.

77. *Ibid.*, p. 111.

78. *Ibid.*, p. 112.

79. *Ibid.*, pp. 113-14.

80. *Ibid.*, p. 116.

81. *Ibid.*, p. 112.

82. A. de Quatrefages, 'Histoire naturelle de l'homme. Unité de l'espèce humaine,' *Revue de Deux Mondes*, XXX (1860), pp. 807-33. In his later work, *The Human Species* (London, 1879), Quatrefages said of the polygenetic theory: 'A dogma supported by the authority of the Book which is held in almost equal respect by Christians, Jews and Musselmans, has long referred the origin of all men, without opposition to a single father and mother. Nevertheless, the first blow aimed at this ancient belief was founded upon the same book. In 1655 La Peyrère, a Protestant gentleman in Condé's army, interpreting to the letter the two narratives of the creation contained in the Bible as well as various particulars in the history of Adam and the Jewish nation, attempted to prove that the latter alone were descended from Adam and Eve; that they had been preceded by other men who had been created at the same time as the animals in all parts of the habitable globe; that the descendants of these *Preadamites* were identified with the *Gentiles* who were always so carefully distinguished from the Jews. Thus we see that polygeneticism generally regarded as the result of *Free Thought* was biblical and dogmatic in origin' (pp. 30-31).

83. Quatrefages, 'Histoire naturelle de l'homme,' pp. 809-11. The quotation is on p. 811.

84. *Ibid.*, pp. 811-13. In *The Human Species*, Quatrefages said that 'in 1844 Mr. Calhoun, Minister of Foreign Affairs, when replying to the representations made to him by France and England on the subject of slavery, did not hesitate to defend the institutions of his country by urging the radical differences which, according to him, separated the Negro from the White Man' (p. 31). See also, Pastine, *op. cit.*, p. 13.

85. Dominick McCausland, *Adam and the Adamite: or, the Harmony of Scripture and Ethnology*, 2nd ed. (London, 1868). The quotations are on pp. 301 and 303.

86. Enoch L. Faucher, 'Was Adam the First Man?,' *Scribner's Monthly*, Oct. 1871, pp. 578-89.

87. Alexander Winchell, *Preadamites; or a Demonstration of the Existence of Men before Adam; together with a study of their condition, antiquity, racial affinities, and progressive dispersion over the earth. With Charts and Other Illustrations* (Chicago, 1880). The illustrations appear on the

frontispiece.88. Prof. Burt Green Wilder of Cornell started the first brain, rather than skull, collection, in the U. S. Wilder was a student of Agassiz. However, Wilder's researches led him to decide that there was no serious difference between the brains of white men and blacks. He came to a similar view about the relationship of male and female brains. Wilder's work came to notice in 1972 when the pickled remains of his collection were noticed in a basement at Cornell. A report (unpublished) by Hedwig Kasprzak, entitled, 'Report on Wilder Brain Collection' is the source of my information on the subject.

89. Winchell, *op. cit.*, pp. 247-249.

90. Charles Carroll, *'The Negro a Beast'* or *'In the Image of God.'* The Reasoner of the Age, the Revelator of the Century! The Bible as it is! The Negro and his Relation to the Human Family. The Negro a beast but created with articulate speech and hands, that he may be of service to his master—the White Man. The Negro not the Son of Ham, published in St. Louis in 1900. There is a photoreproduction edition (Miami, 1969). This work was answered by W. S. Armistead in *The Negro is A Man, a reply to Professor Charles Carroll's Book, The Negro is a Beast* (Tifton, Georgia 1908).

91. Winchell, *op. cit.*, p. 251.

92. *Ibid.*, pp. 454-61.

93. *Ibid.*, pp. 461-74. Dr. David N. Livingstone has shown me a paper he has prepared on Winchell's pre-Adamism, and how it was adopted in the late 19th and early 20th century by some fundamentalist theologians in America in answer to Darwinism and to the rejection of the Bible. Pre-Adamism could still make Adam the pivotal figure in history. Dr. Livingstone's study may lead to others revealing the concern and consideration of Pre-Adamism in this century.

94. I. A. Newby, *The Development of Segregationist Thought* (Homewood, IL, 1968).

95. Edward M. East, *Heredity and Human Affairs* (New York, 1935). The copyright was given in 1927 and the preface is dated in that year.

96. The *Encyclopaedia Britannica* had featured racist articles on why blacks are black and why this makes them inferior to whites from the 3rd edition of 1798 onward. In the famous eleventh edition, Thomas Athol Joyce, in the article 'Negro' repeated some of the previous theorizing, like that of skull development, and then added the importance of sex in the Negroes' outlook. East said on p. 190 that 'Joyce is certainly as favorable to the negro as the facts allow.' See T. A. Joyce, 'Negro,' *Encyclopaedia Brittanica*, 11th through 14th editions. (Vol. XIX, p. 344 of the 13th ed.) The 15th edition has a new and neutral account of the differences of blacks and whites.

97. Robert Bennett Bean, 'Some Racial Peculiarities of the Negro Brain,' *American Journal of Anatomy*, V (1906), pp. 353-432.

98. East, *op. cit.*, p. 198. The one exception was Paul Laurence Dunbar, 'Whose pathetic melodies can hardly be called great poetry.'

99. *Ibid.*, p. 199.

100. The major forms of scientific racism in the last hundred years are treated, somewhat polemically, but carefully in Allan Chase, *The Legacy of Malthus: The Social Costs of the New Scientific Racism* (New York, 1977). See also Stephen Jay Gould, *The Mismeasurement of Man* (New York, 1981).

CHAPTER ELEVEN

1. Otto Zöckler, 'Peyrère's (gest. 1676) Präadimitenhypothese nach ihren Beziehungen zu den anthropologischen Fragen den Gegenwart,' *Zeitschrift für die gesammte Lutherische Theologie und Kirche*, XXXIX (1878), pp. 28-48. Zöckler's *Geschichte der Beziehungen zwischen Theologie und Naturwissenschaft mit besondrer Rücksicht auf Schöpfungsgeschichte* (Gutersloh, 1877), has much material on Pre-Adamism and La Peyrère. Band II, pp. 768ff deals with recent discussions on these subjects.

2. A. J. Mass, 'Preadamites,' *Catholic Encyclopedia*, XII, pp. 370-71.

3. *Ibid.*, p. 370.

4. *Ibid.*, *loc. cit.*

5. *Ibid.*, *loc. cit.*

6. *Ibid.*, p. 371.

7. *Ibid.*, *loc. cit.*

8. É. Amann, 'Préadamites,' *Dictionnaire de Théologie Catholique* (Paris, 1933), XII, pp. 2793-800.

9. A. and J. Bouyssonie, 'Polýgenèse,' *Dictionnaire de Theologie Catholique*, XII, pp. 2520-536.

10. Amann, *op. cit.*, p. 2799.

11. Bonaventura Mariani, 'Poligenismo,' *Enciclopedia Cattolica* (Vatican City, 1952), IX, cols. 1676-680. Two recent works cited were P. C. J. Carles, 'L'unité de l'espeèce humaine,' *Archives de philosophie*, XVIII (1948); and D. Poulet, *Tous les hommes sont — ils fils de Noe?* (Ottawa, 1941).

12. O. W. Garrigan, 'Preadamites,' *New Catholic Encyclopedia* (New York, 1967), XI, p. 702.

13. O. W. Garrigan, 'Polygenism,' *New Catholic Encyclopedia* XI, p. 539.

14. *Ibid.*, p. 540.

15. An example of this literature is the work by David Balsiger and Charles E. Sellier, Jr., *In Search of Noah's Ark* (Los Angeles, 1976). On pp. 216-17, a lengthy list of works arguing a similar theory is given including the *Creation Research Quarterly*. Some writers have been using findings about the Turin Shroud to make a similar argument for the Bible's veracity.

16. Including such scholars as Léon Poliakov, R. H. Popkin, Ira Robinson, H. P. Salomon, Hans Joachim Schoeps, Leo Strauss, and Miriam Yardeni.

17. Sokolow, *History of Zionism*, I, pp. 41-42; and Hans Joachim Schoeps, 'Der Praeadamit Isaak de La Peyrère,' *Der Weg*, No. 51, Dec. 19, 1947, pp. 5-6. At the bottom of p. 5, Schoeps said, 'Warlich, Peyrère ist der erste Zionist gewesen, 250 Jahre bevor Theodor Herzl den politischen Zionismus begründate.'

18. This incident occurred in June, 1970, at a talk sponsored by the Van Leer Foundation at the Israel Academy of Sciences.

19. A. S. Yahuda, *The Language of the Pentateuch in its Relation to Egyptian*, Vol. I (Oxford, 1933) and *The Accuracy of the Bible* (London, 1934). On p. xxxvii of the latter work, Yahuda insisted that the presence of Egyptian elements in the Pentateuch constitutes the best evidence that the Books of Moses were composed in the period when Hebrew was still under Egyptian influence. He also argued that there was no need for a multiple authorship theory of the Pentateuch or any claim that it was written at Ezra's time or later.

20. Yahuda, *Accuracy of the Bible*, p. 214.

21. Yahuda's collection of Newton manuscripts is in the National Library of Israel, Yahuda Ms. Var. 1. There are indications of approval by Yahuda on the manuscripts, as well as in an unfinished manuscript by Yahuda on Newton's religious views, indicating much agreement by Yahuda with Newton's views on biblical chronology. On Newton's views on this topic, see Frank Manuel, *Isaac Newton Historian* (Cambridge, MA, 1963), as well as Isaac Newton, *The Chronology of Ancient Kingdoms*. Professors B. J. Dobbs, Richard S. Westfall, and myself have started the task of editing all of Newton's religious and alchemical manuscripts. This edition will be published by the Cambridge University Press.

22. On Vieira's views, see A. J. Saraiva, 'Antonio Vieira, Menasseh ben Israel et le Cinquième Empire,' VI (1972), pp. 25-56; and Karl Kottman, '16th and 17th Century Iberian Controversy over St. Thomas's Theory of Jus Gentium and Natural Law: The Interpretation of Antonio Vieira, S. J.,' *Atti del Congresso Internazionale*, no. 8, *L'Uomo*, Tome II, pp. 295-305.

23. On this, see Popkin, 'Jewish Messianism and Christian Millenarianism.'

24. La Peyrère, *Men before Adam*, Book V.

25. See, for instance, Marvin Harris, *The Rise of Anthropological Theory* (New York, 1968), p. 87; Francis C. Haber, *The Age of the World* (Baltimore, 1959), pp. 277-78; and Alfred C. Haddon, *History of Anthropology* (London, 1934), pp. 39-40.

26. Concerning Cyril Burt's work, see D. D. Dorfman, 'The Cyril Burt Question: New Findings,' *Science*, 29 Sept. 1978, Vol. 201, pp. 1177-86; Leslie Hearnshaw, *Cyril Burt, Psychologist* (London and Ithaca, NY, 1979), and Nigel Hawkes's review of the Hearnshaw book in *Science*, Vol. 205, 17 August 1979, pp. 673-75.

27. Henri Grégoire, *De la Noblesse de la peau ou du préjuge des blancs contre la couleur des Africains et celle de leurs descendans noirs et sang-mêlés* (Paris, 1826), p. 51. On this, see Necheles, *The Abbé Grégoire*, chap. 13.

28. Alexander von Humboldt, *Cosmos*, I, p. 368.

29. Cited at the end of Alexander von Humboldt's *Cosmos*, I, p. 389, from Wilhelm von Humboldt's *Ueber die Kawi-Sprache*, Band III, p. 426.

BIBLIOGRAPHY

Sources

1. Acosta, Jose de. *Historia Natural y Moral de las Indias*. Mexico: Fondo Cultura Economica, 1940.
2. Adair, James. *The History of the American Indians*. London: E. and C. Dully, 1775.
3. Adams, Hannah. *The History of the Jews from the Destruction of Jerusalem to The Present Time*. London: A. Macintosh, 1818.
4. Agassiz, Louis. 'The Diversity of Origin of the Human Races.' *The Christian Examiner and Religious Miscellany*, XLIX (1850), pp. 110-45.
5. ——, 'Geographical Distributions of Animals, *The Christian Examiner and Religious Miscellany*, XVIII (1850), pp. 181-204.
6. Alexandre, Noel. *Historia Ecclesiastica Veteris Novique Testamenti*. Paris: A. Dezallier, 1714.
7. Alexo de Orrio, Father Francisco Xavier. *Solution to the Great Problem of the Population of the Americas, in which on the Basis of the Holy Books There is Discovered an Easy Path for the Transmigration of Men from One Continent to the Other; and How There Could Pass to the New World, not only Beasts of Service, but Also the Wild and Harmful Animals; and by This Occasion One Completely Settles the Ravings of the Pre-Adamites, which Relied on This Difficult Objection until Now Not Properly Solved*. Mexico: Herederos de Dona Maria de Ribera, 1763.
8. Allen, Don Cameron. *Doubt's Boundless Sea*. Baltimore: Johns Hopkins Press, 1964.
9. ——. *The Legend of Noah*. Urbana: University of Illinois Press, 1963.
10. Amann, E. 'Préadamites.' *Dictionaire de Théologie Catholique*, XII (1933), pp. 2793-800.
11. Anchel, Robert. *Napoleon et Les Juifs*. Paris: Les Presses Universitaires de France, 1928.
12. Armistead, W. S. *The Negro is a Man, a reply to Professor Charles Carrol's Book, the Negro is a Beast*. Tifton, GA: Armistead and Vickers, 1903.
13. Arnauld, Antoine. *Rémarques sur les principales erreurs d'un livre intitulé l'ancienne nouveauté de l'Ecriture Sainte, ou l'Eglise triomphante en Terre. Oeuvres de M. Antoine Arnauld*. Lausanne: B. Alix, 1775-1783. Tome V.
14. Arnold, Gottfried. *Kirchen und Ketzer Historie*. Frankfurt: Thomas Fritsch, 1700.
15. Astruc, Jean. *Conjectures sur les Mémoires originaux dont il parôit que Moyses s'est servi pour composer le livre de Génèse*. Bruxelles: Z. Renan, 1753.
16. Atkins, John. *The Navy Surgeon: Or a Practical System of Surgery*. London: C. Ward and R. Chandler, 1734.
17. St. Augustine. *De Civitate Dei*. Libri XI-XXII, Corpus Christianorum, Series Latina, Vol. 48. Turnhout: Brepols, 1955.
18. ——. *Of the Citie of God: With the Learned Comments of IO. Lod. Vives*. English translation by J. H. (John Healy?), London?: n.p. 1610.
19. Aumale, Duc d'Henri. *Histoire des Princes de Condé*. Paris: Calman-Levy, 1896, Tome VI.
20. Azevedo, J. Lucio d'. *A Evolucas do Sebastinismo*. 2nd. ed. Lisbon: P. Livraria Classica Editora, 1947.
21. Bacher, W. 'Ibn Ezra, Abraham ben Meir, (Aben Ezra).' *Jewish Encyclopedia*. Vol. VI, pp. 520-24.
22. Bachman, John D. D. *The Doctrine of the Unity of the Human Race Examined on the Principles of Science*. Charleston: C. Canning, 1850.
23. Bacon, Francis. 'Of Vicissitude of Things.' *Essays*. London: Oxford University Press, 1958.

24. Balsiger, David. and Charles E. Sellier, Jr. *In Search of Noah's Ark*. Los Angeles: Sun Classic Books, 1976.
25. Bangius, Thomas. *Coelum Orientes et Prisci Mundi Triade. Exercitationum Literariarum Repraesentatum*. Copenhagen: P. Morsining, 1657.
26. ——. *Exercitationes Philologico-Philosophicae quibus Materia de Ortu et Progressu Literarum*. Krakow: J. Laurenti, 1691.
27. Bauer, Bruno. *La Question juive*. In *Karl Marx, La Question Juive*. Edited by Robert Mandrou, Paris: Union Generale d'Editions, 1968.
28. Bayle, Pierre. 'Peyrère, Isaac la.' *Dictionnaire historique et critique*. Amsterdam: Compagnie des Libraries, 1740.
29. ——. *Réponses aux Questions d'un Provincal*. Rotterdam: Chez Reiner Leers, 1704-7. Part V.
30. Bean, Robert Bennet. 'Some Racial Peculiarities of the Negro Brain.' *American Journal of Anatomy*, V (1906), pp. 353-432.
31. Beattie, James. *Essay on the Origin and Immutability of Truth*. Second edition. Edinburgh: W. Creech, 1776.
32. Bendysche, Thomas. 'The History of Anthropology.' *Memoirs read before the Anthropological Society of London*, I (1863-64), pp. 335-420.
33. Berkeley, George. *Alciphron: Or the Minute Philosopher*. London: J. Tonson, 1732.
34. Bernadau, M. 'Notice sur Isaac La Peyrère, auteur Bordelais, extraite du Pantheon littéraire d'Aquitaine, ou Histoire des Hommes illustres nés dans l'ancienne province de Guienne.' *Bulletin polymathique du Museum d'Instruction publique de Bordeaux*, Année 1810, pp. 375-79.
35. Bernus, A., *Richard Simon et son histoire critique du vieux Textament*. Lausanne: G. Bridel, 1869.
36. C. J. Betts, *Early Design in France*. (The Hague 1985).
37. Beverland, Adrian. *Histoire de l'Etat de l'Homme dans le peché originel*. n.p., 1731.
38. Bicheno, James. *The Restoration of the Jews, The Crisis of All Nations to which is now prefixed, A Brief History of the Jews from their first Dispersion to the Calling of their Grand Sanhedrin at Paris, October 6, 1806*. Second edition. London: Johnson, 1807.
39. Blau, Joseph L. *The Christian Interpretation of the Cabbala in the Renaissance*. New York: Columbia University Press, 1944.
40. Blount, Charles. *The Oracles of Reason*. London: Gildon, et al., 1693.
41. Blumenbach, Johann F.. *On the Natural Varieties of Mankind*. Translated by Thomas Bendysche. New York: Bergman Publishers, 1969.
42. Blumenkranz, Bernard. *Juifs et Christiens dans le Monde Occidental, 430-1096*. Paris and The Hague: Mouton, 1960.
43. Bonald, Louis Gabriel Ambroise. 'Sur les Juifs.' *Mercure de France*, XXIII (1806), pp. 249-67.
44. Borst, Arno. *Der Turmbau von Babel*. Stuttgart: A. Miersemann, 1957. Vol. I.
45. Bory de Saint-Vincent, J.B.G. *L'Homme (Homo), Essai Zoologique sur le genre human*. Second edition, Paris: Rey et Gravier, 1827. Vol. II.
46. Boudinot, Elias. *The Age of Revelation Or the Age of Reason shown to be An Age of Infidelity*. Philadelphia: Asbury Dickens, 1801.
47. Bouwsma, William J. *Concordia mundi; the Career and Thought of Guillaume de Postel*. Cambridge: Harvard University Press, 1957.
48. Bowersock, G. W. *Julian the Apostle*. Cambridge: Harvard University Press, 1978.
49. Bouyssonie, A., and J. Bouyssonie. 'Polygénes.' *Dictionnaire de Théologie Catholique*, XII (1933), pp. 2520-36.
50. Braithwaite, William C. *The Beginning of Quakerism*. Second edition, revised by H. J. Cadbury. Cambridge: Cambridge University Press, 1955.
51. Bredvold, Louis I. *The Intellectual Milieu of John Dryden*. Ann Arbor: University of Michigan Press, 1959.
52. Brett, Samuel. *A Narrative of the Proceedings of a Great Council of Jews on 12th October 1650. Harleian Miscellany*. Edited by W. Oldys, London: 1808-1813. Vol. I., pp. 379-85.

53. Brothers, Richard. Pamphlet collection. British Library, BM3185.f.i (1-10).
54. Browne, Sir Thomass, *Pseudodoxia Epidemica*, in *Works of Sir Thomas Browne*, London: Faber and Gwyer, 1928.
55. Browning, Robert. *The Emperor Julian*. London: Weidenfeld and Nicolson, 1975.
56. Bruno, Giordano. *The Expulsion of the Triumphant Beast*. Translated by Arthur Imerti. New Brunswick: Rutgers University Press, 1964.
57. ——. *Cabala del cavallo Pegasco, Dialogo Secundo In Dialoghi Italiani: Dialoghi Metafisici e dialoghi morali*. Edited by Giovanni Aquilecchia, with notes by Giovanni Gentile. Third edition. Florence: Sansoni, 1958.
58. ——. *Spaccio della Bestia trionfante*. In *Dialoghi Italiani: Dialoghi metafisici e dialoghi morali*. Edited by Giovanni Aquilecchia, with notes by Giovanni Gentile. Third edition. Florence: Sansoni, 1958.
59. Bruys, François. *Mémoires historiques, critiques et littéraires*. Paris: Hérissant, 1751. Tome II.
60. Brydone, P. *A Tour through Sicily and Malta in a series of letters to William Beckford*. W. Strahan, 1773. Vol. I.
61. Burnet, Thomas. *Telluris theoria Sacra*. London: R. N. Impensis Gualt, 1681.
62. ——. *The Theory of the Earth*. London: R. Norton, 1684.
63. Burtin, François Xavier. 'Réponse à la Question physique proposée par la Societé de Teyler sur les Révolutions génerales, qu'a subies la surface de la Terre, et sur l'ancienneté de notre globe.' In *Verhandelingen uitgegeeven door Teyler's Tweede Genootschap, zevende Stuk*. Haarlem: 1789, pp. 194-95.
64. [Review of] François Xavier Burtin. *The Monthly Review*, III (1970), p. 543.
65. Cadbury, Henry J. 'Early Quakerism and Uncanonical Lore.' *Harvard Theological Review*, XL (1947), pp. 177-205.
66. Calmet, Dom Augustin. *Dictionnaire historique, critique, chronologique, géographique et littéral de la Bible*. Paris: Emery, Benoist, 1722. Tome II.
67. 'Cantarini, Isaac Vita Ha-Kohen.' *Encyclopedia Judaica*, V (1971), pp. 122-23.
68. Cantel, R. *Prophétisme et Messianisme dans l'oeuvre du Père Vieira*. Paris: Ediciones Hispano Americanes, 1960.
69. Cappel, Louis. *The Hinge of Faith and Religion*. Translated by Philip Marinel. London: Thomas Dring, 1660.
70. Carles, P. C. J. 'L'unité de l'espèces humaine.' *Archives de philosophie*, XVIII (1948).
71. Carroll, Charles. '*The Negro a Beast*' or '*In the Image of God.*' *The Reasoner of the Age, the Revelator of the Century: The Bible as it is: The Negro and his Relation to the Human Family. The Negro a beast but created with articulate speech and hands, that he may be of service to his master—the white man. The Negro not the Son of Ham*. St. Louis: American Book and Bible house, 1900. Photoreproduction edition. Miami: 1969.
72. Carroll, Robert T. *The Common-Sense Philosophy of Religion of Bishop Edward Stillingfleet*. The Hague: Martinus Nijhoff, 1975.
73. Casas, Bartolemé de Las. *History of the Indies*. Translated by Andre Colland. New York: Harper & Row, 1971.
74. Castro, Americo. *La Realidad historia de España*. Mexico: Editorial Porrua, 1954.
75. ——. *The Structure of Spanish History*. Princeton: Princeton University Press, 1954.
76. Chambers, Ephraim. 'Praeadamite.' In *Cyclopedia; Or, An Universal Dictionary of Arts and Sciences*. London: 1786: James and John Knapton, Vol. III.
77. 'Charpy de Sainte-Croix, Nicolas.' Michaud, *Biographie universelle*. Vol. VII, pp. 680-681.
78. Charpy de Sainte-Croix, Nicolas. *L'ancienne nouveauté de l'Ecriture Sainte, ou l'Eglise triomphante en terre*. n.p. 1657.
79. ——. *Le Hérault de la fin des temps ou Histoire de l'Église triomphante*. Paris: Guillaume Desprez,
80. Charron, Pierre. *La Replique de Maistre Pierre Charron sur la Response faite à sa troisième Verité*. Lyon: J. Didier, 1595.
81. Chase, Allen. *The Legacy of Malthus: The Social Costs of the New Scientific Racism*. New York: Knopf, 1977.

82. Christianus, 'Account of Peyrera, Author of 'Praedaminae Rappel des Juifs, etc.' *Gentleman's Magazine*, LXXXII (1812), pp. 432-34.
83. Christianus, 'Further account of Isaac Peyrera,' *Gentleman's Magazine*, LXXXIII (1813), pp. 614-16.
84. Chwolson, Daniel. 'Über die Überreste der Altbabylonischen Literatur in Arabischen Übersetzungen.' In *Académie Imperiale des Sciences de St. Petersbourg, Mémoire des Savants étrangers*. Repr. Amsterdam: Oriental Press, 1968. Vol. VIII, No. 2.
85. *Co-Adamitae, or an Essay to prove the two following paradoxes, viz. I. That there were other men created at the same time with Adam, and II. that the angels did not fall*. London: J. Wilford, 1732. Anon.
86. Cohn, Norman. *The Pursuit of the Millenium*. New York: Harper, 1961.
87. ——. *Warrant for Genocide, The Myth of the Jewish World Conspiracy and the Protocols of the Elders of Zion*. London Harmondsworth: Penguin, 1970.
88. Colabus, Michael. *Disputationes ex capite V Epistolae ad Romanos Contra Praeadamitae*. Rostock: 1656.
89. Conway, Anne. *The Principles of the Most Ancient and Modern Philosophy*. Edited with an introduction by Peter Loptson. The Hague, Martinus Nijhoff, 1982.
90. Coons, Carleton. *The Origin of Races*. New York: Knopf, 1962.
91. Crawford, Charles. *An Essay on the Propagation of the Gospel, in which there are Numerous Facts and Arguments Adduced to prove that many of the Indians in America are Descended from The Ten Tribes*. Philadelphia: James Humphreys, 1801.
92. ——. *Observations upon Slavery*. 1790.
93. Danchin, F. -C.. 'Études critiques sur Christopher Marlow.' *Révue germanique*, IX (1913), pp. 52-68.
94. Dannhauer, J. Conrad. *Praeadamitae Utis, sive fabula primorum hominum ante Adamum conditorum explosa*. Strasbourg: J. Staedelii, 1656.
95. D'Arce, Lom. *Nouveaux Voyages de Mr. le Baron de Lohontan dans l'Amérique septentrionale*. The Hague: n.p., 1703.
96. De Bow, J. D. B.. 'Ethnological Researches—Is the African and Caucasian of Common Origin?' *De Bow's Review*, LX (1850), pp. 243-45.
97. 'Desmarets de Sainte-Sorlin, Jean, 1595-1676.' Michaud, *Biographie Universelle*. Tome X, pp. 532-33.
98. Desmarets, Samuel. *Refutatio Fabulae Prae-Adamiticae*. Groningen: Francisci Bronchartii, 1656.
99. De Larrey, Isaac. *Histoire de 'Angleterre, d'Ecosse et d'Irlande*. Rotterdam: R. Leers, 1713. Vol. IV.
100. Deschamps, Jules. *Rappel futur des Juifs*. Paris: 1760.
101. Desfours de la Génetière, Charles François. *Avis aux catholiques sur le caractère et les signes de temps où nous vivions, ou De la conversion des Juifs, de l'avenément intermédiare de Jésus-Christ et de son régne visible sur la terre*. Lyon: n.p., 1794.
102. Desmoulins, Antoine. *Histoire Naturelle des races humaines du nort-est de l'Europe, de l'Asie boréale et Orientale et de l'Afrique australe*. Paris: Meguignon-Marvis, 1826.
103. Dibon, Paul. 'Lettres de Samuel Des Marets à Claude Saumaise.' *LIAS*, I (1974), pp. 267-99.
104. 'Préadamite.' in *Dictionnaire Universal françois et latin, Vulgairement appelé Dictionnaire de Trévoux*. Paris: Veuve Delaune, 1743. Tome V^e.
105. Diderot, Dénis. 'Préadamites,' in *Oeuvres Complètes*. Paris: Garnier Bros., 1876. Vol. 16.
106. Dietrich, Johann Conrad. *Antiquitates Biblicae*. Gissae-Hassorum: Surtibus Societaris, 1671.
107. Dini, Alessandro. 'La Teoria preadamitica e il Libertinismo di La Peyrère 1594-1676.' *Annoli dell Istituto di filosofia*, Universita di Firenze, Vol. I (1979), pp. 165-235.
108. Dobbs, Francis. *A Concise View from History and Prophecy, of Great Predictions in the sacred Writings that have been fulfilled, also of those that are now fulfilling, and that remain to be accomplished* London: n.p., 1800.

109. ——. *Universal History Commencing with the Creation... in Letters to his Son*. London: n.p., 1787.
110. Dorfman, D. D. 'The Cyril Burt Question: New Findings.' *Science*, 201 (Sept. 29, 1978), pp. 1177-86.
111. Dormay, F. *Animadversiones in Libros Prae-Adamitarum. Paris: n.p.*, 1657.
112. Douglass, Frederick. 'The Claims of the Negro Ethnologically Considered.' Reprinted in *Racial Thought in America*, edited by Louis Ruchames. New York: Grosset and Dunlap, 1970. Vol. I.
113. Dubois, Claude-Gilbert. 'La Mythologie nationaliste de Guillaume Postel.' *Proceedings of the Postel Congress*. Avranches: 1981. Forthcoming.
114. Dubnow, Simon. *History of the Jews*. South Brunswick: T. Yoseloff, 1971. Vol.IV.
115. Duncan, Isabella. *Pre-Adamite Man or the Story of our Planet and its Inhabitants told by Scripture and Science*. Third edition. London: James Nisbit et al., 1860.
116. Dupèbe, J. 'Poursuites contre Postel en 1553.' *Proceedings of the Postel Congress*, Avranches: 1981. Forthcoming.
117. Dupront, Pierre A.. *Daniel Huet et l'exégèse comparatiste au XVIIe siècle*. Paris: E. Leroux, 1930.
118. Dury, John. *A Case of Conscience, Whether it be lawful to admit Jews into a Christian Commonwealth?* London: Richard Wodenothe, 1656.
119. ——. *Israels Call to March out of Babylon into Jerusalem*. London: G. M. for T. Underbill, 1646.
120. East, Edward M.. *Heredity and Human Affairs*. New York: C. Scribner's Sons, 1935.
121. Ebert, Friedrich Adolf. *Allgemeines Bibliographisches Lexikon*. Zweiter Band, Leipzig: F. A. Brockhaus, 1830.
122. Elbogen, Ismar. *History of the Jews after the Fall of the State of Jerusalem*. Cincinnati: Department of Synagogue & School Extension of the Union of American Hebrew Congregations 1926.
123. Ellies-DuPin, Louis. *Nouvelle Bibliothèque des Auteurs Ecclesiastiques*. Second edition, Paris: André Pralard, 1690. Tome I.
124. Englecken, Herman Christopher. *Dissertatio Theologica Praeadamitiste recens incrustati examen Complectens*. Rostock: n.p., 1707.
125. Erdman, David V.. *Blake: Prophet against Empire*. Garden City: Doubleday, 1969.
126. Espagne, Jean d'. *Oeuvres*. La Haye: A. Leers, 1674.
127. Espiard de, La Cour. *Oeuvres Melées....* Amsterdam [Dijon]: n.p., 1749.
128. Evans, Arise. *An Eccho to the Voice from Heaven*. London: The Author, 1652.
129. ——. *Light for the Jews, or the Means to convert them, in answer to a Book of theirs, called The Hope of Israel, Written and Printed by Menasseth Ben-Israel*. London: The Author, 1664.
130. ——. *A Voice from Heaven to the Commonwealth of England*. London: n.p., 1652.
131. Faber, George Stanley. *A General and Connected View of the Prophecies, relative to the Conversion, Restoration, Union and Future Glory of the Houses of Judah and Israel*. London: F. C. and J. Rivington, 1809. Vol. I.
132. Fahd, T.. 'Ibn Wahshiyya.' *The Encyclopedia of Islam*. Leiden and London: E. J. Brill, 1969, p. 964.
133. Faucher, Enoch L., 'Was Adam the First Man?' *Scribners' Monthly*, October, 1871, pp. 578-89.
134. Fecht, J.. *Praeadamitismi recens incrustrati examin*. Rostock: n.p., 1696.
135. Feijoo y Montenegro, Benito Jeronimo. 'Solucion del gran problema historico sobre populacion de la America, y Revoluciones del Orbe Terraques.' In *Teatre Critico Universal*, published in *Dos Discursos de Feijoo Sobre America*. Mexico: Secretaria de education publica, 1945.
136. Feldstein, Stanley. *The Poisoned Tongue*. New York: Morrow, 1972.
137. Felgenhauer, Paul. *Anti-Prae-Adamita. Prüfung uber das Lateinische in Truck Aussgegangne Buch dessen Titul is Prae-Adamitae, Dass, vor Adam auch sollen Menschen gewesen seyn*. Amsterdam: Bey H. Betkio, 1659.
138. ——. *Bonum Nunciam Israel quod offertur Populo Israel &e Judae in hisce temporibus novissimus de MESSIA....* Amsterdam: n. p., 1655.

139. Filleau de la Chaise [Du Bois de la Cour], *An Excellent Discourse Proving the Divine Original, and Authority of the Five Books of Moses*, trans. by W. Lorimer, London: Tho. Parkhurst, 1682.
140. Fell, Margaret, (Fox, Margaret (Askew) Fell). *A Loving Salutation to the Seed of Abraham among the Jews*. London: Tho. Simmons, 1657.
141. Firth, Katherine R. *The Apocalyptic Tradition in Reformation Britain, 1530-1645*. Oxford: Oxford University Press, 1979.
142. Fisher, Samuel, *The Rustick Alarm to the Rabbies*, London: Robert Wilson, 1660.
143. ——. *The Testimony of Truth Exalted*. London: n.p., 1679.
144. Foster, John Wells. *Pre-Historic Races of the United States of America*. Chicago: S. C. Griggs, 1887.
145. Fredrickson, George M. *The Black Image in the White Mind*. New York: Harper and Row, 1971.
146. Freudenthal, Jacob. *Die Lebensgeschichte Spinoza's*. Leipzig: Veit & Comp., 1899.
147. Frothingham, N. L. 'Men before Adam.' *The Christian Examiner and Religious Miscellany*, L (1851), pp. 79-96.
148. Garrett, Clarke. *Respectable Folly, Millenarians and the French Revolution in France and England*. Baltimore: Johns Hopkins University Press, 1975.
149. Garrigan, O. W. 'Polygenism.' *New Catholic Encyclopedia* XI (1967), p. 539.
150. ——. 'Preadamites.' *New Catholic Encyclopedia*, XI (1969), p. 702.
151. *Gazette Nationale ou le Moniteur universal*, 3 Prairial, An. 7, Bonaparte, Napoléon. 'Proclamation.'
152. Gerbi, Antonello. *The Dispute of the New World*. Translated by Jeremy Moyle. Pittsburgh: University of Pittsburgh Press, 1973.
153. Gibbes, R. W. 'Death of Samuel George Morton, M.D.' in *Charleston Medical Journal*, VI (1851), p. 594.
154. Gillispie, Charles C. *Genesis and Geology*. Cambridge: Harvard University Press, 1951.
155. Glaser, Lynn. 'Indians or Jews.' An Introduction to a reprint of Menassah ben Israel's *The Hope of Israel*. Gilroy: R. V. Boswell, 1973.
156. Godwyn, Morgan. *The Negro's and Indians Advocate, Suing for their Admission into the Church: or a Persuasive to the Instructing and Baptizing of the Negro's and Indians in our Plantations*. London: J. D., 1680.
157. Goethe, Johan Wolfgang von. *Conversations of Goethe with Eckermann*. Translated by John Oxenford. London: Dent, 1882.
158. Goldbach, Barthold. *Dissertation Disp. de controversia celebri utrum ante Adamum alii fuerint homines*. Konigsberg: 1682.
159. Good, John Mason. *The Book of Nature*. London: Longman, Rees, Orme, Brown, and Green, 1826. Vol. II.
160. Gossett, Thomas. *Race, The History of an Idea in America*. New York: Schocken Books, 1971.
161. Gould, Stephen Jay. *The Mismeasurement of Man*. New York: W. W. Norton, 1981.
162. ——. 'Morton's Ranking of Races by Cranial Capacity. Unconscious manipulation of data may be a Scientific Norm.' *Science*, 200 (5 May, 1978), pp. 503-9.
163. Graetz, Heinrich. *History of the Jews*. Philadelphia: The Jewish Publication Society of America, 1895. Vol. V.
164. Grégoire, Henri. *De la Littérature des Negres*. Paris: Maradan, 1808.
165. ——. *De la Noblesse de la peau ou du préjugé des blancs contre la couleur des Africains et celle de leurs descendans Noirs et sang-mêlés*. Paris: Baudouin frères, 1826.
166. ——. *Essai sur la regénération physique, morale, et politique des juifs*. Metz: Devilly, 1789; English edition, London: n.p., 1791.
167. ——. *Histoire des Sectes religieuses*. Paris: Baudouin frères, 1828. Tomes II, III.
168. Grotius, Hugo. *Dissertatio altera de origine Gentium Americanarum adversus obtrectatorem*. 1643.
169. Haber, Francis C.. *The Age of the World*. Baltimore: Johns Hopkins Press, 1959.
170. Haddon, Alfred C.. *History of Anthropology*. London: Watts and Co., 1934.

171. Hale, Matthew. *The Primitive Origination of Mankind*. London: W. Godbid for W. Shrowsbery, 1677.
172. Halevi, Judah. *The Kuzari*. Introduction by Henry Slonimsky. New York: Schocken Books, 1964. Part I.
173. Halhed, Nathaniel Brassey. *A Code of Gentoo Laws, or Ordinations of the Pundits, from a Persian Translation, made from the Original, written in Shanscrit Language*. London: Stoupe, 1776.
174. ——. *Testimony of the Authenticity of the Prophecies of Richard Brothers and of his Mission to Recall the Jews*. London: Robert Campbell, 1795.
175. Hallez, Théophile. *Des Juifs en France. De leur état moral et politique*. Paris: G. -A. Dentu, 1845.
176. Hamilton, William T., D. D. *The 'Friend of Moses' or A Defence of the Pentateuch as the Production of Moses and an Inspired Document against the Objection of Modern Skepticism*. New York: M. W. Dodd, 1852.
177. Hanke, Lewis. 'Pope Paul III and the American Indians.' *Harvard Theological Review*, XXX (1937), pp. 65-102.
178. ——. *The Spanish Struggle for Justice in the Conquest of America*. Philadelphia: University of Pennsylvania Press, 1949.
179. Harris, John. *Remarks on some late Papers relating to the Universal Deluge: And to the Natural History of the Earth*. London: R. Wilkin, 1697.
180. Harris, Marvin. *The Rise of Anthropological Theory*. New York: Crowell, 1968.
181. Harrison, John F. *The Second Coming, Popular Millenarianism 1780-1850*. New Brunswick: Rutgers University Press, 1979.
182. Hartlib, Samuel. *Englands Thankfulnesse*. London: Michael Sparke, senior, 1642.
183. Hawkes, Nigel. 'Tracing Burt's Descent to Scientific Fraud.' in *Science*, August 17, 1979, pp. 673-75.
184. Hazard, Paul. *La Crise de la conscience europeenne*. Paris: Boivin, 1935.
185. Hearnshaw, Leslie. *Cyril Burt, Psychologist*. Ithaca: Cornell University Press, 1979.
186. Heidegger, Johann Heinrich. *Historia sacra Patriarchum*. Amsterdam: P. le Grand, 1667.
187. Hempel, Andreas B. *Dissertatio de Praeadamitis*. Helmstadt: n.p., 1714.
188. Hermansson, J. *Dissertation de Praeadamitis*. Upsala: 1730.
189. Hertzberg, Arthur. *The French Enlightenment and the Jews*. New York: Columbia University Press, 1968.
190. Hill, John Edward Christopher. *The Anti-Christ in Seventeenth Century England*. London and New York: Oxford University Press, 1971.
191. ——. *Change and Continuity in Seventeenth Century England*. London: Weidenfeld and Nicolson, 1974.
192. ——. *Puritanism and Revolution*. London: Secker & Warburg, 1965.
193. ——. 'Till the Conversion of the Jews.' Clark Library Lecture, October 1981, To be published in R. H. Popkin, ed. *Millenarianism and Messianism in English Literature and Thought*, forthcoming.
194. ——. *The World Turned Upside Down*. London: Maurice Temple Smith, 1972.
195. Hilpert, J.. *Disquisitio de Praeadamitis*. Utrecht: Johannem Janssonium, 1656.
196. Hobbes, Thomas. *Leviathan. English Works of Thomas Hobbes*. Edited by William Molesworth. London: J. Bohn, 1839. Vol. III, Part III.
197. Hohenheim, Theophrast von (Paracelsus). *Sämtliche Werke*. Edited by Karl Sudhoff. Munich and Berlin: R. Oldenbourg, 1929. Abt. 1, Band 14.
198. ——. *Sämtliche Werke*. Edited by Karl Sudhoff. Berlin: R. Oldenbourg, 1933. Abt., 1, Band 14.
199. Condemnation of the President and Council of *Holland/Zeeland* against *Prae-Adamitae*.' November 26, 1655.
200. Home, Henry, (Lord Kames). *Six Sketches on the History of Man, Containing the Progress of Men as Individuals*. Philadelphia: R. Bell and R. Aitken, 1776.
201. ——. *Sketches of the History of Man*. Glasgow: Thomas Duncan, for Ogle, Allardice and Thomson, 1819. Vols. I, II.

202. Horn, Georg. *Dissertatio de vera aetate mundi qua sententia illorum refellitur qui statuent Natale Mundi tempis Annis minimum 1440 Vulgarem aerem anticipare*. Leiden: Apud Joannem Elsevirium & Petrum Leffen, 1659.
203. Huddleston, Lee Eldridge. *Origins of the American Indians, European Concepts, 1492-1729*. Austin: University of Texas Press, 1967.
204. Huet, Pierre-Daniel. *Demonstratio Evangelica*. Paris: Stephenum Michallot, 1679.
205. Hulsius, Ant. *Non ens praeadamiticum*. Leiden: Johannem Elsevirium, 1656.
206. Humboldt, Alexander von. *Cosmos*. Translated by E. C. Otte. London: Bell, 1888. Vol. I.
207. Humboldt, Wilhelm von. *Ueber die Kawi-Sprache*. Berlin: Druckerei der Königlichen Akademie der Wissenschaften, 1836-39. Band III.
208. Hume, David. 'Of National Characters.' In *The Philosophical Works of David Hume*. Edited by T. M. Green and T. H. Grose. London: Longmans, Green, and Co., 1882. Vol. III.
209. Hunt, James. 'Introductory Address on the Study of Anthropology.' *Anthropological Review*, I (1863), pp. 1-21.
210. ——. 'On the Negro's Place in Nature.' *Memoirs read before the Anthropological Society of London*, I (1863), pp. 1-63.
211. Huygens, Christiaan. *Journal de Voyage à Paris et à Londres*. Edited by Henri-L. Brugmans. Paris: P. André, 1935.
212. Jacob, Margaret. *The Radical Enlightenment: Pantheists, Freemasons and Republicans*. London: Harvester, 1981.
213. Jacquot, Jean. 'Thomas Harriot's Reputation for Impiety.' *Notes and Records of the Royal Society of London*, IX (1952), pp. 164-87.
214. Jessey, Henry, *A Narrative of the Late Proceeds at Whitehall Concerning the Jews*. London: L. Chapman, 1656.
215. Jones, William. 'On the Chronology of the Hindus.' *The Works of Sir William Jones*. Teigmouth ed. London: J. Stockdale, etc., 1807. Vol. IV.
216. ——. 'On the Gods of Greece, Italy and India.' *The Works of Sir William Jones*. Teigmouth ed. London: J. Stockdale, etc., 1807. Vol. III.
217. ——. 'Note to Mr. Vansittart's Paper on the Afgans being descended from the Jews.' *The Works of Sir William Jones*. Teigmouth ed. London: J. Stockdale, etc., 1807. Vol. IV.
218. ——. 'A Supplement to the Essay on Indian Chronology.' *The Works of Sir William Jones*. Teigmouth ed. London: J. Stockdale, etc. 1807. Vol. IV.
219. Jordani, Bruni, Nolani. *Opera Latine Conscripta*. Edited by F. Fiorentino, et al. Naples: 1879-91. Repr. Stuttgart: Fromann, 1962. Vol. I.
220. Joyce, T. A. 'Negro.' *Encyclopaedia Brittanica*. 11th - 14th editions.
221. Julian, Emperor. 'Letter to a Priest.' *Works*. Loeb Library edition, translated by Wilmer Cave Wright. New York: MacMillan Co.; London: William Heinemann, 1913. Vol. II.
222. Jurieu, Pierre. *Histoire critique des dogmas et des cultes*. Amsterdam: F. L. Honoré, 1704.
223. Kames, Lord. See Home.
224. Kaplan, Yosef. 'The Portuguese Jews in Amsterdam. From Forced Conversion to a Return to Judaism.' *Studia Rosenthaliana*, XV (1981), pp. 37-51.
225. ——. 'R. Saul Levi Morteira en zijn geschrift Obstaculus y opociciones contra la religion Xptiana.' *Studies in the History of Dutch Jewry*, I, Jerusalem: 1975, pp. 9-31.
226. Katz, David S., 'Menasseh ben Israel's Mission to Queen Christina of Sweden, 1651-1655,' *Jewish Social Studies*, XLV (1983-84), pp. 57-72.
227. ——. *Philosemitism and the Readmission of the Jews to England 1603-1655*. Oxford: Oxford University Press, 1982.
228. Kidder, Richard. *A Commentary on the Five Books of Moses: with a Dissertation concerning the Author or Writer of the said Books*. London: J. Heptinstall for W. Rogers, 1694. Vol. I.
229. King, Edward. 'Dissertation concerning the creation of Man.' *Morsels of Criticism,*

tending to illustrate some few passages in the Holy Scriptures upon philosophical principles and an enlarged view of things. London: J. Davis, 1800, pp. 70-71.

230. Kocher, Paul. *Christopher Marlowe, A Study of his Thought, Learning, and Character.* New York: Russell & Russell, 1962.

231. Kottman, Karl. '16th and 17th Century Iberian Controversy over St. Thomas' Theory of Jus Gentium and Natural Law: The Interpretation of Antonio Vieira, S. J.,' in *Atti del Congresso Internazionale*, no. 8, *L'Uomo*. pp. 295-305. Tome II.

232. Kuntz, Marion L.. 'Guillaume Postel and the Universal Monarchy.' *Proceedings of the Postel Congress.* Avranches: 1981, Forthcoming.

233. ——. 'Guillaume Postel, and the World State: Restitution and the Universal Monarchy,' *History of European Ideas*, IV (1983), pp. 299-323 and 445-65.

234. ——. *Guillaume Postel, The Prophet of the Restitution of all Things.* The Hague: Martinus Nijhoff, 1981.

235. Labrousse, Elisabeth. 'Vie et mort de Nicolas Antoine.' *Etudes Theologiques et religioses*, III (1977), pp. 421-33.

236. Lane, Edward William. *The Genesis of the Earth and of Man: A Critical Examination of Passages in the Hebrew and Greek Scriptures, Chiefly with a view to the Solution of the Question whether the Varieties of Human species be of more than one origin.* Edited by Reginald Stuart Poole. Edinburgh: A. and C. Black, 1856.

237. 'La Peyrère.' *Bibliographica Gallica.* London: R. Griffiths, 1752.

238. La Peyrère, Isaac. *Apologie de la Peyrère.* Paris: L. Billaine, 1663.

239. ——. *La Bataille de Lents.* Paris: Imprimerie du Louvre, 1649.

240. ——. *Lettre de la Peyrère à Philotime.* Paris: A. Courbe, 1658.

241. ——. *Men Before Adam.* London: n.p., 1656.

242. ——. *Prae-Adamitae.* [Amsterdam], 1655.

243. ——. *Du Rappel des Juifs.* Livres I-V. n.p., 1643.

244. ——. *Recueil de Lettres escrites à Monsieur le Comte de la Suze, pour l'obliger par raison à se faire Catholique,* Paris: S. Piget, 1661.

245. ——. *Relation du Groenland.* Paris: A. Courbe, 1647.

246. ——. *Relation de l'Islande.* Paris: T. Iolly, 1663.

247. ——. *Suite des Lettres escrites à Monsieur le Comte de la Suze, pour l'obliger par raison à se faire Catolique.* Paris: S. Piget, 1662.

248. ——. *A Theological Systeme.* n.p., 1655.

249. Leakey, Louis L. S., and V. M. Goodall. *Unveiling Man's Origins.* Cambridge, MA: Schenkman Publishing Company, 1960.

250. Lecky, William E. H. *The History of the Rise and Influence of the Spirit of Rationalism in Europe.* New York: D. Appleton and Company, 1866. Vol. I.

251. Leclerc, Georges Louis, Comte de Buffon. *Natural History, General and Particular.* Translated by William Smellie. Second edition. London: A. Strahan, 1785. Vol. III.

252. Lefranc, Pierre. *Sir Walter Ralegh, écrivain, l'oeuvre et les idées.* Quebec: Les Presses de l'Université Laval, 1968.

253. León, Nicolás. *Bibliografía mexicana del siglo XVIII*, sección primera. México: F. Díaz de León, 1902.

254. Levi, David. *Letters to Dr. Priestly in Answer to his letters to the Jews, Part II, occaisioned by Mr. David Levi's Reply to the Former Part.* London: printed for the author, 1789.

255. Linnaeus, (Karl Von Linné). *A General System of Nature Through the Three Grand Kingdoms of Animals, Vegetables, and Minerals.* London: Lackington, Allen, and Co., 1806.

256. Livermore, H. V. *A New History of Portugal.* Cambridge: Cambridge University Press, 1966.

257. Lods, Adolphe. 'Astruc et la critique biblique de son temps.' *Révue d'Histoire et de Philosophie réligieuses*, X (1924), pp. 109-39 and 201-27.

258. ——. *Jean Astruc et la Critique biblique au XVIIIe Siècle.* Strasbourg and Paris: Librarie Istra, 1924.

259. Long, Edward. *History of Jamaica.* London: T. Lowndes, 1774. Vol. II.

260. Lovejoy, Arthur O., and George Boas. *Primitivism and Related Ideas in Antiquity.* New York: Octagon Books, 1965.

261. Lucien-Brun, Henri. *La condition des Juifs en France depuis 1789.* Deuxième edition. Lyon: A. Effantin, 1900.

262. Lurie, Edward. 'Louis Agassiz and the Races of Man.' *Isis,* XLV (1954), pp. 227-242.

263. Maas, A. J.. 'Preadamites.' *Catholic Encyclopedia,* XII, pp. 370-371.

264. Mahler, Raphael. *A History of Modern Jewry, 1780-1815.* New York: Schocken Books, 1971.

265. Mahoudeau, P. G.. *Revue anthropologique.* 25e Année, 1915, p. 26.

266. Maimonides, Moses. *The Guide for the Perplexed.* Translation, Introduction and notes by Schlomo Pines. Introductory essay by Leo Strauss. Chicago: University of Chicago Press, 1964. Book III.

267. Maistre, Joseph. *Les Soirées de Saint-Petersbourg.* Paris: Librairie greque, latine et française, 1821.

268. Malo, Charles. *Histoire des Juifs.* Paris: Leroux, 1826.

269. Malot, François. *Dissertation sur l'epoque du rappel des Juifs.* Avignon: Par l'abbé F. Malot, 1776.

270. Manuel, Frank. *Isaac Newton, Historian.* Cambridge, Belknap Press of Harvard University Press, 1963.

271. Marana, Giovanni P., *Letters Writ by a Turkish Spy,* 8 vol. 13th ed., London: A. Wilde, 1753.

272. ——. *Letters Writ by a Turkish Spy,* selected and edited by Arthur J. Weitzman. London: Routledge Kegan Paul, 1970.

273. Margival, Henri. *Essai sur Richard Simon et la critique biblique en France au XVIIe siécle.* Paris: Maillet, 1900.

274. Mariani, Bonaventura. 'Poligenismo.' *Enciclopedia Cattolica.* Vatican City: 1952. Vol. IX, cols. 1676-1680.

275. Marolles, Michel de, and Isaac La Peyrère. *Le Livre de Genese.* n.p., n.d..

276. ——. *Mémoires.* Amsterdam: A. de Sommaville, 1755. Tome II.

277. Marquet, Yves, 'Cycles de la Souveraineté chez les Ihwan Al-Safa,' *Studia Islamica,* XXXVI (1972), pp. 47-69.

278. Maupertuis, P. L. Moreau de. *Venus Physique. Oeuvres de Maupertuis.* Lyon: J.-M. Bruyset, 1756. Tome II.

279. Maurice, Thomas. *Indian Antiquities.* London: The Author, 1794.

280. McCausland, Dominick. *Adam and the Adamite: or, the Harmony of Scripture and Ethnology.* Second edition. London: R. Bentley, 1868.

281. McKee, David. 'Isaac de la Peyrère, a precursor of the Eighteenth Century Critical Deists.' *Publications of the Modern Language Association,* LIX (1944), pp. 456-85.

282. ——. *Simon Tyssot de Patot and the Seventeenth Century Background of Critical Deism.* Johns Hopkins Studies in Romance Literature and Languages, Vol. XI. Baltimore: The Johns Hopkins University Press, 1941.

283. Méchoulan, Henri. 'Menasseh ben Israel au Centre des rapports Judeo-Chrétiens en Hollande au XVIIe siècle dans un lettre inédit d'Isaac Coymasas à André Colvius,' *Studia Rosenthaliana,* XVI (1982), pp. 21-24.

284. ——. and Nahon, Gérard. Introduction to Menasseh ben Israel, *L'ésperance d'Israel.* Paris: Presses Univ. de France, 1979.

285. Mede, Joseph. *The Works of the Pious and Profoundly-Learned Joseph Mede.* London: Roger Norton for Richard Royston, 1672.

286. Meinsma, K. A., *Spinoza et son cercle,* Paris: J. Vrin, 1983.

287. Ménage, Gilles. *Ménagiana.* Paris: Florentin Delaune, 1729. Tome II.

288. Menasseh ben Israel. *Conciliador.* Frankfort: auctoris impensis, 1632.

289. ——. *Esperanca de Israel.* Amsterdam: Semuel ben Israel Soeiro, 1650.

290. ——. *To His Highness the Lord Protector of the Commonwealth of England, Scotland and Ireland. The Humble Addresses of Menasseh ben Israel, a Divine and Doctor of Physick, in behalf of the Jewish Nation.* Amsterdam?: n.p., 1651(?)

291. ——. *The Hope of Israel.* Translated by Moses Wall, London: R. I. for Hannah Allen, 1650.

292. ——. *Spes Israelis.* Amsterdam: n.p., 1650.

293. ——. *Vindiciae Judaeorum, or a Letter in Answer to certain Questions propounded by a Noble and Learned Gentleman, touching the Reproaches cast on the Nation of the Jews, wherein all objections are candidly, and yet fully, cleared.* London: R. D., 1656.

294. Menendez Pelayo, Marcelino. *Historia de la Heterodoxos Espanoles.* Edited by E. Sanchez Keyes, Santander: S. A. de Artes Graficas, 1948. Vol. VII.

295. ——. *Historia de los Heterodoxos Españoles.* Madrid: Consejo Superior de Investigaciones Cientificas, 1956. Vol. I.

296. Mersenne, Marin. *Correspondance du P. Marin Mersenne.* Tome XII, Paris: Editions du Centre Nationale de la Recherche Scientifique, 1972. Tome XIII, Paris: 1977. Tome XIV, Paris: 1980.

297. Mévorah, Baruch. 'Napolean Bonaparte.' *Encyclopedia Judaica,* XII, pp. 824-25.

298. Micraelius, J. L. *Monstrosae de praeadamitis opinionis abominanda foeditas demonstrata.* Stettin: 1656.

299. Mitchell, John. 'An Essay upon the Causes of the Different Colours of People in Different Climates.' *Royal Society of London Philosophical Transactions,* XLIII (1744-45), pp. 102-150.

300. Molnar, Stephen. *Races, Types, and Ethnic Groups. The Problem of Human Variation.* Englewood Cliffs: Prentice Hall, 1975.

301. Momigliano, Arnaldo. 'La Nuova Storia Romana di G. B. Vico.' *Revista Storia Italiana,* LXXVII (1965), pp. 773-790.

302. ——. 'Vico's *Scienza Nuova:* Roman 'Bestion' and Roman 'Eroi'.' *History and Theory,* V (1966), pp. 3-23.

303. Monod, Jacques. *Le Hasard et la necessité.* Paris: Editions du Sevil, 1970.

304. Montalto, Elijah. *Treatise on Isaiah 53,* First Part published in English by 'Philo-Veritas.' London: 1770.

305. Morange, B. *Libri de Praeadamitis brevis analysis, quae paveis totius libri fundamentum exponitur et evertitur.* Lyon: Iullieron and Baret 1656.

306. Morin, Jean-Baptiste. *Refutatis compendiosa errone: ac detestandi libri de Praeadamitis.* Paris: The Author, 1656.

307. Mornay, Philippe de. *Advertissement aux Juifs sur la venue du Messie.* Saumur: T. Portau, 1607.

308. ——. *Reponse pour le Traité de l'Eglise ... aux Objections proposées en un livre nouvellement mis en lumiere intitulé Les Trois Veritez.* Second edition. G. Cartier, 1595.

309. ——. *De la Verité de la Religion Chrestienne contre les Athées, Epicureans, Payans, Juifs, Mahumedisles, et autres infidèles.* Anvers: C. Plantin, 1581.

310. Morton, Samuel. *Types of Mankind: or Ethnological Researches, based upon the Ancient Monuments, Paintings, Sculptures, and Crania of Races, and upon their Natural Geographical, Philological and Biblical History.* Philadelphia: J. B. Lippincott and Co., 1854.

311. Mosheim, John Lawrance. *An Ecclesiastical History, Ancient and Modern.* Translated by Archibald MacLaine. New York: Harper and Brothers, 1880. Vol. II.

312. Nashe, Thomas. *Pierce Pennilesse* and *Christs Teares over Jerusalem. Works of Thomas Nashe.* Edited by R. B. McKerrow, London: A. H. Bullen, 1910. Vols. I, II.

313. Naudé, Gabriel. *Considerations politiques sur les Coups d'État.* Cologne: n.p., 1752.

314. Necheles, Ruth. *The Abbé Grégoire 1787-1831. The Odyssey of an Egalitarian.* Westport: Greenwood Publishing Corp., 1971.

315. Nemo (W. Moore). *Man: Palaelithic, Neolithic and Several other Races, not inconsistent with Scripture.* Dublin: Hodges, Foster, and Co., 1876.

316. Netanyahu, B. *The Marranos of Spain.* New York: Kraus Reprint Co., 1973.

317. Neubauer, A. *The 53rd Chapter of Isaiah.* Oxford: Polyglot, 1876.

318. Newby, I. A. *The Development of Segregationist Thought.* Homewood: Dorsey Press, 1968.

319. Newton, Isaac. *The Chronology of Antient Kingdoms amended,* ed. by J. Conduitt, London. Printed for J. Tonson, 1728.

320. Nicaise to Carrel. *Nouvelles de la Republique des Lettres*. Oct., 1703, pp. 390-91.
321. Nicéron, Jean-François. *Mémoires pour servir à l'histoire des hommes illustres*. Paris: Briasson, 1730. Tome XII.
322. ——. *Mémoires pour servir à l'histoire des hommes illustres*. Paris: Briasson, 1732. Tome XX.
323. Noah, Mordecai Manuel. *Discourse on the Restoration of the Jews*. New York: Harper, 1845.
324. ——. 'The American Indian and the Lost Tribes of Israel.' *Midstream*, May, 1971, pp. 49-64.
325. Noreña, Carlos G. *Juan Luis Vives*. The Hague: Martin Nijhoff, 1970.
326. 'Notes on the Antiquity of Man.' *Anthropological Review*, I (1863), pp. 60-107. Anon.
327. Nott, Josiah C. 'An Examination of the Physical History of the Jews, in its bearing on the Question of the Unity of the Races.' *Proceedings of the American Association for the Advancement of Science*, 3 (March 15, 1850).
328. ——. 'The Mulatto, A Hybrid-Probable Extermination of the Two Races if the Whites and Blacks are allowed to Intermarry.' *American Journal of the Medical Sciences*, VI (1843), pp. 252-56.
329. ——. *Two Lectures on the Connection between the Biblical and Physical History of Man*. 1849. Reprinted New York: Negro Universities Press, 1969.
330. —— and George A. Gliddon. *Types of Mankind: or Ethnological Researches, based upon the Ancient Monuments, Paintings, Sculptures, and Crania of Races, and upon their Natural, Geographical, Philological and Biblical History*. Philadelphia: Grambo, 1854.
331. Oldenburg, Henry. *The Correspondence of Henry Oldenburg*. Edited by Marie Boas Hall and A. Rupert Hall, Madison: University of Wisconsin Press, 1974. Vol. I.
332. Origen. *Origines in Sacras Scriptura*. Notes by Pierre Daniel Huet. Rothomagi: n.p., 1668.
333. Oxenstirn, Gabriel, Count. 'Relation d'un Entretien que j'eus autrefois à Padoue avec un fameux rabin.' In *Pensées de Monsieur le Comte d'Oxenstirn sur divers sujets*. The Hague: Jan Van Duren, 1742. Tome II, pp. 142-44.
334. P., L. *Two Essays, Sent in a Letter from Oxford, to a Nobleman in London*. London: B. R. Baldwin, 1695. *Somers Collection of Scarce and Valuable Tracts, Third Series*. London: Printed for F. Cogan, 1751, Vol. III, pp. 291-308.
335. Pagel, Walter. *Das medizinische Weltbild des Paracelcus, sein Zusammenhang mit Neuplatonisimus und Gnosis*. Wiesbaden: 1962. (Kosmosophie Bd. I).
336. ——. *Paracelsus: An Introduction to Philosophical Medicine in the Era of the Renaissance*. Basel: S. Karger, 1958.
337. Paine, Thomas. *The Age of Reason, Part the Second, being an Investigation of True and Fabulous Theology*. London: H. D. Symonds, 1795.
338. Paracelsus: see Hohenheim.
339. Pascal, Blaise. *Oeuvres Complètes*. Edited by Louis Lafuma. New York: Macmillan, 1963.
340. Pastine, Dino. 'La Origini del poligenismo e Isaac La Peyrère.' In *Miscellanea Seicento, Istituto di Filosofia della Facoltà di Lettere e Filosofia dell' Università di Genova*. Firenze: 1971, pp. 7-234.
341. Patin, Guy. *Lettres de Gui Patin*. Edited by J.-H. Réveille-Parisé. Paris: J.-H. Baillière, 1846. Tome I, II.
342. Patrick, Simon. *A Commentary upon the First Book of Moses called Genesis*. Second edition. London: R. Chiswell, 1698.
343. Patterson, Henry S. 'Memoir of the Life and Scientific Labors of Samuel George Morton.' In *Types of Mankind*. Edited by Josiah Nott and George A. Gliddon. Philadelphia: Grambo, 1854.
344. 'Peyrère, (Isaac la).' *Encyclopaedia Britannica*. Third edition. (Vol. 1-12 ed. by C. Macfarquhar, vols. 13-18 by G. Gleig) 18 vols. Edinburgh: A. Bell and C. Macfarquhar, 1797.
345. Philalethes. 'Peyrerius and Theological Criticism.' *Anthropological Review*, II (1864), pp. 109-16.
346. Pintard, René. *Le Libertinage érudit*. Paris: Boivin, 1943.

347. Poliakov, Léon. *Histoire de l'antisémitisme de Voltaire à Wagner.* Paris: Calmann-Lévy, 1968.

348. ——. *Le Mythe aryen.* Paris: Calmann-Lévy, 1971.

349. Pollock, Frederick. *Spinoza, His Life and Philosophy.* Second edition, London: Duckworth and Co., 1899.

350. Popkin, Richard H. 'Bible Criticism and Social Science.' *Boston Studies in the Philosophy of Science,* XIV (1974), pp. 339-60.

351. ——. 'The Development of Religious Skepticism and the Influence of Isaac La Peyrère's Pre-Adamism and Bible Criticism.' In *Classical Influences on European Culture, A D 1500-1700.* Edited by R. R. Bolgar, Cambridge: Cambridge University Press, 1976, pp. 271-80.

352. ——. 'Divine Causality: Newton, the Newtonians, and Hume.' In *Greene Centennial Studies, Essays Presented to Donald Greene* by Robert Allen and Paul Korshin. Charlottesville, Univ. Press of Virginia, 1984, pp. 40-56.

353. ——. 'The First College of Jewish Studies.' *Revue des Études Juives.* Forthcoming.

354. ——. *The History of Scepticism from Erasmus to Spinoza.* Berkeley: University of California Press, 1979.

355. ——. 'Hobbes and Skepticism.' In *History of Philosophy in the Making, Essays in Honor of James D. Collins.* Edited by Linus J. Thro, S. J. Washington: University Press, pp. 133-48.

356. ——. 'Hume's Racism.' *The Philosophical Forum,* IX (1977-78), pp. 211-26.

357. ——. Review of Margaret Jacob, *The Radical Enlightenment. Journal of the History of Philosophy.* Forthcoming.

358. ——. 'Jewish Messianism and Christian Millenarianism.' Clark Library Lecture. In *Culture and Politics from Puritanism in the Enlightenment.* Edited by Perez Zagorin. Berkeley: University of California Press, 1980, pp. 67-90.

359. ——. 'Jewish Values in the Post-Holocaust Future.' *Judaism* XVI (1967), pp. 273-276.

360. ——. 'La Peyrère, the Abbé Grégoire, and the Jewish Question in Eighteenth Century Culture,' *Studies in Eighteenth Century Culture,* IV (1975), pp. 209-22.

361. ——. 'The Marrano Theology of Isaac La Peyrère.' *Studi Internaxionali di Filosofia,* V (1973), pp. 97-126.

362. ——. 'Menasseh ben Israel and Isaac La Peyrère.' *Studia Rosenthaliana,* VIII (1974), pp. 59-63.

363. ——. 'Menasseh ben Israel and La Peyrère II.' *Studia Rosenthaliana,* XVIII (1984), pp. 12-20.

364. ——. 'A Note on Serrarius.' In French edition of Meinsma, *Spinoza et son cercle,* pp. 277-79.

365. ——. 'The Philosophical Basis of Eighteenth-Century Racism.' *Studies in Eighteenth Century Culture,* III (1973), pp. 245-62.

366. ——. 'The Philosophical Basis of Modern Racism.' In *Philosophy and the Civilizing Arts, Essays Presented to Herbert W. Schneider.* Edited by Craig Walton and John P. Anton. Athens: Ohio University Press, 1974, pp. 126-64.

367. ——. 'Pre-Adamism in 19th Century American Thought: 'Speculative Biology' and Racism.' *Philosophia,* VIII (1978), pp. 205-39.

368. ——. 'The Pre-Adamite Theory in the Renaissance.' In *Philosophy and Humanism, Renaissance Essays in Honor of Paul Oskar Kristeller.* Edited by Edward P. Mahoney. Leiden: Brill, 1976, pp. 50-69.

369. ——. 'Rabbi Shapira's Visit to Amsterdam.' *Dutch Jewish History,* ed. Jozeph Michman and Tirtsah Levie, Tel-Aviv University, Hebrew University, Jerusalem 1984, pp. 185-205.

370. ——. 'Scepticism, Theology and the Scientific Revolution in the Seventeenth Century.' In *Problems in the Philosophy of Science.* Edited by I. Lakatos and A. Musgrave. Amsterdam: North Holland Pub., 1968, pp. 23-25.

371. ——. 'Spinoza and La Peyrère.' *The Southwestern Journal of Philosophy,* VIII (1977), pp. 172-95.

372. ——. 'Spinoza, the Quakers and the Millenarians, 1656-1658.' *Manuscrito*, VI (1982), pp. 113-33.

373. ——. 'Spinoza's Relations with the Quakers.' In *Quaker History*, LXXIII (1984), pp. 14-28.

374. ——. 'The Third Force in 17th Century Philosophy: Scepticism, Millenarianism and Science.' *Nouvelles de la Republique des lettres*, III (1983), pp. 35-63.

375. ——. editor. *Millenarianism and Messianism in English Literature and Thought 1650-1800*. William Andrews Clark Lectures, 1981-1982, Forthcoming.

376. Postel, Guillaume. *Candelabri Typici in Mosis Tabernaculo*. Venice: 1548.

377. ——. *De Foenicium Literis*. Paris: Martinum Iuvenem, 1552.

378. ——. *Les Raisons de la Monarchie*. Moriar: n.p., 1551.

379. ——. *Le Thrésor des Prophetiés de l'Univers*. Introduction and notes by François Secret. The Hague: Martinus Nijhoff, 1969.

380. Proust, Jacques. *Diderot et l'Encyclopédie*. Paris: A. Colin, 1962.

381. Poulet, Donat. *Tous les hommes sont-ils fils de Noé?*. Ottawa: Universitas Catholica ottaviensis, 1941.

382. 'Pre-Adamite.' *Encyclopedia Britannica*. Third edition. (Vol. 1-12, ed. by C. Macfarquhar, vols. 13-18 by G. Gleig), Edinburgh: A. Bell and C. Marfarquhar, 1797.

383. 'Pre-Adamites.' *Naaukeurige Beschrying der uitwendige Godtsdienst-Plichten, Kerk-Zeden en Gewoontens Van alle Volkeren der Waereldt*. Illustrated by Bernard Picart, translated by Abraham Moubach. The Hague, Amsterdam and Rotterdam: Alberts, 1727-1738, Deel VI, pp. 198-208.

384. Prichard, James Cowles. *The Natural History of Man*. London: H. Bailliere, etc., 1848.

385. Pythius, Joannes. *Responsio exetastica ad tractatum incerto authore nuper editum cui titulus Praeadamitae*. Leiden: Johannem Elsevirium, 1656.

386. Quatrefages, A. de. 'Histoire Naturelle de l'homme. Unité de l'espèce humaine.' *Revue de Deux Mondes*, XXX (Dec. 15, 1860), pp. 807-33.

387. ——. *The Human Species*. London: C. Kegan Paul, 1879.

388. Quinn, Arthur. *The Confidence of British Philosophers*. Leiden: E. J. Brill, 1977. Part I

389. Ralegh, Sir Walter. *The History of the World*. London: R. White, et al., 1676. Book I.

390. Ramsay, James. *An Essay on the Treatment and Conversion of African Slaves in the British Sugar Colonies*. Dublin: n.p., 1784.

391. Randolph, Pascall Beverly. *Pre-Adamite Man: The Story of the Human Race from 35,000 to 100,000 years ago*. New York: S. Tousey, 1863.

392. Article on Isaac La Peyrère, *Du Rappel des Juifs* in *Gazette de France*, 28 Aout, 1806.

393. Article on Isaac La Peyrère, *Du Rappel des Juifs*. *Journal de Paris*, 29 Aout, 1806.

394. Rastell, John. *A New Interlude and a Mery, of the Nature of the i i i i Elements*. London: n.p., c.1520.

395. Reeves, Marjorie. *The Influence of Prophecy in the Later Middle Ages*. Oxford: Oxford University Press, 1969.

396. Reimann, Jacob Friedrich. *Historia Universalis Atheismi et Atheorum falso de merito suspectorum apud Judaeos, Ethnicos, Christianos, Muhamedanos*. Hildesiae: Apud Ludolphum Schroeder, 1725.

397. Rénaudot, Eusebius. *A Dissertation on the Chinese Learning*. London: n.p., 1733.

398. Révah, I. S. 'Les Marranes.' *Revue des Études Juives*, CXVIII (1959-60), pp. 29-77.

399. ——. 'Aux Origines de la Rupture Spinozienne: Nouveaux documents sur l'incroyance dans la communauté judeo-portugaise d'Amsterdam à l'époque de l'excommunication de Spinoza.' *Revue des Études Juives*, CXXIII (1964), pp. 357-431.

400. ——. *Spinoza et Juan Prado*. Paris: Mouton, 1959.

401. Réveille-Parisé, J. -H. *Lettres de Gui Patin*. Paris: J.-H. Baillière, 1846.

402. Richelet, Pierre. 'Pré-adamites.' *Dictionnaire de la langue françoise, ancienne et moderne*. Lyon: Duplain frèes, 1759. Tome II.

403. Ricuperati, G. 'Alla origine de Triregno: La Philosophia *Adamito-Noetice*. di A. Constantino.' *Revista Storica Italiana*, LXXVII (1965), pp. 602-38.

404. Rivet, André. *Correspondance intégrale d'André Rivet et de Claude Sarrau*. publiée et an-
      notée par Hans Bots et Pierre Leroy. Amsterdam: APA, 1980.
405. Robinson, Ira. 'Isaac de la Peyrère and the Recall of the Jews.' *Jewish Social Studies*,
      XL (1978), pp. 117-30.
406. Roger, Jacques. 'Boucher de Crevecoeur de Perthes, Jacques.' *Dictionary of Scientific
      Biography*. Edited by C. G. Gillispie. New York: 1978. Vol. XV, Supplement I, pp.
      50-52.
407. Rokeah, David. 'Julian.' *Encyclopedia Judaica*. Vol. 10, pp. 469-70.
408. Romans, Bernard. *A Concise Natural History of East and West Florida*. New York:
      Printed for the Author, 1785.
409. Romanus, Eusebius (Philippe le Prieur; listed in Bibliothéque Nationale as le P.
      Jean Mabillon). *Animadversiones in librum de Prae-adamitis*. Paris: n.p., 1656 (2nd Edi-
      tion 1658).
410. Rondet, Laurent Etienne. *Dissertation sur le rappel des Juifs*. Paris: Lottin l'aine, 1777.
411. Roth, Cecil. *A History of the Jews in England*. Third edition. Oxford: Clarendon
      Press, 1964.
412. ――. *The History of the Marranos*. Philadelphia: Jewish Publication Society, 1941.
413. ――. *A Life of Menasseh ben Israel*. Philadelphia: Jewish Publication Society, 1934.
414. ――. *A Life of Menasseh ben Israel, Rabbi, Printer, and Diplomat*. Philadelphia: Jewish
      Publication Society, 1945.
415. ――. *The History of the Jews in Venice*. Philadelphia: Jewish Publication Society,
      1930.
416. ――. 'New Light on the Resettlement.' *Transactions of the Jewish Historical Society of
      England*, XI (1928), pp. 112-42.
417. Rumpf, Vincent. *Dissertatio Critica de hominibus orbis nostri incolis, specie et ortu avito inter
      se non differentibus*. Hamburg: C. Neumann, 1721.
418. Salden, Willem. *Otio Theologica*. Amsterdam: Apud H. and Viduam Theodori
      Boom, 1684.
419. Salomon, H. P. 'The De Pinto Manuscript.' *Studia Rosenthaliana*, IX (1975), pp.
      1-62.
420. ――. 'Haham Saul Levi Morteira en de Portugese Nieuw-Christenen.' *Studia Rosen-
      thaliana*, X (1976), pp. 127-41.
421. ――. 'The Portuguese Background of Menasseh ben Israel's Father as revealed
      through the Inquisitional Archives at Lisbon,' *Studia Rosenthaliana*, XVII (1983),
      pp. 105-46.
422. Saraiva, A. J. 'Antonia Vieira, Menasseh ben Israel et le Cinquième Empire.'
      Studia Rosenthaliana, VI (1972), pp. 25-56.
423. Sarrau, Claude. *Epistolae*. Orange: n.p., 1654.
424. Schickard, Wilhelmus, *Tarich*. Tubingen: T. Werlini, 1628.
425. Schmid, J. Ant. *Pentas Dissertationum, I. de Praeadamitis ex orbe proscriptis*. Hemstadt:
      n.p., 1716.
426. Schoeps, Hans Joachim. *Barocke Juden Christen*. Bern and Munchen: Francke, 1965.
427. ――. 'Der Praeadamit Isaak de la Peyrère.' *Der Weg*, No. 51, Dec. 19, 1947, pp.
      5-6.
428. ――. *Philosemitismus im Barok*. Tubingen: J. C. B. Mohr, 1952.
429. Scholem, Gershom G. *Major Trends in Jewish Mysticism*. New York: Schocken Books,
      1969.
430. ――. *Sabbatai Sevi, the Mystical Messiah*. Princeton: Princeton University Press,
      1973.
431. Schoock, Martin. *Diluvium Noach: Universale sive Vindicae Communis senteniae quod
      Diluvium Noachicum universae terrae incubuerit*. Groningen: n.p., 1662.
432. Schwarz, Leon. *Diderot and the Jews*. Rutherford, NJ: Fairleigh Dickenson Press,
      1981.
433. Secret, François. 'Introduction.' In Guillame Postel, *Le Thrésor des Propheties de
      l'Univers*. The Hague: Martinus Nijhoff, 1969.
434. ――. *Le Zohar chez les Kabbalistes chrétiens de la Renaissance*. The Hague: Mouton,
      1964.

435. Shulim, Joseph J. 'Napoleon I as the Jewish Messiah: Some Contemporary Conceptions in Virginia.' *Jewish Social Studies*, V (1945), pp. 275-80.
436. Simon, Richard. *De 'l'Inspiration les Livres sacrés*. Rotterdam: R. Leers, 1687.
437. ——. *De 'l'Inspiration les Livres sacrés*. Rotterdam: R. Leers, 1702.
438. ——. *Lettres choisies, de M. Simon*. N, Rotterdam: R. Leers, 1702. Tome II, IV.
439. Slotkin, James S. *Readings in Early Anthropology*. Chicago: Aldine Publishing Co., 1965.
440. Smith, John Pye. *On the Relation between the Holy Scriptures and Some parts of Geological Science*. Third edition. London: Jackson and Walford, 1843.
441. Smith, Stanhope. *An Essay on the Causes of the Variety of Complexion and Figure in the Human Species, to which are added Strictures on Lord Kames's Discourse on the Original Diversity of Mankind*. Philadelphia and Edinburgh: Robert Aitken, 1787.
442. Smyth, Thomas, D. D. *The Unity of the Human Races proved to be the Doctrine of Scripture, Reason and Science with a Review of the Present Position and Theory of Professor Agassiz*. New York: G. Putnam, 1850.
443. Sokolow, Nahum. *The History of Zionism, 1600-1918*. London: Longmans, Green, and Co., 1919. Vol I.
444. Sortais, Gaston. *La Philosophie moderne depuis Bacon jusqu' à Leibniz*. Paris: P. Lethielleux, 1922. Tome II.
445. Spanheim, Friedrich. *Disputatis Theologica de Statu Instituto Primi Hominis*. In *Opera*. Leiden: C. Boutestein, J. Luchtmans, 1703. Tomus III.
446. Spitzel, Theophile (Gottlieb). *Felix literatus ex infelicium periculis et casibus*. Augsburg: Theophil Goebel, 1676.
447. Spinoza, Benedict de. *Works of Spinoza*. Edited by R. H. M. Elwes. New York: Dover Publications, 1955. Vol. I.
448. Stanton, William. *The Leopard's Spots*. Chicago: University of Chicago Press, 1960.
449. Steinmann, Jean. *Richard Simon et les origines de l'exégèse biblique*. Paris: Desclée de Brouwer, 1960.
450. Stillingfleet, Edward. *Origines Sacrae*. London: R. W. for Henry Mortlock, 1661.
451. ——. *Origines sacrae*. Eighth edition. London: R. Knaplock, et al., 1709.
452. ——. *Origines Sacrae*. London: R. W. for Henry Mortlock, 1662. Book III.
453. Stolpe, Sven. *Christina of Sweden*. New York: Macmillan, 1966.
454. Strathmann, Ernest A. *Sir Walter Ralegh, A Study in Elizabethan Skepticism*. New York: Columbia University Press, 1951.
455. Strauss, Leo. *Spinoza's Critique of Religion*. New York: Schocken Books, 1965.
456. Tamizey de Larroque, Philippe. *Quelques Lettres inédites d'Isaac de la Peyrère à Boulliau* (*Plaquettes Gontaudaises*, no. 2). Paris: n.p., 1878.
457. ——. Philippe et A. Communay. 'Isaac de la Peyrère et sa famille.' *Revue critique d'histoire et de littérature*, XIX (Jan. -Juin., 1885), pp.136-37.
458. *Theophilus to Autolycus*. In *Ante-Nicene Christian Library*, Vol. III, 1868.
459. Thomasius, Jacob. *Dissertationes LXIII Varii Argumenti*. Halle: J. F. Zeitleri, 1693.
460. Thorowgood, Thomas. *Jewes in America, or Probabilities that the Americans are of that Race*. London: W. H. for T. Slater, 1650.
461. *The Three Impostors*. Edited by J. Myles. Dundee: n.p., 1844. Anon.
462. Toon, Peter, editor. *Puritans, the Millenium and the Future of Israel; Puritan Eschatology 1600-1660*. London: James Clarke, 1970.
463. *Traité des Trois Imposteurs*. En Suisse: De l'Imprimerie Philosophique, 1793. Anon.
464. Trevor-Roper, Hugh. *Religion, the Reformation and Social Change*. London: Macmillan, 1967.
465. *De Tribus Impostoribus*. Edited by Gerhard Bartsch. Berlin: Akademie-Verlag, 1960. Anon.
466. Trinius, Johann Anton. *Freydenker Lexicon*. Leipzig and Bernberg: C. G. Corner, 1759.
467. Tuveson, Ernest. *Millennium and Utopia*. Gloucester: Peter Smith, 1972.
468. Tyssot, Simon, de Patot. *The Travels and Adventures of James Massey*. London: S. Whatley, 1733.

232 BIBLIOGRAPHY

469. Ursinus, J. H.. *Novus Prometheus Praeadamitarum plases ad Caucasum relegatus et religatus*. Frankfort: C. Hersindorf, 1656.
470. Usque, Samuel. *Consolation for the Tribulations of Israel*. Trans. by Martin A. Cohen. Philadelphia: Jewish Publications Society, 1915.
471. Vake, J.. *Beweisthun dass ein Gott sey, samt Vorbericht von der Praeadamiterey*. Hamburg: C. Neumann, 1696.
472. ——. *Disputatio physica de origine animal humane*. Leipzig: J. Georgi, 1669.
473. Van Amringe, William Frederick. *An Investigation of the Theories of the Natural History of Man by Laurence, Prichard, and Others*. New York: Baker and Scribner, 1848.
474. Van den Berg Jan. 'Quaker and Chiliast: the 'contrary thoughts' of William Ames and Peter Serrarius.' In *Reformation Conformists and Dissent, Essays in honour of Geoffrey Nuttall*. Edited by Buick Knox. London: Epworth Press, 1977.
475. Van der Wall, Ernestine. 'De Hemelsche Tekenen en het rijk van Christus op Aarde. Chiliasme en Astrologie bij Petrus Serrarius 1600-1669.' *Kerkhistorische Studien* (Leiden 1982), pp. 45-62.
476. Vanini, Lucilio. *De admirandis naturae reginae deaque mortalium arcanis*. Paris: Adrianum Perier, 1616.
477. Van Limborch, Philip. *De Veritate Religiones Christianae, Amica collatio cum erudito Judaeo*. Gouda: Apud J. ab Hoeve, 1687.
478. Vereté, Mayir. 'The Idea of the Restoration of the Jews.' Clark Library Lecture, May 1982. In *Essays in Honor of S. Ettinger. Forthcoming*.
479. ——. 'The Restoration of the Jews in English Protestant Thought, 1790-1840.' in *Middle Eastern Studies*, VIII (1972), pp. 3-50.
480. Vico, Giambattista. *Principi di Scienza Nuova*. In *Opere*. Edited by F. Nicolini. Milan and Naples: R. Ricciardi, 1953. Libro Primo.
481. Vieira, Antonio de. *Historia do Futuro, Esperances de Portugal, Quinto Imperio do Mundo*. Lisbon: A. Pedrozo Galram, 1718.
482. Virey, Julian J.. *Histoire naturelle du genre humain*. Paris: F. Dufart, an IX, 1801. Tome II.
483. Vockerodt, M.G. *Historia Societatum et Rei Literariae ante Diluvium*. Jena: aere et impensis Bauhoferianis, 1687.
484. Voltaire, François Marie Arouet de. *Essays on the Bible*. In *A Philosophical Dictionary*. New York: Coventry House, 1932.
485. Voltaire, François-Marie Arouet. *Essai sur les moeurs de l'esprit des nations*. In *Oeuvres completes de Voltaire*. Edited by Louis Moland, Paris: Garnier frères, 1877-85. Tome XI.
486. Voltaire, François-Marie Arouet. *Dictionnaire philosophique*. Edited by Julien Benda, text established by Raymond Naves. Paris: Garnier frères, 1954..
487. Voltaire, François-Marie Arouet. *Philosophical Dictionary*. Edited by Peter Gay. New York: Basic Books, 1962. Vol. II, 480-483.
488. Vossius, Isaac. *Dissertatio de vera Aetate Mundi*. The Hague: Adriani Vlacq, 1659.
489. Waldenfels, Christopher P. de. *Selectae Antiquitatis Libris XII. De Gestes primaevis, item Origine Gentium Nationumque migrationibus, atque praecipius nostratum dilocationibus, ex Sacre Scripturae*. Nuremberg: Wolgangi Mauritii Endteri, et al., 1677.
490. Webb, John. *An Historical Essay Endeavoring a Probability that the Language of the Empire of China is the Primitive Language*. London: N. Brook, 1669.
491. Webster, Charles. *From Paracelsus to Newton*, Cambridge: Cambridge University Press, 1982.
492. ——. *Samuel Hartlib and the Advancement of Learning*. Cambridge: Cambridge University Press, 1970.
493. Webster, Noah. *Effects of Slavery*. Hartford: Hudson and Goodwin, 1793.
494. White, Anne Terry. *Men before Adam*. New York: Random House, 1942.
495. Williamson, Arthur H.. *Scottish National Consciousness in the Age of James VI: The Apocalypse, the Union and the Shaping of Public Culture*. Edinburgh: J. Donald Publishers, 1979.
496. Winchell, Alexander. *Preadamites: or a Demonstration of the Existence of Men before Adam;*

together with a study of their condition, antiquity, racial affinities, and progressive dispersion over the earth. With Charts and other Illustrations. Chicago: S. C. Griggs and Co., 1880.

497. Wing, Donald. *Short-Title Catalogue 1641-1700.* New York: The Index Society, 1948. Vol. II.

498. Worm, Ole. *Olai Wormii et ad eum Doctorum Vivorum Epistolae.* 2 Vols. Copenhagen: n.p., 1751.

499. Yahuda, A. S.. *The Accuracy of the Bible.* London: Weidenfeld, 1934.

500. ———. *The Language of the Pentateuch in its Relation to Egyptian.* Oxford: Oxford University Press, 1933. Vol. I.

501. Yardeni, Miriam. 'La Religion de la Peyrère et 'Le Rappel des Juifs'.' *Revue d'Histoire et de Philosophie religieuse,* LI (1971), pp. 245-59.

502. Yerushalmi, Joseph Hayim. *From Spanish Court to Italian Ghetto, Isaac Cardoso.* New York: Columbia University Press, 1971.

503. Zagorin, Perez. 'Thomas Hobbes' Departure from England in 1640: An Unpublished Letter.' *The Historical Journal,* XXI (1978), pp. 157-60.

504. Zöckler, Otto. *Geschichte der Beziehungen zwischen Theologie und Naturwissenschaften mit besondrer Rücksicht auf Schöpfungs-geschichte.* Gutersloh: n.p., 1877.

505. ———. 'Peyrère's (gest. 1676) Präadamiten-Hypothese nach ihren Beziehungen zu den anthropologischen Fragen den Gegenwart.' In *Zeitschrift fur die gesammte Lutherische Theologie und Kirche,* XXXIX (1878), pp. 28-48.

Unpublished Material

1. Anon. *Whey^re There were any men before Adam 3 pp.* British Library Sloane Ms. 1022 or 1115.

2. Alba, M. Jean. Letters in support of La Peyrère. *Bibliothèque Nationale,* Ms. Fonds Français, 15827, fols. 149 and 162.

3. Christina, Queen of Sweden, *Bibliothèque de l'Ecole de Médicine de Montpellier,* Mss. 258 and 258bis.

4. Desmarets de Sainte-Sorlin, Jean. *Examen d'un livre intitulé, L'Ancienne Nouveauté de l'Escriture Sainte, ou l'Eglise triomphante en Terre.* Colbert collection of the *Bibliothèque Nationale,* Ms. 1659.

5. Du Puy, Christian. Lettre à I. Boulliau, Jan. 5, 1646. *Bibliothèque Nationale* Ms. Fonds francais 9778, fol. 33; Bibl. Nat. Coll. Dupuy 730, fol. 154.

6. Girard, Patrick. *Trois thèmes de recherches sur les origines des doctrines raciales de l'occident moderne.* Paris: 1975, Maison des sciences de l'Homme, Fascicule VIII. Mimeographed.

7. Grégoire, Abbé Henri. 'Analyse de l'ouvrage intitulé *Du Rappel des Juifs,* 1643, dont Isaac La Peyrère est author.' Ms. in the *Bibliothèque de Port-Royal,* Paris 1806.

8. ———. 'Recueil de piéces sur Le Rappel des Juifs'. Ms. in the Bibliothèque de Port-Royal, Paris 1806.

9. Kasprzak, Medwig. 'Report on the Wilder Brain Collection.' Ms., n.p...

10. La Peyrère, Isaac. *Des Iuifs, Elus, Reietés et Rapelés.* Ms. 191 (698), Chantilly: 1673.

11. La Peyrère, Isaac. Letter to Philibert de la Mare, September 9, 1661. *Bibliothèque Publique de Dijon,* Fonds Baudot no. 82.

12. La Peyrère, Isaac. Report to the Prince of Condé, Namur, Oct. 8, 1655. *Chantilly,* Papiers de Condé, P. XV, fols. 347-54.

13. La Peyrère, Isaac. *Reponse de Lapeyrère aux Calomnies de Des Marais (sic), Ministre de Gronigue.* Ms. Bibl Municipale de Dole. Ms. no. 107.

14. Naudé's letter to Cardinal Barberini, 1641. *Biblioteca Vaticana,* Barberini Coll. Latin 6471, fol. 22v.

15. Oddos, Jean-Paul. *Recherches sur la vie et l'oeuvre d'Isaac Laperere (1596? - 1676).* Unpublished thése de 3ème cycle, 1971-1974. Université des Sciences Sociales, Grenoble II.

16. Papiers de Pierre Lenet. *Bibliothèque Nationale* Ms. Fonds français, 6728, Documents divers, No. 20.
17. Rivet, André. Letter to Claude Sarrau, April 4, 1644. *Bibliothèque Nationale* Ms. Fonds français 2390, Part I, fol. 26.
18. Sarrau, Claude. Letter to André Rivet, April 23, 1644. *Library of Leiden University*, Ms. BLP 289/2.
19. Saumaise, Claude. Letter to Father Marin Mersenne. *Bibliothèque Nationale*, Fonds français 6204, fol. 85.

INDEX